THE LAST SUNSET

OTHER LOTUS TITLES

Ajit Bhattacharjea	*Sheikh Mohammad Abdullah: Tragic Hero of Kashmir*
Anil Dharker	*Icons: Men & Women Who Shaped Today's India*
Aitzaz Ahsan	*The Indus Saga: The Making of Pakistan*
Alam Srinivas & TR Vivek	*IPL: The Inside Story*
Amir Mir	*The True Face of Jehadis: Inside Pakistan's Terror Networks*
Ashok Mitra	*The Starkness of It*
Dr Humanyun Khan and G. Parthasarthy	*Diplomatic Divide*
Gyanendra Pandey & Yunus Samad	*Faultlines of Nationhood*
H.L.O. Garrett	*The Trial of Bahadur Shah Zafar*
L.S. Rathore	*The Regal Patriot: The Maharaja Ganga Singh of Bikaner*
M.B. Naqvi	*Pakistan at Knife's Edge*
M.J. Akbar	*India: The Siege Within*
M.J. Akbar	*Kashmir: Behind the Vale*
M.J. Akbar	*The Shade of Swords*
M.J. Akbar	*Byline*
M.J. Akbar	*Blood Brothers: A Family Saga*
Maj. Gen. Ian Cardozo	*Param Vir: Our Heroes in Battle*
Maj. Gen. Ian Cardozo	*The Sinking of INS Khukri: What Happened in 1971*
Madhu Trehan	*Tehelka as Metaphor*
Mushirul Hasan	*India Partitioned. 2 Vols*
Mushirul Hasan	*John Company to the Republic*
Mushirul Hasan	*Knowledge, Power and Politics*
Nayantara Sahgal (ed.)	*Before Freedom: Nehru's Letters to His Sister*
Nilima Lambah	*A Life Across Three Continents*
Sharmishta Gooptu and Boria Majumdar (eds)	*Revisiting 1857: Myth, Memory, History*
Shashi Joshi	*The Last Durbar*
Shashi Tharoor & Shaharyar M. Khan	*Shadows across the Playing Field*
Shrabani Basu	*Spy Princess: The Life of Noor Inayat Khan*
Shyam Bhatia	*Goodbye Shahzadi: A Political Biography*

FORTHCOMING TITLES

M.J. Akbar	*Have Pen, Will Travel*
Peter Church	*Added Value: The Life Stories of Indian Business Leaders*
Michel De Grece	*The Bourbon Rajah*

THE LAST SUNSET

The Rise & Fall of the Lahore Durbar

Amarinder Singh

LOTUS COLLECTION
ROLI BOOKS

Lotus Collection

First published in India in February 2010
Second impression, March 2010
Third impression, April 2010

The Lotus Collection
An imprint of
Roli Books Pvt. Ltd
M-75, Greater Kailash II Market, New Delhi 110 048
Phone: ++91 (011) 40682000
Fax: ++91 (011) 2921 7185
E-mail: info@rolibooks.com
Website: www.rolibooks.com
Also at Bangalore, Chennai, Jaipur, Mumbai & Varanasi

Cover Design: Supriya Saran
Cover Painting: Michael Perry
Pre-press: Jyoti De

ISBN: 978-81-7436-779-2

Typeset in Guardi Roman by Roli Books Pvt. Ltd
and printed at Replika Press Pvt. Ltd

Contents

LIST OF ANNEXURES

Acknowledgements

I wish to thank a large number of institutions and people who made this book possible.

Her Majesty the Queen's archives at Windsor and the India Office Library whose help was most invaluable. I am most grateful to Major General G.S. Malhi VSM, General Officer Commanding the 1st Armoured Division, for his personal interest in getting the maps of the First and Second Anglo-Sikh wars prepared. To the former vice-chancellor of the Punjabi University at Patiala, Sardar Swaran Singh Boparai who put at my disposal all the books and documents in the university library, and his former registrar, Sardar Parm Bakhshish Singh, earlier head of the department of Punjab Historical Studies, who willingly answered all the questions I put to him, as did the grand old man of Sikh history, Dr Kirpal Singh, whose enthusiasm is always infectious and who answered all my questions from memory, and in turn offered many suggestions.

The archives at Kathmandu of the Nepal government, that pointed me in the right direction for information on the twelve-year stay of Maharani Jinda in Nepal and to G.S. Aujla, IPS, the then principal of the Police Training Academy at Phillaur who loaned me a large number of books from their excellent library which were most useful. To the Imperial Hotel, Delhi for use of the photographs of Sardar Hari Singh Nalwa and Sardar Sham Singh Attari. To Major Amardeep Singh, formerly of my regiment, the old Ludhiana Sikhs, and Navneet Sharma who were consistently available to me to resolve issues as they appeared.

To Michael Perry for the painting of Mortal Combat for the cover, and to Ken Hunt for all the wonderful paintings of the Lahore Durbar Army. To David Mathews, general manager at the Wildflower Hall Hotel in Mashobra, Simla, who sent me photographs from the Oberoi Collection of the Indian Army of the period, on display at his hotel.

To Patricia Pugh for her assistance at the time of editing the manuscript and to Ian Bottomley, Tara Pugh and Shoma Choudhury, without whom this book would not have appeared as it does.

And finally, to my former private secretary, when I was chief minister of Punjab, M.P. Singh PCS, who arranged to get me books and documents from the various libraries and archives of Punjab for me to take notes, and to Nirmaljit Singh Kalsi, IAS, the then secretary Information and Technology, who painstakingly facilitated many of the pictures in the book. To them all I offer my grateful thanks.

Declaration

The Lahore Durbar had two principal cities, Lahore and Amritsar. The Fakir Khana Museum at Lahore, houses the most comprehensive collection of Maharaja Ranjit Singh's memorabilia, documents of his period and paintings. As with any museum that wishes to preserve and expand its collection, it has to constantly look to its resources. With the cost of such items and service constantly on the rise, money becomes the major constraint.

At Amritsar, the name that personifies service is that of the late Bhagat Puran Singh's 'Pingalwara' (a sanatorium for 1200 terminally ill people, who are unable to afford medical treatment).

The Last Sunset will be released, apart from in India, at Lahore, Maharaja Ranjit Singh's capital, and in other countries where Punjabis are settled in large numbers.

The proceeds of this book, in both India and Pakistan, will go to their respective institutions, and that from other countries, will be divided between the two as my humble contribution in helping preserve the memory of the great Ranjit Singh in the cities he loved.

THE LAHORE FORT DURING THE SIKH PERIOD
1801-1849

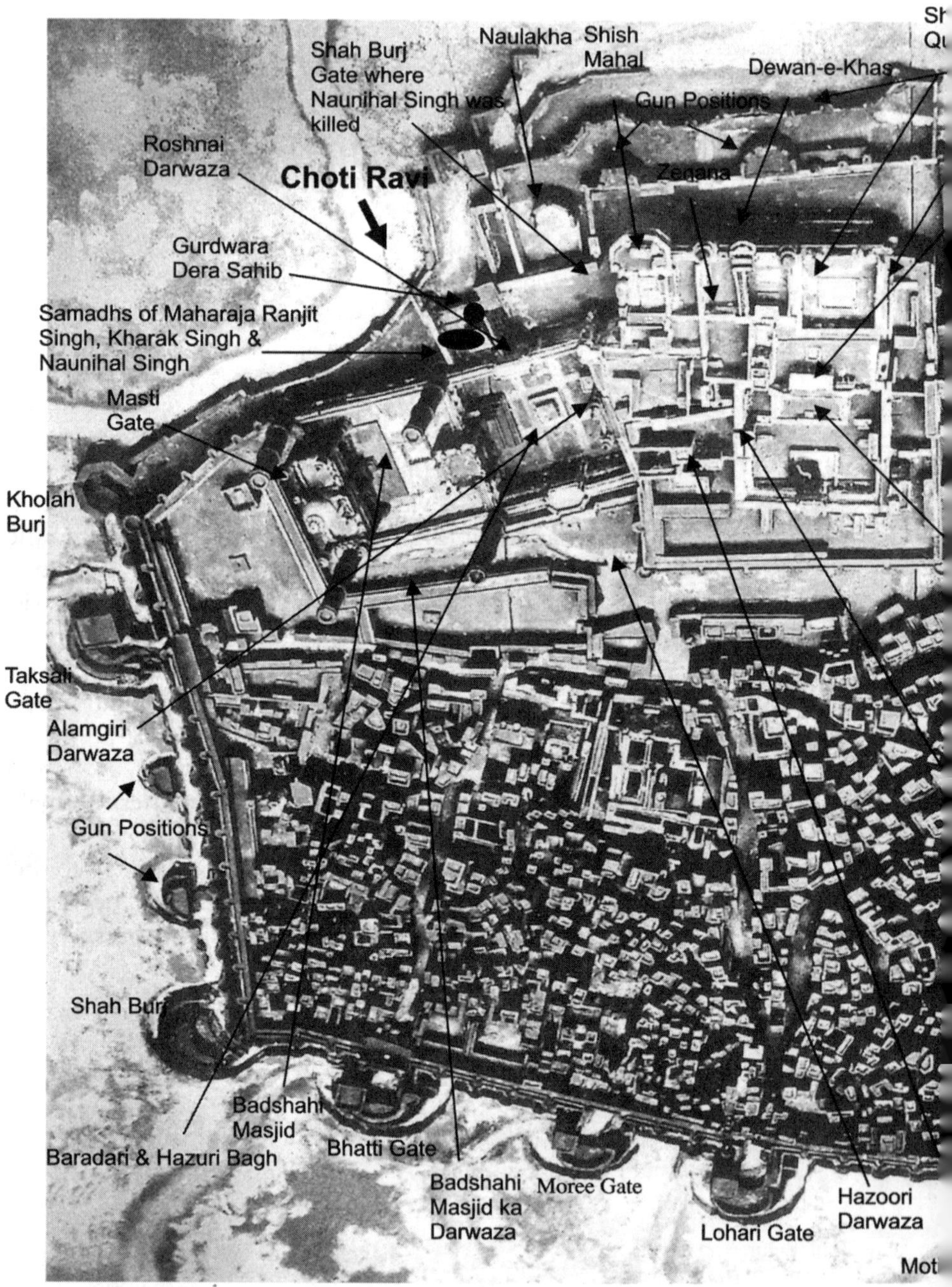

New Sikh Defensive Wall
Raja Dhyan Singh's Baradari
Cashmiree Gate
Gate to the Summan Burj
Khizri Gate or Sheranwala Gate
Gun Positions
Yakki Gate
Delhi Gate
Gun Positions
Akbari Gate
Jemedar Kushal Singh & Raja Tej Singh's Residence
Dewan-e-Am
Gun Positions
Mochie Gate
Point where Raja Dhyan Singh was killed
ah Alam Gate

Introduction

Seldom in history does a man make so great an impact upon the events of his time that, 168 years after his death, he is still being written, spoken and conjectured about as if those events were recent happenings.

Such a man was Ranjit Singh, the maharaja of Lahore. Though illiterate, he was a highly perceptive man. His great intelligence and will to go on learning till his dying day, made him one of the ablest rulers and military commanders in the history of the Punjab and, indeed, of India.

I have sometimes been asked why I have chosen to write this study about a man and his times of whom so much has already been written by very competent men and women in countless books, by military men in their autobiographies or historians covering the more mundane business of government and the national events of a certain period. While autobiography often makes for an absorbing and enjoyable read, the authors, sometimes, have their noses too close to the windowpane to see things in their true perspective. Some autobiographies are written under the pressure of personal prejudice, and thus fail to give an accurate, broad-based, in-depth account of events surrounding the experiences of the authors. As for written history, this is, all too often, written in a monotonous, dry as dust style with which it has, sadly, now become synonymous, making people shy away from it. I have attempted to write about the military aspects of a fascinating period, factual in every respect, I believe, and without prejudice, to produce a story – a human story – to which, I hope, lay readers too, will be attracted.

History seeks to record events as they actually occurred. However, students will find that military biographers, and even historians, are divided down the middle over the story of the years I have covered about events in the Punjab and the activities of the Lahore Durbar.

Contemporary historians, writing while the game was still in progress, bat openly for their own sides. Later historians are, perhaps, more objective, writing with a tongue-in-cheek subtlety which tends to favour their own. This behaviour is inevitable when events have changed the history of a country or a large part of it. Whilst the British can find very little wrong with their own part in the ten years preceding the annexation of the Punjab, the Sikhs write with a bias of their own. Mythology thus created becomes embedded in men's minds over a span of a century and a half. Whilst the victor, be he a general, a staff officer or even the adjutant of a regiment writing up the unit's war diary, seeks to glorify success, the vanquished disappear quietly from the scene, to lick their wounds and brood over disaster until the day dawns when they begin to look back with nostalgia and toy with the idea of what might have been ... if only ...!

Ranjit Singh was unquestionably a great man. As he swept through the Punjab, bringing more and more of it under his own control, he showed his understanding of men, building a team of exceptional administrators to become either his ministers or the holders of key positions, such as the governorship of newly-won territories.

An outstanding military commander, who had learnt the art of war on the battlefield from an early age, he created the Sikh Khalsa Army which the British would come to acknowledge as the best in India, an accolade that would become widely accepted after the two Sikh wars of 1845 and '48. General Sir Charles Gough and Arthur Innes wrote in the introduction to *The Sikhs and the Sikh Wars*, '[...] in the Sikhs we found the most stubborn foe we ever faced on Indian soil since the French were beaten at Wandewash.' That army made possible the remarkable military successes which characterized the forty-two years of Ranjit Singh's reign.

No man is perfect and, as history frequently reveals, it is often apparent that the greater a man's merits and talents, the greater his failings and weaknesses. If that were not so he would be less than human. Ranjit Singh was no exception to this rule. He too had certain qualities which were unworthy of his greatness. Though illiterate, he was highly intelligent and extremely able, and at times showed himself to be cunning, treacherous and quite ruthless. Yet, with one or two particular exceptions, he took no life, except in battle, and rehabilitated all those he vanquished. When it came to the acquisition of treasure, such as the great Kohinoor diamond, or the possession of some object that had seized his imagination, such as the beautiful Persian horse Liali, or even lesser desirable objects, he would cheat and even steal, if need be. If he had decided that he wanted something, he took it, regardless of means or cost.

After his death in 1839, a string of mediocre rulers, ambitious courtiers and an army that had grown aggressively volatile, presented the British with an ideal situation, enabling them to ferment intrigue which took root in that hopelessly fragmented establishment, the Lahore Durbar. It could now be only a matter of time before the kingdom of Lahore met its nemesis.

By 1845, the British, who by then had consolidated their gains in India, saw an opportunity and played their part in the game to perfection. The Lahore Durbar, by then fully infiltrated, also played its part in the impending disaster. Both sides had their reasons but the British completely outplayed the court of Lahore and its regent, Maharani Jinda Kaur.

In the Sikh wars which followed, the British Indian Army, which consisted of a number of British regiments and those of the East India Company, was highly trained and its units experienced in battle. As far as the British elements were concerned, the wars in Europe, America and China were not long over. The Company's sepoys had fought in the various engagements through which the British Empire in India was being established and consolidated and these were not yet over. General Sir Hugh Gough was supported by a string of very experienced divisional commanders, whose subordinates, down to the lowest level, had also learnt their trade on the battlefield or were the product of the cadet colleges in England. Even the governor general, General Sir Henry (later Lord) Hardinge, who had served with distinction under Wellington in the Peninsular wars, offered to serve as Gough's deputy in the field of Ferozshah. As he was well known to be inclined to interfere in military matters, this offer was, perhaps, something of a mixed blessing.

'The Evolution of the Army up to 1839' shows us how Ranjit Singh created his great Sikh Khalsa Army, using a number of battle-hardened European soldiers of fortune, all former officers in Napoleon's armies. It was their skill and experience and their understanding of the immense importance of discipline which would give the Khalsa Army its high quality and reputation.

It is both sad and extraordinary that no Sikh record of the battles of the two Sikh wars exist today, apart from the organizational structure of the Khalsa Army, the names of the three divisional commanders and of their brigade commanders and of the general commanding at each battle. Of tactical deployments and handling, we know very little. Such detailed information about the conduct of the two Sikh wars as did exist was contained in one of the volumes of a daily chronicle written by Sohan Lal Suri, the *vakil* of the camp of Lahore during the reign of Ranjit Singh and the subsequent administrations. However, in his *Umdat-ut-Tawarikh*, the *vakil* records that volume three, the one which, it is believed, would have told us much of what we so badly need to know about the conduct of operations and the tactical handling of the army, was borrowed by an English lieutenant, Herbert Edwardes, and never returned. What was there in that volume which the British wanted to keep under wraps and where is it today?

The circumstances surrounding the onset of the first Sikh war of 1845-46 are obscure but the general situation within the kingdom of Lahore and the state of the Lahore Durbar, combined with the mounting discontent within the army, enables us to make an informed suggestion of the purpose behind it.

By 1845, six years had passed since the death of the army's beloved and revered sovereign, Ranjit Singh. During that time, the magnificent army with which he had achieved so much and which, rightly, had developed an immense pride in those achievements, had received no collective training and had been in virtually no operations. Small wonder then that it had become restless under a series of hopelessly incompetent administrations. Both the Regent and the Lahore Durbar saw it as a real threat to their own positions and the decision was made to contrive a means by which the army could be committed to battle and, hopefully cut down to size thereby. The commander-in-chief, Tej Singh and the wazir of the durbar, Lal Singh, were instructed to initiate appropriate action and launch a strike against the British Protectorate, the Cis-Sutlej Punjab, though the actual objective of this action remained obscure. As the army was being reactivated and mobilized, it was suggested by both the regent and the durbar that the Cis-Sutlej Punjab might be bypassed and a thrust be made at Delhi, hinting at the vast haul of loot that such an operation, if successful, could offer. Could it be that they had second thoughts and saw this latter proposal as a means of getting the army disposed of once and for all? Be that as it may, it was ignored by an apprehensive Tej Singh and the wazir who continued to plan their move across the Sutlej and into British protected territory in order to fight a defensive battle of attrition and thereby to get their army cut to size.

It is difficult to see what the aim of this projected movement really was. With Lal Singh leading a covering force, followed by Tej Singh with some 30,000 men, both men deployed their forces in strong defensive positions, as if awaiting the arrival of the British to eject them. Some years earlier, it had been suggested to Ranjit Singh that he should acquire the Cis-Sutlej Punjab but he had rejected the idea saying, 'I could perhaps push them [the British] back to Aligarh but they would soon push me back across the Sutlej and out of my kingdom.'

No general of the Sikh Army had any professional training. Such knowledge and skills as they had, like Ranjit Singh, they had acquired on the battlefield. Many commanders, particularly those of the Jagirdari Fauj, were still in their teens. The army's mindset seems to have been that of the set-piece battle, perhaps due to their lack of command experience at the highest level. The Sikh overdependence on artillery became apparent as the battles unfolded. All battles were planned and fought in defensive positions under the cover of guns. Of the nine battles fought in the two wars, the Sikhs had superiority in guns, both in numbers and calibres. It was at Gujrat that for the first time the Sikhs were out-gunned.

Ranjit Singh's views on the hazards of invading the Cis-Sutlej Punjab must have been well known and we can only conclude that Tej Singh's concept was that of a war of attrition, to be won principally by the use of his superior strength in artillery, which included a considerable number of heavy guns, closely defended by strong groups of well-trained infantry. It is hard to understand how any general who was well acquainted with the strength and resources of the British Indian Army and the considerable experience of its commanders could have thought that such a scheme would have succeeded, unless of course, the objective was the destruction of their own army. An equally incomprehensible aspect of the Sikh plan was the failure to have any role within it for their cavalry. This was something that would not change during the course of both wars, despite the very effective use made by the British of theirs.

Having crossed the river Sutlej, Lal Singh deployed his covering force in a wooded area at Mudki where he sat and simply waited for Gough to attack him, which Gough did, pushing the Sikhs back, though at heavy cost to his own troops. Lal Singh then followed the same routine at Ferozshah and yet again at Sobraon, as did Ranjodh Singh Majithia at Aliwal. Meanwhile, Tej Singh was also waiting, with his 30,000 men, eying General Littler who had only 6,000 at Ferozepur. Not only did Tej Singh make no attempt to attack Littler but he allowed him to slip away to join Gough's main body at Ferozshah. Tej Singh then waited for twenty-four hours before moving to join Lal Singh. In the battle that followed, both sides suffered heavy casualties but the first day had undoubtedly gone to the Sikhs. Having deployed his infantry to deliver the coup de grace, advancing in extended order, Tej Singh then did something which was quite inexplicable. As his leading troops reached a point some 200 yards from Gough's defensive line, he ordered a halt and a withdrawal just as victory was within his grasp.

The only tactical movement made by the Sikhs in that war was an attempt by a force under Ranjodh Singh Majithia to cut Gough's lines of communication and destroy his supply train. Responsibility for the security of the train lay with a small force under General Sir Harry Smith, whose shrewd generalship lead to a punishing defeat of the Sikhs at Aliwal, where, once again, they had their backs to the river in a defensive position. As at Mudki, a charge by a single regiment of the British cavalry created absolute havoc and loss of a substantial number of guns by the Sikhs.

The Sikhs made their last stand on the British side of the Sutlej at Sobraon, again making the fatal error of having their backs to the river. After a bitter struggle, in which both sides suffered very heavy casualties, the day was won by a British cavalry charge, the Third Light Dragoons, which had already fought magnificently at Mudki. The British now crossed the river and swept on to Lahore, where the war ended with Hardinge, having effectively, become the overlord of the Punjab.

The British had no wish, at that stage, to annex the Punjab, for to do so would have been to take on a massive new administrative and economic commitment, besides the Sikh Army could be effective in the near future in keeping the Afghan designs in check, now that the game of one-upmanship between the Russians and the British had begun in Central Asia. They, therefore, declared it to be a protectorate and set up a Council of Regency on behalf of the young Maharaja Dalip Singh consisting of four Sikhs and four British officials, Colonel Henry Lawrence being appointed the first British Resident in Lahore.

Battered into submission though it had been, the Khalsa Army had lost none of its fierce pride and the determination to strike back at the first opportunity burnt in every soldier's heart. The Multan incident in 1848 provided that opportunity. The first British attempt to reinforce Edwardes had failed when the Sikhs in the force that had been sent to bring Mulraj to justice went over to him. Throughout the Punjab, Sikhs sprang to arms to fight for the Khalsa. Gough now sent General Wish with his reinforced 1st Division to Multan. Three major engagements were then fought at Ramnagar, Chillianwala and Gujrat, the revitalized Khalsa being commanded by a new commander-in-chief, Raja Sher Singh Attari.

Remarkably, Sher Singh followed the very same policy as Tej Singh had two years earlier – the set-piece defensive position, waiting for the enemy to come to him. Again, the cavalry was not used. All three battles were hard fought and the losses on both sides were heavy. At Gujrat, Gough now had a number of heavy guns which were used very effectively to crush the Sikh artillery before his army swept forward and finally put the Sikhs to flight. The pursuit was relentless and some were driven as far as Peshawar. The power of the Khalsa was finally crushed.

There was now no way forward for the British but to accept Governor General Dalhousie's preconceived insistence on the annexation of the Punjab. The sun had set for the last time on the Lahore kingdom.

The story of the ten years following the death of Ranjit Singh is truly tragic. As the story unfolds and the underlying treachery on the part of the Lahore Durbar and the Sikh generals emerges, so does the clear evidence of the gallantry and determination of the soldiers of the Khalsa Army. How else could it have been that the British were so nearly defeated at Ferozshah and Chillianwala and again were given such a bloody nose at Ramnagar and Sobraon. Gujrat was, indeed a famous British victory in the end. Treachery and intrigue apart, at no time did the Sikh generals begin to rival the generalship of the British. This extraordinary story calls for the most relentless research until, at last, the whole truth finally emerges.

Our story ends with the annexation of the Punjab in 1849 and the final demise of the Shukarchakia dynasty, founded by Ranjit Singh's grandfather, Charat Singh, and brought to further greatness by his father Maha Singh before Ranjit Singh himself created a kingdom which finally embraced not only the Punjab in present-day Pakistan but territories to the north and west which even included Jammu and Kashmir and what is now known as the Northern Areas in Pakistan. To these we add the areas of the present Indian Punjab and Himachal Pradesh, the entire area west of the river Sutlej. That extraordinary build-up covered a period of seventy years, finally collapsing with the exile of Maharaja Duleep Singh.

Was it destiny that brought about that downfall or did the prophecy of Sri Guru Gobind Singh come true? Guru Sahib had said at Hazoor Sahib at Nanded, just before his death in 1708, that whoever built a memorial to him would die and his dynasty fade out of history. Ranjit Singh did build such a memorial and at the end of his glorious reign of half a century, the dynasty collapsed through lack of worthy successors. His grandson, Maharaja Kharak Singh's son, Maharaja Naunihal Singh died in an accident without leaving an heir. Maharaja Sher Singh and his son Partap Singh were assassinated, Duleep Singh, the last of his children, was exiled from the Punjab as a ten-year-old boy, never to return and, though married twice with eight children of his own, never saw his grandchildren, as none of the eight, though some were married, had a child. Whatever the reason, it is beyond doubt that the collapse of the dynasty finally paved the way for the complete annexation of India into the British Empire.

It is characteristic of fighting men that despite the intensity of their conflict with a worthy enemy, both sides will develop profound respect for the fighting qualities of their opponents. The Sikh wars were no exceptions to that rule. Thus, within a few years the British would have grounds for deep gratitude to the same Sikhs who they had fought at Ferozshah, Sobraon, Chillianwala, and Gujrat, for their loyal support in the most difficult of times, including during the consolidation of the frontier regions and Afghanistan.

Prologue

The desire to dominate the world and world trade, together with the building of their empire, seems to have pre-occupied the minds of successive kings and queens of England and their governments throughout the seventeenth, eighteenth and nineteenth centuries.

In India, a seemingly innocuous trade agreement was signed in 1615 during the reign of James I and that of the fourth Mughal emperor, Jahangir. This was soon followed by the establishment of the British East India Company, ostensibly to further the economic interests of both countries. As the world knows, it was but the first step towards India becoming an integral part of the future British Empire.

By the middle of the nineteenth century, the British flag was flying high over a large part of the world, signifying British supremacy. In India too, the Union Jack was flying over much of the subcontinent, apart from some minor French and Portuguese enclaves. The defeat of the Jats, under Durjan Saul, in the battle of Bharatpur in 1826, left just one last bastion of Indian rule, the kingdom of Lahore, under its remarkable leader, the Maharaja Ranjit Singh Bahadur, who ruled over virtually the whole of that great state, the Punjab, 'The Land of the Five Rivers'.

In 1857, after the first Indian rebellion, the East India Company's properties passed to the Crown and the rest of India, ruled by 128 princes of large states categorized by gun salutes, and 412 lesser ones, 540 in all, became protectorates, also under the British Crown.

In those days it was commonly said of the British Empire that the sun never set upon it. However, that could not yet be said about India. For that to be true, the whole of it would have to be annexed under British rule and the stumbling block of the Punjab had yet to be brought into line.

The death of Ranjit Singh in 1839 and the consequent decline of his great kingdom, gave Britain the opportunity to stake her claim. If the Punjab were now to fall, the sun would indeed shine upon British interests throughout the subcontinent for generations to come. That fall would truly be 'The Last Sunset'.

The Lion of Lahore

The summer is perhaps the worst time for any traveller to visit the Punjab, particularly during the months of May to July. The dry, searing heat in May reaches an incredible 50 degrees centigrade. July is possibly even worse with temperatures in the upper 30s and 100 per cent humidity.

True to form, 27 June 1839 was hot and humid. The pre-monsoon showers had begun and the humidity was extremely oppressive. That day will remain etched in the history of the Lahore Durbar as the most tragic and fateful day in the brief life of the Shukarchakia dynasty.[1] Though it was not recognized at the time, the countdown to the annexation of the kingdom of Lahore had begun. Its ruler, Maharaja Ranjit Singh Bahadur, had died that morning.

At fifty-nine, Ranjit Singh, born on 2 November 1780, was a remarkable man. He was illiterate, capable only of putting his name down on a piece of paper, and yet a man with a brilliant mind for governance and military strategy. These qualities had enabled him to carve himself a kingdom from a completely hostile environment. These, along with his ability as a statesman, an administrator, and above all, his exceptional military talent, learnt in combat, in which he had been constantly engaged since the age of seventeen.

His kingdom extended in the west to the Khyber Pass, the entry to the kingdom of Kabul. From the north-west to the north, it ran along the Suleiman mountain range of Afghanistan, and then extended south of the Hindukush, Dardistan and Pangi ranges, engulfing the Chitral, Swat and Hazara valleys and other parts of what are now known as the 'Northern Areas'. Sind was to the south of his territory. Towards the north-east, it engulfed the valley of Kashmir and Ladakh and extended to Tibet. To the south-east it extended to the river Sutlej, which separated it from the Cis (south of) Sutlej states of Patiala, Jind and Nabha.

The maharaja had suffered a stroke in 1834 which had left him partly paralysed. His health had been deteriorating ever since. In June 1839 it had worsened and he had hovered between life and death for days and the end was expected. All the Hindu, Muslim and Sikh sardars (nobles) and generals of the kingdom and members of the family had gathered at Lahore. While he was still conscious he had called for his family and principal nobles and indicated that his successor would be his elder son Kharak Singh. Then taking his prime minister, Raja Dhyan Singh's hand in his, he announced that he wanted him to continue as the prime minister after his death, and that he expected him to guide his son with the utmost loyalty. Ranjit Singh then lingered for a few days in a coma until life finally ebbed out of him on the morning of 27 June. A pall of gloom descended on Lahore along with a feeling of uncertainty which usually follows the passing of a great ruler.

The prime minister took control of the funeral arrangements. The maharaja's body was bathed with fragrant waters and dressed in full durbar regalia; the family paid its respects, as did the sardars and generals, and the last prayers were said. Four of his maharanis then declared that they would immolate themselves on the maharaja's pyre in the ancient ritual of sati.[2] Seven slave girls would also immolate themselves, in order to be available to serve their master in his next life. Thousands of rupees were distributed in alms to the poor around the fort, and 22 lakh rupees in cash and 25 lakh in kind were offered in the maharaja's name to the poor around Sikh, Hindu and Muslim religious shrines throughout the kingdom, and to the holy institutions. The historic shrine of Jwalamukhi[3] was offered 250 maunds of ghee (purified butter).[4]

Late that afternoon, the funeral cortege left the palace in the Lahore Fort, led by his son Kharak Singh, now the maharaja, with other male members of the royal family, the four maharanis in golden palanquins, sardars and nawabs of the kingdom, generals, officers and soldiers of the army. In the wake followed thousands of citizens of the kingdom. They passed through the Roshni Darwaza to the north of Hazuri Bagh, the beautiful garden between the Alamgiri Darwaza, the main entrance to the fort, and the Badshahi Mosque; then, under the ramparts of the magnificent fort, to a small garden outside it. The Gurdwara Dera Sahib stood on the other side of this garden, on the spot where the fifth guru of the Sikhs, Sri Guru Arjun Devji had been martyred. The river Choti Ravi ran nearby. A six-foot-high funeral pyre of sandalwood had been prepared, the wood mixed with cotton seed, ghee and other combustible materials. The bier, made of silver and lined with the finest Kashmiri shawls, was placed by the side of the pyre. The sardars then gently removed the maharaja's body from the bier and placed it on top of the pyre.

The maharanis, led by the senior-most of the four, Maharani Mehtab Devi, the elder daughter of the Rajput, Raja Sansar Chand of Kangra, all dressed plainly without any ornaments, ascended the pyre and sat by the head of their dead husband. Mehtab Devi then took his head in her lap.[5] The other three were Hardevi, daughter of Mian Padam Singh of Nurpur, Chand Kaur, daughter of Sardar Jai Singh of Chainpur near Amritsar and Ishar Kaur. The seven slaves of his household – including the famous dancing girl Kaulan – arrayed themselves near his feet.

Before she took her place, Maharani Mehtab Devi caught the prime minister's hand, placed it on her dead husband's chest and made him swear to go by the maharaja's last wish, which was for him to always guide the new maharaja and to be loyal to him. Then turning to Kharak Singh she said it was her husband's last wish that he retain Raja Dhyan Singh as his prime minister, to treat him well, and to always follow his advice.

All were covered by a red cloth which had been dipped in oil and other inflammable materials. The Holy Gita was placed on the maharaja's chest and the granthis (Sikh preachers), pandits and maulvis chanted their last prayers. A final 180-gun salute was fired by his soldiers, his artillery men manning their guns on the ramparts. Maharaja Kharak Singh then lit the pyre. Not a single lady uttered a word, nor was there any murmur or cry of agony. They sat motionless till, mercifully, death finally engulfed them. Even in death, the presence of Ranjit Singh was so absolute that this sad and terrible duty was performed, as was to be expected of the maharanis and ladies of a great ruler, with dignity and courage.

The great Ranjit Singh was gone and his kingdom, from his death in 1839 to the annexation of the Punjab by the British in 1849, would be subjected to intrigue and the ambition of mediocre rulers and courtiers alike. Unable to provide the strong personal and military leadership the Sikhs have required and respected throughout history, the kingdom, built by the abilities of a single man, ceased to exist within ten years of his passing.

Ranjit Singh was born on 2 November 1780, the son of Maha Singh, the head of the Shukarchakia misl, a break-away group from the original Fyzulpurias. His mother was the daughter of Raja Gajpat Singh of Jind and was known as Mai Malwain as she belonged to the Malwa region of Punjab.[6]

The Fyzulpuria misl[7] of Bhatti Rajput descent traces its history back to Jaisalmer in the great Indian Thar desert. The Bhattis moved north to the region of the present east and west Punjab during the twelfth and thirteenth centuries and established themselves across this fertile plain, on stretches of land interspaced and bound by the waters of the five great rivers of the region, the great Indus and its tributaries – the Jhelum, Chenab, Ravi, Beas, and Sutlej, which merge at Harike, before flowing into the Indus, north of Sind. The 'Punjab' derives its name from these five rivers: 'Punj' meaning 'five' and 'Ab' water.

Syad Muhmmad Latif, in his *History of the Punjab*, describes Punjab as,

> [...] an extensive, flat plain, hemmed in by high mountain walls on the south and west, and open to the south and east [...] The north-east angle comprises the alpine region of Kangra, and the north-west angle the Eusafzai, Peshawar, Kohat and Hazara valleys [...] The southern plain belongs naturally to the same level table-land as the thirsty Thar desert of Rajputana and the wild and dry country of Sind. This plain is divided into Doabs, or inter-fluvial tracts, which form the natural divisions of the country [...] Thus the tract between the Beas and the Ravi is called the Bari Doab, that between the Ravi and the Chenab the Rachna Doab, and that between the Chenab and the Jhelum, the Chaj Doab. The space enclosed between the Jhelum and Chenab, on one side, and the Indus on the other, takes its name from the latter river and is styled the Sindh Sagar Doab. The tract enclosed between the last two of the Punjab rivers, the Beas and Sutlej, is called the Bist Jalandhar, this being the fifth Doab.[8]

As time passed most Bhattis married Jat women, simply because there were no Bhatti families around in the region to whom they were not related. As a consequence, the Rajputs refused them recognition and all future generations were known as Jats. All the Jat Sikh misls,[9] of the twelve that were founded during that period have the same heritage. Rajputs throughout history have been known as warriors, while the Jat, though equally adept at fighting and in the use of arms, wield the plough with equal dexterity.

The head of this clan which had moved north was known as Kalu the Bhatti. He established his family in 1470 at a village about 40 miles south-west of Lahore which he called Mouza Pind Bhattian. The family lived there for three generations, except for Kalu who quarrelled with the rest of the family and moved to a village called Sansi, where he died in 1488.

Many generations later, his descendant Bara, at the age of twenty-five, visited Amritsar and entered the Sikh faith. He died in 1679 after spending the rest of his life preaching the faith in the adjoining villages of Kiali and Shukarchak. His nine-year-old son, Buddha, succeeded him. After Guru Gobind Singh created the Khalsa[10] in 1699, Buddha, one of the earlier Sikhs of the region to be baptized, became Buddha Singh.

Buddha Singh was an ambitious and brave man. He quickly took control of all the neighbouring villages, one of which was Shukarchak which he made the headquarters of his estate. His boldness and courage helped him in rapidly expanding his estate but he remained popular with the people. This was the beginning of the expansion of the family.

Buddha Singh died in 1716. He had two sons – Nodh Singh and Chanda Singh. Nodh Singh was married to the daughter of Golab Singh Majithia, and had four sons, the eldest being Charat Singh who was born in 1721. During Charat Singh's rule he ravaged the countryside, ruthlessly expanding his territory and increasing his wealth many times over.

Charat Singh, with growing ambition, now felt that the time was ripe to establish himself as a separate entity. As a first step, he asked his brothers to stay away from their Fyzulpuria misl gatherings. He then moved his headquarters to Raja Sansi, between Amritsar and Lahore. His main ally at the time was Amir Singh of Gujranwala, and both belonged to the Fyzulpuria misl. Charat Singh then married the elder daughter of Amir Singh in 1756 and announced that this union would henceforth be known as the Shukarchakia misl. Their combined strength enabled them to extend their territory further. Charat Singh died in 1774 when the chamber of a rifle he was firing blew, and is reputed to have left his ten-year-old son Maha Singh, born in 1764, an estate which then yielded three lakh rupees annually.

As Maha Singh was too young to run his affairs, his mother Mai Desan managed the estate till he came of age. During her period of regency, she took help from Jai Singh Kanhiya, chief of the Kanhiya misl, and reestablished the fort at Gujranwala which had been destroyed earlier by Ahmad Shah Abdali in 1751-52. Maha Singh's marriage to the daughter of Raja Gajpat Singh of Jind also was of much significance. His wife was later known as Mai Malwain. This marriage raised his standing and many more came to join his flock, thereby increasing his small army substantially.

In 1778, at the age of fourteen, Maha Singh engaged in an undertaking which earned him great fame as a warrior and conqueror. No matter how treacherously the objective was achieved, what seemed to matter was the end result. Rassulnagar, situated on the east bank of the Chenab, was held by a powerful tribe of Mahomedans, the Chathas, also known as Manchurias.[11] The head of the tribe at that time was a Mussalman Jat named Pir Mohammad. Maha Singh, assisted by Jai Singh Kanhiya, attacked the town at the head of 6,000 troops, the pretext being the famous Zamzama gun[12] of Ahmad Shah, also known in history as the 'Bhangian ki Top', which Jhanda Singh Bhangi, after his conquest of the Chathas, had left with Pir Mohammad in deposit, as it was too heavy to be taken across the Chenab. Maha Singh now claimed it as the property of the Khalsa, conveniently forgetting that the Bhangi misl too belonged to the Dal Khalsa. The town of Rassulnagar was besieged, and the blockade continued for four months. The surrounding country, all of which belonged to the Chathas, was depopulated, and according to a contemporary historian, not a grain of wheat was left in the houses of the zamindars. The Chathas sought the help of the Bhangi chiefs who were at the time employed in plundering and conquering Multan and Bhawalpur, but in vain.

The besieged now had no alternative but to sue for peace, and Maha Singh put his seal on the Holy Granth, binding himself not to harm Pir Mohammad if he surrendered in person. Pir Mohammad, on receiving this assurance, came out unguarded, but was treacherously put under arrest. His sons were tied to the mouths of guns and blown and the town of Rassulnagar was plundered.[13] After Rassulnagar, he successfully attacked and captured the Chathas' second city, Alipur. Maha Singh renamed the cities as Ramnagar and Akalgarh (today they exist as Rassulnagar and Akalgarh). He made over Ramnagar to one of his lieutenants, his uncle Dal Singh, to rule as governor in his name, and gave Akalgarh to him in perpetuity.

Following the capture of Ramnagar, Maha Singh attacked Jammu, which was sacked and looted and the palace burnt to the ground. He then took Sahiwal, captured Isa Khel and Musa Khel and then captured Kotli, close to Sialkot.

In 1780, Mai Malwain gave birth to a son who was named Ranjit Singh. Now, with a string of military successes behind him, Maha Singh decided to achieve total supremacy amongst the Sikh misls of his region, the Majha.[14] At first he turned to the Bhangi misl with whom relations had always been strained. In 1784, the dispute came to a head when Maha Singh was snubbed in Amritsar by the powerful Kanhiya misl chief, Jai Singh, who at one time had been his ally and that of his father's, but was now wary of the young Maha Singh's increasing ambition and his growing influence and standing. On the occasion of Diwali that year, when both were to celebrate at the Golden Temple, Jai Singh dismissed Maha Singh and called him a *bhagtia*, a dancing boy. Maha Singh used this insult as an excuse to attack Jai Singh. In a battle that was fought near Majitha, Jai Singh Kanhiya was defeated and was forced to flee across the Beas. He returned later with a fresh army and attacked Maha Singh at Naushera, only to be defeated again, after which he withdrew north to Batala where he lived in seclusion for the rest of his life.

A short while after this battle, Sada Kaur, the astute daughter of the old Jai Singh, in an effort at rapprochement, proposed the marriage of her daughter Mehtab Kaur to Maha Singh's son Ranjit Singh. This proposal was happily accepted by Maha Singh, who, though wary of Jai Singh, was content to have a subjugated Kanhiya misl by his side. The marriage took place in 1774. The powerful Shukarchakia and Kanhiya misls now became a formidable force in the tracts between the rivers Chenab and Beas, encompassing the Ravi. Maha Singh, after an eventful and strenuous life, died in 1792, at the age of twenty-eight. Ranjit Singh was then twelve years old.

His mother Mai Malwain and Lakpat Rai, one of his father's trusted assistants, took over the management of the estate. His mother-in-law, Sada Kaur, also involved herself in its day-to-day running. An ambitious woman, Sada Kaur planned to ingratiate herself with her son-in-law and, with his assistance, take over the Kanhiya misl when her father died, instead of it going to either of her two brothers. A year later, in 1793, this occasion arrived, and as per her designs, Ranjit Singh forced the issue and Sada Kaur became the new chief.

With his estate under this management, he spent the next four years in his favourite pastime of hunting and other leisurely pursuits. He was never taught to read or write and, while still a minor, was married for a second time to Raj Kaur, the daughter of Ram Singh, the chief of the Nakkais.

When he was seventeen, however, he turned against that management. At first the assumed reason was ambition which had given rise to impatience. One day he announced unilaterally that henceforth he would manage his own affairs. He dispensed with the services of his mother, mother-in-law and Lakpat Rai and appointed his uncle Dal Singh, who was then his governor at Ramnagar, as his dewan.

The more compelling reason for this far-reaching decision, however, was not simply ambition. He had lost confidence in his mother and was greatly disturbed with information reaching him regularly about his mother's indiscretions with various paramours. Lakpat Rai was one of those suspected. He was, as a consequence, sent to Katas, allegedly for work, but was assassinated on arrival on Ranjit Singh's orders. Soon after this, he came upon Laik Missar in his mother's apartment one night and, in a fit of rage, drew his sword and killed her. Laik Missar was dispatched by his soldiers.[15]

It is often said that history repeats itself. Maha Singh too, had killed his mother Mai Desan in 1788 in a similar fashion, but with a gun not a sword, to restore his family's honour. One of his companions, a Khodadad Khan of Jelalpur near Gujrat, had killed his own mother and fled his domain with about twenty horsemen, and had joined Maha Singh's outfit while on the run. One day Maha Singh taunted him and asked him how his mother had died. In an angry response, Khodadad Khan told Maha Singh not to worry about his mother but to take care of his own, whose involvement with a Hakikat Singh of Wazirabad was well known to all.

Some days later, this taunt still rankling him, Maha Singh went into the zenana and shot his mother dead and cut off her hand with a sword. He later gave it to Khodadad Khan as proof.[16]

The capture of Lahore had been one of Ranjit Singh's most cherished desires and he had of long been working towards it. Lahore, the centre of power in that region, was at that point in time the symbol of Bhangi supremacy and was ruled by three brothers of the Bhangi misl – Lehna Singh, Gujar Singh and Sobha Singh. Their rule was tyrannical, and, secretly, encouraged by his agents, the nobles of Lahore petitioned Ranjit Singh to take control of the city.

Ranjit Singh and Sada Kaur marched on Lahore. A whisper in the bazaar that they were on their way to a pilgrimage in Amritsar, achieved its objective and the brothers let down their guard. On reaching Amritsar, however, he turned back that very night with 5,000 troops, covering the distance of 14 miles to Lahore in a forced march and reaching it in the early hours of the morning. On receipt of information from one of their outposts, the brothers quickly mustered a force of 200 cavalry to meet him, which Ranjit Singh soon dispersed. On reaching the fort, early on the morning of 6 July 1799, he marched upon the Lahori Gate. It was strongly guarded, under the personal supervision of Lehna Singh's son Chet Singh. Under instructions of Mokham-ud-din, one of Chet Singh's commanders, the guards deceived Chet Singh by the alarming news that Ranjit Singh was attacking the Delhi Gate, which had actually been attacked by the Kanhiya force under Sada Kaur. Chet Singh immediately hurried to the Delhi Gate, and in his absence the Lahori Gate was thrown open.[17]

While the rest of the family fled, Chet Singh shut himself up in a section of the fort with the intention of fighting back. Next morning, however, he offered to surrender after realizing that treachery was at play, and that any attempt to hold the fort would now be futile. Ranjit Singh received him graciously as an equal and gave him a *jagir* of a large village. As agreed, the citizens of the city were treated with full consideration. He had finally occupied Lahore and fulfilled one of his greatest ambitions.

Ranjit Singh's kingdom had by now become so large that he decided to restructure his army and place troops at strategic locations throughout his kingdom. This was his first effort in this direction. Earlier, all moves to counter aggression were made by the force stationed with hi at Lahore. With this decision in 1799, at the age of nineteen, he laid the foundations of what was to become a formidable army till his death in 1839.

Desa Singh Majitha was given command of 400 cavalry, Hari Singh Nalwa was given 800 cavalry and infantry, Hukam Singh Chimni was appointed superintendent of artillery with 200 gunners, Ghouse Khan became the commandant of artillery with 2,000 troops, Baj Singh Moraliwala was the commandant of 500 troops, Milkha Singh was positioned at Rawalpindi with 700 troops, Roushan Khan and Sheikh Ibadulla (of Hindustan) were given 2,000 *najibs,*[18] Nodh Singh was to command 400 troops, Attar Singh Dhari received 500 cavalry, Kurba Singh was given 1,000 troops, and Nehal Singh Attari was to command 500 troops. All the above were made sardars to give them additional authority.

Alongside the units of the regular army as listed above, a feudal army or Jagirdari Fauj, was created. Sardars Jassa Singh and Bhag Singh Hallowalia, sons of Nar Singh of Chammari, were ordered to equip and train 10,000 troops. The Kanhiya sardars had to train 5,000 troops, the Nakkais 4,000 troops, the hill rajas 5,000 troops, and the sardars of Doaba 7,000 troops. They had to do this from their own resources and were all made honorary commanders.

Recognizing the military talent of Dewan Mokham Chand, earlier in the employ of Sahib Singh Bhangi of Gujrat, he appointed him as his commander-in-chief. The appointment upset his existing military leadership and the sardars, but it was an astute decision and was to be of great advantage in the future.

A year later, in 1800, jealousy, past history and a fear of his rising strength, and hence of their own future, forced a coalition of aggrieved nawabs, misl chiefs and sardars, all of whom had been in confrontation with Ranjit Singh at some time or another, to forge an alliance against him. Jassa Singh Ramgarhia, Golab Singh Bhangi of Amritsar, Sahib Singh Bhangi of Gujrat, Jodh Singh of Wazirabad, and Nawab Nizamuddin Khan of Kasur, came together to lay siege to Lahore, to seize it and to finish off Ranjit Singh once and for all. To their astonishment, Ranjit Singh led his troops out of the fort and marched up to his opponents' concentration point at Mouza Pind Bhattian (the village established by his ancestor Kalu in 1470), 40 miles from Lahore, and camped opposite them. There a standoff took place for two months. Ranjit Singh waited patiently for their move which never materialized. Finally, the opposing force struck camp and retired. He then followed them up to Batala where a battle was fought between the Kanhiyas under Sada Kaur, allied with him, against Jodh Singh the son of Jassa Singh Ramgarhia. Jodh Singh was defeated in this battle and Ranjit Singh returned to Lahore in triumph.

The ill feelings and jealousy did not end with this incident. On another occasion in 1790, the then chief of the Chatha clan, Hashmat Khan, also wary of Ranjit Singh's growing power and the fact that his family had already been his victims once earlier, decided to eliminate him personally. One day, knowing the track on which young Ranjit Singh would be returning from a hunting trip, and knowing too, his habit of always riding ahead of his party, he concealed himself in a thicket along the track. As Ranjit Singh crossed his hiding place, he sprang up and delivered a sword blow which missed the young Ranjit but severed his bridle and part of his saddle. Reacting with lightening speed, Ranjit drew his sword and in one stroke severed Hashmat Khan's head. Over the next few days he followed up, attacking and annexing most of the Chatha territory along the Chenab.

Ranjit Singh did not have full faith in his co-religionists in preserving his kingship. He was aware that Sikh youth had betrayed Banda Singh Bahadur, the creator of the first independent Sikh state, and as a consequence had destroyed their own state, their leader and themselves. Hari Ram Gupta, in his *History of the Sikhs*, writes,

> He feared the Sikhs more than he did the Durrani or Barakazi Afghans or frontier Pathans [...] He adopted a threefold policy towards the Sikh Sirdars. The weaker must go to the wall without any compunction. With some of the stronger ones, he made matrimonial alliances and demanded territory and money in dowry, and then put an end to them in due course. With the strongest, he entered into solemn brotherhood by exchanging turbans and taking ritualistic oaths on the holy Granth.[19]

Baron Von Hugel, in *Travels in the Cashmere and Punjab* assessed that:

> [...] his conscience never troubled him whether he robbed the widow or orphan; deprived some unfortunate dependent on his honour of all his property; seized the treasures confined to his care, or claimed the whole fortune of his friend, or even the inheritance of his own son [...][20]

According to Hari Ram Gupta, he toured the country often, always accompanied by a huge army as well as all the subdued chiefs – Hindu, Muslim and Sikh. The small chieftains were overawed by this cavalcade and submitted quietly after offering gifts and promising recruits when required. Others resisted, but eventually yielded.[21]

Even though Ranjit Singh turned a blind eye to any courtesy, nicety or decency and in many cases took ruthless and unethical steps while building his empire, visitors who met him during those turbulent years more or less unanimously acclaim his intelligence. In spite of being illiterate, his great power of assimilating information on a variety of subjects, along with a remarkable memory, left its impression on all those with whom he conversed.

In *A Journey to India*, (1835), Victor Jacquemont describes his meeting with him,

> Compared to Ranjit the most skilful of our diplomats is a complete simpleton [...] His conversation is like a nightmare. He is almost the first inquisitive Indian I have seen; and his curiosity balances the apathy of the whole nation. He asked me a hundred thousand questions about India, the British, Europe, Bonaparte, this world in general and the next, hell, paradise, the soul, God, the devil, and a myriad others of the same kind.[22]

Even during the last few years of his life when W.G. Osborne, a British Army captain, and Emily Eden, the sister of Lord Auckland, the then governor general of India, visited Lahore, that inquisitiveness had not died. As Captain Osborne recorded, 'It is hardly possible to give an idea of the ceaseless rapidity with which his questions flow, or the infinite variety of subjects they embrace. The more I see of Ranjit, the more he strikes me as an extraordinary man.'[23]

Emily Eden gives a rather feministic observation of him:

> He is exactly like an old mouse, with grey whiskers and one eye [...] he had two stockings on at first; which was considered an unusual circumstance; but he very soon contrived to slip one off, that he might sit with one foot in his hand, comfortably [...]

She goes on to add,

> He has made himself a great king; he has conquered a great many powerful enemies; he is remarkable just in his government; he has disciplined a large army; he hardly ever takes away life, which is wonderful in a despot, and he is excessively beloved by his people.[24]

In late 1800, he marched on Jammu, capturing Mirowal and Narowal on the way, and then laid siege to Jassarwal. On reaching Jammu, he camped 4 miles outside the city. Rather than being taken at the point of the sword, the Raja visited him and presented him with a purse of 20,000 rupees and an elephant as *nazrana,*[25] thereby accepting his sovereignty. Ranjit Singh, in turn, bestowed upon him a robe of honour, a *khilat,*[26] and then moved on, reducing Sialkot and then Dillawargarh, held by the Sodhis at that time, and finally returned to Lahore. He now felt that the time had finally arrived for him to declare himself maharaja, ruler of a sovereign state. This he did in 1801, with great pomp, by following all the rituals of coronation. He was then twenty-one ears old.

Maharaja Ranjit Singh had a reliable and consistent strategy to expand his kingdom. At first he consolidated the territory under his control, then laid siege to territory that he intended to capture. If the defender accepted defeat he paid obeisance by offering a *nazarana*. Once his sovereignty was accepted, he in turn offered a *khilat*, acknowledging that tribute, thereby accepting him as a vassal. An annual tribute to be paid was then stipulated. Those who refused to accept his rule or sovereignty were put to the sword. Those who finally accepted his sovereignty after being subdued, were given back their estates but with an increased annual tribute, which they had to pay. Unless a conquered 'friend' failed to pay on a number of occasions, he usually gave them an opportunity to reform.

When the nawab of Kasur, Nizamuddin Khan, raised the standard of revolt in 1802, Ranjit Singh sent Sardar Fateh Singh Kaliwala to deal with him. Rather than face Fateh Singh's forces, the nawab submitted to the terms proposed to him. However, he reneged on five further occasions. Kasur was attacked again in 1807, when the new nawab, Kutub-ud-din, failed to pay the annual tribute and the city was sacked and burnt to the ground. All able-bodied men, women and children were taken away as slaves and the remainder were killed. The nawab saved his life by abandoning Kasur and crossing to his Mamdot estate near Ferozepur, south of the river Sutlej.

On another occasion in the same year, the Bhangi chief, Sahib Singh of Gujrat also raised the banner of revolt. He marched to deal with Sahib Singh. On hearing of the maharaja's approaching army, Sahib Singh shut himself up in the fort, which was duly besieged by the Lahore Army. Sahib Singh sued for peace after the fort was virtually demolished by heavy artillery fire. He was made to pay a large *nazarana*, and to give an assurance of good behaviour. That given, Ranjit Singh returned to Lahore.

For his part, Ranjit Singh entered into treaties and broke them at will. He was prepared to do anything that offered a momentary advantage. On one occasion when he heard that his uncle Dal Singh, his father's old associate and his own dewan, who had since fallen out with him, was likely to join Sahib Singh Bhangi in an expedition against him, he remonstrated with the old man, in his late father's name, and invited him to Lahore. When he arrived he was received with great honour and respect. That night, he was promptly put under house arrest. Having divided the two, he successfully subdued Sahib Singh Bhangi in a great battle, fought 2 miles out of the city of Gujrat, as described above. After the battle, Dal Singh was released but died shortly after reaching his estate in Akalgarh. Ranjit Singh promptly rode to Akalgarh to condole with his widow who was his aunt. On entering the city, however, he arrested her, took over all her treasure, military stores and territory and returned to Lahore, leaving her the revenue of two villages, on which she was to maintain herself and her children.

His treatment of neighbouring rulers was on much the same lines. Shortly after the Dal Singh incident, word arrived that Raja Sansar Chand of Kangra had sacked a part of Sada Kaur's territory. He promptly dispatched his troops to the location and sent word to Fateh Singh Ahluwalia to reach Batala without delay. Sansar Chand, on hearing the news, fled to the hills, while Ranjit Singh seized Naushera and made it over to Sada Kaur with all its revenues. He then marched to Nurpur and captured it. On his return journey, he razed Sansar Chand's fort at Sujanpur, near Pathankot, to the ground.

On his way back to Lahore, he added Dharamkot, Sukalgarh and Baharampur, the old seat of the Pathans, to his territory and then besieged the fort at Band, which soon surrendered to him. He then took Pind Bhatian, which he made over to Fateh Singh. On his return to Lahore, with 400 horses of the famed Dhanni country, word was waiting for him that Uttam Singh Majithia, in charge of the fort at Sitpur, had rebelled. The fort was taken and Uttam Singh brought to him in chains. Ranjit Singh forgave him, but penalized him with a heavy fine. His stick and carrot policy worked well.

In 1802, when he was twenty-two, his wife Raj Kaur gave birth to a son who was named Kharak Singh. A few days later, the incident narrated above about the nawab of Kasur took place and afterwards, Ranjit marched from Kasur to the Jalandhar Doab to subdue the widow of Chuhar Mal of Phagwara, who wanted independence. Phagwara was taken and handed over to Fateh Singh Ahluwalia, while the widow was dispatched to Hardwar to spend the rest of her days in penance. While still at Phagwara, word reached him that Sansar Chand had once again descended to the plains and had taken control of Bijwara and Hoshiarpur. Both cities were recaptured and military posts were established there. Sansar Chand yet again fled to the hills and Ranjit Singh captured a number of villages belonging to him and to other uncooperative Sikh sardars.

Within three months of his return to Lahore, his restless nature once again got the better of him and he crossed the Sutlej for the second time, supposedly to visit Hardwar on a pilgrimage. In fact, he intended to assess the strength and resolve of the Cis-Sutlej states of Patiala, Nabha and Jind in forging a military alliance against him in the event of hostilities. Shrewdly assessing each, he professed friendship and returned to Lahore.

On his return from Hardwar, he decided to capture Multan and led his army there in 1802. After a bloody standoff, the ruler of Multan, Nawab Muzaffar Khan, submitted to him and paid him a large *nazarana* of 1,80,000 rupees and promised to change his allegiance from Kabul to Lahore. Ranjit Singh allowed him to keep possession of his territory and returned to Lahore.

Ranjit Singh's sights were now set on Amritsar, the city of Sri Guru Ram Das, the holy city of the Sikh's with the Durbar Sahib (Golden Temple). Amritsar was still in the possession of the Bhangi misl, which was ruled by Rani Sukhan, the widow of Golab Singh Bhangi. In 1802, he found an excuse to attack it. He wanted to repossess the Zamzama, which was in her possession. Rani Sukhan refused and Ranjit Singh got the opportunity to force the issue. He asked Fateh Singh Ahluwalia to reach Amritsar while Sada Kaur and he moved and besieged the city. Fateh Singh began his operations at the Bridge Gate and Ranjit Singh at the Lohgarh Gate. They managed to enter the city and the Rani took shelter with Jodh Singh Ramgarhia who had earlier been defeated in battle by Ranjit Singh but had been treated honourably. On behalf of the Rani, he persuaded him to give her a source of revenue to maintain herself and her family in exchange for the city. With this, the Bhangi misl ceased to exist forever as an effective force.

In 1803, he moved on Jhang. The chief, Ahmad Khan, was asked to pay a large tribute or be prepared to face military action. On his refusal, Jhang was attacked, the battle lasting two days. The nawab had collected all his relatives and other acquaintances with their forces, all of whom were determined to oppose Ranjit Singh's expansionist policy. These included the Sials, Kharals and Bharwanas. After the second day, the defenders broke and Nawab Ahmad Khan fled to Multan, leaving his city to Ranjit Singh. In subsequent negotiations, Jhang was returned to Ahmad Khan, who agreed to pay an annual tribute of Rs 60,000.

In 1805, Jaswant Rao Holkar, the famous Maratha ruler, pursued by Lord Lake, entered Ranjit Singh's kingdom and asked for military assistance to fight the British. Lord Lake, in the meanwhile encamped on the river Beas at Jelalabad. Ranjit Singh refused this request but negotiated with Lord Lake on the Maratha's behalf and an agreement was reached wherein Jaswant Rao returned to Indore. This was Ranjit Singh's first contact with the British Army and he was deeply impressed with their discipline and military ability.

Sir Lepel Griffin sums up Ranjit Singh's style of conquest and governance with this observation:

> For all his rapacity, Ranjit Singh was not cruel or blood thirsty. After the victory or capture of a fortress, he treated the vanquished with leniency and kindness, however stout their resistance might have been, and there were at his Court many chiefs despoiled of their estates but to whom he had given suitable employment, and who accepted their position with the resignation of eastern fatalism, which takes the sharpest sting out of defeat. The sardars who had been the leaders of several confederacies [misls], which he overthrew were all reduced from equality and rivalship to honourable

> subjugation in this fashion. In addition, there was a large group of Muhammadan Khans and nobles who would have received short shrift earlier, but whom Ranjit Singh attached to his fortunes, thereby materially strengthening his position in the western districts. The heads of the Mussulman tribes of Sial, Ghebas, Tiwanas and Kharals, and the family of Nawab Muzaffar Khan of Multan were included in this group.[27]

Fakir Syed Waheeduddin in his book *The Real Ranjit Singh* adds Sir Lepel Griffin could have added several other names, for example, those of Nawab Kutb-ud-din of Kasur, the nawab of Bhawalpur, Sardar Sultan Mohammad Khan and several other Barakzais and Saddozai princes.

Sir Henry Lawrence sums up the maharaja's considerations in this respect as follows:

> Members of deposed ruling families may be seen in Delhi and Kabul in a state of penury, but in Punjab there is not to be seen a single ruling family whose territories may have been conquered by Ranjit Singh, and which may have been left unprovided by him. Not only the Sikh ruling houses, but those of other faiths, too, were provided for by him with equal munificence.[28]

Ambition, once again getting the better of Ranjit Singh, forced him to cross the river Sutlej for the third time, and foray east to Patiala, seemingly to intervene in a dispute between Raja Sahib Singh and his wife. In fact, he came in response to an invitation from the raja of Nabha, who had a territorial dispute with Patiala and had been defeated in battle over this dispute earlier on. On reaching Patiala, he promptly occupied the disputed territory of Duladi and, to indicate his supremacy, also occupied the neighbouring village of Mansurpur. He then moved on Patiala. A preliminary skirmish and posturing took place, which lasted the whole day.[29] When it ended in stalemate, a peace treaty was concluded between him and Sahib Singh of Patiala and the invested territories were restored to Patiala and Ranjit Singh returned to Lahore.

By now, the Phulkian rulers of the Cis-Sutlej states of Patiala, Nabha and Jind, and the other rulers and sardars of the region were convinced that the constant interference in their affairs by Ranjit Singh, the occupation of Faridkot and the levying of a major fine on the nawab of Malerkotla, meant that he was biding his time before crossing the Sutlej and annexing them all.

In consequence, on 4 March 1808, a meeting was held at Samana, 14 miles from Patiala city, and was attended by the four major chiefs and six important minor sardars of the Cis-Sutlej region. The following resolution was adopted in this meeting.

> We, the rulers of Sirhind province, are placed between two big ambitious powers. We cannot maintain our independent positions for long. The British Government is sure and certain to advance from the Yamuna to the Sutlej. Similarly Ranjit Singh has his eyes upon us. It is certain he will cross the Sutlej. We have to choose between the two evils. To go under the British is like courting tuberculosis (*Tap-e-diq*), which brings gradual but slow death to the patient. The alliance with Ranjit Singh would be fatal, like delirium (*Sarsam*) which finishes the victim within hours.[30]

There was a unanimous vote for an alliance with the British!

The three Phulkian states of Patiala, Nabha and Jind considered Ranjit Singh treacherous. The Jind ruler was Maharaja Bhag Singh, who was Ranjit Singh's uncle. It was his sister, Raj Kanwar, Ranjit Singh's mother Mai Malwain, whom Ranjit Singh had accused of infidelity and had killed. All three rulers being from the same family felt the same repugnance towards him.[31]

They sent their vakil*s* to Delhi to seek British protection against Ranjit Singh. On 7 March 1808, Mr Seaton, the British Resident at Delhi, wrote to the secretary to the governor general.[32]

The Treaty of Amritsar between Ranjit Singh and Charles Metcalfe was signed on 25 April 1809. Article 2 of the treaty states '[…] nor commit or suffer any encroachments on the possessions or rights of the Chiefs (of the Cis-Sutlej) in its vicinity.' Lord Minto, the governor general, ratified the treaty in council on 30 May 1809, and on 12 June, Colonel Octherlony, the British political agent in Ludhiana, issued a proclamation to the Cis-Sutlej chiefs declaring them to be under British protection.

In 1883, a year before he died, Ranjit Singh is described by Captain Osborne as:

> […] his height is rather beneath the usual stature of the Sikhs and a habitual stoop causes him to look shorter than he really is (various estimates put him at anywhere between 5 ft 3 inches to 5 ft 7 inches), he is by no means firm on his legs when he attempts to walk, but all weakness disappears when he is once on horseback. He has still a slight hesitation in his speech, the consequence of a paralytic stroke about three years ago; but those about him assert that his health is much improved within the last twelve months. His long white beard and mustachios give him a more venerable appearance than his actual age would lead you to expect; and at fifty-eight years of age, he is still a hale and hearty old man, though an imaginary invalid.[33]

his personal life was in accordance with the times. His consumption of alcohol mixed with crushed pearls was excessive and would contribute to his early death. Emily Eden wrote, 'Ranjit produced some of his wine, a sort of liquid fire, that none of our strongest spirits approach and, in general, Europeans cannot swallow more than a drop of it'.[34]

He had twenty marriages – ten of these were by traditional ceremony and included five Sikh, three Hindu and two Muslim ladies. A further ten marriages had taken place by the *chaddar* ceremony,[35] which included seven Sikh and three Hindu ladies (Maharani Jinda being one of them). In addition to this, his harem contained twenty-three other ladies, taking the total to forty-three in all.[36]

The two senior maharanis were Mehtab Kaur Kanhiya and Raj Kaur Nakkai, his son Kharak Singh's mother. During the Gurkha invasion of Kangra, Ranjit Singh provided assistance to Raja Sansar Chand, once his great adversary, who now required his assistance to defeat the Gurkha General Amar Singh Thapa. Having defeated and pushed the Gurkhas out of Kangra, he sealed the alliance by marrying two of the raja's daughters – the elder Mehtab Devi, also known as Guddan, who would later commit sati on her husband's death and the younger one being Raj Banso. The two Muslim ladies he married were Moran, who is better known in Sikh history as the lady whom he went to see on arrival in Amritsar, rather than first paying his respects at the Darbar Sahib. As a consequence of which he had to face the wrath of the Jathedar of the Akal Takht.[37] The second story associated with this incident is that Akali Phula Singh, the then Jathedar of the Akal Takht, castigated him on his marriage to a Muslim lady. Which of these two versions is correct is a matter of conjecture for this story has been passed down the years by word of mouth. If it is the latter, then it is difficult to comprehend how, a few years later, he married Gul Bahar, another Muslim. Both these ladies were from Amritsar. Gul Bahar lived the longest, dying in 1863 at Lahore, after the annexation of Punjab.[38] She lived on an annual income of 12,380 rupees provided by the British government, as the maharani of the late Maharaja Ranjit Singh.

Fakir Azizuddin, an ancestor of Fakir Syed Waheeduddin and a minister of Ranjit Singh's, asserts that Moran, a young courtesan whom he married in 1802, a year after he became the maharaja of Lahore at the age of twenty-one, was his favourite. She was the only one in whose name a coin was struck, with a picture of a peacock symbolizing her name. On her request he built a mosque, which still stands near the Mati Chowk at Lahore and became a great centre of learning. She was also very popular with the people of Lahore as she had a kind and benevolent disposition, and as a consequence, earned the affectionate title of Moran Sarkar rather than the more official one of Maharani Sahiba. Moran's wedding, as recorded by Fakir Waheeduddin, started with the description of the *barat* or wedding procession on its way to Amritsar, 'crossing the Shalimar gardens, while the end was still at the Lahore Fort. A procession of elephants, horses, palkis and people on foot.'[39] The ceremony in Amritsar was held at the house of Moran's godfather, a rich merchant, Mian Samdu, as her father did not have the means to marry his daughter to the maharaja, and 'the bride was given away with a dowry of several lacs of rupees worth of jewellery, clothes, household effects, as if she had been a princess'. Ranjit Singh gave Pathankot to her as a *jagir*, where she spent her last days after his death, residing in the Pathankot Fort.

Being fond of dance and music, he kept 150 dancing girls, mostly from Kashmir and the Punjab hills. Apart from entertainment in private or for his guests, they were an integral part of the proceedings of the durbar. The girls were in the age group of twelve to eighteen. After they reached eighteen they were given away in *jagirs*, or given *jagirs* to live on. One of the girls called Kaulan (Lotus) was given seven villages as *jagir* but despite this wealth she was one of the ladies who committed sati on Ranjit Singh's pyre. Carried away by the lifestyle of Lahore, General Ventura, one of the foreign commanders of his army, too kept fifty dancing girls!

He entertained his guests depending on which part of his kingdom he was then in. He had a house in Batala which later became his son Prince Sher Singh's house. This was one of the venues of a great deal of entertainment as it was here, and at Dinanagar, that Ranjit Singh spent the summer months. After the annexation in 1849, it became the Baring High School. Ranjit Singh's grandson Naunihal Singh later lived in a beautiful palace in Lahore, called the Haveli, which had ceilings worked with mirrors and gold, and the walls richly ornamented with glass and artificial flowers. He also built a two-storied building on wheels. It was taken to Dinanagar, where he went often during the summer months, and to Ropar, for a meeting with Lord William Bentinck in 1831.

His architects, Illahi Bakhsh, Allah Yar and his son Mohammad Yar built an exquisite house in Lahore in the arabesque style. It was adorned with small pieces of mirror set in various patterns with enamel. The walls were decorated with flowers and foliage. Another favourite of Ranjit Singh's was Wazirabad, where he built a beautiful building called the Samman Burj which had an exquisite shish mahal and had walls covered with beautiful frescos.

He desired beautiful gardens to be built in the cities of his kingdom and encouraged all his courtiers and sardars to do so. Many had been built before his time and were in a run-down condition, and many new ones were added. He turned the Badami Bagh to the north of the Lahore Fort, into an exquisite garden. Dewan Deenanath's garden, on the old road to the Shalimar, near the tomb of Ghore Shah, was another. The Shalimar gardens themselves, which were in a run-down state, were renovated at considerable expense. Other such gardens were the garden of Dewan Ratan Chand Darhiwala, outside the Shah Alam Gate; Ram Bagh at Amritsar; the Hazuri Bagh at Lahore; and Hari Singh Nalwa's garden around a beautiful house that he had built at Gujranwala. Then there were gardens at Batala, Dinanagar, Multan, the Gheba chief's garden at village Kot, and innumerable gardens of lesser importance at Lahore and in some other cities.

Ranjit Singh's drinking parties were much talked about events, and one day he invited Captain Osborne to one of them. Osborne quotes him as saying, 'You have never been to one of my drinking parties; it is bad work drinking now the weather is so hot; but as soon as we have a good rainy day, we will have one.' Osborne in turn recorded his views:

> I sincerely trust it will not rain at all during our stay, for, from all accounts, nothing can be such a nuisance as one of those parties. His wine is extracted from raisins, with a quantity of pearls ground to powder, and mixed with it, for no other reason (that I can hear) than to add to the expense of it. It is made for himself alone and, though he sometimes gives a few bottles to some of his favourite chiefs, it is very difficult to be procured, even at the enormous price of one gold mohur for a small bottle. It is as strong as aquafortis ... He laughs at our wines, and says that he drinks for excitement, and that the sooner the object is attained the better.[40]

He had seven sons. The eldest was Kharak Singh, born to his second wife, Maharani Raj Kaur. The senior Maharani Mehtab Kaur had two sons – Sher Singh and Tara Singh.[41] Then there was Kashmira Singh and Peshora Singh, the sons of Daya Kaur, and Multana Singh was born to Ratan Kaur. These latter two ladies were the wives of Sahib Singh Bhangi of Gujrat, whom Ranjit Singh defeated in battle in 1810. He brought them back to Lahore and married them by the *chaddar* ceremony. The three sons, of these two maharanies were named by the maharaja to commemorate his victories over Multan, Peshawar and Kashmir. We then have the youngest, Duleep Singh, born to Maharani Jinda, also married by the *chaddar* ceremony, the daughter of a Munoo Singh, belonging to a poor Aulak family of Gujranwala, who had been in Ranjit Singh's service for many years. There is no record of any daughters having been born. After he had a stroke in 1834, his doctors reported that he would be unable to have any more children.

Ranjit Singh's quest for the best went beyond acquiring women. His desire for owning the best drove him to unacceptable behaviour with the once deposed, and soon to be, Saddozai Amir of Afghanistan, Shah

Shuja-ul-Mulk, for example. He first invited the deposed amir to Lahore in 1813 as his guest, then kept him and his family and entourage under house arrest, and released him only after he had been forced to give up what he wanted, the famous Kohinoor diamond – a flawless egg-shaped diamond, an inch and a half long, an inch wide with a half inch depth, valued by Osborne in 1838 at 4.5 crore rupees.

He attacked his own Barakzai governor at Peshawar, Yar Mohammad, in 1829 when he refused to sell him a beautiful Persian horse, Liali. After his defeat and death, the horse, hidden elsewhere, was not found. He then made Sultan Mohammad Khan, the younger brother of the deposed governor, the ruler of Peshawar and demanded that Liali be found and given to him. After much hesitation Liali was finally 'presented' to Ranjit Singh and carried in triumph to Lahore by Sher Singh and General Allard. Baron Von Hugel says that 'He [Ranjit Singh] spent 60 lakh rupees and the lives of 12,000 soldiers to get this horse'. This was the cost of the campaign.

The one aspect of him that can be considered remarkable in those times is, that in his thirty-nine years at the helm of affairs, no death penalty was ever awarded, no matter how heinous the crime, in the civilian or military field. Alexander Burns, in his book *Travels into Bokhara* writes about this as follows,

> The most creditable trait in Ranjit's character is his humanity, he has never been known to punish a criminal with death since his accession to power [...] Cunning and conciliation have been the two great weapons of his diplomacy.[42]

When news reached Ranjit Singh that General Avitabile, his governor at Peshawar, had executed some Muslims who were attempting to foment trouble, he was soundly castigated. In another incident, when 'the maharaja heard of the excesses carried out, also in Peshawar, by Sham Singh Peshoria, a leading landowner, he was summarily dismissed from the durbar and put in chains'. Dr Honigberger, Ranjit Singh's doctor, recalls the maharaja telling him 'We punish but we will not take life'. In 1839, Captain La Font was warned by him not to beat his sepoys.[43]

The punishments meted out in his army were: dismissal or discharge; degradation; deduction of pay; confiscation of a *jagir*; fines; extra duty; amputation of limbs; imprisonment; physical punishments; warnings and reprimands; disbandment, in the case of collective punishment; and the stockade.

In the civilian field, justice covered a wide spectrum of judicial courts: the nazim's court, at the headquarters of a province; the Adalat-e-Ala, at Lahore which was an appellate high court; the ministers' court, pertaining to their own departments; jagirdars' court, a jagirdar had certain civil and military authority to decide cases of his own *jagir*; the Sharia courts, the courts of *kazis* and *muftis*, to decide cases of Muslims, according to the Quran; and the maharaja's court, to hear appeals from the lower courts. Ranjit Singh frequently censured guilty officials for having failed to decide cases honestly. The death penalty was banned. Punishment was meted out in the following order, depending on the crime: fines; imprisonment and mutilation of limbs.

Captain Osborne's comments on the maharaja's court were,

> His executions (of justice) are very prompt and simple, and follow quickly on the sentence: one blow of the axe, and then some boiling oil to immerse the stump in, and stop all effusion of blood, is all the machinery he requires for his courts of justice. He is himself accuser, judge, and jury; and five minutes is about the duration of the longest trial at Lahore.[44]

Ranjit Singh was a good judge of men. His administration was filled with extremely able people, whom he brought in from all over. Raja Dhyan Singh, the second of the three Jammu brothers, was his prime minister and was given the title of Raja Kalan, to distinguish him as the senior raja in the durbar. Jemadar Khushal Singh was the first Darogha-e-Deorhi Mualla, or Lord Chamberlain. Foreign relations or Dabir-ul-Mamlikat was with the extremely competent Fakir Aziz-ud-din, who in addition to his diplomatic skills, was a great scholar and physician. He was most popular with all communities. The auditor general of accounts was Ganga Ram and later Deenanath. Religious endowments were handled by bhais Gobind Singh, Ram Singh and Gurmukh Singh. The court language was Persian (Pharsi).

The state had a population of 35 lakh (3.5 million) in 1831. Administratively, it was divided into eight provinces. Each province was split into *parganas*, each *pargana* into *taluqas* and each *taluqa* consisted of 50 to 100 villages. The eight provinces were Lahore, Jalandhar, Kangra Hills, Jammu, Kashmir, Peshawar, Gujrat or Wazirabad and Multan.

In Multan, after its initial conquest and return to Nawab Muzaffar Khan on his promise of good behaviour, the nawab had reneged on his annual tribute on two further occasions, in 1805 and 1807, and an expeditionary force had to be sent yet again to enforce the payment. When he reneged for the fifth time, in 1810, Ranjit Singh attacked and captured the city and laid siege on the fort of Multan in which the nawab and his family were ensconced. The siege lasted two months, and during the ongoing attempts to occupy it, Ranjit Singh lost one of his trusted commanders, Attar Singh Dhari. Nihal Singh Attari and the up-and-coming Hari Singh Nalwa were wounded. The nawab finally yielded to him and a large tribute of 1,80,000 rupees and twenty horses was extracted from him. Yet again, in 1815, the nawab fell back on his annual payment and once again a force was sent against him. This time a tribute of two lakh was extracted from him. The nawab repeated the same in 1816 and 1817 when forces had to be sent to recover the durbar's dues. Ranjit Singh now decided to end this business once and for all.

On 20 June 1818, Akali Sadhu Singh and his Nihangs forced a breach caused by the famous siege gun Zamzama and was the first to enter the fort. Nawab Muzaffar Khan, gallantly, blocked the breach, along with his four sons. While the nawab and his two sons, Shah Nawaz Khan and Haq Nawas Khan were killed, one of his sons, Sarfaraz Khan, was captured and the fourth, Zulfiqar Khan surrendered. Out of the Multan garrison of 3,000 just 500 survived. The city of Multan was then sacked by the army and Griffen puts the loot taken at 2 million pounds sterling, 2 crore rupees at the then rate of exchange.

Ranjit Singh had suffered three consecutive defeats in his attempts to capture Kashmir, the third attempt being in 1814. Since those defeats, Kashmir remained uppermost in his mind. In 1819, he felt that he was ready to make another attempt. He set up camp at Wazirabad and appointed Missar Dewan Chand as the supreme commander of this operation. Dewan Chand's force comprised 20,000 troops and heavy artillery. As a prelude, he released Sultan Khan of Bhimbar, who had been his prisoner for the last seven years and who agreed to accompany the Sikh Army. The army was divided into three parts. The main force was under Dewan Chand accompanied by Sultan Khan. The reserve force was under Prince Kharak Singh and the second reserve was under Hari Singh Nalwa. Ranjit Singh, with an additional reserve force, was in the rear.

Going over the Toshamaidan Pass, Dewan Chand reached Rajauri in early June 1819. As the raja of Rajauri, Aghar Khan, had fled, he destroyed his fort and gutted the town. He then placed the raja's younger brother Rahimullah Khan on the *gaddi* of Rajauri. Aghar Khan, now joined by the raja of Punch, Rahullah Khan, attacked Dewan Chand's column in the Dhakideo and Maja Passes, where they were soundly beaten. The road to the Pir Panjal now lay open. Kharak Singh marched behind Dewan Chand and set up his headquarters at Sardi Thana. Ranjit Singh established his camp at Bhimber.

On 5 July, Dewan Chand engaged an Afghan force led by Jabbar Khan at Shopian, and defeated them in a few hours. The army entered Srinagar on 15 July 1819.

For twenty years from 1819 to 1839, seven governors ruled Kashmir for Ranjit Singh. The first governor being Dewan Moti Ram, the son of the Sikh commander-in-chief, Dewan Mokham Chand, who was then the governor of the Jalandhar Doab as well, in addition to his duty as commander-in-chief. Two years later, Hari Singh Nalwa became the governor and ruled till Ranjit Singh sent him to Hazara in 1822.

PUNJAB BOUNDARIES AND MAJOR TOWNS PRE 1 JANUARY 1845

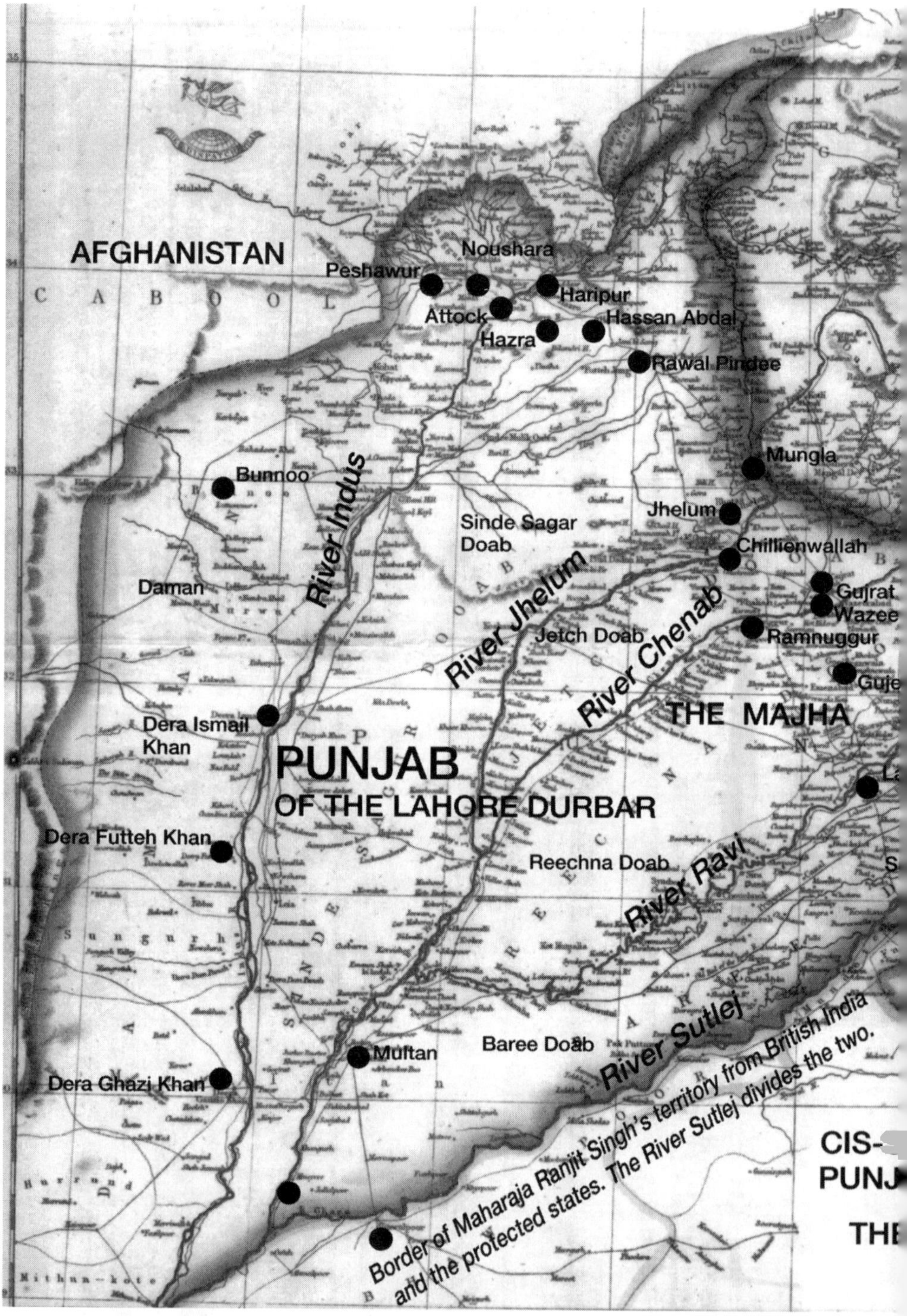

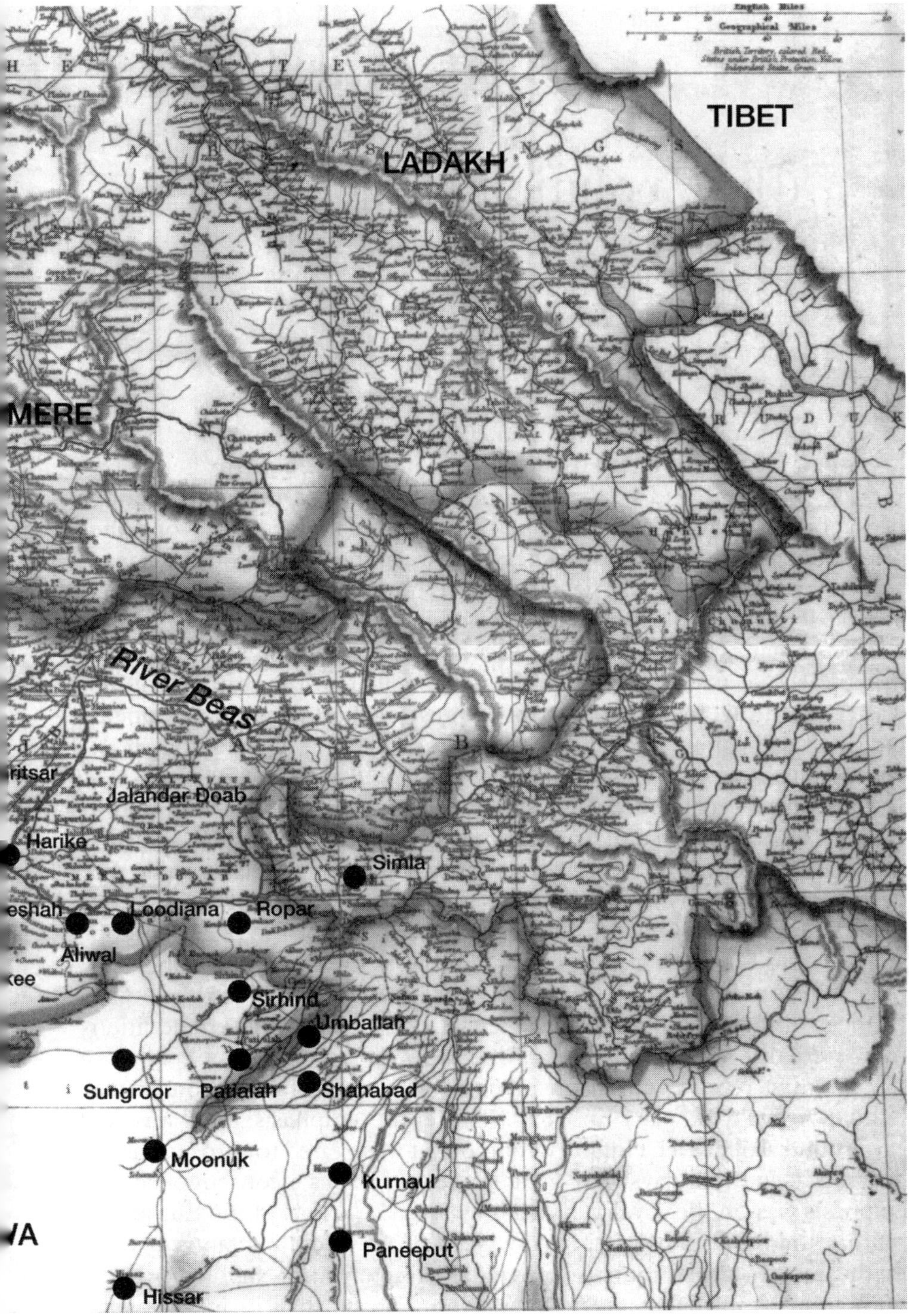
English Miles
Geographical Miles
TIBET
LADAKH
River Beas
Jalandar Doab
Harike
Simla
Loodiana
Ropar
Aliwal
Sirhind
Umballah
Sungroor
Patialah
Shahabad
Moonuk
Kurnaul
Paneeput
Hissar

The Evolution of the Army

Maharaja Ranjit Singh had consolidated his empire by the age of twenty-one. His quest for knowledge, both to better his empire and his army, continued unabated. A contemporary of Napoleon, he was greatly interested in the happenings in Europe, the wars, military organizations, tactics, and weaponry. His inquisitiveness, verging on impatience, was geared towards improving his military arsenal and capability, and thereby his military strength and efficiency. He had the hostile Afghans on the western border and a potential threat, the British, in the east. No matter how friendly and conciliatory the British attitude was at that time, their conquest of the rest of the Indian subcontinent indicated their ultimate objective – the subjugation of his kingdom at an appropriate time.

This period coincided with the end of the Napoleonic wars and a number of European soldiers of repute, formerly of the French Army or those of their allies, looked east in order to soldier on. Persia became the destination for many as Ranjit Singh's reputation had not reached the continent till then. Once in Persia, however, tales of Ranjit Singh and stories of his kingdom and his military prowess drew many to Lahore to offer their services to him. By the end of his reign in 1839, thirty-nine European officers, including six generals, were in his service. In addition there were three doctors.[45]

The first reorganization on modern lines and consolidation of the Lahore Army took place in 1822. The entire emphasis then was on cavalry and artillery. The infantry component was geared towards garrison duty. Sikhs in those days were great horsemen and as a consequence the emphasis was on the cavalry. It was only after the arrival of the European officers and Ranjit Singh being convinced of the role the infantry played in the major battles fought between Wellington and Napoleon, both during the Peninsular wars and in northern Europe, that the infantry was reorganized along the lines of the European armies. As a result, its role in battle was recognized by the Sikhs, many of whom then opted to join it.

The strength of Ranjit Singh's army in 1821 stood at 50,000. The Fauj-e-Khas comprised 11,000 Ghorcharras divided into 15 Derahs led by eminent sardars, amongst them Sham Singh Attari, Gurmukh Singh Lamba, Hari Singh Nalwa, and two by non-Sikhs, the Mulraj Derah and the Dogra Derah. Ten thousand infantry was divided into 16 battalions of 600–800 men, each manned by Poorbiyas of north-central India, Gurkhas of Nepal and other mercenaries with a sprinkling of Sikhs and Muslims. Four regular cavalry regiments called Rajmans were raised totalling 1,200 horse, led by Gurmukh Singh, Hira Singh, Mehtab Singh, and the 4th Rajman. In addition, there were 9,000 irregular infantry for garrison duty, personal guards and constabulary. The artillery, as will be noticed, had only Muslim commanders. As the Sikhs loved the cavalry, the Muslims loved their guns and were excellent gunners. Based on the calibre of the guns and their usage, the artillery was divided into the Topkhana 'Fili', or Elephant Batteries with the heavy siege guns; the Topkhana 'Shutri', with their camel mounted Swivels or Zambooraks; the Topkhana 'Aspi', or Horse Artillery; and the Topkhana 'Gavi', or bullock-drawn field guns. The artillery was under the derahs – Illahi Bakhsh, Mazhar Ali Beg, Ibadullah Khan, and Ghulam Mohammed Khan. In addition, there were 20,000 irregular cavalry and infantry comprising the feudal or Jagirdari Fauj. This comprised 10,000 infantry, mainly hill men, Gurkha and Dogra battalions, and 10,000 Sikh Feudal Horse. The reorganization under European generals took place now and the army was forged into a highly disciplined force trained on European lines.

Ranjit Singh's leadership and army were respected by the British, and they therefore preferred him as an ally, till such time that they had consolidated the rest of India. Even more importantly, they considered him a natural ally in keeping the aggressive designs of the Afghan rulers in check. As a consequence, a mission led by Charles Metcalfe (later Lord Metcalfe) had visited Lahore in 1809 and a treaty of friendship was entered into. Ranjit Singh, in turn, respected British military capability and adhered to the Treaty of Amritsar for the rest of his life. He was a realist and a politically astute man and knew his strengths and shortcomings.

In his autobiography, Colonel Alexander Gardner, Ranjit Singh's American colonel of artillery, who died in the service of the state of Kashmir at the age of ninety-two in 1877 writes:

> An incident occurred during the visit of Mr Metcalfe's mission which brought home to Ranjit Singh's mind a sense of the true value of discipline, and made him all the more determined to build his army on the European model. Among the Sikh troops of 1809 was a turbulent and fanatical group known as the Akalis, or Immortals, whose headlong valour had often served Ranjit Singh and turned the

> fortunes of a doubtful battle. The Akalis, (led by Akali Phula Singh), infuriated by the sight of the religious observance of Mr Metcalfe's escort of Hindustani sepoys, suddenly and without the slightest warning made an attack in overwhelming numbers on the camp of the British mission, which was defended only by two companies of native infantry. Though taken by surprise, the escort quickly rallied and repelled the attack. The Akalis, in turn incurred the wrath of Ranjit Singh more for their ignominious defeat, than for the inconvenience caused by their misconduct in making the attack.[46]

The first two European officers to arrive in Lahore were Ventura and Jean Francois Allard. Both had served in Napoleon's army but after his defeat and exile to St Helena, had moved to Egypt, then Persia, Afghanistan, and finally to Punjab in 1822.

Both these officers had served with distinction up to and at Waterloo. Ventura, an Italian, was a colonel of infantry and Allard had enrolled in the French Army in the ranks of the 23rd Dragoons, a distinguished cavalry regiment, and on commissioning, served in Napoleon's Imperial Guard and the 7 Hussars, ending his career in Waterloo as a captain.

Taking an instant liking to Ventura, Ranjit Singh gave him command, first of two battalions of infantry and soon after that of the Fauj-e-Khas, his model brigade. It would henceforth also be known as 'Francais Campoo'. To indicate the esteem he held him in, he had him accommodated in the famous tomb of Anarkali, which had earlier been home to Kharak Singh, his son and heir apparent. Allard was ordered to raise a regiment of Dragoons on the French pattern.

Next to arrive was Paolo di Bartolomeo Avitabile who had served the king of Naples, Joseph Bonaparte, as a lieutenant of artillery and had commanded a battery of guns. He arrived in the court at Lahore and was immediately employed for the artillery. Very soon, however, Ranjit Singh, a good judge of men, sent him to Wazirabad as governor. After a distinguished career at Wazirabad, Avitabile was sent to Peshawar as governor after a string of Sikh governors had failed to control the city once it came under the durbar. He remained there as governor till 1843.

The fourth officer to arrive was Claude Auguste Court. A graduate of the Ecole Polytechnique of Paris, he had joined the 151st Regiment of line of the French Army as a sub-lieutenant of foot and the next year had been transferred to the 68th Regiment. Five years later he resigned his commission and left for the East, first to Persia from where he reached the Lahore Durbar in 1827. He was appointed to head the artillery, a post which had been vacant after Avitabile's promotion.

Of the four, Ventura had been a French colonel under Napoleon and the other three had been junior officers. All of them, except Ventura who commanded an infantry battalion in battle under Napoleon, had limited combat experience. None had any experience of higher command. Nevertheless, all were appointed generals by Ranjit Singh.

Colonel Gardner lists thirty-nine foreign officers and three doctors. There were six generals. Apart from the above four, there was General Harlan, an American and General Van Cortlandt from England, both infantrymen. There were nine colonels – Ford and Stienbach with the infantry and Foulkes with the cavalry, all three from England; Canora, an American artillery soldier; Mouton of the French cavalry; Hurbon, a Spanish engineer; Thomas, a lieutenant colonel of infantry and the Anglo-Indian son of the famous Irish adventurer Colonel George Thomas who had carved himself a principality at Hansi towards the end of the eighteenth century. There was one Lieutenant Colonel Rattray, also of the infantry, and Gardner himself. There were twenty-four other officers of field rank and below, many of whom later ended up commanding regiments of cavalry or battalions of infantry.

The organization and training of the army was to be on the lines of the French Army, so would be the drill, words of command and tactics employed in battle. The principal formation was a brigade; there was no higher command till much later. Though the French commanders used French tactics and the English commanders used tactics learnt in the British Army, there was no confusion. Both nationalities had recently finished fighting each other in the European wars, and had, undoubtedly, learnt enough from each other during the process to enable them to evolve standard procedures.

To begin with, in 1799, Ranjit Singh's army was, as elsewhere in India, based on the feudal concept. It comprised 2,500 Ghorcharras and the existing derahs including a sprinkling of retainers and soldiers of fortune.[47] The second phase of reorganization was undertaken by Ranjit Singh in 1808, where some semblance of a modern military structure began to evolve. What must be remembered, however, is that in 1808 he was just eighteen years old, uneducated and with no professional military training.

The Lahore Durbar Army

Commander-in-Chief [48]

Maharaja Ranjit Singh
Strength 14,000

A. Ghorcharras: 6,000

i. Original Derahs 2,500
ii. New Derahs 3,500
Ghorcharra Khas Derah
Sham Singh Attariwala's Derah
Gurmukh Singh Lamba's Derah
The Sandhanwalia's Derah

B. Regular Infantry: 1,500

4 Telinga (Poorbiya) Battalions
1 Hindustani (Rohilla) Battalion

C. Irregular Infantry: 5,000
5 Battalions (1,000 men each)

D. Artillery
Field – 35-40 guns of various calibres
Zambooraks – 100 Zambooraks

E. Jagirdari: 1,500
Feudal Infantry
Feudal Horse

By 1831, the third phase of the organization of the army was completed as follows:[49]

	Fauj-e-Ain (The Regular Army)		**Jagirdari Fauj**
Irregular Army		Regular Army	Cavalry
Fauj-e-Sawari (Ghorcharras) 1. Ghorcharra Khas	Fauj-e-Kilajat 1. Static Fort Gunners	Fauj-e-Khas Cavalry Infantry	Artillery Infantry (Feudal Forces of the sardars and nobles)
(Feudals of Ranjit Singh) 2. Missaldar Sowaran (misls subjugated by Ranjit Singh)	2.Garrison Infantry comprising untrained najibs and Ramgoles		Artillery

The command of the army remained with Ranjit Singh till his death in 1839. Army commanders were appointed on a temporary basis for a particular campaign and the requisite force was given to them for the duration of that campaign.

Till the mid 1840s, there was no formation above that of a brigade. The brigades were in fact independent brigades, or in some cases depending on their deployment, they were, what are today called Brigade Groups. In 1844, a decision was taken to raise 4 divisions. By November 1845, according to British Intelligence estimates, 7 divisions, each 8,000 to 12,000 strong, had been raised, though in fact only 4 divisions had been raised. The first, of 4,000 cavalry and 2 Infantry Brigades, was under Sham Singh Attari. The second division was commanded by Raja Lal Singh and comprised 4,500 cavalry and 2 Infantry Brigades, and the third was under Sardar Tej Singh comprising 1,000 cavalry and 4 infantry brigades, including 1 of irregulars. The fourth being the Dogra division under Raja Gulab Singh, and the Raja Dhyan Singh and Raja Suchet Singh's independent brigades comprising 18 infantry battalions and 6 cavalry regiments in all.

Till 1840, a brigade, commanded by a general, was the largest formation employed in the regular army. The organization varied but usually consisted of 3-4 infantry battalions, 1 cavalry regiment and 1-2 artillery batteries. The strength varied between 4,000 and 5,000 troops. When the general's rank was introduced by Ranjit Singh in 1836, eight generals were appointed to command the brigades, Ventura, Court, Ajit Singh, Gujar Singh, Ram Singh, Tej Singh, Misr Sukh Raj, and Mian Udham Singh (Allard was then on leave in France). By 1845 there were 12 brigades (including the Fauj-e-Khas). The remaining brigades were commanded by colonels. In addition to the brigades there were a number of independent battalions and batteries.

The Fauj-e-Khas, or 'Royal Army', or Francais Campoo, or French Legion, the various names by which the model brigade was called, was raised by Allard and Ventura and became the role model from the organizational point of view for the remaining brigades that were subsequently raised. Allard was also appointed to command all of the Fauj-e-Ain cavalry, apart from his Fauj-e-Khas Brigade. The brigade comprised 4 infantry battalions, the older two being the Paltan Khas and Paltan Dewa Singh. In 1823 the Gurkha Paltan was added and in 1824 Paltan Sham Sota. The infantry compliment was increased by Ranjit Singh by 1 battalion in 1826, to 5 battalions. The cavalry compliment, to begin with, comprised 2 cavalry regiments – the Rajman Khas Lancia or the Royal Lancer Regiment and the Rajman Daragun Anwal, or the First Dragoon Regiment. Another cavalry regiment was added in 1826. The artillery compliment was commanded by Illahi Bakhsh and comprised 24 guns.

The Fauj-e-Khas, apart from being the smartest on parade – with meticulous precision in drill to the roll of the drum, on the French pattern – was the best-equipped, best-armed and best-dressed brigade in the army. It also acquitted itself with distinction in the battles fought at Naushera in (1823), Dera Ismail Khan, Multan, and Peshawar in (1837-39), in the conquest of Kulu and Mandi in 1841, and during the first Sikh war in 1845-46. Its strength had reached 5,500 men by 1839, and was about the same at the time of the first Anglo-Sikh war, when it comprised 3,176 infantry, 1,667 cavalry and 855 artillerymen with 34 guns. The cavalry regimental strength had the Dragoons with 730 troopers, the Lancers with 750 troopers and the Royal Lancers with 187 troopers, 1,667 in all.

At the beginning, a colonel commanded a two infantry battalion group, while the Kumedan commanded a battalion. By the end of Ranjit Singh's era, however, the colonels had become battalion commanders, and the Kumedans had fallen to a position of second-in-command.

Each battalion had 8 companies called 'pelotons'. Every two pelotons comprised a 'region' and four regions formed a 'demi-battalion'. A peloton was further divided into two sections. The colonel was assisted by a commandant, a *mahzor*, a *mutsaddi*, one writer, and one *granthi*. The colonel commanded and the commandant was responsible for training and administration with the adjutant assisting him. The *mahzor* was the battalion quartermaster and the *mutsaddi* checked the battalion rolls and reported to the adjutant. A *peloton* had a strength of 1 subedar, 2 jemadars, 1 sarjan, 4 havaldars, 1 furrier, 4 naiks, 1 *tambur mahzor* (drum major), 1bugler, a few *tamburchis* (drummers), and 100 men.

In turn a battalion, called 'bataillon', had 8 subedars, 17 jemadars, 8 sarjans, 32 havaldars, 32 naiks, 8 furriers, 1 drum major, 16 drummers, and 8 buglers – 130 in all. In addition, it had 76 non-combatants enrolled, which included 4 timekeepers, 4 flag bearers, 9 khalasis, 9 artisans, 16 water carriers, 16 cooks, spadesmen or *beldars*, 9 camel drivers, and one runner or *harkarah*. Each battalion had a troop strength of between 600 and 800 men.

The regular cavalry regiments were organized much on the same lines. Having being trained on the French lines by Allard since 1822, the troopers were called Sowaran Francees. The regiments were divided into 'risalas' or troops. The regimental organization was more or less the same as the infantry battalion. At the troop level it varied. A troop was commanded by 1 risaldar and comprised 2 jemadars, 1 nishanchi (ensign), 1 sarjan, 4 havaldars, 4 naiks, 2 trumpeters, and on an average about 150 to 200 troopers. The smallest on record was the Rajman Gobind which in 1839 had just 98 troopers, the average being 250 to 700. In 1839 there were 10 regular cavalry regiments, and in 1845 there were 15. Before the First Sikh War, the British took the average regimental strength at 600 troopers.

The artillery batteries, or derahs, too had a similar organizational structure as an infantry battalion. The battery, however, was of no fixed size.

> By the end of Ranjit Singh's reign, Jinsi batteries consisted of 10 to 30 guns, (some even had 40 and more), while Aspi batteries had between 5 and 10 guns. Of the 32 Aspi batteries recorded in 1845, 14 had 2 to 7 guns, 4 had 8 to 10 and 11 had 11 to 15. For tactical usage, batteries were divided into sections of two guns, but for administrative purposes, a section comprised one gun and limber and one ammunition wagon and limber. The highest rank in the artillery was General, of whom there were four in 1845.[50]

The Aspi guns were 3 pdrs to 6 pdrs (pounders), while the Jinsi's comprised 6 ½ pdrs to 12 pdrs. Heavier guns were 18 pdrs and 24 pdrs. There were so many calibres of guns that at the end of the First Sikh War over 96 different types were captured out of the 250 taken by the British on the field. Most were produced by the foundry set up at Lahore.

Each gun was the responsibility of a jemadar, assisted by a havaldar and a naik. There were between 8 and 11 gunners (*golandaz*) and 5 to 7 non-combatants (*beldars, mistris, saqqas*, etc.) per gun. The total establishment of a 10 gun battery was about 250 gunners and non-combatants, in a fifty-fifty ratio.

Each gun and wagon of a Jinsi battery was drawn by bullocks, camels or cart horses. The Kalan or siege guns were drawn by elephants. A single heavy gun required between 80 and 100 bullocks to move it. The heavy siege guns were all of Mughal origin and were known by their names. The Bhangian ki Top was the famous Zamzama, firing an 84 pound projectile. Then there were the giants 'Fateh Jung' and the 'Kadhe Khan', given by Maharaja Sahib Singh of Patiala to Ranjit Singh on one of his visits. It was deployed during the First Sikh War and was returned by the British to Patiala, after the war. Today it stands in the Patiala Fort, as does the Zamzama in the Lahore Fort.

In a horse-drawn battery there were 6 to 8 horses per gun and limber, and the same number of horses for ammunition. The Zamboorak batteries were more flexible, with 3 gunners per swivel and comprised anywhere between 40 and 105 guns.

The ammunition used by the guns included round shot made of iron, brass or zinc. Chain shot, canister, grape, and shells. The shells were mostly made of brass, copper, pewter, or lead.

At the time of Ranjit Singh's death the regular artillery totalled 192 guns and 4,500 gunners, organized into 14 batteries. The Kila Jat and Jagirdari guns added to this takes the figure up to between 350 and 400. In addition, there were 280 Zambooraks with the regular army and a similar number with the Jagirdari Fauj. After Ranjit Singh, and the army's direct influence in governance, the size of the artillery grew dramatically and had doubled by the eve of the First Sikh War. When Sher Singh died in 1843, there were 232 guns and 6,050 gunners. Under Raja Hira Singh the strength increased to 282 guns, 300 Zambooraks and 8,280 gunners and by 1845, there were 32 batteries with 388 Zambooraks and 11,500 gunners. The Kila Jat and Jagirdari guns are not included in these figures. Cunningham estimates that in July 1844, the Fauj-e-Ain and Jagirdari Fauj together could field 552 guns and 995 Zambooraks. The Fauj-e-Kilajat had an additional 505 guns and 1,428 Zambooraks.

In 1831, when the reorganization of the army on modern lines came into existence, the first signs of the implementation of the European military system became visible.

Commander-in-Chief

Maharaja Ranjit Singh

Strength 84,500

A. Ghorcharras: 10,000

Derah Leaders:

1. Dewan Missar Chand
2. Jemadar Khushal Singh
3. Sardar Lehna Singh Majithia
4. Raja Suchet Singh

5. Sardar Sandhanwalia
6. Sardar Sham Singh Attari
7. Sardar Gurmukh Singh Lamba
8. Ghorcharra Derah Khas
9. Ardaliyan Da Derah
10. Pindiwala Derah
11. Ramgarhia Derah (disbanded and merged with the Derah Khas)
12. Jamwalla Derah (disbanded and merged with the Derah Khas)
13. Mulraj Derah
14. Dogra Derah
15. Naulakha Derah
16. Derah Khas

B. The Fauj-e-Ain or Regular Army (20,000)

Fauj-e-Khas

1. 4 Battalions of infantry of General Ventura
2. 2 Rajmans of cavalry of General Allard
   1st Dragoons
   2nd Lancia (Lancers) Dragoons
3. Horse Artillery Derah Illahi Bakhsh (24 guns)

Regular Infantry

4. 21 Regular Infantry battalions (600–1,100 men each)
5. Several independent infantry companies

Regular Cavalry (3,914, including Allard's two Dragoons in Fauj-e-Khas)

6. i. Rajmans Gurmukh Singh
   ii. Rajmans Hira Singh
   iii. Rajmans Mehtab Singh

C. Irregular Infantry (24,000)

7. i. Garrison Duty
   ii. Personal Guards
   iii. Constabulary

D. Artillery (3,500)

8. i. 32 Topkhana Derahs, Fili, Aspi and Gavi (300 guns)
   ii. 4 Derahs Aspi (300 Zambooraks)

E. Jagirdari Fauj (27,000)

9. i. Feudal Infantry (mainly Hill, Gurkha and Dogra battalions)
   ii. Feudal Horse
   iii. Limited Feudal Artillery

Ranjit Singh had initially appointed Ventura to command two infantry battalions and Allard to raise a regiment of Dragoons on the French pattern. Only after testing Ventura in combat did he give him command of a brigade-level formation, which was to beome the Fauj-e-Khas. Once raised, it became the envy of all for its smartness, discipline, movement, and steadfastness in battle. It also became the model on which all brigades would henceforth be organized and trained.

Soon after Allard was ordered to raise his regiment of Dragoons. Colonel Gardner goes on to say, that one day Ranjit Singh ordered his Ghorcharras, or irregular cavalry, to cross the Indus. The order was immediately obeyed, but no discipline was observed and no precautions were taken. No less than 500 men and horses are said to have been swept away by the torrent and drowned. Allard then mounted an elephant, and directed his cavalry by trumpet-sounds, and moving them in a suitable formation, succeeded in conveying them across the Indus without a single man lost, Allard was immediately promoted to the rank of a general.[51]

Ventura and Allard had been appointed in 1822 and the opportunity to prove themselves came in March of the following year. When Fateh Khan, the wazir (prime minister) of Afghanistan, was killed in internal disturbances in August 1818, Ranjit Singh took advantage of the confusion within Afghanistan and swiftly captured Khairabad and its neighbouring area around the western bank of the Indus that belonged to Feroz Khan, the Khatak chief. He then moved just as swiftly and occupied Peshawar on 20 November 1818. Its governor, Yar Mohammad Khan Barakzai, fled to the Yusafzai country. Ranjit Singh made over the governorship to Jehandad Khan, the former governor of Attock and left for Lahore. Yar Mohammad promptly returned and turned Jehandad Khan out and reoccupied his former domain. Shrewdly, Ranjit Singh did not touch Peshawar for the next four years while he focused his attention on capturing Kashmir, which he achieved in 1819, and then took some time in its consolidation.

Once Kashmir was under control, he turned to Peshawar and demanded Yar Mohammad Khan's allegiance. Yar Mohammad promptly paid 40,000 rupees as *nazarana* and presented Ranjit Singh with six Persian horses. An annual tribute of 20,000 rupees was levied on him, and he in turn promised his total allegiance to the Lahore Durbar.

Upset with this turn of events, Mohammad Azim Khan, the new wazir of Afghanistan, decided to once and for all finish Sikh domination of this territory and called for a Jehad (religious war) to rid Ranjit Singh of Peshawar and the territories west of the Indus that had been conquered by him. The Yusafzais and Khataks joined him in this.

The battle was fought with the Afghans at Naushera or Theri, on 14 March 1823. Colonel Gardner narrates the battle as, 'The Afghans were in great strength – their regular troops holding a position on the right bank of the Kabul (Lunda) river, while 20,000 mountaineers of the Khatak and Yusufzai tribes occupied a strong position on the left bank.'

Ranjit Singh now showed his confidence in generals Ventura and Allard by sending them with a small force of 8 battalions and 2 batteries to keep the regular Afghan troops in check while he with his main strength fell upon the Ghazis. The battle was severely contested, but thanks to the superior command of Ranjit Singh, resulted in a complete victory for the Sikhs. The loss of the victors was estimated by Captain Wade[52] (afterwards Sir Claude Wade) at 2,000 men out of a total force of 24,000. The Afghan tribesman lost more than 3,000 men. Mohammad Azim Khan, the commander of the Afghan regular troops, however, fearing that his treasure and harem might fall into the hands of the Sikhs, struck camp and crossed the Mohmand hills with undignified haste and regained the valley of Jellalabad. As a result, Ranjit Singh occupied the city of Peshawar.

Khuda Bakhsh, the then chief of the Chatha clan, distinguished himself during this battle. His family had fallen on hard times as Ranjit Singh had usurped his family's entire property after an abortive attempt on his life by his ancestor. Khuda Bakhsh had reversed the policy of his ancestors of confrontation with the Shukarchakias, and had waited upon Ranjit Singh, and had been warmly accepted by the maharaja and was appointed a sardar of the Ghorcharras, with a *jagir* given to him which provided 12,000 rupees annually. Since then he had served the maharaja most loyally and gallantly in the battles of Kasur, Multan, Mankhera, Kashmir, and Peshawar. In this battle of Theri too, he served his patron yet again by leading his troops valiantly into the Afghan centre, and during the battle, severing with a single stroke the head of a leading Afghan chief, while he himself took several wounds.[53]

What Colonel Gardner did not state however, was that the ferocious battle nearly ended in a stalemate or with the possibility of a defeat for Ranjit Singh. At a critical moment in the battle, when defeat seemed almost imminent, Ranjit Singh saw Akali Phula Singh and his Nihang and Akali shock troops with their black flags, riding up the hill which was the enemy's main position. With casualties mounting to ferocious plunging fire, Phula Singh ordered his men to dismount and advance on foot. Seeing him move ahead on his elephant, exhorting his troops, the army took heart and also moved forward. Phula Singh was shouting to his men all the while to move or die. When his mahout refused to move forward because of the tremendous fire plunging down on them, he pulled out his pistol and shot him dead, and then with the tip of his sword continued to guide the elephant forward. But he was hit in the forehead by a bullet which killed him immediately, and he fell back in the howdah. Seeing him fall, anger filled both the Akalis and the army, and the men stormed the position and after a severe hand-to-hand battle, captured it. The Afghans fled the scene. Had Akali Phula Singh not taken the initiative the battle of Theri may, in all probability, have been lost. It was his battle.[54]

A mound was erected to commemorate the battle and a gurdwara was built on the spot where Akali Phula Singh fell. It is now a place of pilgrimage where Hindus, Muslims and Sikhs pay their respects. Every Thursday night, Muslim women light a lamp to the hero of the battle of Theri, with a prayer to protect their children.

> The first campaign of the year 1826 was directed against Kotler, the chief command being given to Jemadar Khushal Singh, a favourite officer of the Maharaja. In this campaign a number of Sikh sardars, chiefs and soldiers refused to serve under Ventura and Allard, and threatened to resist their authority by main force. The two generals complained to the Maharaja, who at once proceeded to the army, degraded the mutinous officers, and severely punished the ringleaders of inferior rank.[55]

For the officers commanding various units, the battlefield was the training ground. There was no formal training. Officers were promoted as per their performance in battle. Ranjit Singh had an uncanny ability to make these selections. However, if ever he found anyone wanting in any manner he was just as quick to remove him, 'as he did in the case of Missar Sukh Dayal, brother of Missar Dewan Chand', his loyal and trusted general. 'He was appointed a commandant of artillery in 1825, but was soon after dismissed for incompetence.'[56]

Though Ranjit Singh appointed many generals from amongst the foreign soldiers who came to his durbar, besides the many who had been elevated to this rank from amongst those who had fought his battles for him over the years, his mind was still occupied with the question of his future command. The choice to produce future military leaders fell naturally on his sardars – be they Muslim, Sikh or Hindu – and their sons. Baron Hugel comments on a General Ram Singh: 'He was only fourteen years old, notwithstanding his youth, his talents, vivacity and desire for information promise great things'. However, in a general observation he also states, 'The building completed, the Maharaja does not think the same care necessary for its preservation as for its construction, and boys, simpletons and dotards are here as in older services, creeping into command'. On the contrary, the traveller Mcnaughton records that:

> General Officers have been selected from sons of sardars who have had their children carefully trained in the European system of military tactics. They are generally very young men, not more than seventeen years of age, and some of them whom I have seen are remarkable for their military spirit.[57]

Ranjit Singh had a great eye for choosing his leaders, both civil and military. It is, therefore, difficult to accept the fact that he would choose anything other than able commanders for his troops in his regular army. His successes are proof of this. Perhaps he did wish his sardars to make good soldiers of their sons; however that does not mean, as the two observers have reported, that he would automatically appoint them to regimental or higher command over his tried and tested commanders in the Fauj-e-Ain. Leadership of the derahs and the Jagirdari Fauj was another matter. Those units were based on the existing feudal system, and it was possible that in these cases such young leadership did exist. A young son taking over from a deceased father was how the feudal system worked.

The class composition of the army was as follows.

> In the regular infantry the Sikhs comprised 52 out of the 62 battalions (in 1845). The same was the case in the regular cavalry. There were 4 Dogra battalions and two of Gurkhas. The Gurkhas were put under the command of General Court. One of the sons of the Gurkha General Amar Singh Thapa, who had at first been pushed out of Kangra by Ranjit Singh and had then been defeated by Colonel Ochterlony at Malaun, Bhupal Singh was appointed a Captain and served with the Gurkha troops under Court. In the artillery, however, Muslims were over 50 per cent. The cavalry too had 10 per cent Muslim troopers. The officer class covered the three prominent inhabitants of the state. In 1844, there were 16 generals and senior officers who were Sikh, 13 were Hindus and 3 Muslim and one Englishman.[58]

This was not the case during Ranjit Singh's reign. There were six European generals under him but most left the service after his death and during the unstable period which followed it, including the army unrest of 1842 during Sher Singh's reign. Once the panchayat system took over, the troops virtually dictated as to who would be a general, or who should or should not be promoted. One, therefore, gets a distorted picture of the community-wise list of officers of high rank listed above during 1844. During Ranjit Singh's reign competence, not religious affiliation, brought promotion.

In 1836, after Ranjit Singh suffered a stroke, he appointed General Ventura, in whom he had developed implicit faith, to an appointment called 'Chief General'. What precisely his task was is not clear, he was perhaps a chief of staff or a deputy, as in armies today. As he had been partly incapacitated due to the stroke and his health was a concern, Ranjit Singh perhaps felt it necessary to do so, in case a battle was thrust upon him while he was indisposed.

Captain Osborne records this observation of the Lahore Army,

> [...] the Sikh Army possesses one great advantage over our own – the ease with which it can be moved. No wheel carriage is allowed on a march, their own bazaars carry all they require; and thirty thousand of their troops could be moved with more facility, and less expense and loss of time, than three Company's regiments on this side of the Sutlej [...]

He goes on to give an insight into Ranjit Singh's character as a military commander. He writes,

> He is in a most facetious humour, which rather surprised me, as reports had been received overnight from Peshawar, by no means favourable to the success of arms in that quarter. His old enemy Dost Mohommed Khan, with his Afghans, had attacked and utterly defeated a large body of the Sikh Army under one of Ranjit's favourite generals and had killed and taken prisoner upwards of five hundred of them. The Maharaja seemed to bear the reverse with great equanimity, and, in an answer to some questions I ventured to put to him on the subject, said that a trifling defeat now and then was useful, as it taught both men and officers caution.

During the course of his leadership of the Shukarchakia misl, and later as the maharaja of Lahore, Ranjit Singh's conquest of what would become his kingdom meant a series of battles to capture, occupy and then hold his territory against those who wanted it back, or those who eyed it. If details were to be given of these battles, it would run into half the book, and that is not the objective of this one. Suffice it to say that the kingdom extended in the west to Afghanistan, in the north-west to Badakshan, to the north came Tibet, to the east it extended to the river Sutlej, from the moment it entered India from Tibet through the Shipki La Pass to the point it merged with the Beas at Harike and then with the Indus. To the south lay Sind, on which he had set his eye, but an agreement with the British prevented him from moving south.

In today's terms, the kingdom of Lahore comprised what is today Pakistan, less Sind. To this one can add the entire Jammu and Kashmir including Ladakh, the Indian Punjab up to the river Sutlej and the major part of Himachal Pradesh west of the Sutlej, comprising Kulu, Mandi, Chamba, and the entire Kangra belt.

During the conquest of his territory, he captured Multan in 1818, Kashmir in 1819, subdued the war-like Yusafzai Pathans in Hazara and captured their territory along with Gilgit, Chitral and Swat, which would be known as the 'Gilgit Wazarat' (today known in Pakistan as the Northern Areas). Then came his battles to subdue the other tribal areas in the north, of Akora in 1826, Hazro in 1827, Saidu or Pirpai in 1827, Utmanzai in 1828, and Phulra in 1829.

In 1820, Ranjit Singh fell out with his mother-in-law Sada Kaur. She had been his ally in all battles fought since he was seventeen years old, and had also been one of his closest confidants. In actual fact he was by now wary of her strength and influence. The excuse used was his insistence on her providing part of her *jagir* to her grandsons, Sher Singh and Tara Singh, whom he had refused to acknowledge as his sons. Ranjit Singh now stated that since they were Mehtab Kaur's sons, and as a consequence, Sada Kaur's grandsons, she must therefore give them part of her *jagir*. When she refused, she was arrested, and kept in confinement for twelve years in Amritsar, till she died in 1832.

On the news of her death, Kanwar Naunihal Singh was sent to perform her last rites, while Missar Beli Ram was dispatched to attach all her property to the state. Later Ranjit Singh personally rode over to her house to condole with members of her family. While in her house, he sent for her principal attendant Mai Dasi and ordered her to produce all of Sada Kaur's personal effects. He then returned to Lahore with two lakh rupees and a pearl necklace worth 60,000 rupees. The greater joy for him, however, was the final subjugation of the misls. The Kanhiyas could not have been subjugated as long as she was alive. The subjugation of all misls north of the Sutlej was now complete.

In 1835, still not reconciled to Peshawar being in the domain of the Lahore Durbar, Dost Mohammad, the king of Afghanistan and Ranjit Singh's constant adversary, moved towards Peshawar from Jellalabad, over the Khyber Pass, with an army of 40,000 Afghans and 37 guns. On receiving the news, Ranjit Singh moved north in a forced march reaching Gujranwala on 19 April, Wazirabad on 20, Gujarat on 22, and on 23 April at Rohtas. He reached Rawalpindi on 25 April. On 29, in heavy rain he reached Serai Kala at Hasan Abdal and Attock on the 30th.

He crossed the river Indus on 1 May and reached Naushera on 2 May 1835. After the first battle against the Barakzais and Ghazis, at Ramkani on 4 May, in which they were defeated, he entered Peshawar and Sultan Mohammad, the ruler already allied with Ranjit Singh, received him.

Ranjit Singh then attempted to dissuade Dost Mohammad from attacking Peshawar by sending Fakir Aziz-u-din and General Harlan as his emissaries. The offer was spurned and Dost Mohammad ordered his troops to deploy on the ridge line east of the Khaibar. Ranjit Singh then deployed the French Division comprising 22,000 men under generals Allard, Avitabile, Court, and Ventura at Hashtnagar, which was Dost Mohammad's left flank. The maharaja then led his army of 80-60,000 men forward. Feigning a frontal attack, he pressed the enemy's right flank. Fearing that the Sikh Army had surrounded him, Dost Mohammad panicked and fled. When the Sikhs reached the top of the Khaibar, there was no one to be seen.

In 1837, two years later, Hari Singh Nalwa, who had tamed the wild tribal areas of the north and had remained governor of Hazara for fifteen years from 1822 to 1837, was sent to Peshawar to build a fort at Jamraud, at the mouth of the Khyber Pass, as a permanent check to Dost Mohammad's ambitions and persistent efforts at encroachment. While the maharaja's orders were being implemented, he lived in Peshawar in the new fortress, built on the site of the old Bala Hissar. As the celebrations for the wedding of the maharaja's grandson, Kanwar Naunihal Singh, were on in Lahore, most of the army was camped at Lahore. Hari Singh sent 600 men out of his small command at Peshawar, under Mihan Singh, to Jamraud to protect the builders.

Dost Mohammad who was at Jellalabad, and was himself building a fort at the Khaibar, at Ali Masjid, now saw his chance. With Ranjit Singh preoccupied at Lahore and with just a handful of troops with Hari Singh Nalwa at Peshawar, he sent the best of his army – 7,000 horses, 2,000 matchlock men and 9,000 guerrilla fighters, under his son Mohammad Akbar Khan to capture Peshawar. On the way, they were joined by 20,000 Ghazis.

Hari Singh Nalwa immediately dispatched a report to Ranjit Singh at Lahore, which reached him on 21 April, in which he informed the maharaja that the advance guard of Dost Mohammad's army had crossed the Khaibar and had positioned themselves short of Jamraud.

Ranjit Singh in turn, without delay, sent a force under Tej Singh, generals Allard, Court and Avitabile, Jemadar Khushal Singh, the sardar of Attari, Raja Gulab Singh, Sultan Mohammad Khan and Pir Mohammad Khan with their forces, to reach Peshawar, 500 kilometres away, in a five-day forced march. He decided to follow the force later.

General Hari Singh decided to move forward to Jamraud, to fight a delaying action till the Lahore Army arrived. He left Peshawar for Jamraud early on the morning of 29 April with all the troops available to him – 6,000 infantry, 1,000 regular cavalry, 3,000 irregulars, and 20 guns. Early next morning at Jamraud, he ordered his guns to open fire in a bid to draw the Afghans in. He then feigned a retreat, which worked, and drew the entire army down from the hills, into the plains around Jamraud. The Najib battalion on the ramparts then opened fire on the Afghan troops when they closed in, while Hari Singh led his cavalry straight into the centre of the Afghan force, towards the amir's son. The Afghans realized his intention and began to retreat. At this point the Sikh soldiers thought they had won the day and began looting the dead. Just then an Afghan reinforcement from Ali Masjid arrived and drove Hari Singh's men back with heavy losses. While attempting to rally his men, Hari Singh Nalwa, perhaps one of Ranjit Singh's greatest generals, was hit twice, once in his side and once in the midriff. He was carried into the fort where he soon died, but not before instructing Mihan Singh to carry on the battle till the Lahore Army arrived and also not to let the news of his death reach the troops who were then committed in battle. Mihan Singh took command and continued the battle till General Allard with the advance guard of the Lahore Army turned up. On seeing the Lahore Army arrive, the Afghans disengaged and crossed over the Khaibar to Jellalabad, never to return again. Jamraud remained in Sikh hands. Ranjit Singh occupied Peshawar and General Avitabile who was then governor of Wazirabad, was shifted and appointed governor of Peshawar.

With Sind out of his reach, Ranjit Singh now turned south to the territory up to the Sind border. Battles were fought with the Baluchis, Mazaris, Waziries, Bozdars, and the Bugtis. The cities of Bela Dana, close to Dera Ghazi Khan, Maujgarh, Rajanpur, Mithankot, Amarkot, Rojhan, Gotki, Dajal, Harrand, and Sabzal Kot came into his possession.

Maharaja Ranjit Singh died in 1839. The standing army on his death is listed below.

The Sikh Army 1839[59]

Commander-in-Chief
Maharaja Ranjit Singh
Strength 1,01,949
Chief General
General Ventura

Ghorcharras 21,239
In 12 Derahs

1. Ghorcharra Khas Derah (1320)
2. Derah Sham Singh Attariwala
3. Derah Gurmukh Singh Lamba
4. Derah Sandhanwalias
5. Derah Ardaliyan
6. Derah Pindiwala
7. Derah Mulraj
8. Derah Dogra
9. Derah Naulakha
   ii. Naulakha Khurd – Raja Kesri Singh
   i. Naulakha Kalan – Raja Suchet Singh
10. Derah Khas – Raja Hira Singh (1377)

Regular Infantry 30,000

1. Fauj-e-Khas (French Brigade*)
2. Colonel Amir Singh Mann's Brigade
3. Tej Singh's Brigade
4. Dhonkel Singh's Brigade
5. Missar Sukh Raj's Brigade
6. Court's Brigade
7. Colonel Gulab Singh's Brigade

Regular Cavalry 4,664

1. 1st Regiment of Dragoons
2. 2nd Lancia Regiment of Dragoons
3. Rajman Gurmukh Singh
4. Rajman Hira Singh
5. Rajman Mehtab Singh
6. Rajman Grenadier Horse
7. Rajman Ram
8. Rajman Gobind
9. Rajman Akal
10. Rajman Hazoori

Irregular Infantry 25,000

1. Garrison Infantry
2. Personal Guards
3. Constabulary

Artillery 4,490

1. Horse Artillery, 'Aspi' (1 Battery per Brigade)
2. Heavy/Medium/Field Artillery, (14 batteries of 'Fili', 'Gavi' and 'Aspi' – 192 guns)
3. Garrison Artillery, 'Kila Jat'– 100 guns
4. Camel mounted swivel guns – 'Shutri' ('Zambooraks') – 500 guns

Jagirdari Fauj 27,000

1. Infantry (30 battalions – including Raja Dhyan Singh's contingent)
2. Feudal Horse 11,800
3. Feudal Artillery 500 Zambooraks

** Each brigade comprised 3 to 4 infantry battalions (800 to 1,100 soldiers per battalion), 1 cavalry regiment (200 to 600 troopers), and 1 artillery battery. There were 31 infantry battalions and some independent companies.*

In 1831, Jacquemont after having seen the Lahore Army parade, remarked that the Sikh troops 'were unique in the world on account of their graceful stature, bodily form, composure, garments and arms, and that in the art of drilling they were unparalleled in the world'.

In December,1838, Emily Eden, writes: 'I saw thousands of Ranjit's soldiers. They were all dressed in yellow or red satin. Their horses were all dressed in gold and silver tissues and ornaments and sparkling jewels. I really never saw so dazzling a sight.'

In professionalism, after witnessing the excellent military display and manoeuvres at Ferozepur in 1938, she adds,

> ... a sad blow to our vanities. We drove for 2½ miles through a lane of Ranjit's horsemen. One troop was dressed entirely in yellow satin, with gold scarfs and shawls. The other half were in kimkhab. Their arms were all gold. Many of them had collars of precious stones. Their shields and lances were all studded with gold. They had long beards down to their waists. They all were in silver or gold tissue drapery. They bring it over their heads and pass round their beards to keep them from the dust.
>
> After this there was another long line of troops extending 4½ miles. It was a white wall with red coping. It consisted of 30,000 men.
>
> Then 50 horses were led past us. The first horse had on it emerald trappings, necklaces arranged on its neck and between its ears, and in front two enormous emeralds, nearly two inches square, set in gold frames. The crupper was all emeralds. There were stud ropes of gold. This was valued at 37 lakh. The next horse was simply attired in diamonds and turquoises, another in pearls, and there was one with trappings of coral and pearls that was very pretty. Their saddle cloths have stones woven into them. It reduces European magnificence to a very low pitch.
>
> In enduring fatigue, absence from the prejudices of caste, and patience of discipline, the Sikh is not easily surpassed.

Charles von Hugel in 1836 remarked that 'it was flower of chivalry and nobility of the time'.

Osborne in 1838 considered the Sikh soldiers 'the finest material in the world for forming an army'. He further added, 'No native power has yet possessed so large and well disciplined a corps [...] creditable to any artillery in the world'. After witnessing a military display at Deenanagar in the same year he observed that, 'the steadiness and precision of the Lahore army was extraordinary and greater than that of any troops I ever saw'.

According to Hunter the Sikh Army had no parallel for steadiness and religious fervour since the Ironsides of Oliver Cromwell.

Cunningham sums up the army while referring to the late maharaja,

> He found the military array of his country a mass of horseman, brave indeed but ignorant of war as an art and he left it mustering 50,000 disciplined soldiers, 50,000 well-armed yeomanry and militia and more than 300 pieces of cannon for the field [...]

Before Ranjit Singh, the Punjab had enjoyed international reputation in the seventh century during the reign of Harshvardhana of Thanesar due to the visit of the celebrated Chinese pilgrim Hiuen Tsang. After twelve centuries, it once again came into the limelight under Ranjit Singh, mainly on account of the Sikh Army which was equal to any armed force in the world at that time.

Mohanlal Kashmiri, a young man of twenty, during his travels in Central Asia in 1832 happened to attend a royal durbar at Mashad in Iran, on a national festival day. The presiding prince was Abbas Mirza, father of the king of Iran. The prince asked Mohanlal whether Ranjit Singh's court vied in magnificence with what he now saw before him, and whether the Sikh Army could compare in discipline and courage with His Highness's Sirbaz (regular Iranian troops).

Mohanlal replied modestly but firmly that Maharaja Ranjit Singh's durbar tents were made of Kashmir shawls and that even the floor was made of the same expensive material; and as for his army, if Sardar Hari Singh Nalwa were to cross the Indus, His Highness would soon be glad to make good his retreat to his original government of Tabriz.[60]

Ranjit Singh created his kingdom with the help of this army. He maintained peace and order in the country and checked foreign invasions by it, but the army was not given a position superior to civil authority. The army was not allowed to interfere in administration, nor was it permitted to indulge in political brinkmanship. It did not challenge his authority at any time and nor did it attempt to tyrannize the people.

Every Jat village in Majha, Doaba and Riarki supplied a number of soldiers to the maharaja's army. The village paid state revenues from the salaries of its sons. Having lived in big cities like Lahore and Amritsar, the Sikh soldiers did not lose interest in village life due to their lands. Possession of some cultivable land was an emblem of respect and prestige. Every Jat father while selecting a bridegroom for his daughter attached supreme consideration to his possession of arable land.

On account of army demands, trade, commerce and industry flourished in the country. The standard of living in the villages was considerably raised.[61]

With this army, Ranjit Singh carved out his Punjab, as it remained till 1947, from an entirely hostile environment west of the river Sutlej. A man full of foresight and intelligence. A man who used cunning, treachery and ruthlessness, along with diplomacy and the military might he created, to achieve what he did. Die all mortals must, but few leave a legacy like Ranjit Singh, creating, consolidating and ruling a vast kingdom for thirty-nine years with these extraordinary qualities and an iron fist.

The Decline of the Lahore Durbar 1839-45

Maharaja Ranjit Singh breathed his last on the morning of 27 June 1839. The 'raj tilak' was applied on Kharak Singh's forehead, and he was formally recognized as the maharaja of Lahore, fulfilling the age-old tradition of 'the King never dies, long live the King'. His official installation would take place in due course.

History may have been unkind to Kharak Singh who was born in 1802 and died at the young age of thirty-eight. He has been universally written off, in some cases as an 'imbecile', in others as an 'incorrigible opium addict',[62] and yet in others as 'mentally unsound'. Perhaps, it was the case of a mediocre son growing up in the shadow of a great father, and then for historians to judge him as such. In one history book of the Sikh period covering more than three-hundred pages, less than one page is devoted to him. The reason perhaps was his short and lacklustre rule, indecisiveness and closed mind which responded only to a scheming courtier, who soon put paid to him and his rule. This is quite in contrast to his younger days as the heir to his father when he led armies in campaigns and had his late maharaja's ear on a number of subjects. Perhaps the constant usage of opium, taken twice a day, impaired his mind and made him the weak, vacillating man that he has been described as.

On ascending his throne, he almost immediately came under the influence of Chet Singh Bajwa, a former associate of his and present courtier, who himself lacked intelligence and finesse, but who soon established himself as the only adviser to Kharak Singh, with complete sway over him. Chet Singh foolishly played his cards even before he had consolidated his position. He took on the well-entrenched, experienced and intelligent Jammu brothers, led by Prime Minister Raja Dhyan Singh and his son Heera Singh, the late maharaja's favourite. In his arrogance or naivety, whichever way one may look at it, he taunted the prime minister one day, and in a sarcastic manner indicated that his days were now numbered.

To start with, both the prime minister and Heera Singh were banned from entering the zenana, a privilege accorded to both under Ranjit Singh. The constant gossip of ladies was considered an essential source of intelligence, and denying entrance to them, apart from being viewed as an insult, cut them off from this effective source. Then in a further attempt to insult the prime minister who had been positioned in the durbar by Ranjit Singh as the senior-most courtier, or Raja Kalan, the senior amongst all the rajas, Chet Singh got himself elevated to the position of wazir, with the same order of precedence as that of the prime minister. He then raised two battalions of bodyguards with the object of using them, when required, to eliminate the prime minister and whoever else he considered necessary.

Aware of this plan, the prime minister, well-informed and ever astute, took corrective measures of his own. A story was soon discreetly circulated that Kharak Singh had established contact with the British. He was intending to accept their supremacy and as a consequence their protection. Six annas in the rupee (of 16 annas) had been agreed to, which would be paid for by the durbar to the British for this protection. All Sikh regiments would be disbanded and the sardars deprived of their hereditary powers. The rumour swept the kingdom and the army.

In the meanwhile, Dhyan Singh urgently summoned Kanwar Naunihal Singh, then stationed at Peshawar, to return immediately to Lahore. Raja Gulab Singh who was also in Peshawar at that time, accompanied the prince on the way and, having been thoroughly briefed by his brother, indoctrinated him so effectively during the journey that by the time he reached Lahore, Naunihal Singh had become an avowed enemy of his father.

Dhyan Singh and Gulab Singh then so effectively played their part with Naunihal Singh and his mother Chand Kaur that both of them, along with other prominent sardars brought into the plot, were shown letters purportedly written and signed by the maharaja to the British. This so completely convinced them of the maharaja's treachery that they agreed immediately to assassinate his chief adviser Chet Singh, to depose Maharaja Kharak Singh, and crown his son Naunihal Singh. So thoroughly convinced were they, that they wanted this plan to be executed without delay, lest the kingdom be made over to the British before it was put into effect.

That very night, 8 October 1839, led by Raja Gulab Singh and Raja Suchet Singh, the conspirators, the sardars involved in the plot including the Sandhanwalia sardars, accompanied by Kanwar Naunihal Singh and Raja Dhyan Singh, went to the maharaja's chambers, killing two *granthis* and an attendant emerging from it. But the latter managed to raise the alarm. However, before the guards could take any action, Raja Dhyan Singh went up to the officer in command and showed him his hand with his six fingers on it, a fact generally well known, to prove his identity, and quietly indicated to Kanwar Naunihal Singh who was standing close by him. That was enough for the guard commander to order his troops to ground arms and lie down as ordered.

Entering the bed chamber, the conspirators overpowered Kharak Singh. Chet Singh, who also slept in the maharaja's chamber, had fled after hearing the commotion. He was soon found cowering in an empty room adjoining the chamber, and was killed by the prime minister with his dagger. Kharak Singh was bound and transported under guard to his city mansion, where he had lived earlier, and was put under arrest while the eighteen-year-old Naunihal Singh was anointed with the raj tilak and proclaimed the new maharaja.

Kharak Singh lived for another thirteen months, dying on 5 November 1840, in his thirty-ninth year. He was administered a slow-acting poison under the direction of the prime minister, a combination of 'safeda kaskaree' (white lead) and 'rus camphor' (muriate of mercury).[63] However, it is recorded that Maharaja Naunihal Singh thought his father had died of natural causes. During these thirteen months he went to visit him just once, and that too towards the end despite his father sending him innumerable messages.

When news reached him of the maharaja's death, Naunihal Singh was out hunting in his favourite hunting ground at Shah Bilawal outside Lahore. According to those present, he received the news with joy and continued with his sport for another two hours. His dislike for his father had reached such an extreme that there was widespread belief that the poisoning of his father, supervised by the prime minister, had had his tacit approval.

The funeral of Kharak Singh took place that very afternoon, close to the *samadh* of his father. Two wives and eleven of his slave girls committed sati on the funeral pyre. A final salute was given by 180 guns on the ramparts and Naunihal Singh lit the pyre. Straight after doing so, he walked away towards the Choti Ravi to bathe and change his clothes, as was the custom. He was, however, prevented by the prime minister, as his leaving before all the rituals of the funeral were over would have been frowned upon by the people who were present in large numbers at the funeral, along with generals and sardars of the court.

On such occasions, after the pyre is well under way, *shabad kirtan* or hymns are sung and prayers recited. Naunihal Singh waited for a while, but once again impatiently walked away, before the prayers ended, to take his bath and change his clothes before entering the palace. Having done so at the river, at a point 120 yards away from the cremation site, he started walking towards the palace along with his friend Mian Udham Singh, the son of Raja Gulab Singh and nephew of the prime minister.

The small northern gate (today known as the Khooni Darwaza) of the Hazuri Bagh through which he was to enter the palace, was about 40 yards from the *samadh* of the late Maharaja Ranjit Singh. Both entered it together and as he was about to exit the gate, Naunihal Singh affectionately put his arm around the shoulders of his friend and whispered something to him. Just then large chunks of masonry, loosened perhaps by the vibrations caused by the large guns firing on the ramparts, crashed down on them killing Udham Singh on the spot and severely injuring the young maharaja. The prime minister following at a little distance received an abrasion on his arm.

From here onwards the narratives vary. According to Colonel Gardner who was present, the maharaja was immediately carried by five on-duty artillerymen who belonged to his corps. He was taken to the palace and the only people with him when the doors were barred were the prime minister, two of his close followers and some attendants of his from the Jammu region. No one else, neither his mother Chand Kaur nor his wives, not even his closest relatives, the Sandhanwalia sardars, were permitted entry. Most of all, no doctor was called when just after the accident Dr Honighberger, who was present at the funeral, attended to the prime minister's injury.[64]

The artillery soldiers who carried the palanquin with the injured maharaja in it reported to Colonel Gardner that when he was being lifted on to the *palki* he regained consciousness and asked for water. On reaching the palace they lifted him onto his bed and they all noticed that there was a little blood on the sheet and the head was otherwise intact, indicating a minor injury. When the doors were finally opened some two hours later to admit others, after his death was officially announced, the skull was seen to be smashed in and large quantities of blood and tissue covered the sheet. Interestingly, Colonel Gardner records that of the five gunners who carried the maharaja, two died mysteriously, two went home to Hindustan and were never heard from again and the fifth simply disappeared from the scene.

The gate was in full view of the people gathered for the funeral, which was some 50 yards distant, therefore foul play could be ruled out at this stage. What also supports this theory is that Mian Udham Singh, Raja Gulab Singh's son and the prime minister's nephew was with the maharaja, while the prime minister himself was following closely behind and was also hit by the rubble. What is open to suspicion however, are the prime minister's subsequent actions. Over the years, historians have differed over the event, though the majority view does indict Raja Dhyan Singh in the death of the young maharaja. The people of the Lahore state, however, were more pragmatic in their belief. To them it was divine justice for the treatment he meted out to his father.

Two hours after the accident, the prime minister first took the maharaja's mother Chand Kaur into confidence by telling her that he wished her to be the next ruler. He then swore her to secrecy and warned her that any leakage of this decision would reduce her chances of occupying the *gaddi*. He then officially announced the maharaja's death. Hedging his bet, he then also sent an urgent message to Sher Singh informing him of Naunihal Singh's death. Sher Singh was then at his estate at Kanuwan, near Gurdaspur. He was urged to return immediately, as the prime minister wished him to be the next maharaja. He was asked to come straight to the Shalimar Gardens, where he would rendezvous with him.

Naunihal Singh was cremated the next day, 6 November 1840, close to the *samadh* of his grandfather. Two of his young wives committed sati on his pyre.

The prime minister knowing that a war of succession would now take place, had for the moment played safe by offering to make both Chand Kaur and Sher Singh the new ruler of Lahore.

He had bought time, as he had no intentions of making Chand Kaur the new ruler. He knew both she and her supporters – the Sandhanwalia sardars – disliked him, and that he would be their first victim once they were well ensconced at Lahore. Not quite sure however of how the struggle for succession would end, he left his brother Raja Gulab Singh in Chand Kaur's camp to espouse her cause.

To ensure the support of the Dogra brothers, Chand Kaur then announced that one of Naunihal Singh's maharanis was pregnant and if a boy was born he would be the new maharaja and she the regent and that if it was a girl, she would adopt Heera Singh, Dhyan Singh's son, who had been the late Maharaja Ranjit Singh's favourite, to be the new maharaja after her. As to Sher Singh, she said that she did not acknowledge him as a legitimate son of the late maharaja.

Shrewdly assessing the strength she had gathered by then, which included the Sandhanwalia sardars along with some other chiefs, Raja Dhyan Singh then appeared to be pacified. He quietly advised Sher Singh not to precipitate matters just yet but to wait for an opportune moment to press his claim. He then advised him, for the present, to retire to his estate at Batala. The prime minister then announced that as he was unwell and required rest, he was retiring for some time to his estate at Jammu, and left Lahore. Chand Kaur promptly appointed her ally, the Sandhanwalia sardar Attar Singh as the new prime minister. A four member council was formed to run the day-to-day affairs, and the council was presided over by the prime minister. Raja Gulab Singh now firmly allied himself with the maharani.

At this juncture Dhyan Singh, unsure about Sher Singh's success in staking his claim to the throne, because of the doubt of his being a legitimate son of the late Maharaja Ranjit Singh, played his second card. He informed the British government that Maharani Jinda, one of Ranjit Singh's wives, had given birth to a son, Duleep Singh, on 6 September 1838. This was the first the British government learnt of the existence of another heir to the throne of Lahore.

While the new administration attempted to consolidate its precarious position. Dhyan Singh set in motion events to destabilize it. To begin with, his people in Lahore played on the sentiments of those chiefs and sardars and generals of the army who felt disgruntled with the present establishment. Soon, Dhyan Singh's associates at Lahore informed him that the situation was now ripe and that if Sher Singh and he were to march on Lahore, a large part of the army and a number of chiefs and sardars would be prepared to join them.

Dhyan Singh promptly sent a message to Sher Singh to march on Lahore, but instead of entering the city to camp in the Shalimar Gardens where he would meet him. Sher Singh left Batala immediately and arrived at the Shalimar Gardens with around 300 of his followers. Dhyan Singh was still at Jammu. He had once again decided to watch the reaction of the durbar and the army, and subsequent developments, before finally committing himself to Sher Singh.

In Sher Singh's camp, however, there was disappointment at the turn of events. The dominant voice in his camp at this time was Sardar Jawala Singh. He was Sher Singh's principal counsellor and had his eye on becoming the new wazir. He convinced Sher Singh that Dhyan Singh had not come because his sympathies lay with the maharani through his brother Gulab Singh. He then got Sher Singh's permission to negotiate directly with the army stationed at Mian Mir, and the other chiefs of the durbar.

The army, worked upon over the months by Dhyan Singh's emissaries, were by now completely disgruntled with the maharani and the durbar. It reacted readily to a message from Jawala Singh to meet the following day at Budhu-ka-awa. This was, a disused brick kiln, on the outskirts of Lahore, where General Avitabile had built a *baradari* (known later as Fateh Garh, or the Fort of Victory).[65] This was the place used by the *panches*[66] of the army to hold their regular meetings.

Early on the morning of 14 January 1841, Sher Singh arrived at Budhu-ka-awa where the army had paraded in strength. Sher Singh was soon surrounded by the *panches* of the army and the sardars of the Jagirdari Fauj, who paid homage to him and unanimously proclaimed him the new maharaja. Sher Singh was an imposing personality and a soldier who had taken part in many military campaigns, and was one of the generals of the army from the time of the late Maharaja Ranjit Singh. The artillery fired its salute, and that was the first Maharani Chand Kaur, and the people of Lahore, knew of these dramatic developments.

Chand Kaur immediately ordered the gates of the citadel to be shut and convened a meeting of her ministers, which included Raja Gulab Singh, Jemadar Khushal Singh, Sardar Tej Singh, and the Sandhanwalia sardars. Raja Gulab Singh's troops then at Shadera, were ordered into the fort. The troops of the remaining ministers were also concentrated in the fort. The overall command of the troops in the fort was given to Raja Gulab Singh and the defences were prepared for the inevitable assault. A large sum of money was distributed to the soldiers in the fort and to those at the gate by the maharani in an attempt to secure their loyalty. Each soldier was also asked to swear an oath of allegiance to her, the Muslims on the Koran, the Sikhs on the Guru Granth Sahib and the Hindu soldiers on the Gita.

While preparations were on in the fort on a war footing, Dhyan Singh played his third card. Sher Singh was visited in his camp by the third Jammu brother, Raja Suchet Singh and General Ventura, both of whom pledged their services to him. Two of the three Jammu brothers were now in either camp. Whatever the outcome of the ensuing conflict, their future would be secure. Dhyan Singh now moved to a point close to Lahore, to await developments.

An army of 70,000 soldiers now under Sher Singh marched on the fort. He entered the city at 8 p.m. through a gate which then existed between the Mewa Singh barracks and the Badshahi mosque. The artillery entered through the Yakki and Delhi gates and others by the Taxsali gate. Guarding the gates were the soldiers who had taken money from Chand Kaur the evening before and had sworn an oath of allegiance to her. They now simply accepted more from Sher Singh and opened the gates. By day break the major part of the city was Sher Singh's. He now entered the Hazuri Bagh and also took over the Badshahi mosque along with a large ammunition dump belonging to Gulab Singh. Meanwhile, the soldiers, having made Sher Singh maharaja, considered it their right to loot the various bazaars of Lahore, which they did with a vengeance, besides setting fire to the Chatta Bazaar.

After looting and pillaging all night, the army, 70,000 strong with 50,000 followers, moved on the fort early the next morning. Artillery batteries comprising 230 guns were positioned around the fort. More guns were sent for as this number was considered insufficient. The main part of the besieging force was in the Hazuri Bagh, with 12 guns facing the Hazuri Gate (the western gate), ready to blow it in on orders. The besieged force overlooking the Hazuri Bagh comprised crack Dogra troops of Gulab Singh's force and 1,200 soldiers of Budh Singh Mann, who guarded the fort treasury called the Moti Mandir.

While the besiegers raked the ramparts with musket fire, the order was given for the 12 guns to destroy the gate. All fired simultaneously and the gate – in position since the great emperor Akbar had built the fort – was blown apart. After a hushed silence, 300 Akali shock troops stormed the gate, little realizing that Colonel Gardner was himself manning the guns he had positioned within the fort facing the gate. The first salvo of grape annihilated the attackers, not one was seen to survive. Loading quickly, he fired a second salvo at the 12 guns that had just brought the gate down, and blew them all to bits. Simultaneously, the troops manning the ramparts opened fire on the large concentration of troops below them which soon cleared the Hazuri Bagh of the besiegers. Colonel Gardner has recorded that when the killing ground was finally cleared, bodies of 2,800 infantry men, 200 gunners and 180 horses had to be removed.[67]

The siege continued for five days with neither side making any headway. News then arrived that Raja Dhyan Singh had arrived from Jammu and had established his camp 3 miles from Shadera. Sher Singh in the meanwhile attempted to open negotiations with Gulab Singh, who refused to discuss anything till his brother Raja Dhyan Singh was brought into the negotiations. Having agreed to this, Sher Singh sent 500 Ghorcharras along with several of his chiefs and sardars to Dhyan Singh's camp, along with the raja's younger brother, Raja Suchet Singh, to escort him to Lahore. The next day, escorted by this force and accompanied by his troops from Jammu and his brother Suchet Singh, Dhyan Singh, arrived at Lahore where he was met by the maharaja on the outskirts of the city.

Negotiations began between both the parties. Raja Heera Singh was deputed by Raja Gulab Singh to negotiate on behalf of Maharani Chand Kaur. Heera Singh emerged on the seventh day, accompanied by the Sandhanwalia sardars, and peace was agreed to on the following terms: 1) the maharani would surrender the Lahore Fort to Sher Singh and give up all claim to the throne; 2) Sher Singh would give her a *jagir* providing her 9 lakh rupees annually, which would be managed by Raja Gulab Singh as her regent; 3) Sher Singh would refrain from his wish to marry her by the *chaddar* ceremony; 4) the Dogra troops would be allowed to leave the fort with their weapons, unmolested; and 5) security would be provided to ensure that the agreement was implemented.

The night before the agreement was finalized, Raja Gulab Singh took advantage of the confusion and collected all the jewels and other valuables of the maharani on the pretext of keeping them safe. Then without alerting anyone, he cleared out most of the treasury, taking sixteen carts filled with rupees and other silver coins. Each of his 500 horsemen were entrusted with carrying a bag each of gold *mohurs* (gold sovereigns), and other men were laden with quantities of jewellery and other valuables. He also helped himself to twelve of Ranjit Singh's best horses from the stables, and quantities of the best pashminas and rich dresses from the former maharaja's wardrobe.[68]

Before leaving for Jammu, he met Sher Singh and paid his respects to him as the new maharaja and told him that all that he had done was in good faith, as it was his duty to the late Maharaja Ranjit Singh's memory to protect his daughter-in-law. Then with a flourish he took out the Kohinoor from his pocket and handed it to Sher Singh, saying that in the confusion following the battle he had managed to secure it for him. This pleased Sher Singh no end and he immediately ordered that a royal *firman* (a written order of the durbar) be issued making over 20 villages in the Bhimbar district to Raja Gulab Singh, in perpetuity.[69]

Sher Singh was anointed as the new maharaja on 18 January 1841. All the sardars and chiefs except the Sandhanwalias paid homage to him. Dhyan Singh was brought back as the prime minister. The pay of the soldiers who put him on the throne was raised by one rupee a month. All the jagirs and estates of the Sandhanwalias was resumed by the state and orders issued for their arrest. Maharani Chand Kaur's prime minister, Attar Singh and his nephew Ajit Singh escaped across the Sutlej to British territory, while Attar Singh's younger brother Lehna Singh, was brought to Lahore in chains.

Having made Sher Singh maharaja, the army became increasingly intolerant and the soldiers began to take the law into their hands. Molestation of officers they bore a grudge against became routine. The houses of several of the officers were burnt and some, suspected of harbouring an ill feeling towards any of the troops, were put to death. General Court managed to escape, while Colonel Foulkes was killed and so were Hest and Ford. In Kashmir, the Governor Colonel Mihan Singh, who was the second-in-command of Hari Singh Nalwa at the battle of Jamraud, was killed and his house plundered. In Peshawar, General Avitabile abandoned the town and escaped to Jellalabad to save his life. This was the mutiny of 1842 and discontent continued till British intervention was threatened.

The exodus of foreign officers from the Lahore Army now began. Apart from the three killed in the mutiny, of the total that had been employed by Ranjit Singh, six died during the service and twenty-seven now left the service. When the First Sikh War started in 1846, there were just four who had stayed on – Mouton, Holmes, Hurbon, and Cunaraha.[70]

In matters of state, Sher Singh left the management of the government to Raja Dhyan Singh. Sher Singh passed his days in hunting and other pleasures. The Jammu brothers knowing that he still wished to marry Chand Kaur by the *chaddar* ceremony, became instrumental in keeping them apart, by convincing each that the other was conspiring against him or her. Dhyan Singh did not want her back in favour as his own future was at stake. As for Gulab Singh, he believed that the sooner she was off the scene, the sooner he would become master of her wealth of which he had been appointed custodian by the recent agreement. The seed of bitterness was sown in Sher Singh's mind and nurtured to such an extent that finally he ordered her execution. In early June 1842 when he went to Wazirabad on a routine trip, her maidservants were instructed to kill her. Each would be given 5,000 rupees to perform this task. One morning, on the pretext of grooming her hair, they smashed her skull with a large stone, killing her on the spot.

The Sandhanwalias were eventually forgiven by Sher Singh and their estate restored to them. While Attar Singh returned to his estate, Lehna Singh and Ajit Singh remained at court, and in due course became the maharaja's confidants to the extent that their views were solicited on all matters of state. Raja Dhyan Singh encouraged this relationship and in turn befriended them himself.

In the meanwhile the relationship between Sher Singh and Dhyan Singh had also begun to deteriorate. The Sandhanwalias, aware of this and desirous to see them both off the scene, began to play one against the other. They finally succeeded, by convincing Sher Singh that they had been promised a bribe of Rs 60 lakh by the prime minister to kill him. Sher

Singh, already estranged from his prime minister, readily believed the story and eventually became so thoroughly convinced of Raja Dhyan Singh's treachery that one day he gave permission to both Ajit Singh and Lehna Singh to kill Raja Dhyan Singh. The maharaja gave them a *firman* for this purpose, thereby exonerating them from the act they were going to commit, which, it was written, was being done in the interest of the state.

Both brothers then showed the prime minister this order. He, on the face of it refused to believe it unless it had the personal signature and royal seal of the maharaja. This they soon procured. They now convinced Raja Dhyan Singh that they had shown him his death warrant in good faith, as they only wanted to get rid of Sher Singh. They then got his agreement to kill the maharaja. Raja Dhyan Singh told them they would always have his support and promised them 'a great reward' if they succeeded in their task. He then retired to his residence feigning illness while the conspirators set about their task. It was decided to carry out this murder on the following Friday, the day he was to be at his palace at Shah Bilawal.

On the appointed day, Sher Singh was sitting at the window of the *baradari* at Shah Bilawal, watching a wrestling bout when Ajit Singh Sandhanwalia entered and asked the maharaja if he could show him a new fowling piece (shot gun) he had just received. As Sher Singh stretched out his arm to take it, Ajit Singh emptied both barrels into his chest. With one blow of his sword he then severed his head. The maharaja's young son Partap Singh who was playing close by was also then hacked to pieces by Lehna Singh.

The conspirators now met the prime minister who was outside the fort. Taking him by the hand Ajit Singh asked him to return to the fort so that the new arrangements to run the government could be decided upon. He then asked the prime minister as to who he thought should be the new maharaja. Dhyan Singh replied, 'Duleep Singh, of course', to this the retort was 'He is to become the maharaja and you his wazir. What do we get for all this trouble?' The prime minister expressed his annoyance at these remarks and was about to ride away, when on Ajit Singh's cue he was shot in the back and killed on the spot by one of his men. Another man then dismounted and hacked his body to bits.

On hearing news of the treachery of the Sandhanwalias and of the death of the maharaja and his father, Raja Heera Singh, Dhyan Singh's son, went straight to General Avitabile's *baradari* at Budhu-ka-awa and called on the leaders of the army to collect. The army, fully convinced of the Sandhanwalias treachery, readily agreed to follow him. The conspirators in the meanwhile, in an attempt to appease the army, announced that Duleep Singh would be the new maharaja, but by then it was too late. Raja Heera Singh accompanied by troops of the army and those of generals Avitabile and Ventura, with around 100 guns, marched on Lahore, reaching it an hour after sunset.

The Sandhanwalias now entered the fort and shut the gates. Once again the fort was bombarded by the guns and the first breach was made at 9 a.m. the following morning. The first to enter the breach was the Spanish Colonel Hurbon, followed by his soldiers. The defenders were routed and the battle was over in less than an hour. Ajit Singh managed to escape by climbing down a wall by the means of a rope. Unfortunately for him, a Muslim soldier stationed below saw and recognized him, killing him on the spot. He then severed his head and took it to Heera Singh. Heera Singh, in turn, took it to his stepmother who was then sitting on top of his father's pyre and laid the head at her feet. The pyre was then lit.

The battle over, the search began for Lehna Singh whose body was not amongst the dead. He was finally found hiding in a dark cellar and dispatched by the soldiers who found him. His head too was severed and taken to Heera Singh. All of the Sandhanwalia property was now raised to the ground and lands confiscated and all their relations and associates killed. Attar Singh, who got the news of what had happened while at his estate, immediately moved to the assistance of Ajit Singh and Lehna Singh, but by then information reached him that it was all over. He took his family and crossed the Sutlej into the British territory. To the army who supported him, Heera Singh, who assembled the troops, promised one month's salary as gratuity and an increase in their salary.

Four days later a council of the civil and military leaders was called at the Hazuri Bagh and it was decided that Duleep Singh would be the new maharaja and Heera Singh the prime minister. He was formally anointed a few days later, in September 1843. The new maharaja was five years old and the prime minister had just turned twenty-five.

The next two years saw much political unrest, with two prime ministers, Heera Singh and Jawahar Singh, Maharani Jinda Kaur's brother who succeeded Heera Singh as prime minister, being assassinated. Gulab Singh returned to Lahore and Maharani Jinda Kaur became the regent. By now the army was the de-facto ruler of Lahore. It increased its strength, in all arms. The salaries and perks of the soldiers was decided by the army panchayat, the government was only told what their decision was, and was then ordered to pay it.

During the seven years between the death of the great Maharaja Ranjit Singh in 1839 and the start of the First Sikh War in 1846, three maharajas – Kharak Singh, Naunihal Singh and Sher Singh, one maharani – Chand Kaur, four prime ministers – Jawala Singh, Raja Dhyan Singh, Raja Heera Singh, and Jawahar Singh, and twenty-nine other leading figures of the state were assassinated. Seven more died of natural causes. Of the thirty-seven mentioned above, five were killed on the orders of Raja Dhyan Singh and twelve on those of his son Raja Heera Singh. Virtually the entire leadership of the state built by the great Ranjit Singh ceased to exist.[71]

The durbar was by now mortally afraid of the army. The regent feared for her life and that of her son. Officers lacked total control of their troops. Lal Singh was appointed prime minister, his credentials being his intimacy with the regent. Tej Singh became the new commander-in-chief. Fauja Singh Bajwa in his book *The Military System of the Sikhs*, describes them as follows, 'it was indeed unfortunate that leaders were not worthy of the men, that Tej Singh was faint-hearted and Lal Singh incompetent and only half trusted'. Both were to abandon the field during the first war, leaving their army to fend for itself. The stage was thus set for confrontation with the British.

The First Sikh War 1845-46

I. THE SIKHS

After Ranjit Singh's death, the highly disciplined army that had helped him build and secure his kingdom began to crumble. Throughout history, Sikhs have always responded to good leadership, a characteristic that was missing in Kharak Singh. His reign lasted only four brief months, a period during which the new maharaja, despite his previous active command in the army, spent his days in an opium-induced stupor. His son Naunihal Singh deposed him and together with his prime minister, Raja Dhyan Singh, spent much of his time with the army, continuing his grandfather's policy of troop reviews and regular training exercises. Although keen and considered to be the closest in temperament to the late Ranjit Singh, Naunihal Singh, at eighteen, lacked experience and did not receive the complete respect and support of the army as had his grandfather. He was the last to exercise control over it.

It was during Maharani Chand Kaur's reign that the real breakdown in command began. She occupied the throne for only two months – from November 1840 to January 1841 – and can hardly be blamed for this situation, yet historians attribute the independence of the army from the durbar to have started during her reign. The army began to act in all matters of state, overthrowing her and bringing Sher Singh to the throne. The one important aspect during Sher Singh's reign which deserves a mention and which would later have a bearing in the battle of Gujrat during the Second Sikh War, was the visit of Ranjit Singh's old enemy, the former king of Afghanistan, Dost Mohammad. He arrived in Lahore in February 1843 and signed a treaty of friendship with Sher Singh.

Being indebted to the army for his position, Sher Singh pandered to it in every way. He raised its strength, increased its pay and allowances, and submitted to it on all other matters. In 1842, for instance, Sher Singh increased the pay from 8 rupees to 12 to buy peace during the mutiny. During Maharani Jinda's rule, she raised it to 14. In 1845, Peshora Singh, Ranjit Singh's son, promised the army a pay increase to 15 rupees for an infantryman and 40 rupees to a cavalry trooper. In addition, a further 100 rupees and a gold bracelet would be given to every soldier who helped him seize the throne. Appeasing the army had now become routine.

It was during this period that the panchayat system took root in the army. This system had evolved in the villages, being a council of five elders who decided on matters that needed attention for the collective benefit of the whole. This was a concept that the troops both understood and trusted, and was therefore adopted by them. While this 'democratization' worked as a system of village administration, it caused havoc in the army. What should have been a disciplined force under a strong and effective leadership was now one that was controlled by voting. The council would decide what was right or wrong, or what should or should not be done in the battalion. Each company elected two members to the panchayat, putting an end to the disciplined force that Ranjit Singh had so painstakingly created. Commanding officers would henceforth exercise command on parade and, for whatever they were worth, lead their units in battle, but for administrative matters they had to abide by the decision of the panchayat. Lord Gough describes the panchayats as 'guiding the united action of the soldiery, were able to dictate to their officers, and later on found themselves able to appear to be representing the Khalsa in arms, and to dictate to the durbar, or court itself'.

Sher Singh should have been the last person to accept such a system. He had been a general, had led successful campaigns during the days of Ranjit Singh, and knew the importance of being able to command. However, Ranjit Singh was aware that Sher Singh and his brother, Tara Singh, were not his sons. It was only towards the end of Ranjit Singh's life that Sher Singh was permitted to be seated in the maharaja's presence – Tara Singh was never given this honour. Perhaps because of this background, he turned a blind eye to the functioning of the army and let matters drift. The army realized its strength and now knew, as did the durbar, that if anyone wanted to rule the state it had to gain its approval. Consequently, the army declared itself the representative of Sikh aspirations and called itself the Sarbat Khalsa – the supreme body of the Sikhs, whose decision was binding on all.

As one publication of the period puts it:

> Unsurprisingly under such circumstances, with the Khalsa unwittingly following the example of the Praetorian Guard during one of Imperial Rome's more decadent episodes, government control

> of the army steadily weakened. Men took leave whenever they liked, discipline deteriorated, and training all but ceased. Heera Singh was briefly able to reintroduce regular parades in 1844, but in early 1845 it was recorded that, 'exercise and drill were out of use', and a number of parade grounds were subsequently ploughed up and sown with crops. Many officers were murdered during mutinies in support of one or another political faction and the rest were subjected to methodical harassment and intimidation.[72]

The army mutinied soon after Sher Singh's accession in 1841. One of its demands was the removal of its foreign officers – a demand also supported by the sardars who had, even in the days of Ranjit Singh, felt threatened by them. A few of these foreign officers were killed during the mutiny and most left the army during his reign or later during the prime ministership of Heera Singh. Only four remained on the eve of the First Sikh War; however, none of those who had built the army – Allard, Ventura, Avitabile, Court – were amongst them.

Sher Singh was indifferent towards the events taking place around him. He isolated himself from reality and left the affairs of state to his prime minister. He became slovenly, enjoying his pleasures of dance, music, sports, and hunting, and has been described by some historians as completely debauched. Had Raja Dhyan Singh not exercised some control over events, the government would have collapsed. The army now dictated its strength and its pay – even to the extent of telling the durbar who its leaders should be. The Jagirdari Fauj fared better, as they continued to respond to their traditional leadership. On their own, these leaders increased the strength of their levies. This was done by the chiefs and sardars, more for their own security than necessity, as a consequence of the anarchy that was then prevailing in the army.

Ranjit Singh had left his regular army with a strength of 31 battalions of infantry and 10 regiments of cavalry. The army voted and raised its strength to 45 battalions of infantry under Sher Singh and to 62 battalions by 1845, under Maharani Jinda Kaur. Two additional cavalry regiments were raised during this period, one being added by the time of the First Sikh War, raising the strength to 13. The unit personnel were increased to their authorized strength. For instance, the strength of the Rajman Gobind, which stood at 98 in 1839, was now 528.

With self-enhanced salary and allowances, the government's treasury was under extreme strain. For example, the two regiments of the Fauj-e-Khas – the Dragoons and the Grenadiers – whose strength in 1839 was 732 and 770 men, respectively, and cost 17,627 and 18,408 rupees to maintain, now cost the exchequer 21,945 and 22,313 rupees for a slightly reduced strength of 730 and 750 men, which was an increase of around 21.5 per cent in salaries alone. The artillery, which stood at 21 batteries of field guns, around 200 guns and 100 Kila Jat guns, rose to 232 field guns. During Sher Singh's period, and by the time of Jowahar Singh's premiership in the reign of Maharaja Duleep Singh, the Kila Jat strength had increased to 381 guns, nearly double the strength that existed at the time of Ranjit Singh. The smaller field guns were produced in three foundries that had been set up by Ranjit Singh at Lahore, Amritsar and Kotli Loharan, under the direction of General Court and Lehna Singh Majithia. The powder was manufactured in Lahore under the direction of Fakir Nur-ud-din and Dr Honigberger. All of the large siege guns were from the earlier Mughal period.

Because of the panchayat system, discipline and training suffered in the regular army. Even at the level of the durbar, bribes and money, rather than merit, became the order of the day. Fauja Singh Bajwa, in his *Military System of the Sikhs*, says,

> Though the number of such cases can be easily multiplied, a few examples will do for our purpose. Lal Singh Murariwala was promoted by Jawahar Singh straight away from the rank of Commandant to that of General. Another man, Jiwan Singh, 'the head of fools', was promoted to the rank of 'Sardar'. Megh Raj, who was known as 'Mangloo' and who had no qualifications other than being the brother of the attractive and sought-after slave girl Mangla who had since ingratiated herself with both the Regent and Raja Lal Singh, was appointed a General. Promotions were sold openly or secretly, sometimes even disproportionate to the vacancies. At the time of Heera Singh, Lal Singh was given the title of 'Raja' for a payment of 50,000 rupees. Sher Singh promoted people for money on the very day of enlistment, and Colonel Man Singh was notorious for the sale of promotions in his regiment.

Despite this gloomy situation, the morale of the average soldier remained high. The panchayats had enforced a rigorous discipline of their own and the troops themselves looked forward to a fight with the British. In his book *Sikh Wars: British Army in the Punjab, 1845-49* (henceforth referred to as *Sikh Wars*), Hugh C.B. Cook writes,

> The morale of the Khalsa, which had little use for the Durbar in Lahore, was extremely high and the vast majority were strongly Anglophobe. Now at last was the opportunity to prove once and for all the greatness of the nation Ranjit Singh had built up, to establish it as the most powerful state in India, and to humble forever the proud British and show them that the Punjab could never be theirs. [...] The Sikh soldier was extremely brave and neither gave nor expected quarter. [...] The army's weakness lay in its leadership. [...] The Sikh regimental officers were mostly illiterate and, brave though they might be, were not worthy of the men they commanded. Neither of the two principal Sikh generals were in fact Sikhs, but were Brahmins.[73]

Though the Sikh soldier, following the belief of the late Maharaja Ranjit Singh, had held the British Army and its regiments in high regard, they looked down upon the native regiments of the Bengal and Bombay armies. After the disaster in Afghanistan, during the First Afghan War of 1839, their regard for the British had all but disappeared.

Raja Lal Singh had bought his title from Raja Heera Singh when he was the prime minister of the state. He was a high-class Kothari Brahmin, the son of Jassa Missar, a petty clerk in the Sikh treasury, and was patronized by Raja Dhyan Singh. After Dhyan Singh's death, he rose to be the head of the treasury. He had no military training of any sort, even at the most elementary level, and his only military experience was that he had accompanied an army sent to Jammu against Raja Gulab Singh on Maharani Jinda Kaur's directions. Even this was limited as, after a short battle, Gulab Singh realizing the inevitability of defeat had opened negotiations. A great deal of money was paid to the troops, and 3 lakh rupees offered to the durbar as *nazarana*. He then accompanied the army back to Lahore, patched up with Maharani Jinda Kaur and once again entered the durbar's good books.

Raja Tej Singh was also a high-class Brahmin from north-central India. He was the nephew of Jemadar Khushal Singh, one of the late Maharaja Ranjit Singh's trusted generals. He had only average military ability and owed his retention in the service more to the late maharaja's affection for his uncle rather than to his competence. He was also known to act treacherously when it suited him. Colonel Gardner simply sums him up by saying, 'Tej Singh was never trusted by anyone'.

Ever fearful of the army's takeover of the state, the durbar had the regent, Maharani Jinda Kaur, devise means to minimize its authority. The soldiers were constantly demanding a raise in pay, the treasury was empty and the panchayats were becoming more and more belligerent. A war with the British was a scheme that Maharani Jinda Kaur finally settled upon, hoping it would end the menace from the army once and for all. If the British won, the army's constant threat to her and her son would be over – she assumed that the British would permit her to stay on as regent with Duleep Singh as the maharaja. On the other hand, if the Sikh Army won, they could plunder the whole of India, leaving her in peace. This would also make her a very powerful ruler and she thought she had a win-win situation either way.

To execute her plans, she needed two trustworthy leaders, and she found them in Lal Singh and Tej Singh. She realized that both would be unacceptable to the army and to the sardars, unless she created the right situation. To this end, reports were circulated of the intention of the British to take possession of the Sikh territories to the south of the Sutlej river. On several occasions in open durbar, Lal Singh produced and read papers purporting to be letters from *kardars,* or administrative officers, of the country beyond the river. These fake letters stated that the British Army was already advancing, creating disturbances and annoyance in the Sikh state. This seemingly authentic intelligence created considerable excitement among the troops and people of Lahore, and soon became almost the only topic of discussion. When these rumours had worked their intended effect, Lal Singh summoned a council of sardars, officers and deputies at Shalimar. During this assembly, Dewan Deena Nath read a letter that he claimed had been sent to the durbar by the *kardars* of the states beyond the Sutlej. Its contents started that the British authorities really meant to seize that part of the country, that they were causing great annoyance to the servants of the durbar and had actually given orders to the people of several villages to pay tributes only to the British government, which now claimed sovereignty. Dewan Deena Nath also claimed that great disturbances existed in Kashmir, Peshawar and elsewhere, and that for a long time not a rupee of revenue had been paid in by the *kardars*.

Having thus created alarm and concern in the assembly, the wily dewan went on to remind them that their sovereign was but a child, that there was no recognized head of state and that unless arrangements were made for the governance of the country, ruin must speedily ensue. He then informed them that it was the wish of the maharani that Raja Lal Singh should be the wazir and Sardar Tej Singh the commander-in-chief. It was also stated that she was willing to sanction the march of the army across the Sutlej for the protection of the national honour and would, if they thought proper, order all necessary preparations to be made. The council unanimously confirmed Her Highness's choice.[74]

Earlier, generals Avitabile, Court and Pouvindia, aware of future events, had sent a delegation to Raja Gulab Singh who had returned to Jammu after his forced visit to Lahore. In it, they offered him the position of commander-in-chief, an offer he politely declined. He had also declined the post of prime minister when it had been offered by the regent during his enforced visit to Lahore, commenting to his well-wishers that, 'he wished to live longer than six months'.[75]

The army's acceptance of the regent's decision when they had no confidence in Tej Singh and Lal Singh, as even the British were aware, shows the devious and clever manner in which Maharani Jinda managed the issue through her dewan and courtiers. They played on the sentiments of the army to the extent that her decision to allow them to cross the Sutlej to get to grips with the British became the overriding factor. Once this decision was taken, it did not matter who led them; their objective had been achieved.

The political agent, Major Broadfoot, conveyed his assessment of the situation to the governor general, Lord Hardinge, in his report of 20 November 1845. In a postscript, he wrote,

> It is right to add, that up to the last moment, the regular troops were discussing the propriety of murdering Raja Lal Singh and Sardar Tej Singh, and sending for Raja Gulab Singh to lead them. The two chiefs menaced, look for escape to exciting enthusiasm against the British. This may delay or precipitate invasion.[75]

By this time, Raja Gulab Singh was already in touch with the governor general, offering assistance in the event of hostilities breaking out between the British and the Lahore Durbar and, 'assuring him of his support at all times, and promising that whenever he saw the opportunity, he would throw the whole weight of his influence and power into the scale on the British side.[76]

The maharani had been, for some time, thinking of making Lal Singh the prime minister. He had already crossed the Sutlej with a few followers at the end of August 1845, and had moved along the river on what was obviously a reconnaissance mission. It was also clear by then that her intentions were to cross the river and to provoke British retaliation in a war that would destroy her army. Subsequent statements of marching to Ludhiana, Ambala or even Delhi, were meant to indicate to the army that the durbar had every intention of defeating the British and conquering their territory.

With the durbar's intentions clear, and with her two trusted leaders now in position to carry out this policy, the stage was set for the inevitable disaster. The army leadership at the upper level had no confidence in the two appointees, and at the regimental level the leaders were in complete disarray. There had been no large-scale exercises or training for five years, since the rule of Naunihal Singh who was killed in 1840. All that the troops could now count on – up to the non-commissioned officer (NCO) level – was their high morale. With this one positive attribute in hand, the army prepared for war.

Raja Gulab Singh had tactfully opted out and was at his base at Jammu. Lal Singh and Tej Singh had, at the very beginning, been in touch with the British political agents Major Broadfoot and Captain Nicholson at Ferozepur. Prior to hostilities commencing, they had sent a message to General Littler about the fact that they were not going to attack his small force at Ferozepur. Through his confidential agent, Shamsuddin, Lal Singh sent Lord Gough a full report on the eve of battle of Sobraon and after the Battle of Ferozshah, 'on the position and nature of the entrenchments and an account of disposition of troops and guns'.[77] Evidence that consistent and regular reports were communicated to the British is borne out by the accuracy of the reports of decisions taken by the council in Lahore, which were regularly sent by the political agent Major Broadfoot to the governor general.

Captain Peter Nicholson, Major Broadfoot's political assistant at Ferozepur during this period, wrote that at the very beginning,

> Lal Singh had already in a letter requested the British to consider him and the "Bibi Sahiba" [Maharani Jinda] as their friends and to cut up the "Burchas" [ruffians of the army] for them. So there was no point in Lal Singh and Tej Singh compromising themselves by destroying Littler's small force at Ferozepur.

Nicholson, according to contemporary authorities, had also received a letter from Lal Singh after he had crossed the river, affirming his friendship with the British and asking what he should best do. Nicholson is said to have answered, 'Do not attack Ferozepur. Halt as many days as you can and then march towards the governor general.'[78]

The Sikh Army 1845[79]

The organization of the army on this date was as follows:

Wazir	**Commander-in-Chief**
Raja Lal Singh	Sardar Tej Singh

The Fauj-e-Ain (Regular Army) – 22 brigades
62 infantry battalions, 49,000 soldiers
13 cavalry regiments, 7,800 troopers
32 artillery batteries

1. The Fauj-e-Khas (General Ventura had left the service)
Dewan Ajodhia Prasad Commanding

1. 4 infantry paltans (Sikh). 1 Gurkha paltan (Captain Kuldeep Singh)
2. 2 cavalry Rajmans
3. Shaddilah Risala (Jagirdari cavalry squadron)
4. Artillery of Gen Illahi Bakhsh (34 guns) (Sikh & Muslim)
   12 guns, horse artillery and 22 field guns, under Sikander Khan (Illahi Bakhsh's son), Fateh Khan and Lahora Singh

2. General Avitabile's Brigade (since deceased) (Sikh, Muslim & Dogras)
Dewan Jodha Ram Commanding

1. 4 infantry paltans
2. 1 cavalry Rajman
3. 10 guns, horse artillery under Baland Khan and 8 heavy field guns under Rustam Beg

3. General Kahn Singh's Brigade (Sikh & Muslim)

1. 4 infantry paltans
2. 10 guns, horse artillery

4. General Mehtab Singh Majithia's Brigade

1. 4 infantry paltans (Sikh)
2. 1 cavalry Rajman (mixed)
3. 12 guns, horse artillery (Sikh & Muslim)

5. General Tej Singh's Brigade (Sikh)

1. 4 infantry paltans
2. 1 cavalry Rajman
3. 10 guns, horse artillery

6. General Gulab Singh Paovindia's Brigade

1. 3 infantry paltans (Muslim)
2. 14 guns, horse artillery (Sikh & Muslim)

7. Raja Suchet Singh's Brigade (since deceased) (Dogras & Muslim)

1. 2 infantry paltans
2. 1 cavalry Rajman
3. 10 heavy garrison guns and four guns horse artillery

8. General Gulab Singh Calcuttawala's Brigade (since deceased) (Sikh)

1. 4 infantry paltans
2. 1 cavalry Rajman
3. 16 guns, horse artillery

9. General Jawala Singh's Brigade

1. 2 infantry paltans (Sikh)
2. 4 guns, horse artillery (Sikh & Muslim)

10. General Lehna Singh Majithia's Brigade

1. 2 infantry paltans (Sikh)
2. 2 heavy garrison guns, 3 heavy field guns and 10 guns horse artillery (mainly Sikh)

11. General Bishan Singh's Brigade (mainly Muslim, some Sikh)

1. 2 infantry paltans
2. 3 guns, horse artillery

12. General Gurdit Singh Majithia's Brigade

1. 3 infantry paltan (Sikh)
2. 8 artillery guns (Sikh & Muslim)

13. General Court's Brigade (since resigned)

Colonel John Holmes

1. 1 infantry paltan
2. 10 guns, horse artillery

14. General Dhonkal Singh's Brigade

1. 2 infantry paltans (Dogras)

15. General Courtland's Brigade (since resigned)

1. 2 infantry paltans (1 Sikh, 1 Dogra)
2. 10 guns, horse artillery (Sikh & Muslim)

16. Sardar Nihal Singh Ahluwalia's Brigade

1. 1 infantry paltan (Sikh & Dogra)
2. 11 heavy field guns and 4 guns horse artillery (Muslim)

17. Dewan Sawan Mull's Brigade (mainly Muslim, some Sikhs)

1. 3 infantry paltans
2. 40 heavy garrison guns and 6 guns horse artillery

18. Raja Heera Singh's Brigade (since deceased) (Dogra & Muslim)

1. 2 infantry paltans
2. 1 cavalry Rajman
3. 5 heavy garrison guns and 3 heavy field guns

19. Raja Partap Singh of Punch's Brigade (Sikh)
1. 3 infantry paltans

20. Raja Gulab Singh's Brigade (Dogra & Muslim)
1. 3 infantry paltans
2. 40 heavy garrison guns and 15 guns horse artillery

21. Sheikh Imam-ud-din's Brigade (Muslim)
1. 3 infantry paltans
2. 4 guns, horse artillery

22. Sheikh Ghulam Mohi-ud-din's Brigade
1. infantry paltan (Sikh)
2. 8 heavy field guns and 6 guns horse artillery (Muslim & Sikh)

23. State and Independent Artillery
a. Commandant Bhag Singh – 6 guns horse artillery (Sikh & Muslim)
b. Commandant Shiv Prasad – 8 guns horse artillery (Sikh & Muslim)
c. Missar Lal Singh – 10 guns horse artillery (Sikh & Muslim)
d. Sardar Kishan Singh – 2 heavy garrison guns (Muslim & Dogra)
e. General Kishan Singh – 22 guns horse artillery (Sikh & Muslim)
f. Sardar Shyam Singh Attari – 10 heavy field guns (Sikh & Muslim)
g. Mian Prithi Singh – 56 heavy field guns (Muslim)
h. General Mewa Singh – 10 heavy field guns and 10 guns horse artillery (Sikh & Muslim)
i. Colonel Amir Chand – 10 heavy field guns (Muslim)
j. Artillery of Lahore – Commandant Mal Mistry – 10 guns horse artillery (Muslim & Dogra)
k. Artillery of Amritsar – Commandant Sukhu Singh – 20 heavy field guns and 12 heavy garrison guns (Muslim & Sikh)
l. Artillery of Peshawar – 10 heavy garrison guns (Muslim & Dogra)
m. Miscellaneous – 50 heavy garrison guns (Muslim & Sikh)

Total Strength of the Fauj-e-Ain as listed above stands at:*
1. Infantry 60 battalions of 600 soldiers each – 36,000
2. Cavalry 8 regiments of 600 troopers each – 4,800
3. Artillery 384 guns used in the field, organized into 32 batteries (not inclusive of Zambooraks)

a). Horse artillery – 228 guns
b) Heavy field guns – 156 guns
c) Heavy garrison guns – 171 guns (not used in the field)
d) If the Fauj-e-Ain and Feudal Zambooraks (393 and 500, respectively) are added to the above guns, the total comes to 893.

** It is my belief that these figures are inaccurate. The infantry had 62 battalions and they were up to their authorized strength of 800 men each, giving a total of 49,600 infantry soldiers. The* *cavalry, at 13 regiments of 600 troopers, would add up to a total of 7,800 cavalry. One can assume that, once the preparations for war began, all the units were up to strength.*

In *The Sikhs and the Sikh Wars*, Sir Charles Gough and A.D. Innes state that, 'According to information received from Major Broadfoot late in November, the plan of the Lahore Durbar was to send five out of the seven divisions of the regulars against the British.'

Allowing for the artillery, this would seem to mean a body of 40,000–50,000 men. If the sardars' contingents are added to these, it is possible that the whole Sikh force against the British troops did not fall short of 100,000. No such force, however, was ever collected at one time against the British. It should, perhaps, be noted that Captain Cunningham places the numbers very much lower in his *History of the Sikhs*. It is, indeed, clear from his narrative how numerous he reckoned the Sikh Army which crossed the Sutlej to have been, but he seems to put it between 30,000 and 40,000 regulars, with half the number of irregulars. Gough and Innes add that 'while giving due weight to his (Cunningham's) opinion, however, it must be remembered that he wrote always as an enthusiastic admirer of the Sikhs, with a strong inclination to give the benefit of every doubt in their favour'.[80] Captain Nicholson at Ferozepur put the figure at 3,500.[81] Major Broadfoot's report of the Sikh divisions is incorrect. Though the raising of seven divisions had been approved by the Durbar, only four had been raised by the time the war began. Other than these three, the largest formation during the war were brigade groups and brigades.

The regular cavalry Rajmans on the army rolls were:

1. 1st Dragoon Rajman
2. 2nd Lancia Dragoon Rajman
3. Gurmukh Singh Rajman
4. Heera Singh Rajman
5. Mehtab Singh Rajman
6. Horse Grenadier Rajman
7. Ram Rajman
8. Lal Singh's Sowar Rajman
9. Akal Rajman
10. Gobind Rajman
11. Jagat Singh Rajman
12. Sher Singh Rajman
13. Hazoori Rajman

The Jagirdari Fauj (Feudal Levies)

1. Infantry – Ramghols, Akalis, irregular levies and garrison companies 45,000 men
2. Cavalry – Ghorcharras, Jagirdari and Misldar Fauj
   27,000 troopers

The Ghorcharras themselves were in 18 derahs and not 17, as mentioned, which then added up to 21,239 men. The figures would therefore increase.

The derahs were as follows:

1. Derah Ghorcharra Khas
2. Derah Shyam Singh Attari
3. Derah Gurmukh Singh Lamba
4. Derah Sandhanwalia
5. Derah Ardaliyan
6. Derah Pindiwala
7. Derah Ramgarhia
8. Derah Attariwala
9. Derah Mulraj
10. Derah Dogra
11. Derah Naulakha
12. Derah Khas
    A. Naulakha Kalan
    B. Naulakha Khurd
13. Derah Raja Lal Singh
14. Derah Fateh Singh Jogi
15. Derah Imammudin
16. Derah Mangal Singh
17. Derah Jawahar Singh
18. Derah Mian Bhukam Khan
19. There were an additional 1,613 Jagirdari cavalry. These in themselves were of the same strength of an average Derah. As an example, the Derah Ghorcharra Khas was 1,600 strong – therefore, this strength could really pass as the 19th Derah.

As per my estimate the Sikh Army, in numbers, adds up to the following:

Infantry
Regular: 46,000 and Levies: 45,000 (including garrison troops) Total 91,000

Cavalry
Regular: 7,800 and Ghorcharras: 23,000
Total 30,800

If the personnel of 32 artillery batteries and feudal artillery are added to this figure, the total would come up to around 8,000 gunners. The total strength of the army in numbers would then be 130,000 soldiers, at their units' authorized strength.

When the decision to go to war was taken, the 22 brigades of the army were deployed around the state as below:

1. Peshawar – 2 brigades
2. Hazara – 1 brigade
3. Kashmir – 1 brigade
4. Multan – 1 brigade
5. Nowshera – 1 brigade
6. Jammu – 8 battalions (with Raja Gulab Singh)
7. Samba
    a. Raja Suchet Singh's brigade
    b. Raja Kesri Singh's brigade
    c. Raja Heera Singh's brigade
    d. Mian Labh Singh's battalion
8. Lahore – 11 brigades

It was not possible at this stage to withdraw the brigades deployed throughout Punjab for two reasons. Firstly, all these areas were politically unstable and any reduction of troops would have meant the overthrow of the local government. At the Shalimar meeting, the durbar wanted a third brigade, General Avitabile's, to be sent to reinforce the current brigades at Peshawar as the political situation there was deteriorating. This proposal was defeated by the *panchs*. Secondly, the brigades deployed in Kashmir and Hazara were hemmed in by snow and all passes were closed.

To add to this, Raja Gulab Singh was already in touch with the British offering his support. He had an understanding with Lord Hardinge to retain his division comprising eight battalions at Jammu and his three brigades and one battalion at Samba on some pretext. These formations comprised the Dogra troops.

This adds up to around 11 brigades, a force of around 45,000 men, located at Lahore at the disposal of the army for its operations. Colonel Gardner retained one brigade for the defence of Lahore and the protection of the maharani, leaving the commander-in-chief with an available force of about 40,000. We must also assume that 10 cavalry regiments were not with this force, since it was usual for a cavalry regiment to be dedicated to its parent brigade. As a result, Tej Singh could have had only three cavalry regiments available to him for his operations.

II. THE BRITISH

It took the governor general, Lord Hardinge, who had arrived in India to take over his assignment in July 1844, some time before he was prepared to believe that the Sikhs would cross the Sutlej. Nevertheless, in a memo to the Secret Committee[82] of the East India Company on 30 September 1845, he recorded his views contrary to his personal belief,

> The forbearance of the Government of India has been carried to an extent beyond that which has been customary. Every military precaution has, however, been taken; advice and warnings have been repeatedly conveyed to the Lahore Government in the plainest language; even the risk of giving offence by such language has been incurred, rather than fail in the essential point of clearly defining the nature of our policy, and of having the policy well understood. I am convinced that our decision to see the maharaja's government re-established on a basis of independence and strength, is well known to the most influential and leading chiefs. Their personal interests, endangered by the democratic revolution, so successfully accomplished by the Sikh Army, may induce those chiefs to exert all their efforts to compel the British government to interfere – but these attempts, and any danger resulting from them, will be attributable, not to our forbearance, but to their personal fears for life and property.
>
> You may be assured that, whilst I shall omit no precautions, and be prepared for any event, I shall persevere in the direct course I have hitherto pursued, of endeavouring, by moderation, good faith and friendly advice, to avert the necessity of British interference by force of arms in the affairs of the Punjab.[83]

On 24 October, Hardinge conveyed his views to the commander-in-chief, Sir Hugh Gough, of his intention of being prepared for military intervention if the need arose.

> In the present state of our relations with the Lahore Government, your Excellency is aware that I do not anticipate the probability of any emergencies arising which can require the army, under your Excellency's orders, to take the field this autumn. Nevertheless, having to deal with a mutinous Sikh Army, which has usurped the functions of the government, and whose caprice may, at any time, force on a rupture with our forces on the frontier, I have deemed it advisable to be prepared with the means of movement to the extent noted in the margin.

Orders were then issued for the commissariat department to prepare for the movement of a force listed below, in advance of Meerut.

Troops of horse artillery: 7
Companies of foot artillery: 6
Light field batteries: 4
Regiments of dragoons: 2
Regiments of light cavalry: 3
Regiments of European infantry: 5
Regiments of Native infantry: 13
Companies of sappers and miners: 6
Regiments of irregular cavalry: 2

On 20 November, Hardinge again wrote to the Secret Committee,

> I shall not consider the march of the Sikh troops in hostile array towards the banks of the Sutluj, as a cause justifying hostilities, if no actual violation of our borders should occur. The same privilege which we take to adopt precautionary measures on our side must be conceded to them. Every forbearance shall be shown to a weak government, struggling for assistance against its own soldiers in a state of successful mutiny.

On 4 December, he again writes to the Secret Committee,

> This morning, news up to the 1st instant has been received. The Ranee and Sirdars are becoming more and more urgent that the army should advance to the frontier, believing that, in the present posture of affairs, the only hope of saving their lives and prolonging their power is to be found in bringing about a collision with British forces.

On 11 December, lead elements of the Lahore Army crossed the Sutlej.

British Garrison Sirhind (Administrative) Division 11 December 1845

The Sirhind Division was the entire Cis-Sutlej Punjab up to Delhi. Meerut lay 40 miles north-east of Delhi and was not in the Punjab but in the United Provinces.

Commander-in-Chief
General Sir Hugh Gough

Ferozepur (7,000 troops)
Major General Sir John H. Littler, KCB

1. HM 62nd Foot
2. 12th Bengal Native Infantry
3. 14th Bengal Native Infantry
4. 27th Bengal Native Infantry
5. 33rd Bengal Native Infantry
6. 44th Bengal Native Infantry
7. 54th Bengal Native Infantry
8. 63rd Bengal Native Infantry
9. 8th Bengal Light Cavalry
10. 3rd Bengal Irregular Horse
11. 2 Troops Bengal Horse Artillery (6x4 pdrs each)
12. 2 Light Field Batteries (6x9 pdrs each)

Ludhiana (5,000 troops)
Brigadier Hugh Wheeler

1. HM 50th Foot
2. 11th Bengal Native Infantry
3. 26th Bengal Native Infantry
4. 42nd Bengal Native Infantry
5. 48th Bengal Native Infantry
6. 73rd Bengal Native Infantry
7. Detachment Native Cavalry Regiment
8. 2 Troops Bengal Horse Artillery (6x4 pdrs each)

Ambala (10,000 troops)
Major General Sir Walter Raleigh Gilbert

1. HM 9th Foot
2. HM 31st Foot
3. HM 80th Foot
4. 16th Bengal Native Infantry
5. 24th Bengal Native Infantry
6. 41st Bengal Native Infantry
7. 45th Bengal Native Infantry
8. 47th Bengal Native Infantry
9. HM 3rd Light Dragoons
10. 4th Bengal Light Cavalry
11. 5th Bengal Light Cavalry
12. Governor General's bodyguard

Meerut (10,000 troops)
Major General Sir John Grey

1. HM 10th Foot (less 1 company on garrison duty)
2. HM 53rd Foot
3. 43rd Bengal Native Infantry
4. 59th Bengal Native Infantry
5. 3rd Bengal Native Infantry (to be left behind for garrison duty)
6. HM 9th Lancers
7. HM 16th Lancers
8. 3rd Bengal Light Cavalry
9. 4th Bengal Irregular Horse
10. 4 artillery batteries (26 guns)
11. 1 Company Sappers and Miners

Kasauli
HM 29th Foot

Sabathu
1st Bengal European Light Infantry

Hansi
8th Bengal Irregular Horse

Dehra Dun
Sirmoor Gurkha Battalion

Jutogh
Nasiri Gurkha Battalion

III. THE TERRAIN AND BATTLEFIELD

The battles of the First Sikh War were fought on the south bank of the river Sutlej. The Sutlej enters India from Tibet through the Shipki La pass in the present Indian state of Himachal Pradesh. It then flows through the Himalayas entering the Punjab plains at Ropar. It continues through Indian Punjab, west of Ludhiana, meeting the river Beas at Harike. The two combined rivers, still called the Sutlej, continue to flow south until it enters Pakistan close to Fazilka. In Pakistan, it flows south-west, past the city of Bhawalpur, joining the Indus north of the Pakistan city of Uch.

This river divided the kingdom of Lahore, before the annexation of the Punjab, from the rest of India. The area south of the Sutlej with which we are concerned, was called the Cis-Sutlej Punjab, which extended to the border of Delhi and included the states of Patiala, Nabha, Jind, and Malerkotla.

In 1846, the transport network was primitive. Roads were few and far between and those approaching the Sutlej from Delhi were narrow and unsurfaced. Two roads linked Ambala with the rest of India. The first, the Grand Trunk Road, ran from Delhi, 100 miles away, while the second ran from Meerut, 120 miles away.

From Ambala westwards there were four road systems: the first, a continuation of the Grand Trunk Road, ran from Ambala for 38 miles westward to Sirhind, and then to Ludhiana 28 miles further on. At that point it turned north for 8 miles to Phillaur on the Sutlej – the river being the border with the Lahore kingdom. The second approach road continued south of the Sutlej, linking Ludhiana with Dharamkot, a distance of 45 miles. This continued a further 37 miles to Ferozepur on the Sutlej. After a further 9 miles, this road divided at Talwandi, going 22 miles north-west to Harike. Beyond the river, the road continued to Amritsar via Taran Taran, both in the territory of the Lahore Durbar. Another minor road from Harike then continued straight to Lahore via Pittee and Bheranha, both towns being within the Lahore Durbar territory. The third road branched west from Sirhind, linking Malod 38 miles on, Raikot a further 22, Wudnee another 23, and Moodki a further 29. Ferozshah was another 11 miles on and, finally, Ferozepur was a further 17 miles. The fourth went straight from Ambala to Patiala 22 miles distant, then Malerkotla a further 28, and then joined the road mentioned above at Raikot, 23 miles from Malerkotla. The Patiala stretch of the road was also of low quality. From Ferozepur the road continued to Lahore via Kasur, Luliani and Lakhpat, all in Lahore Durbar territory.

Other than the land that was cultivated, it was a difficult terrain inundated with jungles, trees and shrubs. This was more so along the northern link road, the soil of which was loam to clay-loam. Towards the southern approach were sand dunes with kikar (tamarisk) and ber (jujubi) trees and bushes, along with other intertwined shrubs – in all some 22 different species covered some of the plains between these sand dunes.[84] All of the trees were covered by thorns, the kikar being the worst – the thorns on mature trees grew up to 2 inches in length, very pointed, thick and a perfect obstacle to horse and man. The roads and countryside was sand to sandy-loam. High elephant grass grew along the seasonal water courses. The banks of the water courses, particularly of the larger ones and the Sutlej, could be as high as 20 feet as the water eroded the bed continuously, pushing the sand banks higher until they finally collapsed, widening the river through erosion.

The temperatures in December and January, the season when the winter rains arrive, were in the region of 10–15 degrees centigrade during the day, sometimes falling to below freezing point at night. Under these conditions the ground froze and it was common to see ponds and still water puddles along the water courses covered in ice.

Other than the Sutlej and its tributary the Beas, both of which are fed by glaciers higher up in the Himalayas, none of the water courses carried water during the winter unless it had been an exceptionally wet one. During the monsoon season, from end-June to early-September, the water courses turned into fast-flowing torrents. Because of the water velocity, lives have been known to have been lost in them, while crop damage was fairly routine.

There were no canal systems in those days, the first one in the area being the Sirhind canal built by Maharaja Narinder Singh of Patiala after the Sikh wars in 1853. During the wars, the only sources of drinking water were limited to Persian or open wells. Usually one or two common ones were used by the entire village. The more affluent would perhaps have a well on their land for irrigation of the crops, whatever little could be managed by such a system. Smaller villages also had open wells where water was drawn by the means of a bucket attached to the end of a rope. Each village had ponds. These were usually depressions into which the village drains emptied and they were also used by the village water buffaloes, the main source of milk, to wallow in during the hot dry season.

IV. THE INITIAL MOVES

The appointments of Prime Minister Lal Singh and Commander-in-Chief Tej Singh were duly announced at a council meeting held in Shalimar in early November. Subsequent to this, a meeting of *panchs* was summoned to the samadh of the late Maharaja Ranjit Singh and oaths of loyalty to Maharaja Duleep Singh and obedience to Raja Lal Singh and Sardar Tej Singh were sworn by all – on the Guru Granth Sahib in the gurdwara adjoining the samadh by the Sikhs, on the Koran by the Muslims and on the Gita by the Hindus. Orders were now issued for the march to the Sutlej.

Lal Singh was to command the Ghorcharras with three to four batteries of artillery. The Fauj-e-Ain as a whole would march towards

Ferozepur under Tej Singh. The logic for this division is not clear. The importance of infantry and artillery in sufficient numbers was inculcated into the Lahore Army by its French generals, and effectively employed during the battles fought by the late Maharaja Ranjit Singh. For Tej Singh and Lal Singh not to have understood the importance of commanding such a balanced force in what was then modern warfare, and after having seen the usefulness of such a composite formation during past battles, was strange. It was not the days of Ghengis Khan, when Mongolian horsemen galloped across the steppes of Mongolia marauding, pillaging and raping settlements that were unfortunate enough to fall in their way. Had Lal Singh taken even one brigade group with him to Mudki, out of the 10 brigades accompanying Tej Singh, the outcome could very well have been different.

Preparations were undertaken to put the army on a war footing. Units began frantically making good their deficiencies, without which they felt they wouldn't be fully operational. At the same time, the soldiers began to speculate on the loot they were going to take when they ransacked Delhi, Benaras, Mathura and other cities. Some even planned to take over land and settle down to rule territories![85] The army was so excited that when Tej Singh decided that Ventura's brigade should be sent to reinforce the two brigades already in Peshawar to put down trouble that was brewing, the *panchs* present vetoed the proposal, saying that no one was going anywhere until the war with the British was over. They were confident that it would only take a few days.

The troops, by now overly excited and optimistic, sent frantic word to their relatives to join them, as they would be required to help carry home the booty they hoped to plunder as soon as they crossed the river. It was later estimated that when the army reached the Sutlej, there were around 200,000 eager followers in its wake. Many of these were fully armed! Morale was sky high.

On 23 November, Lal Singh left Lahore with his 23,000 Ghorcharras and 40 bullock-drawn field guns. He marched 15 miles from the city and established his camp. The same day the regular army, under the orders of Tej Singh, started its approach on various lines of march to the Sutlej. Tej Singh himself remained behind to complete various arrangements and only reached the army on 16 December, after lead elements had already crossed the Sutlej and the various commanders of the army and the sardars had written to him to come and take command of the army in person. Meanwhile, Lal Singh had moved his camp to 9 miles short of Harike.

With the army on the move, a meeting took place between Lal Singh and Tej Singh, with their sardars and brigade commanders, to decide what their objectives were going to be. Wazir Lal Singh and Commander-in-Chief Tej Singh played their parts to perfection. Lal Singh wanted to cross the river and move on Ludhiana, where there was a British force estimated to be 5,000 strong under Brigadier Wheeler. Tej Singh, at Ferozepur, wanted to move on Ambala. The conference, by now duly impressed by the sincerity of both commanders, ordered Lal Singh to ignore Ludhiana and to move south to join Tej Singh at Ferozepur, and then attack Ambala. Lal Singh, however, crossed the Sutlej at Harike and established his camp south of the river.

Six days later, on 17 December, while still encamped near Sutlej, news reached Lal Singh that a British force in 'moderate numbers' had been sighted approaching the village of Mudki.

In the meantime, Governor General Hardinge had reached Ambala and joined C-in-C Gough on 3 December. By 6 December, he had reached Ludhiana via the Cis-Sutlej states, meeting with the chiefs of the region on the way. By 13 December, while still at Ludhiana, news reached him that the lead elements of the Lahore Army had crossed the Sutlej on 11 December and that the main force had followed the following day. This had been anticipated in a report from Captain Nicholson that had reached him on 9 December. The Sikh breakout finally convinced him of the duplicity of the durbar. In response, he issued a directive to Gough to carry out full mobilization and to bring forward the Meerut Division, comprising around 17,000 troops with 69 field guns. Gough decided to move forward to meet up with Littler's force of 7,000 at Ferozepur. On 2 December, Littler had asked for an additional British infantry battalion to strengthen his position. HM's 80th Foot moved from Ambala for Ferozepur on 10 December by which time it was too late as the Sikh Army had cut the road to Ferozepur.

On 13 December, the governor general issued a Proclamation amounting to a declaration of war against the Lahore Durbar:

> In the year 1809, a treaty of amity and concord was concluded between the British government and the late Maharaja Ranjit Singh, the conditions of which have always been faithfully observed by the British government, and were scrupulously fulfilled by the late Maharaja [...] The Sikh Army has now, without a shadow of provocation, invaded the British territories. The Governor General must, therefore, take measures for effectively protecting the British provinces, for vindicating the authority of the British government, and for punishing the violators of treaties and the disturbers of public peace [...][86]

General Gough began to move. The same day an officer, caked with dust, galloped up to him to inform him that the Sikh Army, consisting of 50,000 troops with about 100 guns, had crossed the Sutlej on 11 December. Gough responded by quickening the pace of the march, covering the 114 miles in five days in 'blinding dust and parched air'. The supply train was unable to keep pace, leaving the troops to manage on what they could carry.

This supply train, or 'tail', had in it about four times as many men as the brigade.

THEATRE OF OPERATIONS DURING THE FIRST ANGLO-SIKH WAR, 1846-47

Map published in 1845

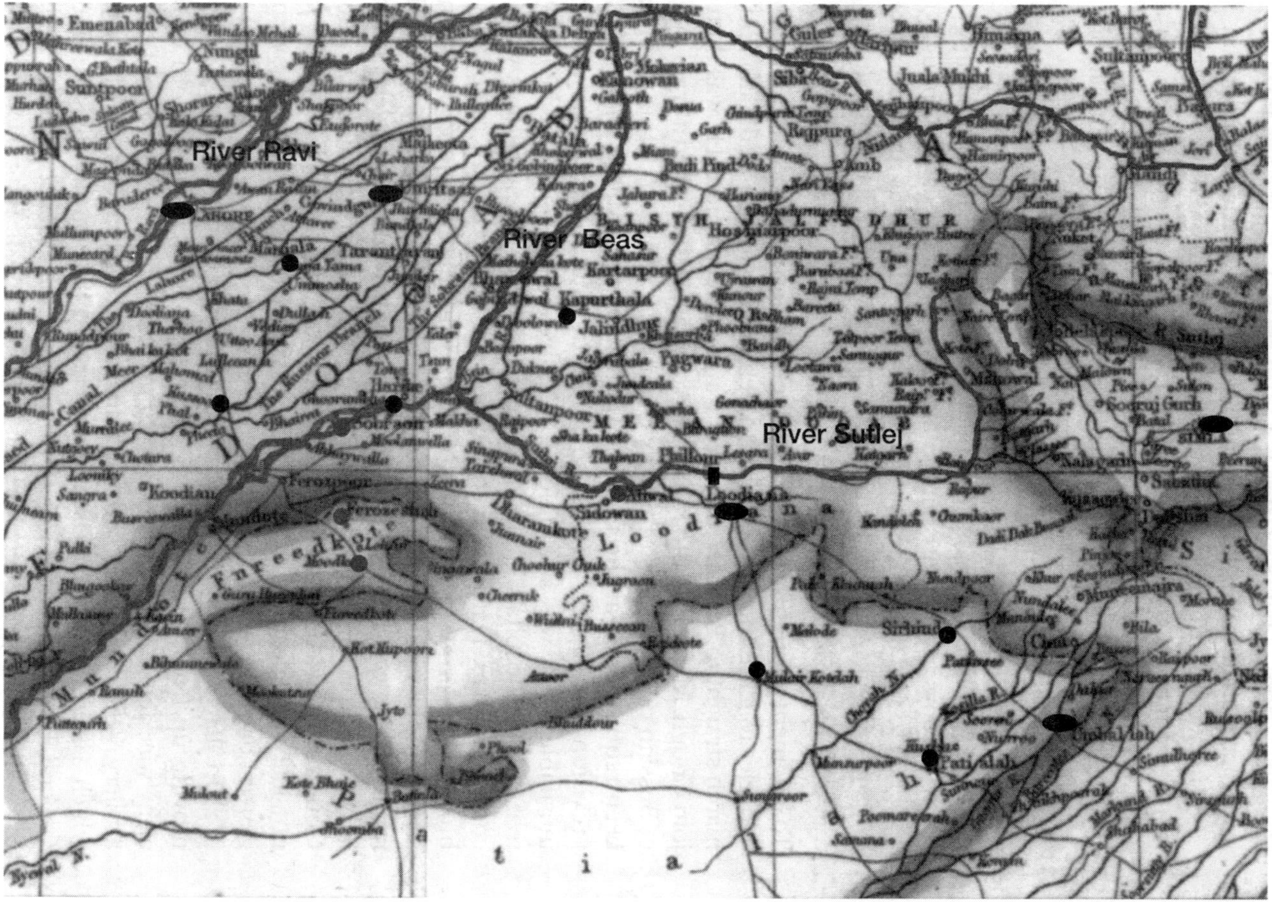

> Every officer was allowed from 20–25 personal servants to look after his clothes, his equipment and his laundry; to pitch his tent, prepare, cook and serve his food and his drinks as well as to oversee all those who performed these tasks. If he kept a palanquin – and senior officers often reclined in them rather than ride all day in the hot sun – he needed six bearers. For every horse he was allowed two servants, a groom and a grass cutter; and for every elephant another two. For every three camels he hired to carry his personal belongings, he had one servant – camels and elephants were marks of status and senior officers would have 40 or 50 of each.
>
> As if these were not enough, every regiment was accompanied by 600 stretcher or dooly bearers; camel-doctors, water carriers, saddlers, blacksmiths, cobblers, tailors, milk girls, and often for entertaining the sepoys, nautch girls and fiddlers. 6,000 camels carried enough grain to feed 8,000 horses for a month, but thousands more camels and bullocks carried ammunition, gunpowder and rations, apart from special personal baggage.[87]

To augment Gough's army, Hardinge, in Ludhiana, ordered Brigadier Wheeler to leave the sick and infirm behind to garrison Ludhiana and to march straight to Bussian to protect the food depot there. He was then to join Gough. Major Broadfoot had, in great haste, established a grain dump at Bussian on the orders of the governor general. Much of this grain had been requisitioned at the point of the bayonet. Hardinge had made no provision for supply dumps, since he did not believe that war was inevitable. What was also unforgivable, because of this same belief, was that no field hospitals had been ordered forward. These failures were to cost many lives. Hardinge also ignored Gough's constant reminders to build up his army to what he considered the requisite force for such a campaign, by ordering troops forward from other stations in India. The news of the governor general's orders to Brigadier Wheeler and his subsequent personal recconnaissance to the border at Phillaur, without Gough's knowledge, elicited a dry and cryptic response, 'I really do not like your position. It would be a fearful thing to have a governor general bagged.'[88]

On 17 December, Wheeler's Brigade met up with Gough's force moving up from Ambala at a village called Chirik. The strength of the army was now 12,000 troops – 5 regiments of cavalry, 5 troops of horse artillery, 2 field batteries with 40 guns, and 13 battalions of infantry, of which 4 were British. It was now brigaded into 1 cavalry division under General Thackwell and 3 infantry divisions under Generals Harry Smith, Sir Walter Raleigh Gilbert and Sir John McCaskill. Only Harry Smith's division was up to strength, the other two being of brigade strength.

At dawn on 18 December, the governor general was basking in the early morning sun and eating his breakfast under a tree after a cold,

THEATRE OF OPERATIONS – FIRST ANGLO-SIKH WAR 1845-46

Roads, cities, villages and rivers are spelt as in 1845

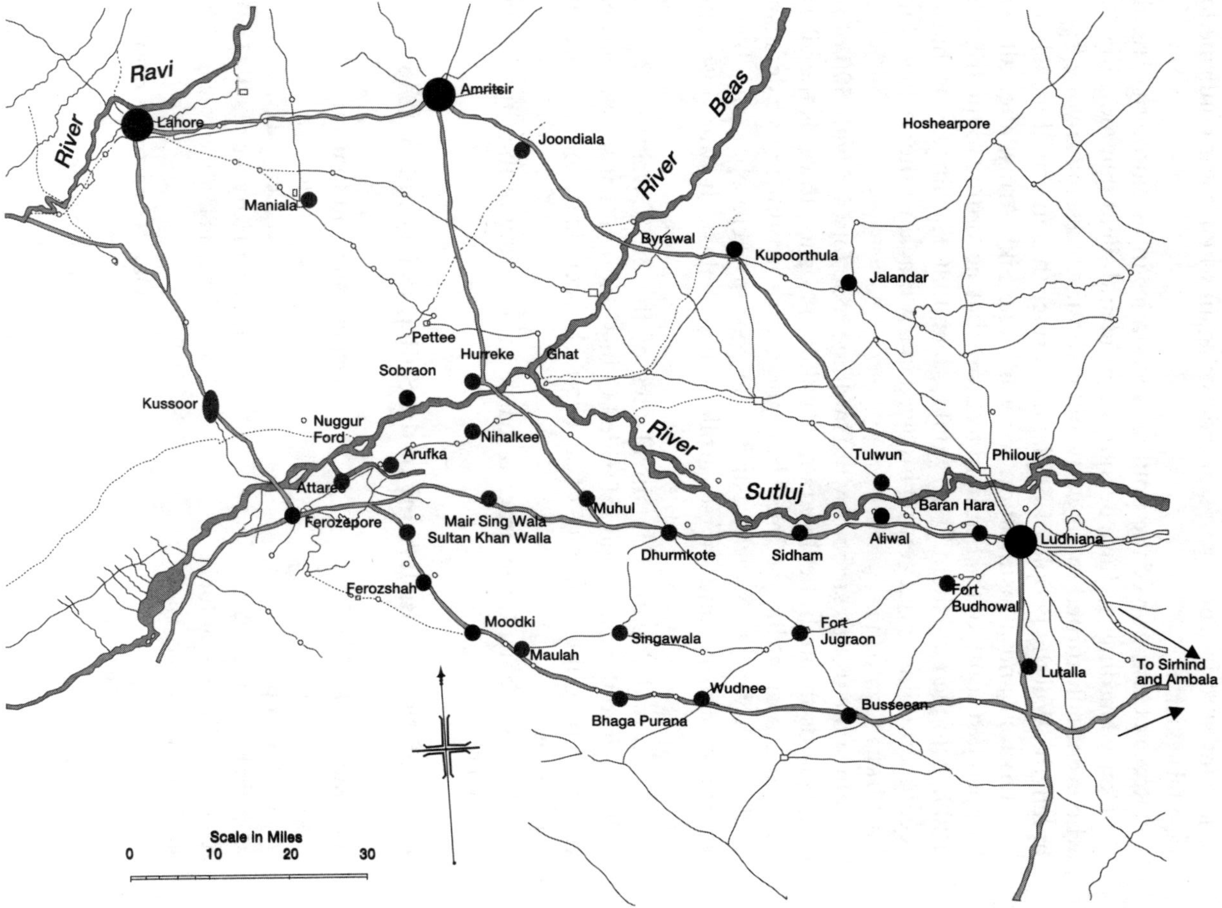

wretched night. Quarter Master Crabtree of the 3rd Dragoons came galloping in with a message from Major Broadfoot, who had been out with the 3rd Dragoons that morning probing forward to make contact with the Sikh forces. His message was that the Sikhs were moving forward. The army stood to, but soon stood down again when it was confirmed to be a false alarm.

Robert Cust, one of the political secretaries in his entourage, recalls Sir Henry Hardinge to have been thoughtful and silent that morning, but who eventually turned to his party and without addressing anyone, spoke at length: 'Will the people of England consider this an actual invasion of our territory and a justification for war? The Sikh Army, after all, was camped just south of the Sutluj in territory that, according to the treaty of 1809, belonged to them.'[89] It would seem that Hardinge was having second thoughts about getting involved in a war against the wishes of the East India Company.

Once the troops stood down, Hardinge rode forward with 500 of his bodyguards through the 'low tamarisk (kikar) bushes, towards the village of Mudki, a large village of mud huts and a fort surrounded by a defensive wall, north-west of which, astride the road to Ferozepur, the British advanced cavalry and horse artillery had halted. It was just after mid-day.'[90]

At around 3 p.m., Captain Haines of the 3rd Cavalry once again galloped into the camp and informed C-in-C Gough that the Sikhs were now marching ahead. Clouds of dust could be seen on the horizon around 3 miles away.

At this moment, the order of battle of the army of the Sutlej stood as under.

Order of Battle British Army of the Sutlej, 18 December 1845[91]

Commander-in-Chief
General Sir Hugh Gough
Aide-de-Camp
Captain H.B. Edwardes
Governor General of India
Lt General Sir Henry Hardinge
Aides-de-Camp
Brevet Major W.R. Herries
Brevet Captain G.E. Hillier
Lt John Munro
Adjutant General: (vice, Major General Sir James Lumley [ill])
Lt Col M. Barr
Deputy Adjutant General
Major Patrick Grant
Quartermaster General (vice, Major General Sir Harry Smith – 1st Div.)
Major General Sir Robert Henry Sale, GCB
Deputy Quartermaster General
Lt Col Garden
1st Infantry Division
Major General Sir Harry Smith
Deputy Assistant Adjutant General:
Captain E. Lugard
1st Brigade
Brigadier (Lt Col) Samuel Bolton, CB
HM 31st Foot Regiment – Lt Col J. Byrne

24th BNI Regiment
47th BNI Regiment
2nd Brigade
Brigadier (Lt Col Hugh M. Wheeler, CB)
HM 50th Foot Regiment
42nd BNI Regiment
48th BNI Regiment
2nd Infantry Division
Major General Sir Walter Raleigh Gilbert
Assistant Quartermaster General:
Major R. Codrington
1st Brigade
2nd Bengal (Grenadiers) Native Infantry Regiment
45th BNI Regiment
2nd Brigade:
16th Bengal (Grenadiers) Native Infantry Regiment
3rd Infantry Division:
Major General Sir John McCaskill, KCB and KH
1st Brigade
Brigadier (Lt Col) Newton Wallace
HM 9th Foot Regiment
HM 80th Foot Regiment – Lt Col T. Bunbury
26th BNI Regiment
73rd BNI Regiment
Cavalry Division: (OC and most staff not present at battle)
Major General Sir Joseph Thackwell
Brigadier (Lt Col) M. White, CB (Officiating)
Assistant Adjutant General:
Captain Tritton
Brigade Major:
Lt (Brevet Captain) T.L. Harrington
1st Brigade
Brigadier (Lt Col) W. Mactier
9th (Christie's Horse) Bengal Irregular Cavalry Regiment – Captain Christie
4th BLC (Lancer) Regiment (2 sqdns)
2nd Brigade
Brigadier (Lt Col) J.B. Gough
Governor General's Bodyguard – Lt Charles Digby Dawkins
5th Bengal Light Cavalry Regiment – Major Alexander
3rd Brigade
Brigadier (Lt Col) M. White, CB
HM 3rd Light Dragoon Regiment
4th Bengal Light Cavalry (Lancer) Regiment (2 Sqdns)
Army Troops:
Army Artillery:
Brigadier (Lt Col) George 'Bully' Brooke, 1st Brigade, BHA
Brigade Major:
Brevet Captain Murray Mackenzie
5.33 Troops, Bengal Horse Artillery (attached to the Cavalry Brigades):
Brevet Major Frederick Brind's European Troops (1/3)
Captain Francis Dashwood's European Troop (1/1) (replaced by 2nd Captain C.E. Mills)
Brevet Major Elliot D'Arcy Todd's European Troop (2/1)
Captain G.H. Swinley's European Troop (3/1)
Captain Hubert Garbett's Native Troop (4[N]/3, BHA)
1st Division, Brevet Major J.T. Lane's European Troop (2/3) – Lt G. Moir
Including:
1st Troop, 1st Brigade, BHA (Dashwood)
2nd Troop, 1st Brigade, BHA (Todd)
3rd Troop, 1st Brigade, BHA (Swinley)
1st Troop, 3rd Brigade, BHA (Brind)
1st Div, 2nd Troop, 3rd Brigade, BHA (Moir)
4th (Native) Troop, 3rd Brigade, BHA (Garbett)
2 Field Batteries, Bengal Artillery: (possibly superintended by Horsford)
7th Heavy Field Battery – Captain Jasper Trower (replaced by 2nd Captain J. Fordyee)

9th Heavy Field Battery – Captain R. Horsford. LFBs were manned by:
3rd Company, 4th Battalion, Bengal Artillery (#7 LFB)
2nd Company, 6th Battalion, Bengal Artillery (#9 LFB)

Once information reached the Sikhs that the British were advancing, the army divided into two. Tej Singh remained opposite Ferozepur to keep pressure on Littler, resisting repeated attempts by his subordinates to push him into attacking Littler's command of 7,000 troops. His attitude was that a C-in-C's job was to fight with the opposing C-in-C and not to become engaged with a mere major general and his small command. The brigade commanders accepted this reasoning. Tej Singh's treachery would become apparent later, but for the moment he got his way. If he really wanted to fight Gough and the governor general, then he should have moved to Ferozshah. He was, it seems, following Captain Nicholson's advice, 'to wait as long as possible and to march on the governor general',[92] or even more likely, he was following the regent's decision to pitch her army against the British and have them cut down to size. What better way but to throw them into battle piece by piece? He had enough military experience, as did his commanders, to have realized that there was every likelihood of a major clash with a highly professional army led by experienced generals and, therefore, the requirement of a sufficiently large and balanced force being made available at Ferozshah was an absolute necessity.

Lal Singh and his Ghorcharras moved to Ferozshah where they began to build an all-round defensive position with entrenchments and a waist-high wall enclosing their position. This was the site he had chosen, during his reconnaissance in August. He now received information from his scouts that a British force, in moderate strength, had reached Mudki in the early hours of 18 December.

Lal Singh had received news from his intelligence sources the day before about the British strength and that their objective was to be Mudki. The sardars of his feudal levies and Ghorcharras now demanded that they move to Mudki to meet the British. At first he was reluctant, insisting on fighting the battle at Ferozshah in a prepared position covered by sufficient artillery. From the information given to him by his scouts, he believed the British force did not have sufficient guns and would certainly be outgunned. The insistence of his Jagirdari Fauj commanders to meet the British head-on finally prevailed and Lal Singh committed himself to Mudki. He immediately sent a detailed report to Tej Singh telling him of his intention and asking him to reinforce his Jagirdari Fauj with elements of the Fauj-e-Ain. Tej Singh sent him the bare minimum – 1,200 infantry troops – detachments from his regular brigades, and 16 horse artillery guns.

Lal Singh left half his force behind at Ferozshah to complete the entrenchment and fortifications. As he had told his Jagirdari chiefs, it was always wise to plan on a fall-back position. We must remember that the feudal levies were commanded, at times, by hot-headed, young, inexperienced feudal leaders, sometimes just fourteen or so years old, and the Ghorcharras were all irregular cavalry with no proper military training.

The strength of the Lahore troops under Lal Singh was put at between 40,000 by Gough and Innis, and 3,500 by Captain Nicholson, who was then at Ferozepur and should have been the most accurate. I have taken a middle view by assuming Cunninghan to be correct, where he puts the strength at, 'about eight to ten thousand Ghorchurras, 2,000 infantry and 22 guns'.[93] The strength at Mudki should have been in line with Captain Nicholson's estimate of 3,500 troops, as their task ordinarily would have been one of covering troops to establish contact with Gough's army (about 8,000-10,000 strong), and then to fall back on their main position at Ferozshah, 8 miles to the rear where the final battle would be fought.

Lal Singh had taken 16 horse artillery guns from Tej Singh because his 40 bullock-drawn ones were too cumbersome to move and were left at Ferozshah. Cunningham puts the number of Sikh guns at Mudki at 22. As Lal Singh did not carry any of his original guns with him, and had only taken 16 from Tej Singh, I put the gun strength at 16 instead of the 22. If he was advancing to Mudki to give battle, Tej Singh should have given him a larger number of guns and infantry of the regular army, if possible, a brigade group or brigade of the 10 he had with him opposite Ferozepur. Taking the requisite strength was imperative in case he did get involved in a pitched battle, as finally did happen. The fact is, there was no regular army commander with this force and no experienced feudal leader to know any better and the only troops he had under command was feudal cavalry, the Ghorcharras.

Lal Singh moved on the morning of 18 December. Around noon, he reached the outskirts of Mudki and established camp. Indecision then got the better of him. With no military or campaign experience of any kind, he refused to take a decision to deploy until the sardars and chiefs, 'reproached him with cowardice, and declared their intention to fight whether he led them or not'.[94]

V. THE BATTLE OF MUDKI

Gough saw the dust clouds on the horizon, even before Captain Frederick Haines, his military secretary who had been sent forward by him, had returned. Haines had met up with Captain Quinn of the 3rd Dragoons, who pointed out the dust cloud and sounds of moving troops and then galloped back to inform Gough. Gough gave the order for the army to deploy. Just then Major Broadfoot arrived saying excitedly, 'There, your Excellency, is the Sikh Army'.[95]

The troops, tired after the continuous forced march over five days, were also hungry. They had not eaten for 36 hours because their supply train of camels and carts had not yet caught up with them. Worse than the hunger was the thirst that parched their throats. They and their horses had drunk from the only available source, the village pond into which the village drains emptied and the buffalo wallowed. It was either that or die of thirst. An hour earlier, the camels carrying their rations had started arriving and the men had lit fires and started to cook their meals from whatever those camels and carts carried. The bugles sounded the 'stand to' suddenly. Leaving their half-cooked meal, the hungry and tired troops rushed and fell in with their weapons.

As Cook wrote in *Sikh Wars:*

> Two factors to be borne in mind are that the men were all tired and hungry, and that the deployment was carried out very hurriedly at a moment when everyone was starting to relax. There had been no time to issue detailed orders and few people really knew what was happening. It is a tribute to good discipline that there was not more confusion. An account from one British regiment tells of men falling in in their shirtsleeves and of some officers with drawn swords and no sword belts.

Lal Singh's scouts had informed him of the British position on the other side of Mudki. By now he also knew that his advance had been spotted by the British cavalry patrols – the dust his Ghorcharras were throwing up indicating his position. Therefore, he decided to deploy his 16 guns, covered by his infantry, within a forest of tamarisk bushes and trees which lay between his camp and Mudki. The Ghorcharras were divided and positioned on either flank with around 4,000-5,000 on each side. He chose this position for two reasons – the jungle provided cover, depriving the British of an exact target, and the tamarisk, being heavily thorned, provided an effective obstacle for the advancing infantry. It also kept the cavalry at bay on the same principle as barbed wire is used in modern warfare.

The first to move on the British side was Brigadier Brooke, the commander of artillery, who limbered up his 12 field battery 9-pounders and 30 horse artillery 6-pounders. His orders were quite simple. 'Now my men,' he said to them, 'when at the gallop, if you see me drop the point of my sword like so, go as if the devil were after you: when I raise it so, pull up; and when I give the flourish, so, come about and unlimber.'[96] Then riding to the front he gave his order to, 'advance in column of troops from the right'. The 5 horse artillery troops galloped in line to the front with the field battery of 9-pounders following. When they had advanced half the distance, the Sikh guns opened up on them from cover. Although they could hear the guns and could see smoke rising from the jungle, they could not pinpoint their position. Round shot began rolling into them, breaking the legs of a number of horses. One young lieutenant, Wheelright, thought he would catch one and throw it back, only to be severely wounded in his right hand. He was reprimanded sharply by the battery commander for bad language and ordered to the rear! The guns under the brigadier then galloped up to the edge of the forest, unlimbered and opened fire on the smoke and sound.

What Gough calls 'the well-directed fire of our artillery' at the smoke rising from the jungle had its impact and the Sikh fire slackened. The Ghorcharras on both flanks were now seen to be moving forward in an enveloping move. Seeing the danger of this move, Gough ordered Brigadiers Gough and White on the right, and Brigadier Mactier on the left, to deal with this threat. Gough himself galloped forward 200 yards to the right front with Brigadier White, ordering the 3rd Dragoons and two squadrons of the 4th Light Cavalry to stop the Sikh threat at all cost.

On Gough's orders, Brigadier White ordered the 3rd Light Dragoons and two squadrons of the 4th Lancers forward. The Bodyguard and the 5th Light Cavalry under Brigadier Gough, also on the right, began their advance. On the left Brigadier Mactier's regiments, the remaining squadrons of the 4th Light Cavalry and the 9th Irregular Cavalry, swept out as well.

The Ghorcharra force saw the British cavalry bearing down on them and took no action, though their enveloping movement came to a halt. They stood bunched up and looked on in confusion, unable to take any counter measures of their own. The most fatal tactic for cavalry is to receive a cavalry charge while stationary, more so when the British cavalry horse was heavier in weight to that of the Ghorcharras'. Where Lal Singh, the commander of the battle, was at this moment, is not known. Since he was not with the Ghorcharras, one must assume that he was with his guns and infantry in the forest, or in his camp a short distance from the forest. Being subsequently 'blind', he would have had no control over the Ghorcharras on either flank. He had obviously not seen the development taking place on the field ahead and, once having given them the earlier 'envelopment' order, he had probably left the Ghorcharras to their own fate under their inexperienced feudal chiefs. Nearly 4,000-5,000 Ghorcharras on each flank really meant 3 to 4 feudal levies on either side, with none accepting the leadership of the other. This was a clear-cut recipe for confusion and disaster.

The Native Cavalry lancers with their heavy bamboo lances lowered, and the Dragoons with their sabres drawn, ploughed into the Ghorcharras. After the shock of the impact, the Ghorcharras recovered sufficiently to engage in hand-to-hand fighting. Hardinge later wrote in his *Despatches* that a sort of, 'Balaclava melee now took place among the opposing cavalry, except the Sikhs made a more determined stand than did the Russians against Scarlett's Heavy Brigade'. The leaderless Ghorcharras finally broke and withdrew on both flanks.

The 3rd Dragoons particularly distinguished themselves in this charge, earning themselves the name 'Mudki Wallas'. The cavalry now turned both flanks while the 3rd Dragoons disappeared around the jungle, sweeping behind the Sikh gun position, sabreing gunners and infantrymen as they galloped past.

Gough now cantered forward with his staff, anxious to be up front. Just then Havelock, who was in the van, had his horse, Feroze, shot from under him. Broadfoot found another and both soon caught up with Gough. An hour later, Havelock once again had the fresh horse shot dead under him and yet again Broadfoot conjured up another horse for him, remarking, 'It appears to be of no use to give you horses, you are sure to loose them.'

In the meantime, the cavalry, having succeeded in breaking up the Ghorcharras, took post on either flank of the horse artillery. Brigadier Mactier was on the left with his 9th Irregular Cavalry and his two squadrons of the 4th Lancers, while Brigadiers Gough and White were on the right with their regiments.

The twelve battalions of infantry had formed from echelon of brigades into a line, forward of Mudki, and had started their mile long advance to the Sikh position from the forward assembly area – Sir Harry Smith's Division on the right, Major General Gilbert's in the centre and Sir John McCaskill's on the left. The divisions were composed of the following:

Sir Harry Smith	Maj. Gen. Gilbert	Sir John McCaskill
Brig. Bolton	1. 45th NI	1. HM 9th Foot
1. HM 31st Foot	2. 2nd Grenadiers	2. HM 80th Foot
2. 24 NI	3. 16th Grenadiers	3. 26th NI
3. 27th NI		4. 73rd NI
Brig. Wheeler		
1. HM 50th Foot	2. 42nd NI	3. 48th NI

For Gough, the elimination of the Ghorcharra concentrations on either flank left only the Sikh artillery and infantry to deal with. The nature of the ground, covered in tamarisk trees and bushes interspersed by other tall trees, prevented him from using the cavalry to exploit their success by taking the guns on their own. The infantry would be needed to do that.

The cavalry had started its operations at 3 p.m. Last light on 18 December, two days short of the shortest day, was 5.30 p.m. The cavalry charge and the dispersal of the ghorcharras was in daylight. By the time the infantry, which started its advance at around 3.30 p.m., had covered the mile to the Sikh position under fire, it was beginning to grow dark. India has a very short twilight, perhaps half an hour at the most, and with sunset at around 5 p.m., last light would be around 5.30 p.m. By 5 p.m., however, the evening dust and smog that hangs in the air all over the

Punjab in winter, together with the dust raised by the cavalry and infantry and the smoke of battle, must have made it impossible to see anything, even before sunset.

As the infantry edged up to the forest, the Sikh guns opened fire again. Hunched over in the hope of making themselves smaller targets, the infantry regiments soon reached the edge of the forest and started to move forward into the jungle in the face of severe and continuous grapeshot. As Featherstone recorded in *At Them with the Bayonet,*

> Soon, the superiority of the Sikhs over the sepoys became apparent. The Company's Indian troops showed a marked reluctance to throw themselves against the half hidden enemy, of whom little could be seen in the deepening dusk, but the red flashes of their muskets. Perhaps this reluctance was logical enough, but it instilled in young William Hodson of the 2nd Grenadiers [who later raised Hodson's Horse] fighting in his first battle, a persistent lack of confidence in Native Infantry. It is recorded that he spent much of the battle within a few yards of three guns which were mowing down his men with grapeshot, as he tried unsuccessfully to get them to follow him to take the position with the bayonet.

Cust, Hardinge's political assistant, moving forward with the governor general, noted with dismay '[...] that the sepoys were panic-stricken and firing their muskets in the air to their right and left. One native battalion turned suddenly towards the rear and began to retire'. Gough sent Havelock to try and stop them. He cantered around to face them saying, 'The enemy are in front of and not behind you.' There is no record of whether he succeeded in turning them or not.

In the Sikh force, there was no sign of Lal Singh or any other commander giving orders. With the Ghorcharras gone, the battle was now sustained by the Muslim gunners and Sikh infantry, both from the Lahore regular army. The infantry was firing as rapidly as it could and the Muslim gunners continued to serve their guns, oblivious of the fact that the British guns and infantry were now concentrating on them. Sikh sharpshooters had climbed trees to pick off British officers and anyone exercising any semblance of command. It soon developed into a fierce hand-to-hand struggle in which the men could not have fought in a more gallant manner than they did. The British cheers were intermingled by the 'Jaikaras' of the Sikh troops and 'Allah ho Akbar' of the Muslim gunners and the infantry battle was fought virtually blind from start to finish. By the time the British Infantry reached the guns, it was already dark.

> The Sikhs were fighting well, their gunners standing nobly to their beloved guns. The intensity, rapidity and precision of their artillery and musket fire indicating that Britain had met a foe, superior to any previously encountered in India. In Wheeler's Brigade, the 42nd and 49th NI, which had been threatened at the outset by the advancing

> Sikh cavalry and had formed a square, would not obey Sir Harry Smith's order to reform line and advance. They were firing wild in all directions, and many in the brigade's third battalion, the 50th Foot which was then advancing claimed to have been hit in their backs by panicky sepoys.[97]

Harry Smith's second brigade, commanded by Brigadier Bolton, was also facing pressure. Bolton, a Peninsular war veteran of the HM 31st, which was now in his brigade, rode forward on his grey charger, his bugler by his side. 'Steady the 31st, steady!', he roared, 'Fire low for your lives.'[98] A few seconds later Bolton, his horse and his bugler all fell. Hardly had the 31st started to advance again, when their commanding officer, Lt Col John Byrne, was severely wounded, and the two officers carrying the Colours together with the rest of the Colour party, were killed. Quarter Master Sergeant Jones, who raised the Colours and then carried them throughout the remainder of the battle, was given a field commission. The 31st now reeling under very heavy and continuous fire was in danger of being wiped out. Gough, who had ridden up to them, now shouted, 'We must take those guns.'[99] Young Lieutenant J.P. Roberts of the 31st, hearing him cried out, 'But where are they?' Hardinge's secretary, Major Somerset, then put his hat on the tip of his sword, crying out to the 31st around him to follow him. Riding into the smoke, followed by officers and the men of the 31st, they fell on the Sikh guns, clashing with the gunners and infantry in hand-to-hand combat. Numbers finally prevailed and the guns were taken. Refusing to abandon their guns, the Muslim gunners fell in heaps around them as did their infantry support.

The 9th Foot was also hotly engaged. Once the fighting died down slightly, the voice of an Irishman hit in his stomach by a spent rifle ball, which knocked him down but did not penetrate him, was heard calling to his officer, 'Mr O'Conner, Mr O'Conner! I'm kilt! I'm kilt!' There was a roar of laughter as the officer replied, 'Then kindly lie down and keep still my man.'[100]

On the right, Brigadier Wheeler now fell. Seeing this, Gough dashed forward on his black Arab charger, Jim Crow, and seized the Colours of 50th Foot, taking it into the heart of the Sikh position. The momentarily wavering 50th, seeing the C-in-C's feat, cheered and charged furiously after him to capture the guns in their front. Still further left, Sir John McCaskill fell, shot through the heart. In Gough's entourage, Sir Robert 'Fighting Bob' Sale, veteran and hero of the Afghan War of 1839 as a brigadier, now Gough's Quarter Master General, was also cut down.

In Hardinge's despatch, he states that, 'the Sikh Infantry, through sheer lack of numbers, were rather thinly extended in their centre, which materially aided the British attack'. The battle continued for another 90 minutes in the dark. Herbert Edwards, later to become a field marshal, wrote in his memoirs,

THE BATTLE OF MUDKI, 18 DECEMBER 1845

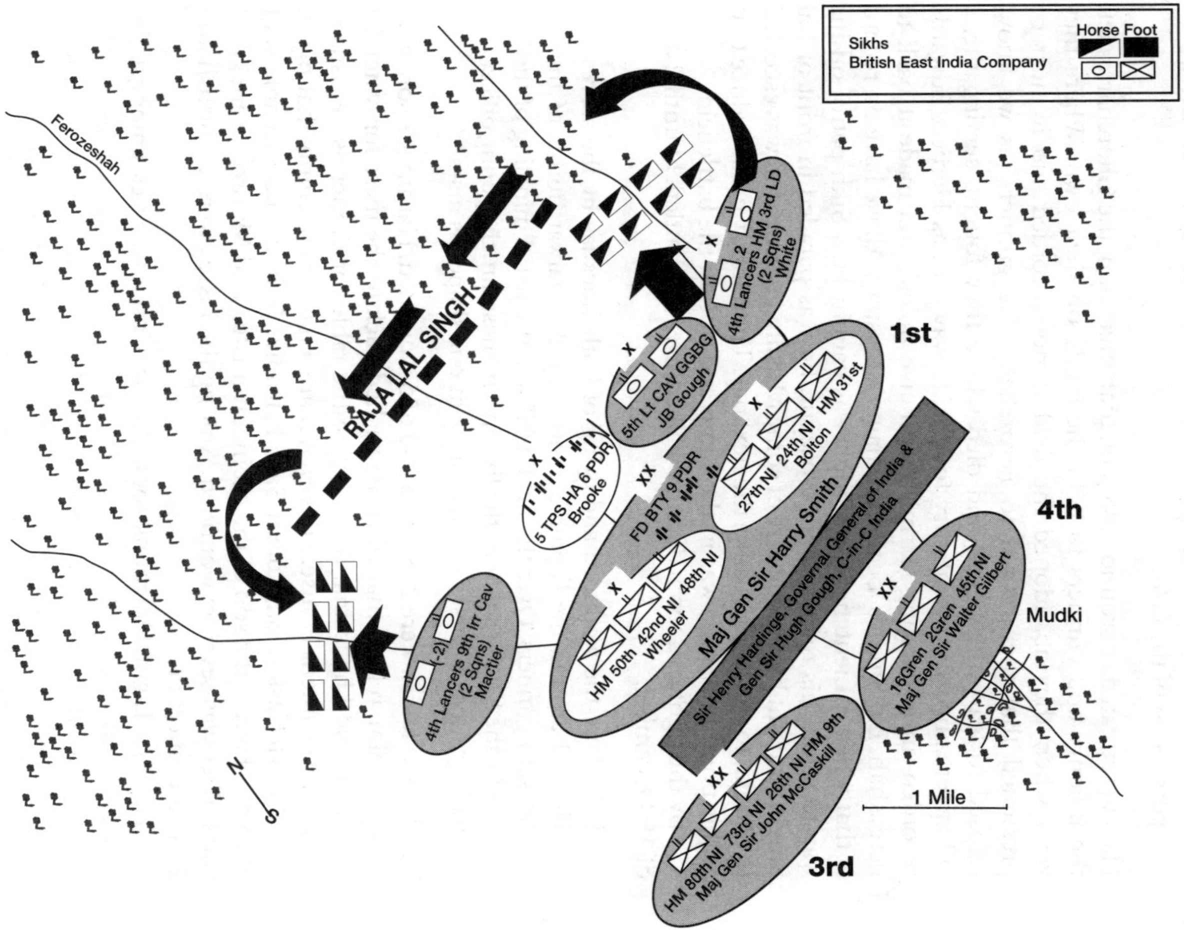

> The last two hours of battle were a series of dogged stands and skirmishing retreats on the part of the Sikh troops, of sharp shooters, gun capture and recapture, and a British pursuit over five miles of the worst ground that ever two armies fought for. Night closed the contest, or rather the pursuit, and the British Army was left in possession of the field.

Having retreated at around 3.45 p.m. that afternoon, the Ghorcharras left the infantry and gunners to fight the battle on their own. Where they went when they abandoned the field is not recorded and it must be presumed that they retired to Ferozshah. The gunners, as we know, refused to leave their guns and died where they fought, serving them. What remained of the infantry fought its way out, as Herbert Edwards recorded, in a 'running skirmish over five miles', and made it back to Ferozshah. Lal Singh's location remains a mystery. All we have on record is that when a Lieutenant Biddulph was caught by a Sikh patrol on his way to rejoin his regiment at Ferozepur, he was paraded in front of Lal Singh, who put him in the care of some Muslim gunners and was escorted to Mudki, to the British camp, the next day. Therefore, we can deduce that at this point Lal Singh was in the camp and not on the battlefield.

By the light of a torch, Gough walked over the battlefield until 2 a.m. of 19 December,

> [...] where the wounded and dying of both sides lay by the scores. Heaped around the captured canon, lay the stalwart forms of the Muslim gunners. Over the field itself was the usual mingling of the dead – the Khalsa soldiery, the European linesman, the young officer, with groups of horses, camels, all lay in one shapeless mass.[101]

The British losses were 215 killed and 655 wounded. Hardinge's son, who was with him, relates that when he rushed back to the mess for water, he found the old khansama, Baxu, laying the table for dinner as he usually did at Government House. However, many chairs were empty that night. Sir John McCaskill, Sir Robert Sale, Brigadier Bolton, and two able staff officers – Herris, the son of the cabinet minister, and Munro – were killed and Hillier was severely wounded. Among the losses were 13 British and 2 Indian officers.

The 3rd Light Dragoons took the heaviest casualties amongst the cavalry regiments. In relation to their numbers, 494 men went into battle, they lost 3 officers, 58 men, 5 officers' chargers and 100 troop horses, while 3 officers, 34 men, 2 officers' chargers and 21 troop horses were wounded.[102] The 4th Lancers, 5th Cavalry and the 9th Irregular Cavalry lost 1 officer and 20 men, while 35 men were wounded.

In the infantry, the 31st Foot lost 156 all ranks, HM 50th Foot lost 125 all ranks. The 47th NI together with the 31st Foot lost 15 men. General Gilbert's Division lost 118 all ranks. In McCaskill's Division, the only officer killed was the GOC. The HM 80th Foot lost 24 men, HM 9th Foot 52 men and the 26th and 73rd NIs lost 11 men between them. In Gilbert's Division, the 2nd Grenadiers took 71 casualties and the 42nd NI in Wheeler's Brigade took 89 casualties.

The Sikh losses were severe, but there are no official figures available. In war, it is usually assumed that the attacker takes three times the casualties to that of the defender. We can assume that the Sikh casualties were in excess of that, as the brunt of the attack was borne by the gunners and infantry who stood fast to the end. All 16 Sikh guns were captured. The British infantry superiority of 1:6 finally prevailed. It was 13 British and NI battalions to 1,200 Sikh infantry, which added up to perhaps one-and-a-half to two battalions in strength. All were detachments taken from Tej Singh's regular brigades for this battle, as were the 16 guns of horse artillery. The Sikh's artillery was definitely out-gunned, with Brigadier Brookes having 12 9-pounder field guns and 30 6-pounder horse artillery deployed in the battle. The 16 Sikh guns were also horse artillery, the calibres being unknown.

> Part of the loss must be ascribed, not only to the courage, but to the fanaticism of the Sikhs. Their gallantry and discipline in the fighting evoked admiration from all – but, brave as they were, they expected no mercy and gave none. [...] The Sikh losses were severe, the ground covered by their dead and wounded – although one account claims that it is possible that their casualties did not exceed those of the British. [...] The Sikhs had also lost the field of battle, but they had not lost their honour, having been less decisively beaten than were most Indian armies.[103]

Once the battle was over, two men of the 9th Foot were found skulking in the village of Mudki. One was from Liverpool and the other from Cornwall – they had hidden in the village of Mudki when the battle began. Paraded before their regiment after the action, the Liverpool man asserted that, 'He didn't like shooting folks', and the Cornishman answered, 'Why should I kill the Seeks? They didn't kill I!'[104]

The exhausted troops reached their camp at 12.30 a.m. that night. The gunners unlimbered, threw blankets over their harnessed horses and threw themselves on the ground along with the rest, wrapped in their cloaks or a blanket. Once again they slept hungry, being exhausted and lacking the strength to cook. All that they wanted was sleep. That day they had marched 20 miles, fought a battle and now, without having eaten or drunk since the evening before, they slept.

Many of the wounded of both armies were to die that night because of the lack of a field hospital. Regimental surgeons did all that they could, but Sikh sword cuts, with their heavy talwars, which were heavier than the British cavalry and infantry swords, created fearful wounds. The Sikhs did not merely strike with the edge, but simultaneously drew the weapon back with a cutting motion that trebled the wound's length and depth.

During the morning of 19 December, the troops had their first meal in 48 hours. Afterwards, they sat in the hot sun smoking their pipes and chatting about the battle and lost comrades. Parties were sent out to bring in any wounded still on the battlefield. Cavalry patrols were sent out, as information had come in that the Sikhs were probing forward again.

One of the most important events to happen on that day took place in the evening, when Sir Henry Hardinge, who was junior in rank to Gough, waived his rank as governor general and volunteered to serve as his second-in-command. Sir Hugh Gough reports in his *Despatch,*

> This evening, in addition to the valuable council with which you had in every emergency before favoured me, you were pleased yet further to strengthen my hands by kindly offering your services as second-in-command in my army. I need hardly say with what pleasure the offer was accepted.[105]

During the battle, Hardinge had taken command of the 3rd Division after its GOC McCaskill was killed.

VI. THE BATTLE OF FEROZSHAH

The day passed in rest and recuperation. A false alarm of the approach of a large body of Sikh cavalry during mid-morning proved abortive and the army, which had 'stood to', finally stood down around noon. The cavalry, perhaps on a reconnaissance, then returned to Ferozshah. That evening, reinforcements arrived led by HM 29th Foot and were marched into camp by the bands of the regiments who fought at Mudki. HM 29th Foot, 900 strong, had covered 180 miles, from the hill station of Kasauli, on the way to Simla and close to Ambala, in nine days with just one day's halt. From Sabathu, another hill station close to Kasauli, came the 1st Bengal European Light Infantry – the company's European regiment 800 strong. The 11th NI arrived from Ludhiana and the 41st NI escorted the large siege gun train from Ambala. They had 1,500 men between them. The siege train commanded by Lt Col G.G. Deniss, comprised 2 x 8in howitzers manned by the 2nd Company, 4th Battalion Bengal Artillery and 2 x 18-pounder elephant-drawn guns manned by the 4th Company of the 4th Battalion BA.

Meanwhile, the Sikhs were strengthening their defensive position at Ferozshah. Entrenchments were being dug and protective walls were being thrown up. Their experience at Mudki was being kept in mind. Their defensive position was oval in shape, one-and-a-half miles in length and about a mile across, around the village of Ferozshah.

Gough, in the meantime, had been reinforced by four fresh infantry battalions and by large-calibre guns. His troops were rested, the ration trains had come in, and he was restless and wanted to attack without delay – before Tej Singh's large force of 30,000 troops of the regular army could link up with Lal Singh's 20,000 reinforced garrison at Ferozshah. He rightly believed that the combination would then be too strong for them to deal with. Secondly, he also feared that the longer he delayed, the better would be the Sikh defensive structure, making it even more formidable to breach and causing higher casualties as a result. He ordered preparation to be made for an attack. Surprisingly, however, it was decided to leave the newly arrived 18-pounder guns behind at Mudki. Why this decision was taken is not known. Reports indicated that the Sikhs had moved large-calibre guns, 24, 32 and 48-pounders, into the Ferozshah defended sector. Gough should have moved the 18-pounders forward to counter these heavy guns.

Meanwhile, the commanders who fell at Mudki had to be replaced. Colonels Ryan and Hicks replaced Wheeler and Bolton as brigadiers in Sir Harry Smith's 1st Division, Brigadier Wallace replaced General McCaskill and the 2nd and 3rd Divisions were now under Gilbert and Wallace, respectively. Both had just one brigade each at Mudki – their strength was also reinforced.

Gough put his proposition of attacking, without any delay, to Hardinge, who just as promptly rejected it. He argued that a larger force was required than they had at present, and that unless Littler's 7,000 men joined them from Ferozepur, the attack would be futile. Despite having offered to be Gough's second-in-command the previous evening, Hardinge, as the governor general, was now threatening to reject Gough's plans. Gough's reasoning was sound. It was 21 December, the shortest day of the year and it would be dark by 5 p.m. or so. If they did not attack soon, it would be a repeat of Mudki, where the confused night fighting had increased the casualties through 'friendly fire'. Gough wanted to attack without delay, keeping Littler's force, which had been delayed, as army reserve when it showed up.

To Gough, what was critical was daylight, not the addition of Littler's force. Events would prove him correct. As George Bruce puts it in his *Six Battles for India:*

> However, any argument on this score proved academic, for no sooner had Gough given out his plan than Hardinge took him to one side and, assuming again his position as governor general, vetoed any attack before Littler's division had joined. He was no doubt influenced by the unexpectedly tough Sikh resistance at Mudki and, realizing that the coming battle could be decisive, he felt that the British must be at maximum strength. Gough had no option but to agree. It was an embarrassing position for a C-in-C to be in, and it is to Gough's credit that, when subsequent events proved him to have been right, he never permitted himself to say, "I told you so."

Later, Bruce sums it up:

> Sir Henry had placed himself in an unenviable position. First, having been ordered by the secret committee to avoid war, he had let himself be led into it by a total diplomatic failure. Secondly, he had weakened his Commander-in-Chief's army by countermanding orders absolutely necessary for the safety of the British position – including those early in December for the 9th Lancers to move up to Ludhiana from Meerut. [Sir Henry had sent them back and they were now moving up for the second time, their absence a general subject of regret for, as Captain Humbly observed then, "It is not possible to calculate the value of the services which this strong corps might have rendered in the hour of need."] Having thus weakened the army, Sir Henry, using his powers as Governor General, for the first and only time in British-Indian history, overruled the plans of his Commander-in-Chief while in face of the enemy.

The decision having been taken, a message was sent to Littler to move quietly out of Ferozepur and to link up with Gough at 1.30 p.m. at a village called Misriwala, some 3,000 yards south-west of the Sikh position.

Orders were issued to the divisional and brigade commanders. The company commanders were told at around 9 p.m. that they must brief their companies accordingly. The troops were to be roused quietly at 1 a. m., camp struck and the army was to move out an hour later at 2 a.m. The troops breakfasted that morning on coffee, onions and elephant lugs – huge cakes of rice, bran and chopped straw used to feed the elephants, which were now being fed to the soldiers. What sustenance straw provided to humans is not explained! At 10.30 a.m., when the Sikh position came in sight, the troops halted for a quick haversack lunch, while the C-in-C made his reconnaissance. Littler arrived at 12 noon, and his troops linked up with the C-in-C's force at Misriwala at 13.30 p.m.

Other than two regiments of Native Infantry left behind to guard and look after the Mudki wounded, who were now within the walls of the Mudki village, the entire force had marched that morning with Gough.

Order of Battle, British Army at Ferozshah, 21 and 22 December 1843[106]

Commander-in-Chief
General Sir Hugh Gough
Aides-de-Camp
Captain the Honorable C.R. Sackville-West (AMS)
Lt F.P. Haines

Governor General of India
Lt General Sir Henry Hardinge

Military Secretary
Brevet Major Arthur William Fitzroy Somerset

Officiating Deputy Secretary to the Government
(Assistant Military Secretary)
Captain William Hore

Aides-de-Camp
Lt Col Wood
Brevet Major W.R. Herries
Brevet Captain G.E. Hillier
Lt John Munro
Lt Peel (Acting)

Army Staff
Deputy Adjutant General
Major Patrick Grant
Judge Advocate General
Lt Col Birch
Military Board
Colonel Benson (Acting ADC)
Assistant Adjutant General
Captain J.R. Lumley

Quartermaster General's Department
Captain Abbot
Captain Mills (took command of Todd's Battery)
Lt Arthur Beecher
Lt Lake
Political Agent
Major George Broadfoot

1st Infantry Division
Major General Sir Harry Smith

Aide-de-Camp
Lt E.A. Holditch

Deputy Assistant Adjutant General
Captain E. Lugard

Deputy Assistant Quartermaster General:
Lt A.J. Galloway

1st Brigade
Brigadier (Lt Col) George Hicks

Brigade Major
Captain J. Garvock
HM 31st Foot – Major Spence
24th BNI – Major Griffin
47th BNI – Captain Pott

2nd Brigade
Brigadier (Lt Col) Thomas Ryan, CB and KH

Brigade Major
Captain Pringle O'Hanlon
HM 50th Foot – Lt Colonel Petit
42nd BNI
48th BNI – Captain Palmer

2nd Infantry Division
Major General Sir Walter Raleigh Gilbert

Aides-de-Camp
Captain R. Houghton
Lt F.M. Gilbert (Extra)

Deputy Assistant Adjutant General
Captain F.W. Anson

Deputy Assistant Quartermaster General
Lt T.S. Rawson
Deputy Assistant Judge Advocate General
Captain G. Carr

1st (3rd) Brigade
Brigadier (Lt Col) James McClaren, CB
1st Bengal European Light Infantry
26th BNI
45th BNI

2nd (4th) Brigade
Brigadier (Lt Col) Charles Cyril Taylor, CB

Brigade Major
Captain J.O. Lucas
HM 29th Foot
HM 80th Foot
41st BNI

3rd Infantry Division
Brigadier (Lt Col) Newton Wallace, 73rd BNI

Deputy Assistant Adjutant General
Captain J.R. Pond

Brigade Major: (6th Brigade)
Brevet Captain P. Garden

HM 9th Foot – Lt Col Abraham Beresford Taylor
2nd Bombay (Grenadiers) NI
16th Bombay (Grenadiers) NI
73rd BNI Regiment

4th Infantry Division
Major General Sir John Littler

Aides-de-Camp
Lt Harvey
Lt W. Fullerton (Acting)

Deputy Assistant Adjutant General
Major P. Innes

Deputy Assistant Quartermaster General
Captain John Francis Egerton

Commissariat Department
Captain W.J. Thomson

Political Officers
Captain Nicolson
Col Van Cortlandt (ex-Sikh Army)

Chief of Artillery
Lt Col Edward Huthwaite

1st (7th) Brigade
Brigadier (Lt Col) Thomas Reid

Brigade Major
Captain C.F.J. Burnett
HM 62nd Foot – Major Shortt
12th BNI – Lt Col Louis Bruce
14th BNI – Lt Col Gardner

2nd (8th) Brigade:
Brigadier (Lt Col) the Hon. Thomas Ashburnham
33rd BNI – Captain Sandeman
44th BNI – Major Wake
54th BNI – Major Osborn

Divisional Artillery:
Lt Col Edward Huthwaite, 3rd Brigade, BHA
Bengal Horse Artillery: (10 x 6 pndrs, 2 x 12 pndr howitzers)
Captain G. Campbell's European Troop (3/3)
Captain E.F. Day's Native Troop (5[N]/1)
5th (Native) (Shah Shuja's) Troop 1st Brigade, BHA
3rd Troop, 3rd Brigade, BHA
Bengal (Field) Artillery: (7 x 9) pdrs, 1 x 24-pdr howitzer)
#6 Heavy Field Battery (half) – Lt A.G. Austen
#19 Light Field Battery (Bullock) – Captain J. Fordyce manned by:
2nd Company, 7th Battalion, BA (#6)
4th Company, 6th Battalion, BA (#19)
detachment, Bengal Sapper and Miner Company – Lt Goodwyn
Garrison of Ferozepur: (not present)
Lt Col Wilkinson
27th BNI – Lt Col Carnegy (Town)
63rd BNI – Lt Col Wilkinson (Cantonment)
#6 Heavy Field Battery (half) (town) – Lt J.S. Tulloh

Heavy (Garrison) Battery (2nd {Reserve} Company, 2nd Battalion, BA) – Lt Angelo (Trenches)
Detachment, Bengal Sapper and Miner Company (Town)

Cavalry Division: (GOC and staff not present at battle)
Major General Sir Joseph Thackwell.
Brigadier (Lt Col) D. Harriott (Acting GOC, Cavalry Division)

Deputy Assistant Quartermaster General
Captain C.F. Havelock

1st Brigade
Brigadier (Lt Col) J.B. Gough

Governor General's Bodyguard
5th BLC

2nd Brigade
Brigadier Harriott

3rd BLC
8th Irregular Horse – Brevet Captain Beecher

3rd Brigade
Brigadier White

3rd Light Dragoons
4th BLC

Gough deployed his army facing the narrow end of the oval-shaped Sikh defensive position, which had the city of Ferozshah at its middle. The road from Mudki linked up at Ferozshah, as did the road from Ludhiana to Ferozepur, which passed through Ferozshah. All three roads were encompassed by the defences.

Gough positioned his formations in a half moon, with Gilbert's 2nd Infantry Division of two brigades to the right, astride the Mudki road and extending to just short of the Ludhiana road. Brigadier Taylor was to the right of the road with his three battalions, HM 29th, HM 80th and the 41st NI, all three in extended order. Brigadier Maclaren was deployed left of the road with his 45th NI, 1st ELI and the 26th NI also in extended order. The 3rd Infantry Division under Brigadier Wallace, comprising one brigade, the 73rd NI, 2nd Bombay Grenadiers, the 16th Bombay Grenadiers, and the HM 9th Foot was in the middle, once again in extended order. He had two troops of horse artillery with a further two troops on his left. The heavy guns, comprising two batteries of 9-pounders and two batteries of 8in howitzers on his right. To their left, extending to just short of the Ferozepur road, was General Littler's 4th Infantry Division with his two brigades. Brigadier Reid was in a two-up formation, with his HM 62nd and 12 NI in front with the 14th NI in reserve, adjoining Wallace. Brigadier Ashburnum was to Reid's left, extending short of the Ferozepur road. All his battalions were up in extended order – the 33rd NI, 44th NI and 54th NI. To his right, he had two troops of horse artillery, and to his left two batteries of 9-pounders. Sir Harry Smith's 1st Infantry Division was in reserve, with Brigadier Hicks positioned behind Gilbert's Division with the HM 31st, 24 NI and the 47th NI, and Brigadier Ryan was positioned behind Littler's division with the HM 50th, 48th NI and 42nd NI. He had a troop of horse artillery with him. The gap between his two brigades was around one mile.

The cavalry brigades were deployed as follows: Harriott was forward of the village of Misriwala with his 3rd Lancers and 8th Irregular Cavalry, positioned to the rear left of Littler's Division and covering the left flank. Gough, with the Governor General's Bodyguard and the 5th Light Cavalry, was also behind Reid's Brigade of Littler's division and forward of Ryan's brigade. White was on the extreme right flank of the deployment, with his 3rd Light Dragoons and 4th Light Cavalry and a troop of horse artillery.

The Sikh Army was divided into two wings. Tej Singh was still sitting watching Littler at Ferozepur, while Lal Singh, having withdrawn from Mudki to his main position at Ferozshah, was in the process of building and strengthening his defence. In the meantime, Tej Singh had sent substantial reinforcements of elements of the Fauj-e-Ain, to strengthen the Ferozshah defences. As to his watch on Littler at Ferozepur, it was impossible for Littler not to have been spotted withdrawing during daylight hours. However, Tej Singh, abiding by his promise to Captain Nicholson and going by the direction of the regent to get their army cut to size, remained at Ferozepur and did nothing to interfere with Littler's withdrawal and his link up with Gough's army at Misriwala.

At Mudki, the Ghorcharras had proved ineffective, mainly due to a confused chain of command – the 10,000 Ghorcharras having almost no effect on the outcome of the battle. The British cavalry, much weaker in numbers, charged straight through them on more than one occasion. Finally, they abandoned the field altogether, riding back to Ferozshah while the battle was still on, leaving the fighting to the 1,200 regular infantrymen protecting the 16 guns, and the gunners themselves.

When Lal Singh moved to Mudki, he had left his 40 cattle-drawn field guns at Ferozshah and also 10,000 Ghorcharras to prepare the entrenchments and the defensive perimeter. Three regular brigade groups of the Fauj-e-Ain now joined this force. The first was that of General Ventura, the Fauj-e-Khas, now under Dewan Ajodhia Prasad, comprising four infantry battalions, two cavalry regiments and one additional Jagirdari cavalry regiment. General Ilahi Bakhsh's artillery comprising 12 Aspi and 12 Jinsi guns were attached to it, making it a substantial force of 3,147 infantry, 2,136 cavalry and 720 gunners – a total of 6,003 men and 22 guns, far in excess of a brigade group. The second was Mehtab Singh's brigade comprising 4 infantry battalions, a lancer regiment and 12 Aspi and 13 Jinsi guns – 25 guns in all – a combined strength of 3,388 infantry, 490 cavalry and 750 gunners, with 25 guns. The third was Bahadur Singh's brigade, comprising 4 infantry battalions and a cavalry regiment with 11 aspi guns – a total strength of 3,760 infantry, 540 cavalry and 11 guns.

To this should have been added the 20,000-odd Ghorcharras of Lal Singh's original force, less the minor casualties sustained at Mudki. Each derah also had a substantial number of zambooraks with it, however only six derahs, comprising 11,527 Ghorcharras, were deployed at Ferozshah. It is possible that the 10,000-odd from Mudki were withdrawn from Ferozshah and redeployed elsewhere because of their poor performance in the battle of Mudki. This is, however, conjecture as there is no record of this. To this were added 7 Jagirdari cavalry regiments totaling 4,012 all ranks and 42 regular army jinsi guns manned by the 1,260 gunners.

The overall strength of the army of the Lahore Durbar at Ferozshah now stood at 12 regular infantry battalions, comprising 10,285 all ranks, 4 regular cavalry regiments comprising 3,166 all ranks, the strength of the Jagirdari cavalry regiment being in addition to the total of the 4. To this, we add 60 guns and 1,800 gunners. To this is further added the Fauj-e-Gair strength. The Jagirdari Derah's of 11,527, the irregular cavalry of 4,012 and 1,260 gunners. Therefore, the total strength at Ferozshah adds up to 15,251 regulars and 16,799 irregular militias – a fighting strength of 32,050 all ranks of the infantry, cavalry and artillery, with 102 guns of the regular artillery. This is inclusive of the 40 cattle-drawn field guns left behind at Ferozshah when Lal Singh moved on Mudki.

The Order of Battle is given below:

Raja Lal Singh's Wing, The Sikh Army, Ferozshah, 21 and 22 December 1845[107]

Commanding General:
Raja Lal Singh (The Wazir)

Fauj-e-Ain: (ex-General Ventura's)
Dewan Ajodhia Prasad

Fauj-e-Khas Brigade
Paltan Khas (812)
Gurkha Infantry Paltan (693)
Dewa Singh Infantry Paltan (824)
Sham Sota Infantry Paltan (818)
Dragoon Rajman (722)
Horse Grenadier Rajman (716)
Shadi Lal's Sowar Risala (Jagirdari)
Artillery Attached
General Ilahi Bakhsh
Aspi (Field Artillery) (360) (12 guns)
Jinsi 1 (Mixed Horse and Field Guns (360) (12 guns)
Beldar (Engineer) Company

Mehtab Singh's Brigade
1st Infantry Paltan (847)
2nd Infantry Paltan (847)
3rd Infantry Paltan (847)
4th Infantry Paltan (847)
Lancia (Lancer) Cavalry Rajman (490)
Artillery:
Aspi (360) (12 guns)
Jinsi (390) (13 guns)
Beldar (Engineer) Company

Bahadur Singh's Brigade
1st Infantry Paltan (940)
2nd Infantry Paltan (940)
3rd Infantry Paltan (940)
4th Infantry Paltan (940)
Artillery:
Aspi (330) (11 guns)
Beldar (Engineer) Company

Fauj-e-Gair: (Militia)

Ghorcharra Sowar's Cavalry:

Jagirdari Fauj

Ardalian Derah
Ghorcharra (2,866)
Mohamed Shah's Mounted Swivels (Zambooraks) (73 men)

Derah Khas
Ghorcharras (2089)
Swivels (figures unknown)

Naulakha Kalan Derah
Ghorcharra (2,096)
Abdur Ramin's Swivels (127)

Naulakha Khurd Derah
Ghorcharra (2,096)

Pindiwala Derah
Ghorcharra (1,060)

Raja Lal Singh's Derah
Ghorcharra (1,039)
Jalal Din's Swivels (61)

Jagirdari (light) Derahs
Kanh Singh Kahnya's Derah (536)
Makhan Khan's Sowar Regiment (664)
Ganda Singh Kunjahia's Sowar Regiment (546)
Mandi Derah (767)
Kanh Singh Mokal's Derah (325)
Kanh Singh Majithia's Derah (557)
Sardar's Attar Singh's and Chattar Singh Kalianwala'a Sowar Regiment (617)

Regular Army Artillery
Howitzer Derah:
Jinsi (360) (12guns)
Makhi Khan's Battery Derah
Jinsi (450 (15 guns)
Amir Chand's Battery Derah
Jinsi (450) (15 guns)

Source: Dewan Ajudhia Parshad, *Waqai-Jang-i-Sikhan*: *Events of the First Anglo-Sikh War* 1845-46. V.S. Suri (tr) Chandigarh: Punjab Itihas Prakashan, 1975.

It was 3.30 p.m. on 21 December – the shortest day of the year – before Gough was finally ready to move. This left him just two hours before last light to enable him to fight and conclude the battle, though he had intended to fight the battle during daylight hours to prevent a replay of what had happened at Mudki.

> The 18,000 men stood ready and waiting, the declining sun casting long shadows over the plain, the blood-stained regimental Colours and the long scarlet and white plumes of the Dragoons drooping in the quiet air. There had been no thought of probing for weak points in the enemy lines, or reconnaissance in force expanding into a strong attack as in modern warfare. This was pitched battle. Tense and excited, praying that they might live, the men waited to advance coolly into the holocaust.[109]

At 4 p.m., an hour before sunset, the bugle sounded the advance and the battalions, deployed in extended order, began to move forward. They

THE BATTLE OF FEROZSHAH, 21 & 22 DECEMBER 1845

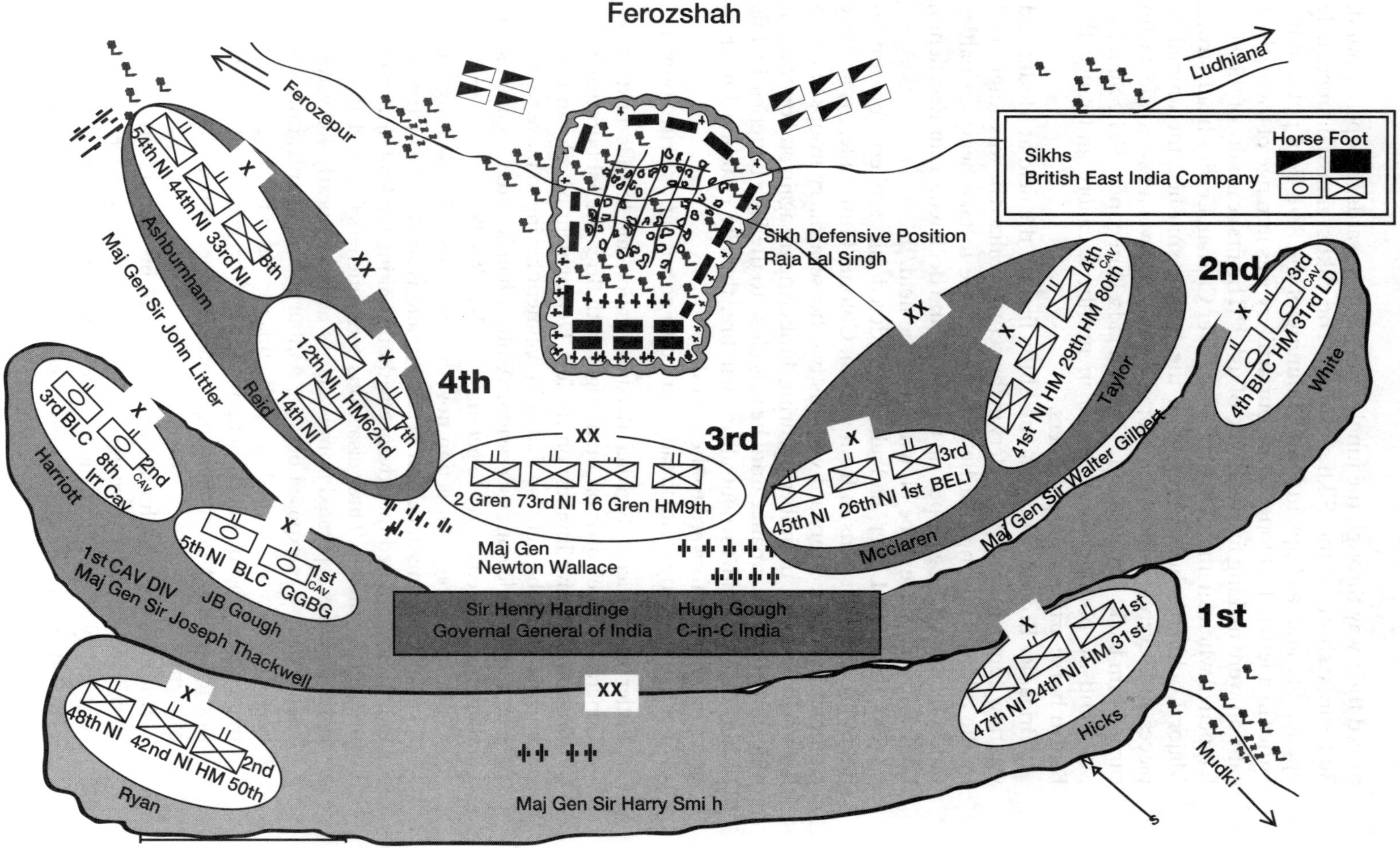

forced their way through the jungle and scrub towards the open ground, 300 yards short of the Sikh position. The Sikhs almost immediately opened fire and, as Captain John Cumming of the 80th Foot put it to his father in a letter, '[...] long before our artillery was in range of them, their cannon were making fearful havoc of us'.[110] The first casualty of the 80th happened when an immense ball passed over Captain Lewis's head, struck Major Lockhart's horse straight in the breast, smashed the animal to pieces and severely injured the Major. Fainting between two soldiers who carried him back, he called out, 'Fight on lads, I am gone.'[111] The Sikh 24-, 32- and 36-pounders outgunned in numbers, calibre and range the British horse artillery's 6-pounders.

Brigadier Brooke, who was one of the first on the field at Mudki and was now commanding the artillery in the centre, realized he was outgunned by the Sikhs. Knowing that he would continue to take heavy casualties unless he moved, he galloped up to Gough and declared, 'Your Excellency, I must now advance or be blown out of the field.'[112]

On the left, Littler had already ordered his artillery forward to neutralize the Sikh guns in front of him. Colonel Huthwaite, his artillery commander, dashed forward with his two horse-artillery troops and two light field batteries, unlimbering, firing, limbering up again and once again repeating this performance until he was close to the Sikh batteries. By this action, he managed to neutralize their fire, thereby enabling Littler to order his infantry forward to the assault.

For Littler, things had already started to go wrong, as Bruce puts it:

> Littler had ordered Bigadier Reed to station his brigade next to General Wallace's division, on his right, with Brigadier Ashburnham's Brigade of Native Infantry on his left. Deployment of column into line was from the right, so that each regiment having to move to the left, must deploy in succession. Ashburnham's three regiments, therefore, needed longer to get into line than Reed's.
>
> But Littler, eager for action now that his guns were silencing the Sikhs, placed himself behind Reed's Brigade as soon as the men were in line, and ordered the advance without waiting for Ashburnham's Brigade to come up. Three disastrous consequences followed: Reed's right flank was separated from Wallace's troops by nearly 400 yards, his left flank was exposed because Ashburnham's men had not yet been able to catch up, and the Sikh guns were able to bring down a tremendous blast of grapeshot upon these two brigades alone directly as they emerged from the jungle into the open within 300 yards of them.
>
> Brigadier Reed, frightened for the lives of his men in this hail of shot, gave the order to charge the batteries almost at once. HM 62 Foot, led by Major Short, ran forward on the right, with the 12th and 14th Native Infantry on their left, over the open space whistling with

> grape. But the two sepoy regiments hung back under the tremendous fire, the 62nd taking the brunt of it alone, and in two or three minutes, 17 out of 23 officers and 250 men were killed or wounded. The remainder, exhausted even before they charged, refused to go on, threw themselves down near the enemy batteries and began ineffectually firing. Lieutenant Gubbins and Kelly ran forward to the batteries, but were cut down. Reed, Short and the remaining three officers made desperate efforts, pointing out the short distance the men had to go to drive the Sikhs off their guns and win the day, but in vain. Reed reported, "I (then) took the responsibility of ordering them to retire, which they did in perfect order". The 14th NI under their Adjutant Lieutenant Paton, who with their Colours joined HM 9th and took part in the subsequent action.

Ashburnham now ordered his brigade forward, but all three battalions, the 54th, 33rd and 44th NI, hesitated. When a well appeared in their front, the ranks broke while the sepoys, crazy with thirst, fell over themselves to get a drink of water. As Ashburnham recalled later, he got the brigade in some semblance of order and resumed the advance, but by then he was down to two-thirds of his strength. Being more or less intact, the 33rd NI took part in the action. When the brigade finally came in the range of the Sikh guns the battalions disintegrated and retreated in sixes and sevens. At this point, about 50 men of the 33rd NI under Sandeman joined the 26th NI in Wallace's Division to continue the fight.

Brigadier Brooke, having asked the C-in-C to allow him to move his guns forward, was still with Gough when the sound of intense rifle fire carried over the sound of guns. This was Littler's battalions firing on the move. Brooke looked towards them and realized that the attack in the present form would not succeed. Gough then gave the order for the general attack to start, even though some of the battalions were not yet deployed. If Littler's attack was to succeed, this support was essential.

Harry Smith's division, fully deployed, commenced its advance. The GOC galloped forward to get a better look at the Sikh defences and met up with Hardinge, who had also ridden forward. Unable to see the formation engaged in rifle fire because of the undergrowth, Hardinge asked Harry Smith who it was. Having seen the advance, he told him that it was Littler's attack and added that it seemed to lack the necessary impetus to succeed. Hardinge then ordered him to move his division forward quickly. Smith led his division up to the left of Gilbert's division in place of Littler's.

As Brooke's howitzers were the only artillery pieces having any impact on the Sikh guns, Gough ordered them forward to engage them. Brooke, in turn, ordered his horse and light field gunners to move as close as 200 yards from the Sikh guns, so they might have some impact. The lead troops galloped forward under their battery commander, unlimbered and laid their guns. Dismounting, the Major laid the first gun himself to check the range. Having fired it, he turned to his horse, found it dead and at that moment a round shot took his head off.

At this point, the battle was going in favour of the Sikhs. Their triumphant 'Jaikaras' and shouts of 'Allah ho Akbar' rang out above the sounds of battle. They had repulsed Littler and Ashburnham, and were winning the artillery battle. The attackers were being mown down in swathes. Morale was high and they intended doing the same to the other divisions. Gilbert on the right, under Gough, and Wallace on the left, led by Hardinge, both in echelon of brigades, now assaulted the Sikh entrenchments with Taylor's Brigade, consisting of the 29th and 80th, leading the way.

Captain Cummings of the 80th, later wrote:

> We advanced against a hailstorm of round shot, shells, grape and musketry. To heighten the destruction, mines had been dug before the trenches and sprung up under our feet – the slaughter was terrible. Yet our fellows pressed nobly on with the charge, and with the bayonet alone rushed over the entrenchments and captured the guns in front of us. The Sikh and Muslim gunners flinched not an inch, but fought till they died to a man at their guns. Our further advance was checked by bursting mines setting their camp on fire, and we retired a short distance to be clear of it.[113]

The 1st European LI of McLaren's brigade moved first. Major Birrell in the centre, Captain Box, the second-in-command, on the right and Captain Seaton on the left. Ensigns Salisbury and Moxon were carrying the Colours. As they advanced through the forest, Sikh fire intensified, destroying not only the undergrowth and shattering trees, but also cutting the advancing troops down in droves. Captain Box was shot in the face and killed, while Captain Kendel, leading No 6 Company, and Captain Clark of No 1 Company, were both mortally wounded. The eighteen-year-old ensign Salisbury, who was carrying the Queen's Colour, fell. Ensign Innes seized the Colours just as the regiment assaulted. Jumping ditches and obstacles in front of the entrenchment, they scrambled up the 10 ft high bank and were soon on the guns amidst a chaotic scene of hand-to-hand combat with the gunners in an atmosphere blacked out by smoke and dust. The 16 Bombay Grenadiers kept up with the 1st ELI, but the 45th NI held back.

As the troops got the better of the Sikh and Muslim gunners, who fell while defending their guns, the British came face to face with Sikh infantry formed, awaiting the outcome before opening fire. The Sikh infantry had waited for the right moment. Once the gunners had been overcome, they opened fire, cutting down the reforming British troops. As the rear British companies linked up with their forward companies on the guns, the Sikhs threw down their rifles, drew their swords and charged the reforming troops.

Time and again during the two wars, this preference for the sword over the bayonet gave the British the advantage in hand-to-hand combat over the Sikh infantryman.

Gilbert's division, now under Gough's personal command, was fully involved in hand-to-hand combat with the Sikhs along their entire line. The bayonet finally prevailed and the Sikhs began to give way. When they did, they rushed back to their rifles, loaded and began volley fire yet again. At that moment, the Sikh cavalry was seen to be forming up to charge Gilbert's division, just as it was reorganizing on the first line of Sikh defences which it had occupied. Seeing the impending danger to Gilbert, the 3rd Light Dragoons, along with a troop of horse artillery led by Brigadier White, charged in through the heavy gun and musket fire straight into the massed Sikh cavalry. The heavier British cavalry horses and their speed created havoc amongst the Sikh riders and horses, who were thrown to the ground. This impetus and the skilful use of the heavy sabre by the Dragoons carried the charge through the Sikh Ghorcharras until they broke.

Once through, the Dragoons reformed and attacked another defensive position to their front. The fire there was so intense that they were forced to withdraw, leaving many dead men and horses behind. It was this charge by the Dragoons, to disperse the Sikh cavalry threatening Gilbert on the late afternoon of 21 December, that saved the day.

On Gilbert's left, from where Littler had earlier retreated, Wallace had continued to advance against the western and southern Sikh defences. Smoke, dust and the late evening haze had obscured the view of the Sikh guns to their front. As they came closer, the Sikh gunners, seeing them through the haze, poured in grape. One of the first to fall was Colonel Taylor, along with many of his junior officers and men. The fire was so intense that the battalion fell back in confusion. On the right, the other battalions of the brigade managed to assault the guns to their front and took them. Harry Smith, advancing as per Hardinge's orders, now had to contend with the withdrawing troops falling back on him.

At that moment, the political agent, Major Broadfoot, rode over to give Smith fresh intelligence about a Sikh counterattack to be led by the Fauj-e-Khas, led by Dewan Ajudhia Prasad. As Smith wrote later in his *Memoirs*,

> To resist this attack, which was being made to take advantage of our check, and penetrate our line between Littler's right and Wallace's left, I must bring up the right of my brigade. I endeavoured to do so, and with HM's 50th Regiment, I partially succeeded under a storm of musketry and cannon which I have rarely, if ever, seen exceeded.

Advancing through a thick haze towards both the Sikh western and southern positions, Harry Smith was caught in a murderous crossfire. Captain Abbot's horse was shot from under him. As he rose from under his dying horse, he was hit in the shoulder and left arm. Broadfoot called to him to get up and at that moment, as he was riding forward with Hardinge and his depleted staff, he too was hit in his thigh and was simultaneously thrown from his horse. He managed to remount and soon after was hit in the arm and almost immediately received a bullet through his heart.

The only option left for Harry Smith was to assault or be shot out of the field. He put himself at the head of HM 50th, and along with Colonel Petit and Colonel Ryan, attacked the forward trenches with bayonets. The Sikhs broke and withdrew, leaving the forward position in the hands of HM 50th Foot.

Smith, with Ryan's Brigade, now pushed on deeper into the Sikh position to the western part of the Sikh tented camp. Ferozshah was 400 yards ahead. He was joined by stragglers from Wallace's division on his right. Being unclear about whether the Fauj-e-Khas attack had gone in, and if so where, as well as worrying about his exposed left flank, he decided to move ahead and take Ferozshah in order to secure himself.

Gough on the right, with Gilbert's division, having taken the guns in their front to the south and right of the Sikh defences, advanced onto the Sikh camp. Mclaren's Brigade, led by the 1st European LI, charged down the centre street of the camp towards Ferozshah. Half a mile to their left, Harry Smith had also made Ferozshah his objective. They had hardly begun their advance when a powder magazine blew up. As Ensign Innes later put it, 'As the smoke cleared away, exposed to view was a horrible and appalling scene, numbers of our men having fallen frightfully burnt and mutilated, and in some instances their pouches ignited, causing terrible wounds, agony and loss of life'.[114]

The explosion of the Sikh powder magazine led to other magazines exploding as the flames reached them, scattering battalions who had to reform in the glow of the fires. Smith continued his advance on Ferozshah and was joined by Captain Seaton who had managed to get around 150 men together in the confusion. Smith adds,

> I speedily seized this village, filled with infantry, cavalry and horses [...] I planted one of the Colours of HM 50th on the mud walls. A scene of awful slaughter here ensued, as the enemy would not lay down his arms. The village was full of richly caparisoned horses and there were camels innumerable around it. By this time, many detachments belonging to the regiments composing the left of the main attack joined me.

Dismounted Ghorcharras and Akali shock troops, led by a big man under a large black flag, attacked the 80th, who had by this time reached the camp. The fiercest fighting with the bayonet and sword took place around the man with the black flag. He was presumably the Akali shock troop leader, as it is they who carried black flags into battle – one must recall the battle of Theri and the attack of Akali Phula Singh on the Afghans. The black flag was finally taken by Colour Sergeant Kirkland, who was commissioned for gallantry in the field. Today, this flag hangs above the 80th's Sikh war memorial in Lichfield Cathedral in Surrey.

Noting that Gough had secured his front, Harry Smith decided to consolidate his own advance by seizing the enemy camp about half a mile beyond Ferozshah. By now his force had swollen to around 3,000 men. However, he noted that far from being defeated, the Sikhs faced him on his right and to his front, and that his position was becoming critical as he had advanced far beyond the Sikh Army still entrenched in strength to his right.

He now quickly built a defensive circle in front of the Sikh camp with the 50th Foot, the 9th Foot under Major Barwell, the 1st European LI under Captain Seaton, the 24th NI under Major Bird and the 19th, 23rd, 28th, and 73rd NIs. Realizing how weak and isolated he was, the Sikhs attacked his right where the 24th NI gave way. Smith contracted his circle and managed to hold, but the Sikhs, under their fierce war cry, closed in. Both officers and men were desperately tired by now and casualties had begun to mount. The Sikhs had brought up guns and began firing grapeshots from behind, closing in in high spirits from all sides. Realizing that he was now in trouble, Harry Smith managed to simulate an attack and successfully withdrew by regiments through Ferozshah and back.

Gough too, realized that the situation was grim. Although his army had driven the Sikhs out of some of their defensive positions and occupied parts of their camp, apart from Littler's earlier retreat, there had been no further repulse. The confusion in the dark could lead to his regiments firing on each other. Therefore, he ordered the buglers to sound the retreat and the army was ordered to fall back 300 yards from the Sikh entrenchments and to bivouac for the night.

The ELI was still fighting the Sikhs in their tented camp, as ordered earlier. Desperately thirsty, they had come upon a well and the thirsty troops frantically seizing the tin can from each other, continued to drink even when the Sikhs opened fire on them, preferring death to the terrible thirst. Bunched up around the well, they made a perfect target and took many casualties. It was then discovered that their Colours had disappeared. Ensign Innes ran up to the barricade they had just attacked and found Ensign Philip Moxon lying dead with the blood-drenched Colours under him. Lieutenant Greville then led an attack on the barricade, as well as on the street leading to the village, clearing both. One of Gough's ADCs arrived and ordered them to retire. The bugles of the various regiments began sounding their regimental calls for retreat. Greville led his men over the entrenchments they had taken earlier and made his way to where his regimental call was sounding assembly.

The Sikhs immediately reoccupied all the entrenchments they had lost that day. Had there been another hour of daylight, Gough felt he would have consolidated his position and driven the Sikhs out of the remaining entrenchments. Had he attacked when he wanted to, without having to wait for Littler to arrive from Ferozepur, the situation could have been very different. He had been over-ruled by Hardinge in his capacity as governor general. As to Littler's division, after his retreat at the start of the battle, he took no further part in it.

That evening there was gloom in the British camp. Harry Smith marched his 3,000 men back over the entrenchments on to the plain. He soon came across officers of the HM 62nd and other units, who had retreated with Littler that afternoon, sitting around a fire. They advised a withdrawal to Ferozepur. Smith is reported to have answered, 'The C-in-C with his army is not far from us meditating an attack as soon as it is daylight, and find him I will if in hell, where I will join him, rather than make one retrograde step'.[115]

Continuing his move in the direction of the C-in-C, he came across around 2,000 men from all regiments, including the horse artillery, once again grouped around fires. He stopped and got his men a swig of rum. He was now accosted by a Captain Lumly, assistant adjutant-general of the British Army acting as the adjutant general while his father was ill. The following conversation is recorded in Bruce's *Six Battles for India.*

> "Sir Harry Smith, you are the very man I am looking for. As senior officer of the Adjutant General's department, I order you to collect every soldier and march to Ferozepur."
>
> "Do you come from the C-in-C with such an order? If you do, I can find him for, by God, I'll take no such order from any man on earth but from his own mouth. Where is he?"
>
> "I don't know, but in my official position, these are the orders."
>
> "Damn the orders, if not the C-in-C's," Smith growled. 'I'll give my own orders and take none of that retrograde sort from any Staff Officer on earth. But why to Ferozepur? What's the matter?"
>
> "Oh, the army has been beaten, but we can buy the Sikh soldiers."
>
> "What! Have we taken no guns?"
>
> "Oh yes, 50 or 60."
>
> "Thank you. I see my way and want no orders."

Captain Christie who commanded a regiment of Irregular Cavalry, then stepped forward and offered to guide him to the C-in-C. After his departure, Lumley ordered the 8th Light Cavalry to Ferozepur. Not being of Harry Smith's mettle, the commandant duly marched off his regiment to Ferozepur as ordered, depleting Gough's army further.

In the meantime, Gough and Hardinge were trying to re-establish some semblance of command and control. They ordered the regiments to form squares in case the Sikhs resorted to a night attack with their cavalry or infantry. The hungry and thirsty officers and men lay down on a freezing ground to sleep in their greatcoats, unable to light fires which would attract Sikh grapeshot. The feeling of defeat was in each man's mind, and some of Gough's own senior officers also suggested a withdrawal to Ferozepur.

Later, Gough recalled that night.

> Were I to have taken the strenuous representations of officers, some of rank and in important situations, my honour and my army would have been lost [...] Two said they came from the Governor General. I spurned the supposition, as I knew it could not be well founded. My answer was, "Well, I shall go to the Governor General, but my determination is taken rather to leave my bones to bleach honourably at Ferozshah than they should rot dishonourably at Ferozepur."

Gough and Hardinge discussed the situation by lantern light in a small hut he had made his headquarters. Both agreed that retreat was out of the question. As to the future course of action, there was just one option – the attack would have to be resumed at first light. Hardinge was quite aware that the army's morale was low and that the troops would not be able to face a similar battle to that they had just fought. Casualties had been too high and the Sikh artillery fire crippling. Gough's army was outgunned, both in numbers and calibre. The army's morale was not helped by the jubilant Sikh war cries and their continuous bombardment. Despite the blowing up of a number of Sikh magazines that evening, they seemed to have unlimited ammunition, while his own artillery was down to a few rounds per gun.

Assuming the worst, Hardinge sent messages to his political secretary Robert Cust and to Frederick Currie to destroy all papers of the state. Cust wrote in his diary,

> News came that our attack had failed and that Mr Currie was to destroy all papers of State. Affairs appeared to be very gloomy indeed, and though the news was kept quite secret, we were concerting measures to make our unconditional surrender, to save the wounded in the fort.[116]

To Lieutenant Bellars of the 50th, the night was one of horrifying uncertainty.

> A burning camp on one side of the village, mines and ammunition wagons exploding in every direction, the loud orders given to extinguish the fires as the sepoys lighted them, the volleys given should the Sikhs venture too near, the booming of the monster guns, the incessant firing of the smaller ones, the continued whistling noise of the shell, grape and round shot, the bugles sounding, the drums beating, and the yelling of the enemy, together with the intense thirst, fatigue and cold, and not knowing whether the rest of the army were the conquerors or conquered – all contributed to make this night awful in the extreme.[117]

Gough and Hardinge spent the night visiting the various squares to talk to the men. In one of them, Colonel Bunbury, the commanding officer of the 80th, was sitting on his horse in the middle of the square. Hardinge lay down and asked him why he didn't dismount and lie down too. Bunbury shrugged and said it was as safe on the horse as lying on the ground. Soon after, the Sikhs brought down fire from a 48in gun, whose sound terrified the troops and caused heavy casualties. Hardinge immediately shouted, 'Take that battery', and ordered Colonel Bunbury to silence it. The colonel led a detachment of his regiment, accompanied by another detachment under Major Birrell of the 1st ELI. In response to this move, the Sikhs sent out an infantry detachment and both blazed away in the dark. Bunbury met the Sikhs in a charge, broke through to the guns and hammered iron spikes into their vents and then fought themselves back, losing a few men in the process. But they had silenced the 48in gun and a few smaller ones alongside it.

Brigadier Asburnham recorded later, 'I paced up and down, and thought how the very fate of the British Empire seemed hanging on a thread.'[118]

There is no record of events in the Sikh camp. Morale was undoubtedly high, as the Sikh war cries, intermingled with the blowing of bugles and the beating of drums, indicated. From the Sikh point of view, Littler had retreated that afternoon and all the British gains had been reversed after their withdrawal in the evening. They clearly outgunned the British, and British casualties were also undoubtedly high. The attack of a British regiment, HM 62nd· had been repulsed in Littler's division, as had his NI battalions, and all three NI battalions of Ashburnham's brigade had retreated.

Lal Singh's role that night is not known, but as he was the only one who knew the regent's orders, he undoubtedly played a role. Despite the high morale during the previous evening and the night, the following morning, the Sikh response was subdued when the British attacked. This was despite the fact that the Sikhs were aware that Tej Singh's army would come to their aid that day, and that their casualties had been far fewer than those of Gough's army.

As to Lal Singh, he made no effort to command. A series of conferences were held that were more often than not inconclusive, and local formation commanders were left to their own judgement. At some point during the night of 21 and 22 December, Lal Singh abandoned his army and left Ferozshah, as did most of the Ghorcharras. Surprisingly, Lal Singh did not cross the Sutlej to Lahore, but went into British territory to Ludhiana. Colonel Gardner, then at Lahore to protect the royal family, puts it as follows:

> He fled, hid himself in a hayrick, skulked off from the army. Swapping his handsome horse for a tattoo (a small half-bred village horse), and

> smearing over his face with ashes like a poor fakir, he hid himself in an oven belonging to an old bakeress at Ludhiana. The Rani Jinda led him a dreadful life at first, when he returned to Lahore after 20 days' absence, jeering at him for his cautious behaviour – but he being her favourite, orders were given to stop any further hilarity.

At first light, Gough quietly formed up his army, after what has been described as the most desperate night ever spent in India by a Commander-in-Chief. Harry Smith had earlier brought in his men, with the guns in front and the infantry in two lines behind them. With bayonets fixed, they waited for Gough to give the order to advance. As the sun rose and the early morning mist dissipated, Gough gave it.

Captain Mills led his three troops of horse artillery forward at the gallop, unlimbered and opened fire on the Sikh guns. The Sikhs' forward guns responded, immediately blowing up three of the artillery ammunition wagons. At that point, for some unknown reason since they had not taken any collateral damage, the Sikh gunfire reduced. At the same time, instead of waiting for an opportunity to attack Gough's troops, the Akali shock troops turned on their own C-in-C, Lal Singh, and raided his camp for loot. They blamed him for not providing the requisite leadership, by leaving command to the local brigade commanders. They were repulsed by the troops guarding the camp, but the rot had set in. By that time, unknown to them, Lal Singh had left the camp.

Gough led the right wing and Hardinge the left. The infantry, facing less resistance than the previous day, carried the trenches to their front on the southern and eastern faces of the defensive perimeter. Then, moving rapidly, they swept forward and captured Ferozshah and the Sikh camp before turning left and sweeping along the gun positions. By 1 p.m., the Sikh position had fallen, and all the guns, stores and the camp had been taken – a complete rout of the Sikhs, who offered virtually no resistance in contrast to the previous day.

The Sikhs withdrew through the jungle north of Ferozshah and a regiment of cavalry was sent to keep contact with their retreat. They crossed the Sutlej at Naggar Pathar and Tilli, some marching up river to cross at Harike Pattan. Food and water now became the chief requirement of Gough's army. A well was found in which the Sikhs had thrown dead bodies. The bloodied water was nevertheless drunk. Thirst was so extreme that the men even made the C-in-C wait for a drink. As to food, all that was found in the Sikh camp were a few oranges, a supply of grain, dried peas and a little sugar, reinforcing the belief that the Lahore Durbar had used every possible means, even starvation, to destroy its army.

As the feeling of relief began to sooth tensions and the troops began to unwind, cavalry scouts galloped in to report to Gough that the regiment in contact with the Sikh retreat had been checked by a large force advancing from Ferozepur. As Bruce puts it in *Six Battles for India*: 'Battered and disorganized, Gough's troops now faced another attack by Tej Singh's fresh army from Ferozepur. Only a miracle could save them, for they were quite without strength to fight again.'

Tej Singh had promised Nicholson that he would not attack Littler at Ferozepur and would, as per his advice, march on the C-in-C. The battle of Mudki was over on 18 December. Tej Singh had reinforced Lal Singh prior to Ferozshah, with three regular army brigade groups on the previous day. He was aware at that point that the next battle would be at Ferozshah, which had started on 21 December. Despite all this, he waited until the battle was over on 22 December at 1 p.m. before arriving at Ferozshah at 1.30 p.m., after Lal Singh's army had been defeated and had dispersed. The distance from Ferozepur to Ferozshah was just 20 miles, less than a day's march, and he was aware of the latest intelligence at all times. Had he come to join battle on the 21, or even on the morning of 22, the outcome would have been very different. It is obvious that, once again, the orders of Maharani Jinda Kaur – that of the destruction of their army – had been kept in mind.

Tej Singh's army comprised 5 regular army brigade groups of the Fauj-e-Ain, 21 infantry battalions, 4 regular cavalry regiments and 134 artillery guns. In addition, he had substantial Fauj-e-Gair (militia) units, inclusive of the Ghorcharras and Jagirdari Risala. The strength of this militia is not known. His overall strength was far in excess of that available to Lal Singh, and in excess of that available with Gough. His order of battle is given below:

Sardar Tej Singh's Wing, The Sikh Army, Ferozshah, 22 December 1845[119]

Commander-in-Chief
Sardar Tej Singh

Fauj-e-Ain: (Regulars)

Shamsher Singh's Brigade: (3,170)
1st Infantry Paltan (600)
2nd Infantry Paltan (600)
3rd Infantry Paltan (600)
4th Infantry Paltan (600)
Ram Rajman (500)
Artillery
Aspi (Field Artillery) (270) (9 guns)
Beldar (Engineer) Company

Rattan Singh Man's Brigade: (4,830)
1st Infantry Paltan (915)
2nd Infantry Paltan (915)
3rd Infantry Paltan (915)
4th Infantry Paltan (915)
Hazoori Rajman (540)
Artillery
Aspi (360) (12 guns)
Jinsi (270) (9 guns)
Beldar (Engineer) Company

Kahn Singh Man's Brigade (4,192)
1st Infantry Paltan (778)
2nd Infantry Paltan (778)
3rd Infantry Paltan (778)
4th Infantry Paltan (778)
Allard's (Cuirassier) Rajman (540)
Artillery
Aspi (270) (11 guns)

Jinsi (270) (9 guns)
Beldar (Engineer) Company

Chattar Singh's Brigade: no details found, assumed to be Court's or Suchet Singh's Brigade.
Approximately 4,500 troops, which are organized as below:
4 Infantry Paltans
1 Rajman
Artillery:
1 Aspi
Belder (Engineer) Company

Mewa Singh's Brigade: (4,735)
1st Infantry Paltan (785)
2nd Infantry Paltan (785)
3rd Infantry Paltan (785)
4th Infantry Paltan (785)
5th Infantry Paltan (785)
Artillery:
Aspi (270) (9 guns)
1st Jinsi (270) (9 guns)
2nd Jinsi (270) (9 guns)
Belder (Engineer) Company

Fauj-e-Gair (Feudal Militia)
Ghorcharra Cavalry Brigades: units and numbers not known
Jagirdari (Light) Cavalry Regiments: units and numbers not known

Regular Army Artillery: Only one derah present. The rest at Ferozepur
Tara Singh's Derah:
Jinsi (360) (12 guns)

Khair Ali Khan's Derah
Ghubar's Topkhana (360) (12 guns)
Lala Jawahir Mal's Artillery Brigade:
Ishwar Khan's Jinsi (300) (10 guns)
Imam Shah's Jinsi (390) (13 guns)

Source: Dewan Ajudhia Parshad, *Waqai-Jang-i-Sikhan*: *Events of the First Anglo-Sikh War* 1845-46. V.S. Suri (tr) Chandigarh: Punjab Itihas Prakashan, 1975.

Even Gough's indomitable spirits fell. His men were exhausted, the cavalry horses so tired and hungry that they could barely gallop; worst of all, his artillery ammunition was almost finished. Yet advancing upon him, great red and gold banners streaming, was another Sikh Army, ready and eager for battle which he could not avoid. 'The only time I felt doubt,' he wrote to his son, 'was towards the evening of the 22nd when the fresh enemy advanced, with heavy columns of cavalry, infantry and guns, and our cavalry horses were thoroughly done up'.[120]

The roles were now suddenly reversed. Gough ordered his army into a defensive square around Ferozshah along the lines of the earlier Sikh entrenchments to receive the inevitable attack. The exhausted horse artillery moved forward into action. Two troops under Colonel Huthwaite trotted through the jungle, engaging the Sikhs from the left of the village. They got an immediate response as the Sikhs replied with fierce cannon fire. Major Brind then went into action with a further two troops and was also on the receiving end of a very aggressive cannonade. Colonel Geddes followed suit with his two troops and received the same response. Colonel Huthwaite withdrew when he was left with only a few rounds of ammunition. Major Brind was driven back by fierce enfilade fire, and

Colonel Geddes retired with his ammunition expended. All three entered the square determined to fight as infantry.

As the Sikhs closed in on them, the gunners fired the few remaining rounds they had, only to receive a reply from about 40 guns that pummelled the area, killing a large number of infantry in a twenty-minute response. At that point, a large number of Sikh cavalry were spotted coming out of the jungle and forming up for a charge on the square.

It was 2 p.m. when Gough ordered the infantry to change front to the north in echelons of regiments and to form a square four deep to receive the Sikh cavalry. The infantry was also virtually out of ammunition. The Sikh cavalry, now only 200 yards away, began its trot forward with lances lowered and sabres flashing in the sun. Suddenly, the 3rd Light Dragoons appeared at full gallop, supported by elements of the 4th Light Cavalry. Under the Colonel of the Dragoons and led by Brigadier White, they were joined in the charge by the GOC. General Gilbert himself galloped straight into the advancing Sikh cavalry. A fierce hand-to-hand battle ensued and the Sikh cavalry finally gave way. The surviving Dragoons regrouped, but their horses, without feed, water or rest, were now beyond another charge. All the Sikh guns now deployed and began a severe cannonade of the squares, killing the infantry in droves. Once again, the Sikh cavalry began to reform in advance of its infantry for a charge on the squares.

At that moment, unable to protect his men from the slaughter, Gough, in his white fighting coat, galloped forward on his well-known horse, along with his ADC, Captain Sackville-West, and made himself a target to draw part of the fire off his squares. He managed to do this as some of the guns targeted him, but more importantly, this gesture had its impact on the morale of his hard-pressed troops who cheered him on.

As Gough was galloping in front of the enemy, he suddenly noticed that his artillery wagons and his cavalry were galloping off to Ferozepur. Riders were immediately sent to recall them, but to no avail. It was Captain Lumley, the acting adjutant-general yet again, who had sent the ammunition wagons off to replenish at Ferozepur along with the cavalry as escort. The infantry squares now braced for what surely would be their last moment in this world.

Once again, the bugles sounded retreat, this time on the side of the advancing Sikh Army. The advance hesitated then halted, and finally the cavalry moved to the flanks and the infantry turned around. As incredible as it sounds, Tej Singh and his army moved off to Ferozepur, saving Gough's army and changing the very course of history. His subsequent explanation was that the British cavalry had gone in the direction of Ferozepur and was planning to attack him from behind. He had, in fact, saved Gough and his army as per the orders of the regent. In this strange way, the battle of Ferozshah ended at 4 p.m. on 22 December.

Had Lumley not given the order to the troops to fall back on Ferozepur, Tej Singh would not have had an excuse to halt the advance and to retreat.

Then the outcome could have been very different. Gough owed his victory to this eccentric officer. When next day he was summoned by the governor general, he appeared in his pyjamas. When asked the reason for this mode of dress, he said that his uniform was so riddled by shot the day before that it had fallen off! He was given the choice of resignation or to appear before a court martial. He resigned.

Having abandoned the field, Lal Singh left the Sikh Army leaderless and its morale plunged. In his *Despatches* to the governor general on 22 December, Gough states that out of the Sikh commanders, 'Bahadur Singh is killed, Lal Singh said to be wounded [which was incorrect], Mehtab Singh, Ajodhia Prasad and Tej Singh, the late governor of Peshawar have fled with precipitation'.[121]

Bahadur Singh was one of the Sikh brigade group commanders, Ajodhia Prasad was commander of Avitabile's Fauj-e-Khas and Mehtab Singh also commanded a Sikh brigade group. The Tej Singh being referred to is presumably the C-in-C of the Sikh Army. Once Lal Singh abandoned his command, his army's morale fell. Despite all the positives in favour of the Sikhs, the British virtually walked into their defensive position the next day. Why Lal Singh took this decision is not recorded, but it seems to be part of the overall design to get the army cut to size, otherwise there is no explanation. The British had taken a beating the day before with heavy casualties. The Sikh morale was exceedingly high, and there was ammunition and stores in plenty. In addition, Tej Singh and his army were expected the next day. Perhaps it was because Lal Singh knew that Tej Singh was on the way that he abandoned the field. Certainly the combined armies of both of them would, in all probability, have defeated Gough.

The British had taken 75 Sikh guns in this encounter, but at a cost of 2,415 casualties – about a seventh of their entire force. Of this number, 694 were killed. Five of the governor general's staff were killed and two were wounded. Brigadier Wallace was killed and Brigadiers Harriott, Taylor and White were wounded.

The total killed included 37 British officers, 17 Indian officers, 630 NCOs, drummers and other ranks. The wounded numbered 1,721, which included 78 British officers, 18 Indian officers, three warrant officers and 1,607 other ranks. The casualties were the highest in the HM regiments, the 62nd leading the list, followed by 9th, 80th, 31st and 50th Foot. The 1st European Light Infantry of the East India Company, which had performed brilliantly, took heavy casualties. However, the pride of place must go to HM 3rd Light Dragoons as, despite their gallant performance and the heavy casualties taken by them four days previously at Mudki, they again performed to perfection. At Mudki, out of a total strength of 494 all ranks, they had lost 3 officers and 58 men, with 3 officers and 34 men wounded. In addition, 5 officers' chargers and 100 troop horses were killed and 2 officers' chargers and 21 troop horses were wounded. At

Ferozshah, the Dragoons had 2 officers and 53 men killed, and 7 officers and 86 men wounded, a total of 9 officers and 139 men as casualties. The chargers of 9 officers and 98 troop horses were killed and 60 troop horses wounded. In four days between Mudki and Ferozshah, the Dragoons had lost 15 officers and 111 men and 17 officers' chargers and 179 troop horses as casualties.

The Sikh casualties have been put at around 2,000. As evidence of this, the heirs of 1,782 men of the regular army claimed balance of pay et cetera, after the war.[122] As no tactical information with regard to the Sikh battle is available, no comment can be made other than the fact, consistently brought out time and again, of the bravery of the gunners standing by their guns to the end.

The treachery of the Sikh regent, her wazir and C-in-C, together with a mad British officer saved Gough from near certain defeat.

Night fell on the field. Shivering, exhausted men huddled around blazing fires. Wandering cattle were slaughtered, crudely grilled in the flames and devoured ravenously. Camels loaded with the canteen stores now arrived, ending their long march from Ambala. The troops ate their fill and then, while sentries patrolled, slept the thankful contended sleep of men who have held their lives in their hands and lived.

Captain John Cummings recalled the bitter cold of the night and the grim early morning sight of the battlefield where many wounded still lay.

> I awoke as the reveille was sounded on the morning of the 23rd to find myself stiff with cold, my clothes covered with a hoarfrost and my limbs so benumbed that I could not rise. After my servant had chafed and squeezed them, I got on my legs. A walk was necessary to bring me round and I staggered through the entrenched camp – a horrible sight, as death was there in its most hideous forms, and men dying in all the most excruciating agonies. Walking about was still dangerous, for Sikh mines were exploding now and then as fire happened to reach them.
>
> I wandered along in a confused way in search of something. I hardly knew what it was that I wanted. At length, behind a curtain in a Sikh tent, I saw a large earthen vessel full of pure cold water. This is what I had been looking for! I flew upon it, and plunged my head and arms into it, clothes and all. I drank until I could drink no more, then stood up and drank again and again.[123]

Gough set up camp about 10 miles north of Ferozshah at Sultan Khan Wala, while Hardinge accompanied Littler and his division to Ferozepur. Reinforcements, particularly of heavy guns and ammunition, were sent for from Delhi, Meerut and Kanpur. Both men decided that until these arrived they would not confront the Sikhs, even if they again crossed the Sutlej, behind which they had already retired. They did, however, believe that the possibility of attacking Ludhiana existed. Ranjodh Singh Majithia was encamped with a sizeable force close to Phillaur on the Sutlej, which in itself was around 8 miles from Ludhiana. Brigadier Godby was dispatched to Ludhiana to take command of the station and the three infantry battalions – the Sirmoor and Nasiri battalions of Gurkhas and the 38th NI – that had reached Ludhiana from their normal bases in and around Kasauli in the Simla Hills. In addition, there was a cavalry regiment. His task was to hold Ludhiana and the fort there, just in case the Sikhs moved in that direction.

VII. THE BATTLE OF ALIWAL

At Sultan Khan Wala, Gough's scouts had given him information that, although the Sikh Army had withdrawn across the Sutlej to Lahore, a fresh force remained south of the Sutlej and had entrenched itself about 10 kilometres east of Harike at Sobraon. As he had agreed with the governor general, Gough decided to wait for his reinforcements to arrive before taking any action. In the meantime, he kept the Sikh position at Sobraon under strict watch.

While awaiting the arrival of the reinforcements, particularly the heavy siege guns that were lumbering up the Grand Trunk Road, Gough received reinforcements of about 10,000 troops of Sir John Grey's division, who had left Meerut in mid-December. His division comprised the 9th Lancers, 16th Lancers, 3rd Bengal Light Cavalry, 4th Irregular Cavalry, 2 Batteries of Artillery, HM 10th Foot, 3 NI Regiments, the 45th, 59th and 68th, and a company of sappers.

Sobraon lay to the north, across the Sutlej towards Lahore. However, the Sikh position was south of the river, with its back to it, at a prominent bend. Well-built high embankments with entrenchments on top were thrown across the front, linking with the river at both ends. A bridge of boats connected both shores. The defences were very well built and had been supervised by Colonel Huberon, a Spanish engineer officer who was one of the four remaining European officers still with the Sikh Army. The opposite rear bank was higher than the front bank and was being prepared as a position for the heavy guns, so they could cover an attack from any direction.

While plans were being made to attack the Sikh Army there, Gough decided to clear the two forts still in Sikh possession – both to the north and slightly to the rear of his position, at Futtehgarh and Dharamkot, on the road between Ludhiana and Ferozepur. He was on the second link road connecting Ambala, Sirhind and Ferozepur, positioned around 3 miles short of the junction of these two roads. On 16 December, Gough sent for Harry Smith and told him that these two forts were to be cleared. He suggested that a brigade and a regiment of cavalry should suffice, and asked him to suggest someone for this task. Harry Smith promptly answered that he would take it on himself. 'When will you march?' asked Gough, delighted with this reply. 'There's no hurry,' was the response. 'Soon after this time tomorrow, I will be writing my report that I have reduced them both.'

Gough laughed and said, 'Why, the distance to Dharamkot is 26 miles from your right.' Smith answered, 'I know that. Still, what I say shall be, provided the engineers supply me in time with the powder I want, to blow the gates in the case of necessity.'[124]

Smith marched two hours before sun up on 17 January, having collected all the animal transport he could lay his hands on and loading them all night along with his supplies and ammunition. The defenders of the first fort to be encountered, Futtehgarh, abandoned it and retreated on his approach. He then carried on to Dharamkot, reaching there by 2 p.m. Its gates were closed and the Lahore Durbar flag was flying.

As the infantry was yet to catch up with him, Smith immediately invested it with his cavalry – the 3rd Bengal Light Cavalry and the 4th Bengal Irregular Cavalry. The garrison commander came out to talk to Smith and laid down a number of conditions for surrendering the fort. Smith cut him short by saying, 'You may march out with your arms, ground them on the glacis, and I will endeavour to secure all hands six weeks' pay. Go back to the fort. I give you twenty minutes to consider, after which I shall make no terms, but open my cannon upon you.'[125]

When no response came on the expiry of the twenty minutes, Smith ordered the howitzer and 9-pounders to open fire. The Lahore flag was immediately hauled down and replaced with a white one. The garrison marched out, laid down their arms and were taken as prisoners of war. The fort was immediately occupied and its defences shored up.

While Harry Smith was engaged at Dharamkot, Gough received a message from his scouts that Ranjodh Singh Majithia, along with Raja Ajit Singh of Ladwa, had crossed the Sutlej with a force of around 10,000 men and had reached Ludhiana. He had entered the city and had burnt part of the cantonment.

Ranjodh Singh's task had been to cut the British line of communication along which substantial reinforcements were travelling in a twenty-mile long column that included the heavy siege guns. While Ranjodh Singh wasted his time with Ludhiana, Gough, concerned for the safe arrival of the convoy, sent Harry Smith orders to advance from Dharamkot to Ludhiana via Jagraon without delay, and to intercept Ranjodh Singh. He also sent him reinforcements comprising the HM 16th Lancers, the 3rd Bengal Light Cavalry, a troop of horse artillery and HM's 50th Foot, then positioned at Bussean.

Smith's own scouts, keeping Ranjodh Singh in sight, reported that he was presently at Baran Hara, 20 miles west of Ludhiana on the Dharamkot road. The Ludhiana to Dharamkot road and the Bussean to Jagraon road both had their junction at Dharamkot. Gough had also received information about Ranjodh Singh's whereabouts, as he too had suggested an approach to Ludhiana via Jagraon. Smith knew that the Sikhs still had a small garrison of infantry and a few hundred cavalry at Badhowal, 7 miles from Ludhiana, where the Jagraon to Ludhiana and the Bussean to Ludhiana roads met. Another strong force, inclusive of guns, was positioned in the fort at Ghungrana – 12 miles from Ludhiana on the Malerkotla road and about 10 miles south of Badhowal.

Smith left Dharamkot with the infantry on 19 January and met up with the reinforcements sent by Gough the same day at Kokari Kalan, about two-thirds of the way to Jagraon.

At 12.30 a.m., on 21 December, Smith left his wheeled guns and heavy baggage behind to follow under an escort of two NI companies, marching in bright moonlight to Jagraon. He continued his march, covering 18 miles by sunrise, leaving him 2 miles short of Badhowal. He intended to skirt Badhowal to the north to avoid a chance of being interfered with by Sikh troops from Ghungrana to the south of it. While on the march, he continued to send messages to Godby at Ludhiana every two hours, with orders to join him, with the strongest possible force, at Sunet, halfway between Badhowal and Ludhiana. By then Godby had received information from his own intelligence sources that Ranjodh Singh had marched from Baran Hara and was now positioned in strength at Badhowal. He managed to get a message to Smith just in time, giving him the new disposition of the Sikhs. Had this message not arrived, Smith would have been in trouble, as Ranjodh Singh's force, 10,000 strong with 40 guns, was well deployed at Badhowal and he would have walked into a trap.

Expecting the Sikhs to march on him any moment, Smith ordered his men to advance in battle order over sand dunes and the softer sand between them. The effort to move forward in this terrain was exhausting. Nevertheless, the close proximity of the Sikh Army compelled Smith to order his army to move in this formation because the Sikh column was marching parallel to him along the village roads. As they were travelling on better terrain, the head of the Sikh column outflanked him by about a mile, while his infantry and guns, to the rear, were also outflanked by the same distance. He remained under continuous Sikh artillery harassing fire throughout.

As Smith recalled,

> With great celerity he brought to bear on my troops a considerable number of guns of very heavy metal. The cavalry moved parallel to the enemy, protected from the fire of his guns by a low ridge of sandhills. My 18 guns I kept together close in rear of the cavalry, in order to open a heavy fire on the enemy and to check his advance [...] This fire, which I continued for some ten minutes, had a most auxiliary effect, creating slaughter and confusion in the enemy's ranks. The enemy's cannonade upon the column of infantry had been furious previous to this. As the column moved on under this cannonade, which was especially furious upon the rear of the infantry, the enemy, with a dexterity and quickness not to be exceeded, formed a line of seven battalions directly across my rear, with guns in the

> intervals of battalions, for the purpose of attacking my column with his line. This was a very able and well-executed move, which rendered my position critical and demanded nerve and decision to evade the coming storm.[126]

Smith now decided to pre-empt Ranjodh Singh and attack his line. He ordered HM 31st to form up, but changed his mind because the men were exhausted after their march through the deep sand. He then changed front on the centre of HM 31st and HM 53rd, and ordered the infantry to march on Ludhiana in echelon of battalions, ready to receive his order to 'Halt Front' if the Sikhs attacked. The cavalry was ordered to move in echelon of squadrons, the two arms mutually supporting each other. The guns were to be placed to the rear of the cavalry. The Sikhs watched the move, but did not leave their entrenchment at Badhowal to engage or interfere. Smith soon reached Ludhiana, camping close to the city rather than close to the Sikhs, as clear water for his troops was now the priority. He established strong outposts to keep a watch on Ranjodh Singh's moves and also had strong patrols out, all the while probing the gaps between them and right up to their position.

This advance to Ludhiana cost Harry Smith dear. He took heavy casualties without once closing with the Sikhs throughout the advance – 69 men were killed, 68 wounded and 77 were taken prisoner, which was a total of 214 men. The Sikhs attacked his baggage train, which had lagged behind, or at least those parts of it that had not returned to Jagraon. All his baggage and supplies were looted and most casualties, particularly the prisoners, were taken during this attack. Smith justified this by saying, 'Had I not affected a junction with the troops at Ludhiana, they and the city would have fallen, and next our treasure, battering train, ammunition, etc. would have been captured or scattered and lost to the army'.[127] On the contrary, the outcome may have been different had he appreciated this danger to his convoy and left a sizeable escort, rather than just two NI companies, knowing full well that his convoy was moving up behind him in an isolated manner.

Ranjodh Singh's orders were to cut the British lines of communication and to prevent the strong supply train and siege guns from reaching Gough at Sultan Khan Wala. From the outset, he wasted time in burning the Ludhiana cantonment, without any military objective, and then withdrew to Badhowal to entrench himself there. He was aware that two roads went west from Ludhiana, while only one, the Grand Trunk Road, came to Ludhiana from Delhi. Therefore, it would have been more appropriate for him to have positioned himself east of Ludhiana, across the Grand Trunk Road, if he intended to be an effective check on the advancing supply train. That he did not was perhaps due to a lack of regular troops with him. The alternative was to have attacked Harry Smith on the march up to Ludhiana while his troops were exhausted. He lost both opportunities.

Cunningham in his *History of the Sikhs* adds,

> The Sikhs did not pursue, for they were without a leader, or without one who wished to see the English beaten. Ranjodh Singh let his soldiers engage in battle, but that he accompanied them into the fight is more than doubtful, and it is certain that he did not essay the easy task of improving the success of his own men into the complete reverse of the enemy. The mass of British baggage was at hand, and the temptation to plunder could not be resisted by the men who were without orders to conquer. Every beast of burden which had not got within the sight of Ludhiana, or which had not, timorously but prudently, been taken back to Jagraon, when the firing was heard, fell into the hands of the Sikhs.

Smith rested his troops on 22 January and made plans to attack Badhowal the next day. However, on the 22nd he got news that the Sikhs had moved north to a prominent ford on the Sutlej, 15 miles west of Ludhiana at Tulawan, close to the villages of Aliwal and Bhundri. Smith immediately moved and occupied the former Sikh position at Badhowal on the morning of the 23 January. Both armies were now reinforced. A regular brigade of the Fauj-e-Ain under Jodha Ram, comprising three infantry battalions – Rup Singh's, Bhagat Singh's and Jiwand Singh's paltans – one cavalry regiment, the Gobind Rajman, and 18 guns, 12 Aspi and 6 Jinsi, joined Ranjodh Singh on 26 January. Gough also sent Harry Smith's second brigade forward to join him, and Brigadier Wheeler reached Badhowal on 27 January with HM 50th, 48th NI, the Sirmoor Gurkhas and a battery of 18 elephant-drawn 14-pounders, along with 25 bullock-drawn wagons of ammunition.

On 27 January, Harry Smith in turn received intelligence that Ranjodh Singh was preparing to march early the next morning, his objective being either to attack Badhowal or to march on Ludhiana. Smith decided to pre-empt Ranjodh Singh and left Badhowal well before dawn, marching north-west towards the Sikh position. The cavalry led in line of squadron columns with two horse artillery batteries in the centre. The infantry followed in continuous columns of brigades at intervals of deploying distance, the artillery within the intervals, with the two elephant-drawn 8-inch howitzers bringing up the rear. Strong cavalry patrols under Major Bradford and Captain Waugh were well out in front.

When he was 6 miles from Badhowal, he received a report that Ranjodh Singh was on the move and was heading for Jagraon. Smith nevertheless maintained his direction and, 4 miles on, arrived at the village of Purain. Dismounting, he climbed the highest house to see things for himself, and there ahead of him was the Sikh Army marching across his front.

Harry Smith recorded his first view of the battle field in his memoirs.

> Directly opposite my front, on a ridge, of which the village of Aliwal may be regarded as the centre [...] a level grassy plain two miles long and a mile wide lay below the ridge upon which [I stood], leading to a slight rise upon which were two villages – Aliwal, slightly fortified, facing the right, and Bhundri, facing the left, covered by a thin grove of trees.[128]

When the cavalry topped the Purain height and showed its presence, the Sikhs halted, turned to their left and occupied the rising land facing Smith. The Sutlej was barely a mile away. Ranjodh Singh had his back to it and, as Harry Smith noted with delight, 'He had no room to manoeuvre'.

Tom Pierce, this being his first battle, remembered,

> We reached the summit of a high hill and came to an extensive level plain [...] and about 1,800 yards ahead was the Sikh Army in battle array, drawn up in line, guns in front, drums beating [...] Our troops had only just time to deploy in line before they boomed forth their murderous fire.[129]

Gough and Innes in *The Sikhs and the Sikh Wars* describe the day and the field as follows.

> It was now 10 o'clock, and the whole scene most striking. The morning was clear and beautiful, the country open and hard grassland – a fair field for all arms. There was no dust and the sun shone brightly. Brigadier Steadman commanded the cavalry on the right: the 1st and 5th Regiments of Bengal Native Cavalry, the Governor General's Bodyguard, the Shekhawati Cavalry and the 4th Irregular Cavalry. Then came Godby's Brigade, the Gurkhas of the Nuseeree Battalion, and the 36th NI; next, Hicks's Brigade, HM 31st, and the 24th and 47th NI; on their left and in the centre of the line the two 8in howitzers and a large battery of 18 guns; then Wheeler's Brigade, HM 50th, the 48th NI, the Sirmoor Gurkha's [Brigadier Wheeler had so much confidence in his own regiment the 48th, that he placed it in the centre of the brigade: the corps fully justified his opinion], then two batteries of artillery [12 guns]; then Wilson's Brigade of HM 53rd, 30th NI and the Shekhawati Infantry; then on the extreme left HM 16th Lancers and the 3rd Light Cavalry.

This was the order of battle of the two opposing forces at Aliwal:

The Army of the Sutlej at Aliwal, 28 January 1846[130]

General Officer Commanding	**Aides-de-Camp**
Major General Sir Harry Smith	Lt Holditch

Lt H. Tombs (Acting)
Assistant Adjutant General
Captain E. Lugard

Deputy Assistant Adjutant General
Lt A.W.C. Plowden
Engineering Staff
Lt Strachey
Lt Robert Baird Smith
Commissariat General's Dept
Captain Mainwaring
Captain Williamson
– Captain Jack (824)
The Shekawati Infantry – Major H. Forster (781)
Principal Medical Officer
(Field Surgeon) Dr Murray
Political Officers
Major Mackeson
Captain J.D. Cunningham
Lt Lake

1st Infantry Division
Maj Gen Sir Harry Smith/Brigadier (Lt Col) Hugh M. Wheeler, CB
Deputy Assistant Quartermaster General
Lt A.S. Galloway
1st Brigade
Brigadier (Lt Col) George Hicks
Brigade Major
Captain P. O'Hanlon/Captain Palmer
HM 31st Foot Regiment – Lt Col Spence (544)
24th BNI Regiment – Major Bird (481)
47th BNI – Captain Corfield (713)
2nd Brigade
Brigadier (Lt Col) HM Wheeler
Brigade Major: Captain Garvock
HM 50th Foot Regiment – Lt Col Ryan, KH (494)
48th BNI Regiment – Captain Troup (857)
Sirmoor Gurkha Battalion – Captain Fisher (781)
3rd Brigade
Brigadier (Lt Col) Archibald Wilson
Brigade Major: Captain Loftie
HM 53rd Foot Regiment – Lt Col Phillips (699)
30th BNI Regiment
4th Brigade
Brigadier (Lt Col) G. Godby
Brigade Major: Lt Vanrenen
36th BNI Regiment – Captain Fleming (571)
Nusiri Gurkha Battalion – Brigadier (Lt Col) Nicholas Penny (586)
2 Field Batteries
2 8in Howitzers

Cavalry Division: (ad hoc)
Brigadier (Lt Col) Charles Robert Cureton, CB
Deputy Assistant Quartermaster General:
Captain Waugh
1st Cavalry Brigade
Brigadier (Lt Col) McDowell, CB
Brigade Major: Lt Pattinson
HM 16th Lancers Regiment – Major J. Rowland Smyth (530)
3rd BLC Regiment – Major Angelo (372)
2nd Cavalry Brigade
Brigadier Stedman
Governor General's Bodyguard
1st BLC
5th BLC
The Shekhawati Cavalry
4th Bengal Irregular Cavalry – Captain Hill (398)
3 Batteries horse artillery – Major Laurenson

Order of Battle of the Sikh Army at the battle of Aliwal, 28 January 1846

Commander-in-Chief:
Ranjodh Singh Majithia

Fauj-e-Ain: (Regulars)
Jodha Ram's (Avitabile's) Brigade: (4627)
Rup Singh's Infantry Paltan (936)
Bhagat Singh's Infantry Paltan (901)
Jiwand Singh's Infantry Paltan (870)
Gobind Cavalry Rajman
Artillery
Baland Khan's Aspi (360) (12)
Rustem Beg's Jinsi (180) (6)
Beldar (Engineer) Company

Ranjodh Singh's (Ex-Lena Singh's) Brigade: (1360)
1st Sirdar's Infantry Paltan (500)
2nd Sirdar's Infantry Paltan (500)
Artillery
Jinsi (360) (12 Howitzers)

Fauj-e-Gair: (Militia)

Ghorcharra Cavalry Brigades
Ghorcharra Khas Derah
Ghorcharra (1600)
Jay Singh's Swivels (76)
Fateh Singh Jogi's Derah
Gorcharra (863)
Gurmukh Singh Lamba's Derah
Ghorcharra (995)
Imam-ud-din's Derah
Ghorcharra (993)
Jawahar Singh's Derah
Ghorchurra (960)
Mul Raj's Derah
Ghorcharra (921)
Jagirdari (Light) Cavalry Regiments
Rajah of Ladwa's Sowar Regiment (approximately 200)

State (Army) Artillery

Fateh Singh's/ Mubarak Khan's Artillery Brigade
1st Jinsi (360) (12 pcs)
2nd Jinsi (270) (9 pcs)
Mortar Derah
Aspi (120) (4 Heavy Mortars)
Unknown Derah
Jinsi (360) (12 pcs)

Source: Dewan Ajudhia Parshad, *Waqai-Jang-i-Sikhan: Events of the First Anglo-Sikh War* 1845-46. V.S. Suri (tr) Chandigarh: Punjab Itihas Prakashan, 1975.
Sikh Army List (compiled from Bajwa and other sources)

On completing his deployment, Harry Smith ordered his cavalry brigades to wheel off and deploy on either side of his infantry, which in turn was deployed in line, in the middle, at the start of the long plain. Then, noting that the Sikhs outflanked him to the left, Smith took ground on the left to cover his position and faced the front again. This movement was conducted with parade-ground precision, the fixed bayonets and drawn swords glinting in the morning sun. He then gave the order to advance.

The Sikhs, who were positioned around 850 yards from the British troops, waited until the line had advanced about 150 yards and then opened fire with their artillery. Tom Pierce recorded this moment, his baptism under fire: 'The first man that was killed stood only a few yards from me, a 9 pound shot took his head from his body. I felt rather sick at seeing the men fall by threes and fours around me.'

As the army advanced closer to the Sikh position, Harry Smith was able to observe the position from close up. He decided that Aliwal, on the right, appeared to be the weakest position of the Sikh line and felt it was the key to the situation. If he could carry it, he would be in a position to make a general attack on the left and centre. He therefore ordered Brigadier Godby and Brigadier Hicks to take Aliwal. Both brigades attacked and captured it without much difficulty and with minimum casualties. They also captured two large guns positioned there. Aliwal was garrisoned by Dogra Irregulars who gave up without a semblance of a fight. As J.D. Cunningham says in *History of the Sikhs:*

> The Sikh ranks were steady and the play of their guns incessant; but the holders of the post were battalions of hill men, raised because their demeanour was sobre and their hearts indifferent to the Khalsa, and after firing a straggling volley, they fled in confusion, headed by Ranjodh Singh, their immediate leader, and leaving the brave Sikh and Muslim artillerymen to be slaughtered by the conquerors.

Smith now gave the order for the attack to commence on the Sikh centre and left. By advancing the line at the run for a short distance and then lying down, to coincide with the firing of the Sikh salvos, they managed to make themselves as small a target as possible.

As the distance reduced, the intensity of the Sikh fire increased and the guns began firing grape and chain shot. Major Lawrenson was commanding the horse artillery with Brigadier Stedman's brigade, and seeing the infantry and his own men and horses fall, raised his sword and galloped forward with his batteries without waiting for orders, to within 200 yards of the Sikh guns. At this point, the guns were wheeled around, unlimbered and fired. By this means, they increased the intensity of their fire and gave the infantry an oportunity to attack. The charge of Wilson's brigade on the left succeeded and the Sikh line to their front collapsed. The guns were spiked as soon as they were taken. The Ghorcharras moved forward in an attempt to fill the gap in the line. Seeing this move develop, Smith in turn ordered Stedman to clear the Ghorcharras. Stedman promptly led his brigade in a charge, preventing the Sikh irregulars from entering the gap, and then managed to push the Ghorcharras back to the river. The Sikh infantry, which had fallen back from this position, now formed squares about 400 yards to their rear.

In the centre, Wheeler continued a steady advance, halting just once to allow Wilson on the left to deal with the Sikhs' right flank, which was pivoting on Bhundri with the help of their irregular cavalry. Brigadier Cureton, the GOC of the Cavalry Division, watching for the right moment to launch his cavalry, saw his chance when Wilson was preparing to charge the Sikh infantry and the guns to his front. He immediately ordered Macdowell to launch a squadron each of the 16th Lancers and the 3rd Bengal Light Cavalry at the Sikh position to assist Wilson. With his squadron of the 16th Lancers, Captain Bere was first off the mark and at full gallop dashed straight into the mass of Ghorcharras. At first it seemed as if the far greater numbers of Sikh irregular horse had swallowed them up, but the momentum and the heavier weight of the British chargers carried the charge through. They were soon seen to reform after having fought their way through the Sikhs. Being now close enough to the Sikh position, Wheeler ordered his brigade to charge the Sikh position to his front. His troops moving forward rapidly, fired one volley and then assaulted the Sikh position. The Sikh infantry of the Fauj-e-Gair broke at the first charge and withdrew. The regular army gunners, as always, defended their guns to the last. After the infantry had abandoned its position, the gunners advanced on a number of occasions to meet the British infantry and engage in hand-to-hand combat. The HM 50th, which came up against the largest of the Sikh batteries, had a very tough fight with the gunners.

On reaching the heights of the ridge upon which the Sikh defences were positioned, Harry Smith finally saw the Sikh camp. He ordered Godby to change front to their left front and rear, and to take the camp – a task the sepoys and Gurkhas soon accomplished.

Wheeler's brigade, led by HM 53rd, followed up to seize the village of Bhundri. Black smoke swirled in the narrow streets and bayonets and talwars clashed until finally the village was taken. Major Lawrenson now turned his guns, loaded with grape, on the fleeing Sikh irregulars. Just then, about 1,000 Sikh irregulars, hidden from view in a ravine below the ridge, suddenly appeared and opened fire on the 53rd with the long matchlocks with which the Fauj-e-Gair were armed, causing heavy casualties. The 30th NI was ordered by Smith himself to take the position. The 30th carried out its task gallantly, coming to the aid of HM 53rd and pushing the Sikh irregulars back. As Smith later recorded, 'this native corps nobly obeyed my orders'.[131]

In *Sikh Wars*, Cook describes the larger picture of the battle to perfection.

> Wilson's Brigade was originally deployed in dead ground, and the Sikh position came into view as it advanced. It then moved forward in a series of short rushes, doubling for some distance, then lying down, then doubling forward again, HM 53rd being directed on the village of Bhundri. The brigade received excellent support from Turton's and Alexander's troops of horse artillery, which kept well forward on its flank. HM 53rd, which attributed its slight losses to its method of advance, stormed into Bhundri and soon cleared the village. Between it and the river were drawn up the Avitabile battalions [Fauj-e-Khas Brigade under Jodha Ram]. The British cavalry, who

> had earlier brushed aside the Sikh Horse opposing them, now threatened them. The leading squadron of the 3rd Light Cavalry, sheered off at the sight of the Sikh regular units, which had thrown themselves into a square, but a squadron of HM 16th Lancers led by Captain Bere and another by Captain Fyler charged the square and went right through it. The square had barely time to recover before the squadrons turned around and charged through it again.

As Cunningham puts it in his book, 'The charge was wisely planned and bravely made, but the ground was more thickly strewn with the bodies of victorious horseman than of beaten infantry'.

Cook continues,

> Meanwhile, the remaining two squadrons of the 16th Lancers, led by Major Smyth and Captain Meick, were ordered to charge a strong battery which was still engaging the British troops. While this was going on, the 30th NI, which had been on the left of HM 53rd and had driven through to the river, was now ordered to wheel and attack the Avitabile squares – Jodha Ram's regular brigade. It carried out its task by striking the Sikh square in the flank, and forcing it to give way. These troops, apart as usual from the Sikh gunners, seem to have been the only units prepared to fight to the last. The rest of the Sikh forces stampeded for the ford, only the Avitabile battalions, Jodha Ram's regulars, holding together in some form of order. The 53rd, in strong support of the 30th NI, streamed in among the fugitives. Few of those who failed to escape across the ford survived and victory was complete.

Pushed against the river, the Sikh Army tried to cross by boat or foot, only to be engaged by all the guns that could be brought to bear – in particular, the 8in howitzers, which caused the most damage. The Sikh artillery commander had unlimbered 9 guns to cover the withdrawal. Having fired one salvo, however, the gunners joined the withdrawing mass of Ranjodh Singh's army. Having reached the opposite bank, the fleeing forces tried to regroup, but the lack of command and the continuous fire prevented that from happening. The battle of Aliwal ended as darkness engulfed the field at 5.30 p.m., having started that morning at 10 a.m.

Fifty-four Sikh guns were taken, 11 sunk in the river and 2, which were positioned on the opposite bank, were spiked by a party sent across for this purpose. In total, the Sikhs lost 67 guns. Their camp, supplies and animals were also taken. The cost to Harry Smith was 151 men killed, 413 wounded and 25 missing, which added up to 589 in all. The Sikh casualties were put at 3,000 – a figure that is difficult to accept. Even though the guns fired continuously on the river as the army withdrew across it, the figure of 3,000 is, I believe, exaggerated. If we recall, the Sikh casualties were put at only 2,000 at Ferozshah, which was the heaviest engagement so far.

The most casualties taken by a British regiment was HM 16th Lancers, whose charge against the Sikh Ghorcharras, guns and a Sikh square cost them 2 officers and 57 men killed, and 6 officers and 77 men wounded – a total of 8 officers and 134 men. Sixty-six horses were killed and 35 wounded. In the infantry, HM 50th took 77 casualties, 10 officers and 67 men.

Once again, the Sikh leadership in the field was lacking. Lal Singh ran away at Mudki, Tej Singh abandoned the field at Ferozshah, and as Captain J.D. Cunningham, states in his *History of the Sikhs*, 'Ranjodh Singh Majithia abandoned the army after Smith's first charge at Aliwal and left the army to its own resources'. Ranjodh Singh had been in Tej Singh's wing at Ferozshah and had abandoned the field with Tej Singh on the second day of the battle. Once again he chose the same path as his commander-in-chief, then at Ferozshah. Major Mackeson, also of the same agency, substantiates this in a letter to Frederick Currie, secretary to government, with this remark: 'However well a force without leaders may defend itself in its trenches, when required to move or manoeuvre in the plain without a directing head, it will be completely helpless and at our mercy.'[132]

According to the official report of Punjab Intelligence, Tej Singh wrote to Harry Smith just prior to Aliwal, 'I don't wish to fight, and will not, and will be willing to come to terms, but the men do not obey my orders'.[133]

Ranjodh Singh Majithia cannot have known of the Lahore Durbar's conspiracy to decimate its own army. Knowledge of this decision was restricted to Maharani Jinda Kaur, the C-in-C Tej Singh, and the wazir Lal Singh. In all probability, it was Ranjodh Singh's timidity that forced him to act in the manner he did. He was not an experienced or even a well-known Sikh general, and had not taken part in any previous battle. Why he was given the important task of cutting the British supply lines is not known. Perhaps his appointment fitted the larger game plan, to put a timid general in command without an adequate force to carry out his orders. He opted out of attacking Harry Smith while he was at Badhowal, when Smith was at his most vulnerable with an exhausted army. One cannot, however, agree with Harry Smith who later recorded: 'He should have attacked me with the vigour his French tutors would have displayed and destroyed me, for his force compared to mine was overwhelming.' This is not correct. Until the time that Jodha Ram's regular brigade of three infantry battalions and one cavalry regiment, with 18 guns, joined him at Aliwal, Ranjodh Singh's comprised one regular brigade of two regular battalions and 12 guns. The remainder of his army was composed entirely of the Fauj-e-Gair irregulars. At the battle of Aliwal, after being reinforced twice, Harry Smith's army was superior both in strength and composition as the above order of battle indicates.

After the battle, Wheeler's Brigade remained near the Aliwal ford. Harry Smith took his division back to join the main army at Sultan Khan

THE BATTLE OF ALIWAL, 28 JANUARY 1846

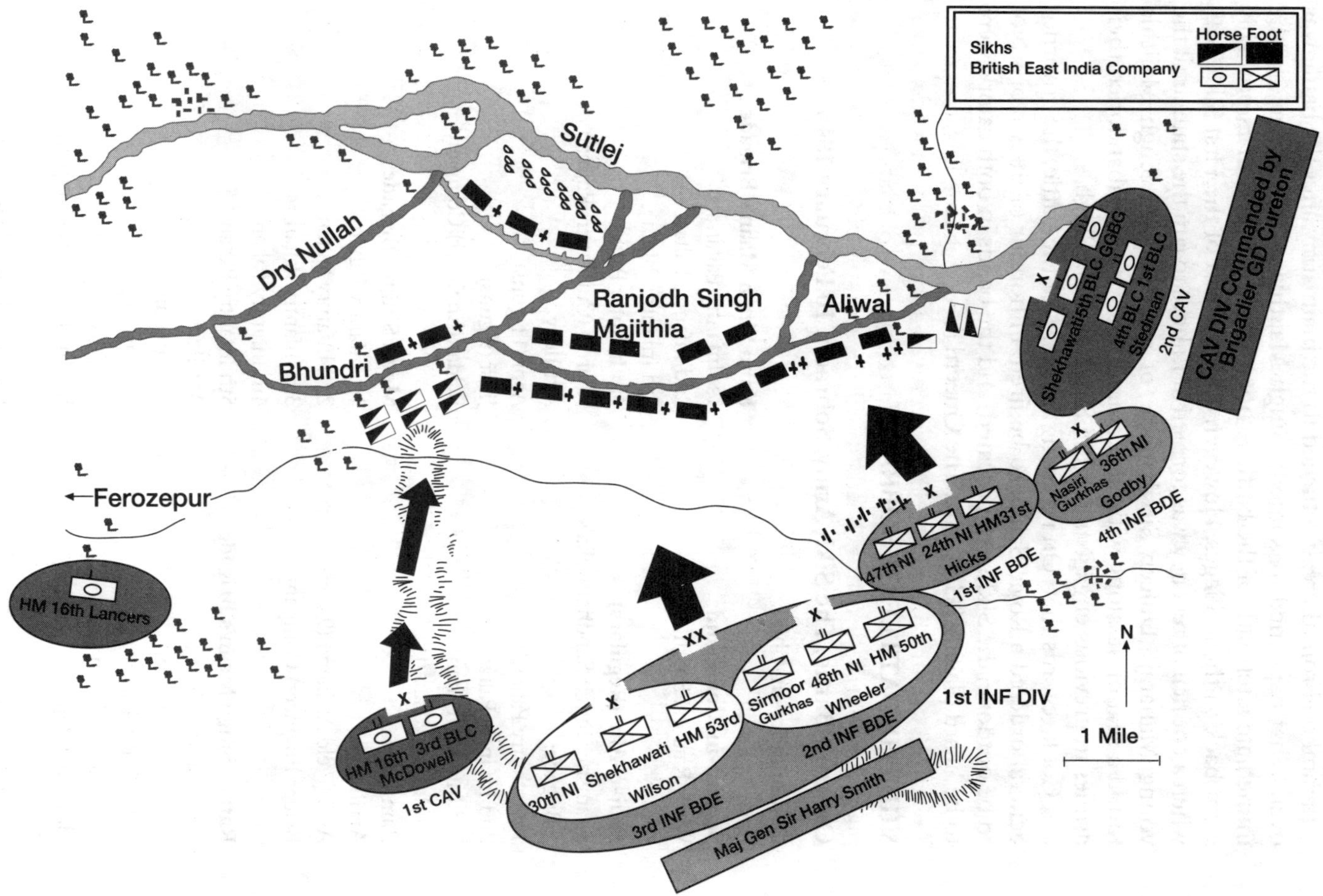

Wala, while Taylor's Brigade, which had been sent forward by Gough to further reinforce Harry Smith prior to the battle, reached as far as Dharamkot. From there, it returned to the main army after the battle was over. What happened to Ranjodh Singh Majithia, or to his army, in the immediate aftermath of the battle is not known. The irregulars probably went back to their villages. However, after the end of the First Sikh War, when a council of regency was formed at Lahore to run the state until the young Maharaja Duleep Singh came of age, Ranjodh Singh Majithia found a seat on it, along with his compatriots who had abandoned their armies in previous engagements, Tej Singh and Lal Singh.

Cook records that 'On receiving the news of the battle, the governor general ordered a Royal Salute to be fired, in honour of the victory. Not to be outdone, the Sikhs reciprocated, and the bands in both camps were to be heard playing "God Save The Queen!"'.

VIII. THE BATTLE OF SOBRAON

Order of Battle, The Sikh Army, Sobraon, 10 February 1846 [134]

Commander-in-Chief:
Raja Tej Singh
Second-in-Command:
Wazir Raja Lal Singh

Fauj-e-Ain: (Regulars)
Shamsher Singh Sandhanwalia's Brigade:
1st Infantry Paltan
2nd Infantry Paltan
3rd Infantry Paltan
4th Infantry Paltan
Ram Rajman
Artillery
Aspi (Field Artillery) (9 guns)
Beldar Engineer) Company

Rattan Singh Maan's Brigade
1st Infantry Paltan
2nd Infantry Paltan
3rd Infantry Paltan
4th Infantry Paltan
Hazooree Rajman
Artillery
Aspi (12 guns)
Jinsi (9 guns)
Beldar (Engineer) Company

Kahn Singh Maan's Brigade
1st Infantry Paltan
2nd Infantry Paltan
3rd Infantry Paltan
4th Infantry Paltan
Allard's (Cuirassier) Rajman
Artillery
Aspi (11 guns)
Jinsi (9 guns)
Beldar (Engineer) Company

Mewa Singh's Brigade
1st Infantry Paltan
2nd Infantry Paltan
3rd Infantry Paltan
4th Infantry Paltan
5th Infantry Paltan
Artillery
Aspi (9 guns)
1st Jinsi (9 guns)
2nd Jinsi (9 guns)
Beldar (Engineer) Company

Fauj-e-Khas Brigade: (remnants)
Paltan Khas
Gurkha Paltan

Dewa Singh Paltan
Sham Sota Paltan
Dragoon Rajman
Horse Grenadier Rajman
Shadi Lal's Risala (Jagirdari)
Artillery (Detached, see below)
Beldar (Engineer) Company

Mehtab Singh's Brigade (remnants)
1st Infantry Paltan
2nd Infantry Paltan
3rd Infantry Paltan
4th Infantry Paltan
Lancia (Lancer) Rajman
Artillery (no longer present)
Beldar (Engineer) Company

Bahadur Singh's Brigade (remnants)
1st Infantry Paltan
2nd Infantry Paltan
3rd Infantry Paltan
4th Infantry Paltan
Akal Cavalry Rajman
Artillery (no longer present)
Beldar (Engineer) Company

Jiwan Singh Toshakhania's Brigade
1st Infantry Paltan
2nd Infantry Paltan
Artillery
Aspi (360) (12 guns)
Jinsi (270) (9 guns)

Fauj-e-Gair: (Militia)
Ghorcharra Cavalry Brigades:
Derah Ardalian:
Ghorcharras
Mohamed Shah's Zambooraks
Derah Khas: (no details available)
Naulakha Kalan Derah:
Ghorcharras
Abdur Ramin's Zambooraks
Naulakha Khurd Derah:
Ghorcharras
Pindiwala Derah:
Ghorcharras
Raja Lal Singh's Sowar Derah:
Ghorcharras
Jalal Din's Zambooraks
Sandhanwalia Derah
Ghorcharras (888)
Sardar Mangal Singh's Derah
Ghorcharras (992)
Jagirdari Cavalry Regiments:
Ganda Singh Kunjahia's Sowar Regiment
Mandi Derah
Sardar Attar Singh's & Chattar Singh's Kalianwala's Sowar Regiment
Kanah Singh Khosia's Derah (549)
Bohkan Khan's Sowar Regiment (349)
Bela Singh's Sowar Regiment (478)
Sardar Tej Bahadur's and Sardar Krishan Singh's Sowar Regiment (360)
Kanah Singh Majithia's Derah (549)
Sham Singh's Attariwala's Sowar Regiment (599)
Bohkan Khan's Sowar Regiment (349)
Bela Singh's Sowar Regiment (478)
Sardool Singh Man's Sowar Regiment (472)
Rattan Singh Ghurjakia's Sowar Regiment (720)
Gulab Singh Kanhiya's Derah (476)
Shamser Singh's Sandhanwalia's Sowar Regiment (392)
Lachi Ram's Sowar Regiment (314)
Partap and Thakar Singh's Sowar Regiment (385)
Ganda and Nihal Singh's Sowar Regiment (629)
Hukam Singh Malwai's Sowar Regiment (100)

State Artillery
Topkhana of Sultan Mahmood:
Bakhtwar Khan's Battery (390) (13 guns)
Mohamed Bakhsh Khan's Battery (360) (12 guns)
Lal Jawahir Mal's Artillery Brigade:
Ishwar Khan's Jinsi (300) (10 guns)
Imamj Shah's Jinsi (390) (13 guns)

Khair Ali Khan's Artillery Brigade:
Ghubar Khan's Battery (360) (12 guns)
General Ilahi Bakhsh's Detachment:
(from Fauj-e-Khas Brigade)
Jinsi #1 (Mixed Horse and Field guns)
Fateh Din Khan's Howitzer Derah
Jinsi (360)(12 guns)
Tara Singh's Howitzer Derah
Jinsi (360)(12 guns)
Jai Singh's Howitzer Derah
Jinsi (360)(12 guns)

Source: Dewan Ajudhia Parshad, *Waqai-Jang-i-Sikhan*: *Events of the First Anglo-Sikh War* 1845-46. V.S. Suri (tr) Chandigarh: Punjab Itihas Prakashan, 1975.
Sikh Army List (Compiled from Bajwa and other sources)

Order of Battle, Army of the Sutlej, Sobraon, 10 February 1846[135]

Commander-in-Chief:
General Sir Hugh Gough
Personal Staff:
Military Secretary
Captain F.P. Haines (Wounded)
Captain the Honorable C.R. Sackville-West (AMS)
Persian Interpreter
Lt Col Henry Havelock, CB
Personal Medical Officer
Assistant Surgeon J.E. Stephens, MD
Aides-de-Camp
Lt Bagot
Lt Edwards
Cornet Lord James Brown
Governor General of India
Lt General Sir Henry Hardinge
Personal Staff
Military Board
Colonel Benson
Military Secretary: Lt Col Wood

Political Agent
Major Lawrence
Secretary to Government (political)
F. Currie, Esq.
Private Secretary
C. Hardinge, Esq.
Assistant Political Agents
Captain Mills (Honorary ADC)
Captain Cunningham, BE
R. Cust, Esq.

Judge Advocate General
Assistant Adjutant General
Major Patrick Grant
Deputy Assistant Adjutant General:
Captain Anson
Captain Tucker
Deputy Commissary General
Lt Col Parsons
Assistant Commissary General
Major W.J. Thompson, CB
Deputy Assistant Commissary General Major Curtis
Lt Col Birch
Attached:
Field Surgeon J. Steele, MD
Aides-de-Camp
Captain Grant
Lord Arthur Hay
Captain Peel
Captain Hardinge
Personal Surgeon
Dr Walker
Army Staff
Acting Quartermaster General (Officiating)
Lt Col J.B. Gough, CB
Assistant Quartermaster General
Lt Col Garden
Deputy Quartermaster General
Lt Col Drummond, CB
Surgeon Graham, MD
Foreign Military Observers

Prince Waldemar of Prussia
Count Oriola
Count Grueben
Postmaster:
Lieutenant Sandys
Superintending Surgeon
Surgeon B. MacLeod, MD
Deputy Assistant Quartermaster General
Lt Arthur Beecher
Acting Adjutant General: (Officiating) Lt Col M. Barr

1st Infantry Division
Major General Sir Harry Smith, KCB
Deputy Assistant Adjutant General:
Lt A.S. Galloway
ADC
Lieutenant E.A. Holdich
1st Infantry Brigade
Brigadier (Lt Col) George Hicks
Brigade Major:
Lt Robert Hay / Captain Combe
HM 50th Foot – Brevet Lt Col Thomas Ryan, CB/Lt Col P.J. Petit
42nd BNI – Major T. Polwhele
2nd Infantry Brigade
Brigadier (Lt Col) Nicholas Penny
Brigade Major:
Captain J. Garvock
HM 31st Foot – Lt Col Spence
47th BNI Regiment – Captain Corfield
Nasiri Gurkha's – Captain C. O'Brien

2nd Infantry Division
Major General Sir Walter Raleigh Gilbert
Assistant Adjutant General:
Captain R. Houghton
Deputy Assistant Quartermaster General: (Officiating)
Lt T.S. Rawson
ADC: Lt F. MacDonald Gilbert
3rd Infantry Brigade
Brigadier (Lt Col) Charles Cyril Taylor, CB, HM 29th Foot
Brigade Major:
Captain A.G. Ward
HM 29th Foot – Captain Stepney
41st BNI – Major Sibbald
68th BNI – Brevet Major Marshall
4th Infantry Brigade:
Brigadier (Lt Col) James McClaren, CB
Brigade Major:
Lt G.H.M. Jones
1st Bengal European Light Infantry – Major Birrell
Sirmoor Gurkha's – Captain J. Fisher /Lt Reid
16th NI (Bombay Grenadiers) – Brevet Major Graves

3rd Infantry Division
Major General Sir Robert Henry Dick, KCB, KCH
Deputy Assistant Adjutant General:
Captain J.R. Pond
Deputy Assistant Quartermaster General (Officiating)
Lt J.S. Paton
ADC: Lt R. Bates
5th Infantry Brigade:
Brigadier (Lt Col) the Honorable Thomas Ashburnham
Brigade Major:
Captain J.L. Taylor
HM 9th Foot – Lt Col Davis
HM 62nd Foot – Major Shrtt
26th BNI – Major Hanscombe
One Company, Bengal Sappers and Miners (attached)
6th Infantry Brigade:
Brigadier (Lt Col) Wilkinson
Brigade Major: Captain Gordon
HM 80th Foot – Lt Col Bunbury
33rd BNI – Captain Sandeman
63rd BNI
7th Infantry Brigade:
Brigadier (Lt Col) Stacy, CB and Brigadier (Lt Col) Orchard, CB

Brigade Major: Lt H.F. Dunsford
HM 10th Foot – Lt Col Franks
HM 53rd Foot – Lt Col Phillips
43rd BNI – Brevet Lt Col Nash
59th BNI – Brevet Lt Col Thompson

4th Infantry Division (Minus)
Major General Sir John Grey CB
1st Task: (To hold Atari, and to watch the fords west of Sabraon)
8th BLC
45th BNI – Captain Short
41st BNI
68th BNI
2nd Task: (To hold the ford at Harike)
59th BNI – Lt Col Thompson
Brigadier Wheeler (To hold Ludhiana and to watch the fords in its vicinity)
48th BNI
Maj Gen Sir John Littler's Division (To hold Ferozepur City and the ford)
Cavalry Division
Major General Sir Joseph Thackwell, KCB
Deputy Assistant AG: Captain J. Tritton
Deputy Assistant QM
Captain C.F. Havelock
ADC Lt T.J. Francis
1st Cavalry Brigade:
Brigadier (Lt Col) T. Scott, CB
Brigade Major:
Brevet Captain T.L. Harrington
HM 3rd Light Dragoon's – Lt Col Michael White, CB
8th Bengal Irregular Horse
9th Bengal Irregular Horse – Captain Christie

2nd Cavalry Brigade
Brigadier (Lt Col) Alexander M. Campbell, CB KH
Brigade Major:
Captain A. Spottiswoode
HM 9th Lancer – Lt Col Fullerton
2nd Bengal Irregular Cavalry – Captain Leeson
2 Troops HA
4th Cavalry Brigade:
Brigadier (Lt Col) Charles Robert Cureton, CB
Brigade Major:
Lt R. Pattinson
HM 16th Lancers – Captain Pearson
3rd BLC – Major Angelo
4th Bengal Irregular Cavalry
5th BLC
Army Artillery
Brigadier (Lt Col) G.E. Gowan, CB, Commander 2nd Brigade, BHA
Deputy Assistant Adjutant General
Captain E. Christie
Deputy Assistant Quartermaster General
Lt H.H. Maxwell
Commissaries of Ordnance:
Captain Pillans
Brevet Captain W.K. Warner
Bengal Horse Artillery
Brigadier (Lt Col) E. Biddulph, 2nd BHA
2nd Company 6th Battalion Bengal Artillery (#9HFB)
4th Company, 6th Battalion, Bengal Artillery (#19 LFB)
Major of Brigade: Captain EG Austen
Brevet Lt Col J.T. Lane's Troop, BHA (2/3)
Captain E.F. Day's Troop, BHA (5[N]/1)
Brevet Lt Col J. Alexander's Troop, BHA (3/2)
Captain Hubert Garbett's Troop, BHA (4[N]/1)
Captain H.G. Swinley's Troop, BHA (3/1)
Captain J. Turton's Troop, BHA (1/2)
Brevet Major G. Campbell's Troop, BHA (3/3)
Captain R. Waller's Troop, BHA (2/1)
Brevet Major Frederick Brind's Troop

BHA (1/3)
Brevet Major C. Grant's Troop, BHA (2/2)
Horse Artillery Troops
1st Troop, 2nd BHA
3rd Troop, 2nd BHA
2nd Troop, 3rd BHA
3rd Troop, 3rd BHA
Bengal Foot Artillery
Brigadier (Lt Col) G.G. Denisss
Major of Brigade:
1st Lieutenant E. Kaye
Special Purpose Batteries:
Brigadier (Lt Col) George "Bully" Brooke
Major of Brigade
Brevet Captain Murray Mackenzie
Superintendence: Brigadier Biddulph
Mortar Battery – Lt Col Wood
6 x 8in
5 x 5.5in
18 Pndr Battery (5) - Major G.S. Lawrenson manned by:
2nd Company, 2nd Battalion, BA
Lt J.A. Angelo
3rd Company, 3rd Battalion, BA
Captain E.P. Master
4th Company, 3rd Battalion, BA
Captain J. Anderson
2nd Company, 4th Battalion, BA Lt.
HR Countenay
Howitzer Battery (6 x10in)
Brigadier Deniss (manned by 1/3BHA)
8" Howitzer Troop (8) - Lt. Colonel Edward Huthwaite (manned by 2/1 & 3/1, BHA)
Independent Artillery Units
Rocket Troop – Lt Col W. Geddes (manned by 2/1, BHA)
12-pndr Elephant Battery (12) – Captain EF Day (Manned by 4[N]/1 & 5[N]/1)
Heavy Field Battery – Brevet Major C. Grant (2/2) 4 x 24 pndr howitzers x 9 pndr cannon
#9 Heavy Field Battery – Captain R. Horsford/Lt. T.E. Kennion
#19 Light Field Battery – Captain Fordyce including
Engineers:
Brigadier (Lt Col) Smith, CB
Bengal Sappers and Mineers – Major BY Relly
Bridge, Park and Train – Major F. Abbot
Along as Observers:
Brigadier (Lt Col) Irvine RE:
Brigade Major, RE:
Major Charles Napier
The Governor General's Escort
Governor General's Bodyguard – Brevet Captain Quin
Detached Troops:
(Rodawalla-baggage protection)
73rd BNI
Army Reserve
4th BNI
5th BNI

Sources: *Artillery*, Vol 3
Hughes, MG BP. *The Bengal Horse Artillery*
Official despatches, *The First Sikh War*
Wylly, Memoris, Thackwell Angelsey, *Marquess of, History of the British Cavalry*, Volume 1
Featherstone, Victorian Colonial Warfare – *India – At them with the Bayonet*
Fortescue, *History of the British Army*, Vol. 12
Stubbs, *History of the Bengal Cavalry*
Bruce, G. *Six Battles for India*
Gough/Innes, *The Sikh Wars*

After the battle of Ferozshah, on 21 and 22 December, the Sikh encampments south of the Sutlej had been abandoned. The army had withdrawn north of the river, except for a defensive enclave that had been maintained south of the river at Sobraon. At the time of the battle of Ferozshah, Sobraon had been occupied, and a defensive position was being prepared there under the supervision of a Spanish engineer Colonel Huberon, assisted by Colonel Mouton, a French cavalry officer of the Napoleonic army, who was now with the Sikhs. Although Cunningham says in his book that these two officers were too junior to influence the building of these entrenchments, they were professionally built, and achieved their task in holding back the British brigades until they were finally breached by the engineers. Besides, Mouton could not have been that junior because during the battle he held one of the four sectors at Sobraon. Huberon also held the same rank of colonel, and both were trained professionals.

At the junction of Punjab's two major rivers, the Sutlej and Beas, and 11 miles upstream of Sobraon lay Harike – Ferozepur was a further 21 miles downstream. The village of Sobraon was north of the Sutlej. Another breakaway portion of this village, called Chota Sobraon, lay south of the river with the river Sutlej between them. At this point, there was a prominent bend where the Sikh defences were positioned. The fortifications were to the south of it, spanning the bend in a three-mile semicircle, with both ends extending to the river. The front of the fortifications faced south, with the river to the rear, and a ford about 400 yards wide. Anticipating normal winter rains, during which period the river was usually full, this defensive position was also linked to the northern bank by a bridge of boats.

In *Sikh Wars*, Cook describes the Sikh deployments as follows:

> The Sikh position lay across a bend of the River Sutluj and was shaped like a bow, with both flanks "refused" towards the river, more particularly on the right, where the line of entrenchments reached the bank very nearly at a right angle to the front. There were three lines of defences, the front line on the left and centre being based upon a ditch and a bank about 10ft high, well riveted with wood. To the right, however, where the ground was much sandier, the defences were less formidable and the bank only reached a height of 6ft. There were also deep ditches below the banks [as per Bruce in his book, *Six Battles for India*, the walls of the entrenchments at this front were 10–12ft). In addition to the ford, the position had been linked with the far bank by a bridge of boats. On the far side of the river, where the banks were much higher, the Sikhs had massed artillery to cover both flanks of their position and enfilade any attack upon them. In view of the fact that their right was obviously the most vunerable part of their defences, it is somewhat surprising that they concentrated

> their irregular troops on that flank (including 200 Zambooraks) and held the centre and left with regular units, massing also the main part of their artillery in the centre.

After the battle of Ferozshah, Hardinge and Gough had decided not to take offensive action against the Sikhs, unless they provoked one, till the arrival of the siege train. This was on its way from Delhi with the large-calibre guns, reinforcements, ammunition, and supplies. As we know, Ranjodh Singh Majithia had in the meantime made an unsuccessful attempt to intercept the siege train, culminating in the battle of Aliwal. The train finally lumbered into Gough's camp, which had moved to Nihalke close to Sobraon, on 7 February. They now had all the heavy guns and reserves of ammunition, except the 24-pounders, which lagged behind because of their size and weight.

While waiting for the train to arrive, the British officers felt bored with nothing to do. As a remark of Herbert Edwards, ADC to Gough reveals, the army was becoming impatient and, 'was sickening from want of a battle; a malignant fever of epidemic horrors must have broken out at Sobraon had it been delayed another week'.[136] To relieve that boredom, they now indulged in one of their favourite sports, which was pig-sticking, as there were numerous wild boar in the sarkanda reeds along the river. The Sikhs sportingly held their fire and encouraged them on.

Other than on such occasions, Sikh snipers continued to be active. In the defended area of the HM 80th, a tall tower afforded a good target to any one climbing it to look at the Sikh position. Therefore, the sentries were told to warn people off if they intended climbing it. An amusing anecdote recorded a time when Gough came to take a look one day and, after the sentry had remonstrated agitatedly with him several times, replied, 'Sure, my good man, aren't I the commander-in-chief and can't I do what I like?'

In a letter to Gough dated 13 January, the governor general had earlier authorized the movement of 13 24-pounders, 5 18-pounders, 6 10in howitzers and a 8in howitzer, with 500 charges per gun, along with 27,000 rounds for the existing 9 and 6-pounders. In the letter, he had also confirmed their decision that, 'no movement across the Sutluj towards Lahore can be made before the arrival of these guns', and also reiterated their resolve that, 'the existence of the Sikh Army on its present Republican system cannot be permitted to remain as it is'.

At Lahore, Gulab Singh had finally been persuaded to return and on his arrival on 27 January was appointed wazir. The following day, on 28 January, Ranjodh Singh was defeated at Aliwal.

> The representatives of the Khalsa had earlier implored the Raja, whose military skill was considerable, to lead them against the enemy, but according to British spies at the court, Gulab Singh merely taunted them for their stupidity in fighting allies to whom Ranjit

> Singh had been loyal for more than a quarter of a century. "I refrained from joining you against the English when you first crossed the Sutluj," he told them. "Why should I help you now when you face certain defeat?" When they offered to murder Lal Singh and Tej Singh and make him Commander-in-Chief instead, he merely laughed at them.[137]

At the same time, Gulab Singh opened communications with the British through an emissary, Doctor Bansi Lal Ghose, making the following requests: to confirm him and his family forever in possession of their present estates and lands, and to leave him in possession of all the territories then under his rule (which included Kashmir), contenting themselves with a tribute of four annas in every rupee of revenue. Hardinge was quite prepared to negotiate with the Lahore Durbar while Gulab Singh represented it, since he believed that with the summer fast approaching, it would be more prudent to resolve the position through negotiations. The unbearable heat through the summer months all but ruled out the possibility of laying siege to the principal cities of Lahore, Amritsar, Multan and Peshawar. He also felt that a prolonged campaign could have political repercussions in other parts of India.

> Negotiations with Gulab Singh were therefore opened. It was made clear to him, that provided the Khalsa was disbanded, or greatly reduced in strength, Sikh sovereignty in Lahore would still be acknowledged. According to Punjab Intelligence, Gulab Singh then ordered the Khalsa at Sobraon to withdraw north across the Sutluj into Lahore territory. His order caused much uncertainty and low morale, and it was not obeyed. So Gulab Singh let the British know he could not control the Khalsa. It was, therefore, agreed that the Sikhs should be attacked and beaten by the British, who would then cross the Sutluj and advance on Lahore without opposition, the Khalsa being refused [additional] arms and [was] ordered to stay where it was at Sobraon, more or less disowned by its own government. A few days later what were said to be plans of the Sikh defences around Sobraon found their way into the hands of Major Lawrence.[138]

Captain Cunningham adds in his *History of the Sikhs,*

> It was under such circumstances of discreet policy and shameless treason that the battle of Sobraon was fought [...] Hearts to dare and hands to execute were numerous, but there was no mind to guide and animate the whole: each inferior commander defended his front according to his skill and means [...]

In their defensive position, the Sikh regular units and artillery were massed in the centre along with Mehtab Singh Majithia, who had earlier commanded his brigade with distinction at Ferozshah. Sardar Sham Singh Attari commanded the left flank and Colonel Mouton, who also commanded the irregular cavalry, the right. Tej Singh was in overall command and was positioned within the defensive perimeter, between the second and third line of entrenchments. Lal Singh commanded the major part of the cavalry across the river on the north bank. 'The position allowed the Sikhs no room to manoeuvre, and should they have to retreat, the river behind them was danger, despite the boat bridge.'[139]

The Sikh defences were based on eight brigades of the regular army. Of these, three were below strength – the Fauj-e-Khas, Mehtab Singh Majithia's and Bahadur Singh's brigades – having taken part in the battle of Ferozshah where Bahadur Singh had been killed. None of them had their complement of guns with them, having lost them at Ferozshah. The total strength within the Sobraon defended sector was put at 20,000 men, of which 15,000 were combatants and 67 guns, all Aspi or Jinsi.

The artillery detachment of the Fauj-e-Khas, under General Illahi Bakhsh, had lost its guns at Ferozshah. As he was detached from his parent brigade, the Fauj-e-Khas at Sobraon, and is listed under the army artillery, he was probably commanding a detachment of heavy artillery on the north bank under Lal Singh. The total number of Sikh guns deployed in the battle, both north and south of the river, were reported to be 103, of which 36, mostly of heavy calibre, belonged to the army artillery, which were deployed on the north bank. Various accounts put the guns within the Sobraon defended sector at 67 (the number captured), but the formation-wise artillery detachments of the five intact Sikh brigades as per their order of battle, add up to 98 guns within the Sobraon enclave. As the British took only 67 guns, this figure is most likely correct as the Sikhs removed no guns from the enclave during or after the battle. It is also possible that some of the guns of these brigades may have been withdrawn before the battle, to strengthen other formations not deployed at Sobraon. This is substantiated by article 8 of the Treaty of Lahore, entered into on 9 March 1846, which states: 'The Maharaja will surrender to the British government all the guns, 36 in number, which have been pointed against the British troops, and which, having been placed on the right bank of the River Sutluj, were not captured at the battle of Sobraon.' The 67 within the defended sector and the 36 on the north bank add up to 103 guns. Despite Hardinge's reservations to the contrary, the delay in the arrival of the heavy 24in guns persuaded Gough to attack on Tuesday 10 January. Hardinge earlier felt that a sizeable force should cross the river west of Harike, at the ford at Ganda Singh Wala, and then turn left and hit the defences on the northern bank. Doing that would isolate the Sikh defensive enclave south of the river. Gough disagreed, siting Sikh vigilance and the fact that, if warned in time, the Sikh regular cavalry with Lal Singh on the north bank could effectively oppose such a river crossing. On the other hand, if an unopposed crossing was successful, the Sikh

Army on the north bank could then easily fall back on Lahore, and the war would then become a series of sieges, which Hardinge was already vehemently opposed to.

Hardinge now consulted all the artillery officers present at Sobraon on Gough's decision to carry out a heavy bombardment and then make a frontal attack. Even though he continued to remain Gough's second-in-command, he again decided, as he had done at Ferozshah, to exercise his prerogative as governor general to take the final decision. Finally, he gave Gough his approval. This decision was conveyed to Gough, who was already fuming with frustration, through a letter that read, 'Upon the fullest consideration of this question, if the artillery can be brought into play, I recommend you to attack. If it cannot and you anticipate a heavy loss, I would recommend you not to undertake it,'[140] – a complete hands-off decision, which Gough readily accepted.

Gough decided to make the main thrust against the Sikh right, commanded by Colonel Mouton, because it was held by irregular forces and he considered it the weakest point of the Sikh defensive position. Simultaneously, he would initially feign attacks upon the Sikh centre and left. Reveille was at midnight and at 1 a.m., the troops were roused and given their breakfast and a stiff ration of rum. The columns began to form at 2 a.m., and at 3 a.m. the formations marched in the dark to their respective positions – their difficulties of marching in the dark being further compounded by mist.

Gough's deployment was made more difficult by two villages – Rodawala and Kodiwala, which were on high ground in line with the left centre of his deployment and around 2,500 yards from the Sikh position. Both were also Sikh outposts. Chota Sobraon lay closer to the Sikh position, around 500 yards from the Sikh lines and to the right of Gough's line of deployment. To maintain secrecy about their deployment and intentions, it became necessary to take the two villages. Therefore, two companies of HM 62nd were sent on the night of 9 and 10 February to attack and occupy Rodawala and Kodiwala. Approaching them in a silent march, they found them unoccupied. Gough knew the past practice of the Sikhs, which was similar to that of the British, to withdraw their outposts at sunset and send them forward again at dawn. Because the Sikhs knew that they would be attacked, Gough had presumed they would maintain their outpost in these two villages on a 24-hour basis.

Gough had now firmed up his plans and had decided that the attack would need to be made by three divisions: Harry Smith's 1st Division on the right, facing the Sikh left under Sham Singh Attari; Sir Walter Raleigh Gilbert's 2nd Division in the centre, opposite Court and Mehtab Singh Majithia; and Robert Dick's 3rd Division, on the left opposite Mouton. As he elaborated in his *Despatches*, Gough describes his deployment as,

> On our left, two brigades of Major-General Dick's division, under his personal command, stood ready to commence the assault against the

THE BATTLE OF SOBRAON, 10 FEBRUARY 1846

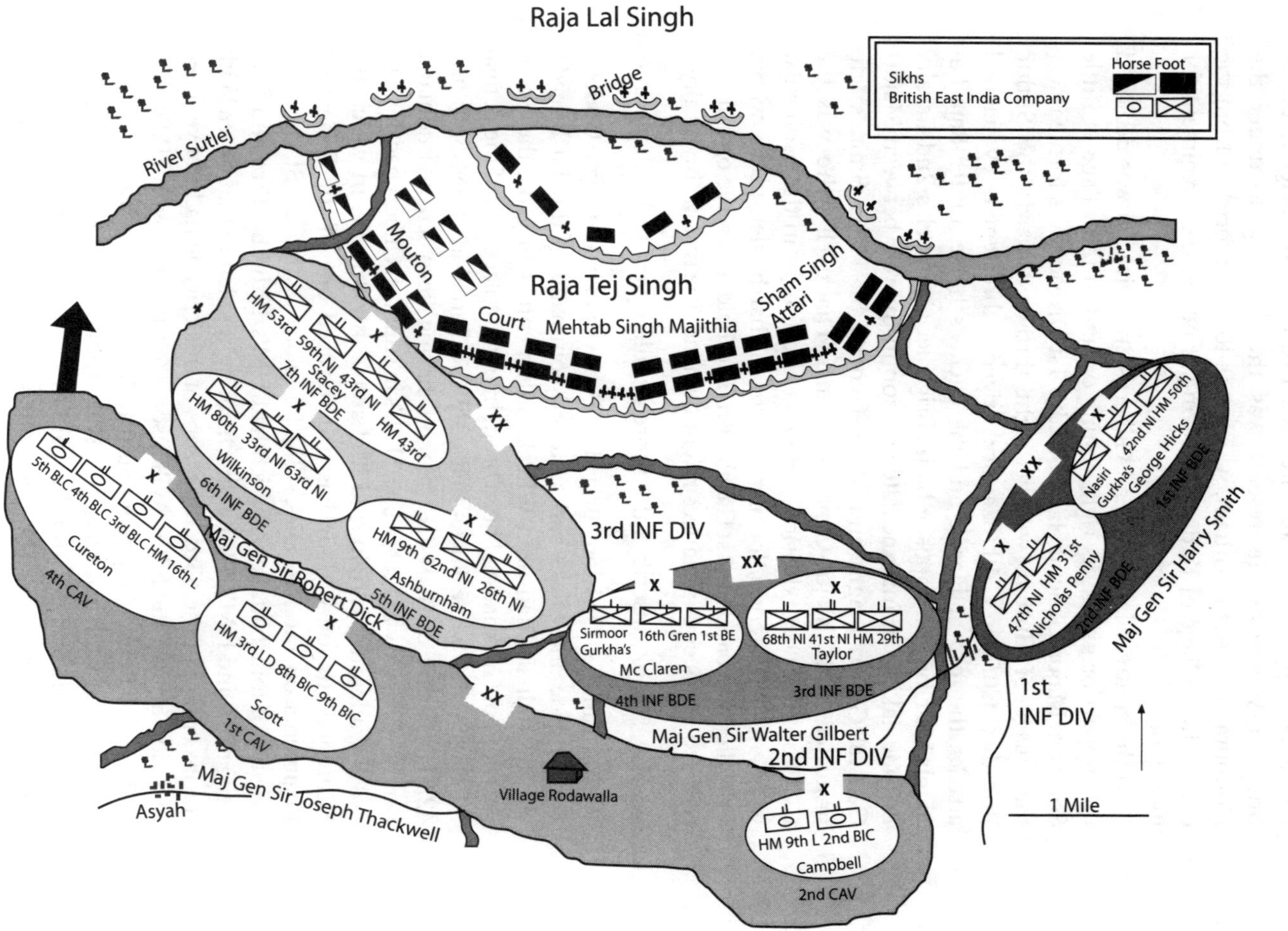

> enemy's extreme right. His 7th Brigade, in which was the 10th Foot, reinforced by the 53rd Foot and led by Brigadier Stacey, was to head the attack, supported, at 200 yards distance, by the 6th Brigade, under Brigadier Wilkinson. In reserve was the 5th Brigade under the Honourable T. Ashburnham, which was to move forward from the entrenched village of Kodiwala, leaving, if necessary, a regiment for its defence.
>
> In the centre, Major-General Gilbert's 2nd Division was deployed for support or attack, its right resting on and in the village of Little Sobraon. Major-General Harry Smith's 1st Division was formed near the village of Guttah, with its right thrown towards the Sutluj. Brigadier Cureton's 4th Cavalry Brigade, threatened, by feigned attacks, the ford at Harike and the enemy's horse, under Raja Lal Singh Misr, on the opposite bank. Brigadier Campbell's 2nd Cavalry Brigade, taking an intermediate position in the rear between Major-General Gilbert's right and Major-General Sir Harry Smith's left, protected both. Major-General Thomas Thackwell (who was the GOC of the cavalry division, who had also fought in the peninsular wars and at Waterloo, loosing an arm in that battle), under whom Brigadier Scott and his 1st Cavalry Brigade, held in reserve on our left, ready to act as circumstances might demand, the rest of the cavalry.

In *Sikh Wars*, Cook describes the more detailed part of the deployment.

> Within Smith's Division, Brigadier Penny had taken over Godby's 2nd Brigade and Hicks had assumed command of the 1st Brigade, which originally had been Wheeler's. In Penny's Brigade, the Nasiri Battalion of Gurkhas had been brought in to replace one of the Bengal NI Regiments, while Hicks had only two battalions (HM 50th and 42nd NI), one of his NI Regiments having been left at Ludhiana. Penny's Brigade was first in line, Hick's in support. Gilbert had Taylor's 3rd Brigade on the right and McLaren's 4th Brigade, in which the Sirmoor Battalion of Gurkhas had replaced one of the Bengal NI Regiments on the left. Dick's 3rd Division was led by Stacey's 7th Brigade of four battalions, which had HM's 10th, the 43rd and 59th Bengal NI, and HM's 53rd in line from right to left in that order. With the exception of the 53rd, the troops of this brigade had not yet been in action against the Sikhs. Wilkinson's 6th Brigade, with HM's 80th and the two Bengal NI Regiments (the 33rd and 63rd), was in support, while further back in reserve was Ashburnham 5th Brigade with HM's 9th and 62nd and the 26th Bengal NI. This brigade was used in the initial stages to cover the deployment of the guns. Two other NI Regiments (the 4th and 5th NI) were also in reserve on this flank, while the 73rd Bengal NI was left at Rodawala. On Stacey's left, ready to exploit success, was Scott's 1st Cavalry Brigade with HM's 3rd Light Dragoons and the 3rd and 9th Irregular Cavalry.

The 9th Lancers, whose officers had substituted chain bridles for leather ones on learning that the 3rd Light Dragoons had had a number of their bridles cut away by talwars in the previous battles, were together with the 2nd Irregular Cavalry, positioned behind the hamlet of Chota Sobraon, which lay about 500 yards in front of the Sikh left, ready to support Smith or Gilbert. The remainder of the cavalry under Cureton was dispatched to watch the Hurrekee fords behind the British right flank, over which it would have been possible for Lall Singh to lead his Sikh cavalry against the British rear, once the troops were committed to the attack.

Just behind Chota Sobraon, between Smith and Gilbert, were eight heavy guns or howitzers, while a field battery was in the centre. Eight 8in howitzers supported the main attack. Six 10in howitzers and five 18-pounders, while to their left was a rocket battery. There were not enough men to man the heavier guns and, in consequence, gunners were drawn from the horse batteries, and their men also manned the rocket battery. This decreased the number of horse-artillery guns available to go forward with the advancing infantry, although the horse gunners were to revert to their proper role at a later stage of the battle.

Early on 10 February, heavy rain was followed by a mist that built up and remained until it was dissipated by the heat of the rising sun. Because of the rain, the river level also rose making it impassable, other than by the bridge or boats.

Gough had intended 'H' hour to be at dawn, which was at 6 a.m., but the thick mist delayed the moment of the guns opening fire. It was imperative for the gunners to see the fall of shot and correct their fire. While inconvenient in the approach and deployment of the army, the mist benefited Gough by concealing his movements. When the sun rose and the mist finally dissipated, the Sikhs were astonished to see Gough's army fully deployed opposite them.

Gough positioned three batteries of his heavy guns in support of Robert Dick's division to neutralize the Sikh right. There were six 18-pounders under Lt Col Lawrenson, six 10in howitzers under Brigadier Deniss and eight 8in howitzers under Lt Col Huthwaite. To their left forward was the rocket battery under Lt Col Geddes. The heavy guns were located about 1,300 yards from the Sikh position. The guns were in position, as was the army before first light, and the gunners awaited orders to open fire. The order to commence firing was finally given at 6.30 a.m.

The 1st European Infantry history records the event as:

> The rising sun rapidly dispelled the fog, when a magnificent picture presented itself. The batteries of artillery were seen in position ready to open fire and the plain was covered with our troops, the fortified village of Rodawala on our left being strongly held by our infantry.

> Immediately, the guns opened a heavy fire. The enemy appeared suddenly to realize their danger, their drums beat the alarm, their bugles sounded "To arms!" and in a few minutes their batteries were manned, and pouring shot and shell upon our troops.[141]

The bombardment continued for two hours, but appeared to be having little effect. The artillery officers had wanted to position their guns 600 yards closer to the Sikhs, behind parapets, but Gough had refused this. He reasoned that he would lose the element of surprise and put them in range of the Sikh artillery. At 1,300 yards his 18-pounders were only reaching the defensive parapets at extreme range and the howitzers had been fused to burst too early and were doing little damage. The Sikhs stood to their guns answering shot for shot and, as Cunningham writes,

> The round shot exploded tumbrels, or dashed heaps of sand into the air; the hollow shells cast their fatal contents fully before them, and the devious rockets sprang aloft with fury to fall hissing among a flood of men; but all was in vain, the Sikhs stood unappalled, and "flash for flash returned, and fire for fire".

Just then, the Sikh cavalry, Mouton's Irregulars, was seen to be preparing to charge the rocket battery. The rockets were directed towards this cavalry concentration, doing serious damage to men and horse and the cavalry withdrew.

Finally, the guns began to have some effect on the defences. Harry Smith wrote,

> To our astonishment, at the very moment of this success our fire slackened and soon ceased altogether, when it was ascertained that the ammunition was expended, the officer in command of the artillery not having brought half the quota into the field which was ordered by the Governor General and the Commander-in-Chief. Thus there was no time to be lost.

Only four rounds per gun were left. This was reported to the C-in-C at a little after 8.30 a.m. Gough ordered his nephew, Colonel J.B. Gough, quartermaster-general, to order General Sir Robert Dick to launch his attack at once on the Sikh right front. In face of this alarming news that reversed his plans, Gough's determination threatened the lives of thousands of his troops and put the outcome of the battle in doubt. The news also spread to the men, for reports agree that a rumour ran like lightening among the waiting red coats, 'that old Gough had been told that there were only four rounds left per gun, and says, "Thank God! Then I'll be at them with the bayonet".'[142]

In his *Despatch*, Gough says, 'The effect of the cannonade was, as has been since proved by an inspection of the camp, most severely felt by the enemy; but it soon became evident that the issue of this struggle must be brought to the arbitrement of musketry and the bayonet.'

Just then, Colonel Benson, one of Hardinge's staff officers, rode up to Gough with a message to say that if he didn't feel confident of success without great loss, he had better withdraw Sir Robert Dick's attack and instead work up the enemy's defences by regular approaches. Gough answered, 'Loss there will be, of course. Look at those works bristling with guns, and defended as they will be; but by God's blessing, I feel confident of success.'

Benson, nevertheless repeated the message and received the same answer. When he foolishly gave it the third time, Gough shouted, 'What! Withdraw the troops after the action has commenced, and when I feel confident of success. Indeed I will not. Tell Sir Robert Dick to move on, in the name of God!'

The order was conveyed to Dick at exactly 9 a.m. and he moved immediately.

Brigadier Stacy's 7th Brigade led Dick's 3rd Division on the Sikh right, about 2,000 yards to his front. Colonel Lane's troops of horse artillery and Captain's Horsford's and Fordyce's field batteries galloped forward, unlimbering at 800 yards and firing. They then moved forward again to within 300 yards of the Sikh position, supporting the infantry, HM's 10th and 53rd and the 59th and 43rd NIs with suppressive fire during their advance. Fortunately for Stacy, the Sikh guns were firing high and even though they changed to grape when the brigade came to within 500 yards of their guns, Stacy did not suffer many casualties. Many of HM 53rd fell to an enfilading Sikh battery firing from the north bank, but the line pressed on and stormed the Sikh right with their bayonets, pushing the gunners back to their inner line of trenches. At this point, HM 10th also suffered from a Sikh battery, which had swung its guns around and opened fire on them.

Generals Gilbert and Smith now launched their feints, but the Sikhs saw through them and instead rushed reinforcements to check Robert Dick's division that had penetrated their defences. Colonel Mouton launched a counterattack to clear Stacy's brigade from the foothold it had achieved and a fierce hand-to-hand battle ensued. While the desperate British looked over their shoulders to see whether the remaining two brigades of their division, the first about 400 yards behind them, were coming to their aid. Colonel Mouton pressed home his counterattack, firing volley after volley. At this moment, Brigadier Wilkinson and his brigade caught up with Stacy, and HM 80th also reached HM 10th, and both led by General Dick attempted to stabilize the position. When General Sir Robert Dick was killed with a bullet to the head, Stacy's brigade was finally dislodged and fell back. Gough's first attack had failed.

Meanwhile, Gough had ordered Smith and Gilbert to convert their feints into storming attacks. The troops moved forward, only to be halted by high, well-built ramparts, which Captain Cunningham describes as, 'higher and more continuous than the barriers which had foiled the first efforts of their comrades'.

On the Sikh's extreme left, Brigadier Penny's 1st Brigade led Harry Smith's division followed by Hick's 2nd Brigade. Penny met the same fate. Unable to cross the formidable height of the ramparts, the brigade fell back exhausted and retired through Hick's brigade, which was now moving into the attack. Once again, unable to cross the high ramparts and being under continuous fire from above, this attack failed too, and Hick's Brigade also fell back and took cover in a dry gulley close by in order to reorganize. While in this position, they witnessed Sikhs coming off the ramparts and dispatching their wounded with their talwars.

Anger at the killing of their wounded comrades gave a fresh impetus to Hick's Brigade. Backed by HM 31st of Penny's brigade which had joined them, it launched its attack and this time the troops scaled the ramparts by standing on each other's shoulders. HM 31st lost its ensign carrying the Queen's Colour, Ensign Tritton having been shot through the head, as was Ensign Jones carrying the Regimental Colours. Lt Noel seized the Queen's Colour while Sergeant McCabe picked up the Regimental Colour from the ground. Together they scrambled up the rampart and planted the flags firmly on top. Shouting their battle cry, the 31st stormed the position, pushing the Sikhs back and establishing a foothold.

In the centre, Gilbert's Division began its advance in response to Gough's order. In their counterattack, the Sikhs, having repulsed Dick's division led by Stacy's brigade, now turned on Gilbert's division and McLaren's brigade. Watching their move, Gough shouted, 'Good God, they'll be annihilated.'

The Sikh centre under Mehtab Singh Majithia was the strongest and, as Ensign Innes later wrote,

> The air, charged with sulphur, was stifling and so heated that it was almost unbearable. Now on rushed the Bengal European Regiment [2nd European Light Infantry] with a determination which promised to carry everything before it; soon reaching the ditch which formed the outer defences, and springing into it, they found themselves confronted by the massive walls, which in the distance had appeared less formidable, for they now found these works too high to escalade without ladders. To retire again was to encounter the storm of fire through which they had just passed, to remain in their present position was annihilation; therefore the Regiment, mortified and chagrined, was forced to seek shelter under cover of the bank of the dry river which it had left but a short time before.[143]

Meanwhile, Hick's brigade had entered into Sham Singh Attari's defences, but was hard put to hold on. Smith later described this as,

> By dint of the hardest fighting I ever saw, I carried the entrenchments [...] Such a hand-to-hand conflict ensued, for 25 minutes I could barely hold my own. Mixed together, swords and targets against

> bayonets, and a fire on both sides [...] We were at it against four times my numbers, sometimes receding (never turning around, though) sometimes advancing. The old 31st and 50th laid on like devils [...] This last was a brutal bulldog fight.

As Colonel G.B. Malleson states in his book, *The Decisive Battles of India*, 'Smith's Division had lost 489 men and Gilbert's division had lost 685 men in about half an hour.'

Smith's foothold on the ramparts was weak, and a determined Sikh counterattack could have pushed him off the entrenchments as well, but Gough's plan had begun to work. Sir Robert Dick had been killed, and however hard-pressed to hold the centre and left, the Sikhs had thinned their right, after the repulse of Stacy's first attack, to strengthen their centre and left, which was being attacked. Dick's division now attacked again, secured a foothold and entered the Sikh position, cutting down the gunners. Gilbert's division once again attacked the left of centre, but was again repulsed. General Gilbert was wounded and so was the brigade commander, Brigadier McLaren. A third attempt was made, and this time the troops, standing once again on each others shoulders, secured a foothold, enlarged it and assaulted the guns, bayoneting the gunners and spiking the guns. Gilbert's second brigade commander, Brigadier Taylor, was at this moment also shot in the head and killed, having been wounded earlier when he received a sword cut on his face.

All three divisions had now secured a foothold in the Sikh position and before the Sikhs could consolidate and renew their counterattacks, Gough ordered General Thackwell and his cavalry division to sweep the entire defensive perimeter, silencing the guns. The engineers created a gap on the Sikh right and General Thackwell personally led the 3rd Dragoons through in a single file. They then formed up, turned left, and galloped along the Sikh gun positions, cutting down the gunners and infantry who were attempting to form squares. Just then, a Sikh battery changed direction and opened grape on the Dragoons bringing them to a halt until the 4th and 5th Bengal Cavalry Regiments joined them. Jointly they charged and silenced the battery. Yet once again, an outer battery, which still manned its guns, turned them inwards and opened fire on the Dragoons.

At this moment, the Sikh C-in-C, Tej Singh, was seen once again deserting his command. He crossed the boat of bridges to the north bank and to safety, damaging the central span, either by mistake or intent, leaving his command to their fate. Sham Singh Attari, the commander of the Sikh left who was opposing Harry Smith's 1st Division and was in his first battle, realized the desperate situation they were now in. He had volunteered to be part of Tej Singh's army after the Sikh defeats at Mudki, Ferozshah and Aliwal, and had left his village of Attari, having taken a vow in his gurdwara, along with the followers of his feudal levy, to either return victorious from Sobraon or to die in the attempt. He now came forward on the ramparts with a white robe (the colour of sacrifice) over his clothes, calling to his troops to rally around him. There followed a hand-to-hand battle, the bayonet against the sword until Sham Singh fell mortally wounded and died on the ramparts. There his body lay alongside those of his men until it was taken back to Attari the following day – 53 other men from his village who had taken the vow with him were also cremated at the same site.

Witnessing the extreme gallantry of Sham Singh and his men, Gough was to later record his feelings:

> Policy, however, precluded me publicly recording my sentiments on the splendid gallantry of our fallen foe, or to record the acts of heroism displayed, not only individually, but almost collectively by the Sikh Sardars and army; I declare, were it not from a deep conviction that my country's good required the sacrifice, I would have wept to have witnessed the fearful slaughter of so devoted a body of men.

As the fighting penetrated deeper into the Sikh defences, the British guns and men were able to pour through the gaps now prepared by the engineers and as Bruce writes,

> Lashed by a merciless fire, attacked by cavalry and infantry on three sides, the Sikhs only stubbornly yielded, fighting bitterly to the death, until at last they could take no more. First a few, then all gave way, until a retreat became a rout and finally a desperate stampede. Soon they were hemmed in a mass at the head of the bridge, there to be shot down or hurled into the river below, which the heavy rains had made no longer fordable.

The governor general's son, Arthur Hardinge, who was his father's ADC, later wrote,

> I saw the bridge at that moment overcrowded with guns, horses, and soldiers of all arms, swaying to and fro, until at last with a crash it disappeared in the running waters, carrying with it all those who had vainly hoped to reach the opposite shore. The river seemed alive with a struggling mass of men. The artillery, now brought down to the water's edge, completed the slaughter. Few escaped; none, it may be said, surrendered.

Cunningham adds,

> No Sikh offered to submit, and no disciple of Gobind asked for quarter. They everywhere showed a front to the victors, and stalked slowly and sullenly away, while many rushed singly forth to meet assured death by contending with a multitude. The victors looked with stolid wonderment upon the indomitable courage of the

> vanquished, and forebore to strike when the helpless and the dying frowned unavailing hatred.

Gough describes the last moments as,

> In their efforts to reach the right bank through the deepened water, they suffered from our horse artillery a terrible carnage. Hundreds fell under this cannonade; hundreds upon hundreds were drowned in attempting the perilous passage. Their awful slaughter, confusion and dismay were such as would have excited compassion in the hearts of their generous conquerors, if the Khalsa troops had not, in the earlier part of the action, sullied their gallantry by slaughtering and barbarously mangling every wounded soldier whom, in the vicissitudes of attack, the fortunes of war left at their mercy.

Harry Smith describes the battle of Sobraon as, the hardest fight in his life except Badajoz, Waterloo and New Orleans.

The battle was over by noon. Cunningham put the Sikh losses at 5,000–8,000 (heirs of 3,125 regular soldiers claimed arrears of pay, et cetera), out of an effective fighting force in the defensive enclave, which he estimates at 15,000 – the remainder being camp followers. These casualties amount from one-third to a half of the troops committed to battle. The Sikhs took the maximum casualties during the withdrawal across the river. The Sikhs lost their great general, Sham Singh Attari, and sardars of the Jagirdari Fauj, Ghulab Singh Koopta, Heera Singh Topee and Kishan Singh (the son of late Jemadar Kooshal Singh) and commanders of the Sikh artillery, generals Mubaruck Ally, Elahi Buksh, who had been part of Ranjit Singh's army from its inception, and Shah Nawaz Khan (the son of Futteh-u-Din Khan of Kasur).

The British losses amounted to 13 British officers killed and 101 wounded, 3 Indian officers killed and 39 wounded, 301 warrant officers, NCOs and ORs killed and 1,913 wounded, 3 NCEs were killed and 10 wounded. A total of 320 killed and 2,063 wounded – 2,383 in all. The killed included Major General Sir Robert H. Dick, KCB KCH, a veteran of the Peninsular Wars and the Waterloo campaign, and Brigadier C.C. Taylor CB. The wounded included Major General W.R. Gilbert, Brigadier C.B. Stacy, Brigadier N. Penny, CO of the Nasiri Gurkhas, then commanding the brigade, Brigadier C.B. McLaren, Lt Col J.B. Gough, the acting QMG, Lt Col M. Barr the officiating AG and Lt Col K.H. Ryan, the commanding officer of HM 50th Foot and Lt Col Petit also of the 50th, and Captain John Fisher commanding the Sirmoor Gurkhas.

HM 50th took the heaviest casualties of 12 officers and 221 other ranks, followed by the 1st Bengal European Infantry who took 14 officer and 185 OR casualties. Amongst the cavalry, the 3rd Dragoons, whom Gough refers to as, 'that regiment which no obstacle usually held formidable by horse appears to check',[144] took 5 officers and 26 men, and 2 officers' chargers and 14 troop horses, as casualties.

The Sikhs lost 67 guns and over 200 Zambooraks deployed within the Sobraon defensive enclave. A further 36 guns on the north bank were handed over to the British after the signing of the Lahore Treaty.

Hardinge's secretary to government (political affairs), Robert Cust, sums up the feelings in aftermath of the battle.

> It was an awful scene, a fearful carnage. The dead Sikh lay inside his trenches – the dead European marked too distinctly the line each regiment had taken, the advance. The living Europeans remarked that nought could resist the bayonet [...] As the place was becoming dangerous from the explosion of mines, I passed out of the trenches and rode along the dry nullah that surrounds it and marked the strong defences which the enemy had thrown up [...] Our losses were heavy and the ground was here and there strewn with the slain, among whom I recognized a fine and handsome lad whom I had well known, young Hamilton, brother of Alistair Stewart. There he lay, his auburn hair weltering in his blood, his forehead fearfully gashed, his fingers cut off. Still warm, but quite dead. Flames were spreading over the Sikh camp, igniting the powder besides each gun and the air was rent with terrific explosions. The guns were now nearly all removed and our dead were being buried. We rode slowly home.

The cost of the First Sikh War to the British was 105 officers killed and 315 wounded. Those killed included 3 major generals, Sir Robert Sale, Sir John McAskil and Sir Robert Dick and Brigadier Wallace and the wounded included Major General Gilbert and 3 brigadiers, Taylor, White and McLaren – 1,290 other ranks were killed and 4,547 were wounded.

Sikh casualties have not been recorded. The vanquished never record their history and so was it with the Sikhs. However, what is on record is that the Sikhs lost 257 guns during the four battles of the First War.

IX. THE AFTERMATH

Gough lost little time in putting his troops across the Sutlej. Wilkinson's 6th Brigade was marched 25 miles, and crossed the river via the Harike ford that night. Part of the army crossed by the repaired bridge of boats that evening, and still more were sent via Ferozepur to Kasur, 16 miles into Lahore territory, which they reached on 12 February. The remainder of the army moved up the next day. As Robert Cust recorded: 'Our camp followers alone must have amounted to 100,000 – beasts of burden, elephants, camels, horses, bullocks, mules, etc, to an amount frightful and incredible.'

Hardinge now sent a message to the wazir, Raja Gulab Singh, to say that, if Ranjit Singh's kingdom was to survive as an independent state, it was necessary for him to come for negotiations without delay. The next day, 15 February, Raja Gulab Singh and a deputation of sardars came to

Kasur to discuss terms. Also, on that same day, the governor general issued a proclamation that the British objectives had been achieved.

Gulab Singh, accompanied by a number of chiefs and nobles each on his own elephant and with his own entourage, had arrived at Kasur for negotiations. He was regarded as the most astute person in the durbar, and was now the most powerful man in the Punjab. He had distanced himself during the First Sikh War, and was now going to claim his reward. He went into the governor general's durbar tent alone to hear and discuss the surrender terms. The other chiefs were left sitting on their elephants. Occasionally, he would come out to confer with the other chiefs. It was well past midnight when he finally agreed to the terms.

Hardinge had decided not to annex the Lahore state. The Sikhs still had a formidable army – despite having been decisively beaten in the four battles of the war. Those on the north bank, under Lal Singh, still had 36 guns, and those who had escaped from the Sobraon enclave along with the rest of the army that was garrisoning the rest of Punjab. 25,000 troops and 50 guns were in the various garrisons of Amritsar and Lahore, in addition to those garrisoning Peshawar and Multan. Hardinge thought it more prudent to weaken the state militarily and territorially, while letting it remain a friendly independent government supervised by a British resident, rather than obtaining total subjugation by fighting a protracted war.

Gulab Singh had agreed to: (1) secession to the British of the Jullandhar Doab (the territory between the rivers Sutlej and the Beas) covering the districts of Jullundhar, Hoshiarpur and Kangra, an area of 11,480 square miles, all the territory of the Lahore Durbar south of the Sutlej, in the Malwa region, thus moving the British Indian borders, around 60 miles closer to Lahore; (2) the payment of one-and-a-half crore of rupees (£1.5million) as indemnity for the expenses of the war; (3) the reduction of the Lahore Army to 20,000 infantry and 12,000 cavalry; (4) the surrender of the 36 guns used against them on the north bank at Sobraon; and (5) the British to have complete control of both banks of the Sutlej.

The Lahore treasury was all but empty and Gulab Singh knew the durbar could not pay the indemnity. It agreed, no doubt once again at Gulab Singh's behest, to part with its hill territory in the north, between the rivers Indus and the Beas, also encompassing Kashmir and Hazara. This Hardinge promptly sold to Gulab Singh for £750,000. This understanding had been reached when Gulab Singh's emissary, Dr Ghosh, had met Hardinge on his behalf with this request, prior to the battle of Sobraon. It was now forced on the Lahore Durbar as part of the Lahore Treaty (Appendix I, Article 12) and later as a separate treaty with Gulab Singh, which was entered into with Gulab Singh at Amritsar on 16 March 1846 and signed by H. Hardinge, F. Currie and H.M. Lawrence (Appendix III). He was recognized as the maharaja of Jammu and Kashmir in this treaty.

On 4 March 1846, Hardinge wrote to the Secret Committee in London justifying this act as follows:

> While the severance of this frontier line from the Lahore possessions materially weakens that State and deprives it, in the eyes of other Asiatic powers, of much of its pride of position, its possession by us enables us at once to mark our sense of Raja Gulab Singh's conduct during the later operations, by regarding him in the mode most in accordance with his ambitious desires; to shew forth, as an example to the other chiefs of Asia, the benefits which accrue from an adherence to British interests; to create a strong and friendly power in a position to threaten an attack, should it be necessary to do so, the Lahore territories in their most vulnerable point; and at the same time to secure to ourselves that indemnification for the expenses of the campaign.

Gulab Singh had stayed aloof from the war and had kept his army intact for the governance of the northern territories and Kashmir, which he hoped to get as per the assurance given to him by the governor general. His army would also be available to the British whenever required, which was also part of his understanding with Hardinge. The order of battle of the Lahore Durbar Army, which had not been engaged in any of the battles during the First Sikh War (given below), indicates how thoughtfully the Dogra elements of the regular army and the feudal levies of Gulab Singh and his allies were kept aloof from the war by him. Some Dogra irregulars took part in the battle of Aliwal, but no Dogra regular troops were deployed in any of the battles. Other than Court's, Pouwindia's, Arjan Singh's, Gen Suchet Singh's and the Ahluwalia brigades of the regular army, and four derahs of the Fauj-e-Gair, who were not committed during the war, being on garrison duties in other parts of Punjab, the remainder belong to the Dogras of the regular army, Raja Gulab Singh's division and the Jasrotia, Raja Suchet Singh, General Suchet Singh and Raja Dhyan Singh's brigades, amounting to 18 infantry battalions, 6 cavalry regiments and 72 guns.

Order of Battle, Sikh Regular Army & Feudal Forces not Engaged by the British During the First Sikh War, 1845-46[145]

Fauj-e-Ain (Regulars)

Arjan Singh's Brigade (4,288)
1st Infantry Paltan (847)
2nd Infantry Paltan (847)
3rd Infantry Paltan (847)
4th Infantry Paltan (847)
Cavalry Rajman (540)

Artillery
Aspi (360) (12 guns)

Court's Brigade (Chattar Singh Attari in Command) (4,292)
1st Infantry Paltan (848)
2nd Infantry Paltan (848)
3rd Infantry Paltan (848)

4th Infantry Paltan (848)
Cavalry Rajman (540)
Artillery
Aspi (360) (12 guns)

Raja Dhyan Singh's Brigade (Hara Singh in Command) (5,738)
(HQ: Jesrota)
1st Jesrota Infantry Paltan (833)
2nd Jesrota Infantry Paltan (833)
3rd Jesrota Infantry Paltan (833)
4th Jesrota Infantry Paltan (833)
5th Jesrota Infantry Paltan (833)
6th Jesrota Infantry Paltan (833)
Jagirdari Sowar Regiment (500)
Artillery: Jesrota Aspi (240) (8 guns)

Raja Gulab Singh's Division (NWF & Kashmir) (10,430)
Infantry
1st Nowshera Infantry Paltan (600)
2nd Nowshera Infantry Paltan (600)
1st Jammu Infantry Paltan (600)
2nd Jammu Infantry Paltan (600)
3rd Jammu Infantry Paltan (600)
4th Jammu Infantry Paltan (600)
5th Jammu Infantry Paltan (600)
6th Jammu Infantry Paltan (600)
7th Jammu Infantry Paltan (600)
8th Jammu Infantry Paltan (600)

Cavalry Brigade
1st Jagirdari Sowar Regiment (750)
2nd Jagirdari Sowar Regiment (569)
3rd Jagirdari Sowar Regiment (672)
4th Jagirdari Sowar Regiment (759)
Jai Singh's Zamburak's (76)

General Suchet Singh's Brigade (4,816)
1st Infantry Paltan (979)
2nd Infantry Paltan (979)
3rd Infantry Paltan (979)
4th Infantry Paltan (979)
Cavalry Rajman (540)
Artillery
Aspi (360) (12 guns)

Artillery Brigade
Nowshera Aspi (300) (10 guns)
1st Jammu Aspi (360) (12 guns)
2nd Jammu Aspi (360) (12 guns)
1st Jammu Jinsi (360) (12 guns)
2nd Jammu Jinsi (360) (10 guns)

Gulab Singh Pouvindia's Brigade (3,824)
1st Infantry Paltan (866)
2nd Infantry Paltan (866)
3rd Infantry Paltan (866)
4th Infantry Paltan (866)
Artillery
Aspi (360)(12 guns)

Raja Suchet Singh's Brigade (3,040)
1st Samba Infantry Paltan (600)
2nd Samba Infantry Paltan (600)
3rd Samba Infantry Paltan (600)
4th Samba Infantry Paltan (600)
Jagirdari Sowar Regiment (400)
Artillery
Samba Aspi (240) (8 guns)

Sardar Aloowalia's Brigade (2,860)

1st Kurpoothulla Infantry Paltan (600)
2nd Kurpoothulla Infantry Paltan (600)
1st Jagirdari Sowar Regiment (676)
2nd Jagirdari Sowar Regiment (676)
Kapoorthulla Aspi (360) (12 guns)

Fauj-e-Gair

Ghorcharra Cavalry
Attariwala Derah
Ghorcharras (870)
Derah Khas
Ghorcharras (2,089)

Derah Kalan
Ghorcharras (1,600)
Ramgariah Derah
Ghorcharra's (740)
Fyshushshi's Zamburak's (101)

Source: Dewan Ajudhia Parshad, *Waqai-Jang-i-Sikhan: Events of the First Anglo-Sikh War* 1845-46. V.S. Suri (tr) Chandigarh: Punjab Itihas Prakashan, 1975.
Sikh Army List Compiled from Bajwa and other sources

After Gulab Singh had finalized the terms with Hardinge on 18 February, Hardinge 'directed' that the young eight-year-old Maharaja Duleep Singh should come to his camp in person, which he did the following day.

Robert Cust, the secretary of political affairs to Hardinge, describes Duleep Singh, 'as a child of an intelligent and not unpleasing appearance'. The usual salutes and welcoming ceremonies over, Duleep Singh was ushered in to the governor general's durbar tent, made hot and stuffy by the officers wanting to witness this event. Protocol demanded that the maharaja offer presents to the governor general. This offer was pointedly ignored by Hardinge until, as tutored, Duleep Singh asked Hardinge's pardon for the offences done by his durbar. He agreed to accept the British terms, then asked to be restored to their friendship. The ice was broken, cordiality restored and the atmosphere became visibly relaxed. Hardinge then readily accepted the maharaja's presents.

Next day, the maharaja received the governor general in his durbar tent set up within his own camp. Cust describes the event as follows.

> [...] a beautiful scene, of which the two chief characteristics were order and magnificence. Shawls and cashmere carpets on the floor. The Maharaja sat on a silver chair with his ministers and nobles standing behind him. There was no crowding, no confusion, all were handsomely dressed – the carpets most beautiful and one side of the tent being thrown open admitted air and light [...] On the whole it presented as mortifying a contrast to our durbar as can be imagined.

The governor general and the commander-in-chief then accompanied the maharaja. All were seated on elephants and proceeded in procession to Lahore. In a strict order of precedence, the procession was escorted by Brigadier Cureton and his cavalry brigade comprising four cavalry regiments, horse artillery, et cetera. They were received a mile outside the city by Wazir Gulab Singh, Sikh sardars, ministers, and nobles, and salutes were fired to welcome the visitors to the capital of the Lahore state.

With the governor general's permission, Gulab Singh, now planning to go back to Kashmir, resigned as wazir and Lal Singh was again appointed wazir and Tej Singh the commander-in-chief of the reduced army – suitable rewards for their treachery. The atmosphere in the city and the countryside was so hostile to both, and to the regent Maharani Jinda, that the durbar was forced to ask the British for a 'protecting force' to stay on in the capital. This was exactly what the British wanted and readily agreed to. They had got themselves a weak, dependent and pliable government in Lahore.

The Treaty of Lahore (Appendix I) was signed on 8 March in the new British Resident designate, Major Henry Lawrence's tent, during which ceremony a letter from the eight-year-old maharaja was read aloud, asking for this 'protecting force'. The next day, the treaty was ratified in which it was stated that on the maharaja's request a British force would remain at Lahore for a year (Annexure II) until the Council of Regency, headed by the C-in-C, Tej Singh and comprising six 'eminent' members, could reorganize its army in accordance with the treaty (Article 7). The Council of Regency comprised: Bhai Ram Singh, a spiritual leader; the wazir, Raja Lal Singh, who had abandoned the field at Mudki and Ferozshah; Sardar Tej Singh, the C-in-C, who had abandoned his army both at Ferozshah and Sobraon; Sardar Chattar Singh Attari, a family of repute that was close to the young maharaja, to whom his daughter was betrothed; Sardar Ranjodh Singh Majithia, who had abandoned the field at Aliwal; Dewan Deenanath and Fakir Nur-ud-din, the respected member of the Fakir family, whose members had served Ranjit Singh devotedly throughout his life.

With Hardinge's ominous address to the durbar still ringing in their ears, 'Success or failure is in your own hands; my co-operation shall not be wanting; but if you neglect this opportunity, no aid on the part of the British government can save the State', the ministers and nobles dispersed to their homes in a sombre and reflective mood. Henceforth, British influence in the functioning of the Lahore Durbar would be absolute.

The proceedings of the durbar held at Lahore on 9 March 1846 quotes Hardinge as saying, 'I leave my political agent, Major Lawrence, assisted by Major McGregor and a most able General Officer Sir John Littler, to command the British troops. These officers possess my entire confidence'.

Article 15 of the Lahore Treaty further states:

> The British government will not exercise any interference in the internal administration of the Lahore State, but in all cases or questions which may be referred to the British government, the Governor General will give aid of his advice and good offices for the furtherance of the interests of the Lahore Government.

Nine months later, on 16 December 1846, this was drastically modified in a fresh agreement between the British and the Lahore Durbar, which states as follows: 'A British officer, with an efficient establishment, shall be appointed by the governor general to remain at Lahore, which officer shall have full authority to direct and control all matters in every department of the State.'[146]

The Council of Regency was amended to include eight individuals, instead of the six that had existed since the Treaty of Lahore. They were to be: Tej Singh, Sher Singh Attari, Dewan Deenanath, Fakir Nur-ud-din, Ranjodh Singh Majithia, Bhai Nidhan Singh, Attar Singh Kaliwala, and Shamsher Singh Sandhanwalia. The stage was now fast being set for the Second Anglo-Sikh War.

For services rendered during the war, on the orders of Queen Victoria, Lieutenant General Sir Henry Hardinge, GCB was granted the dignity of Viscount, General Sir Hugh Gough, Bart GCB was granted that of Baron and Major-General Sir Harry Smith GCB, was granted that of Baronet. The prime minister, Sir Robert Peel, moved a resolution in the Commons on 4 May 1846, granting Hardinge an annuity of £3,000 and to Gough one of £2,000 'and the two next heirs male of their bodies'.

The East India Company made a presentation of its own – a pension for life of £5,000 to Hardinge and a similar pension for life of £2,000 to Gough.

Multan
1848-49

I. THE AFTERMATH OF THE FIRST SIKH WAR – LAHORE UNDER BRITISH INFLUENCE

The Lahore Durbar had been dismembered. Ranjit Singh's kingdom, built by his efforts and the sacrifice of his armies, was now to lose those territories. The rich and fertile Jullundur Doab, yielding an annual revenue of £400,000, with a population of around 40,000 inhabitants and encompassing the cities of Jullundur, Philaur, Phagwara, and Sultanpur, was taken over by the British. Kashmir had been sold to Gulab Singh for 75 lakh rupees. Those considered traitors by the average people in the kingdom, whether it was Gulab Singh, Tej Singh, Lal Singh, or Ranjodh Singh Majithia, were now ruling them by proxy, as the Council of Regency. The regent was considered to have compromised herself. It was generally felt that if the British troops were not stationed at Lahore, neither the regent nor her son, the young maharaja, could be safe outside the walls of the fort without a British escort.

The army, 100,000 strong, had been cut down to 32,000, leaving 68,000 trained and angry men to roam the countryside without a job and with no prospects. In addition to these regular soldiers, there were the irregular levies, the Jagirdari Fauj, the Ghorcharras, the Derahs, and all of the Fauj-e-Gair who had also been disbanded. The prevalent feeling amongst the soldiers was that the army had not lost, it had been betrayed by its leaders and by its durbar; those very leaders were now feathering their nests with the help of the British, while the common soldier was out in the cold. The average soldier knew no other profession and felt humiliated. His religion gave him the sword, and Ranjit Singh had provided the leadership under which he had prospered; he was not going to turn to the plough now.

THEATRE OF OPERATIONS DURING THE BATTLE OF MULTAN 1848

Map published in 1845

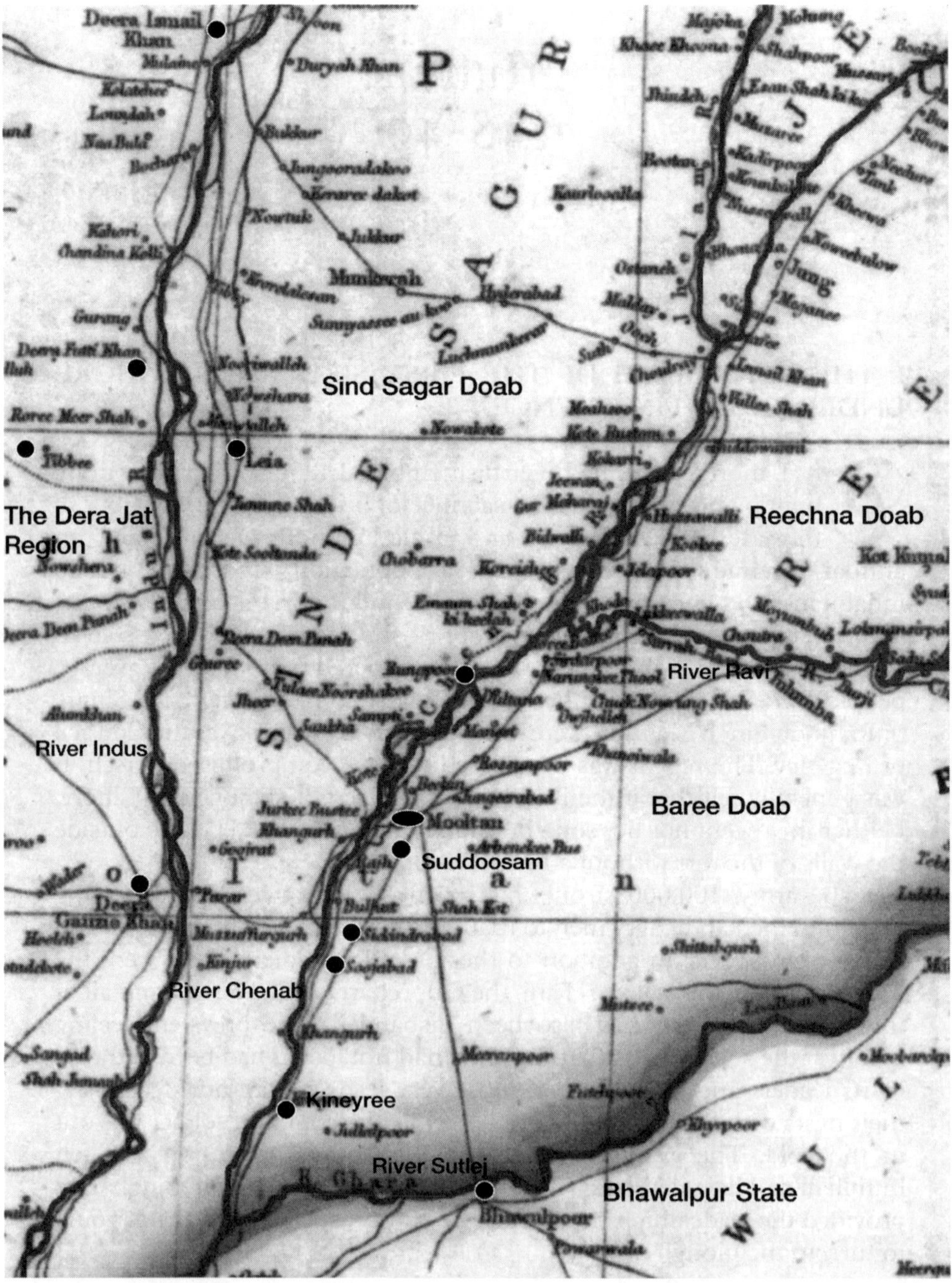

The Lahore Durbar had a maharaja, a prime minister, a government, and an army, all dependent upon a foreign power to keep the peace. No Sikh could accept the fact that their maharaja and government were in any way independent, or were able to give them the strong leadership that they now required.

To add fuel to fire, Sir Henry Lawrence had initiated measures of land reform, introducing the practices that were being carried out elsewhere in India. He also abolished sati and the punishment of mutilation. However laudable these reforms, all they achieved were to further convince the landowners and the common citizens alike of the blatant interference in the affairs and customs of an independent state. Alongside this, Lawrence hoped to smooth the ruffled feathers of the sardars and chiefs, who held large tracts of arable land, by starting the construction of the Bari Doab canal that would irrigate the land between the rivers Beas and Ravi.

Another irritant was the sale of Kashmir. The Lahore Durbar had been made to accept this 'sale' by incorporating it in the enforced ratification of the Lahore Treaty. To add to this insult, Gulab Singh was formally installed by the British as the maharaja of Jammu and Kashmir in Amritsar on 15 March 1846.

The first sign of revolt appeared when the governor of Kashmir, Sheikh Imam-ud-din, refused to hand over control to Gulab Singh when he arrived to take over his new kingdom. A mixed force of British and Lahore troops, under the resident, Henry Lawrence, marched on Kashmir to enforce the governor general's decision. The governor surrendered without firing a shot, professing his innocence, claiming that he was under orders from the Prime Minister Raja Lal Singh, not to give possession of the Kashmir administration to Gulab Singh. He showed Lawrence the written orders he had received. After returning to Lahore, Lawrence had Lal Singh put on trial, during which the former governor of Kashmir produced written evidence. Raja Lal Singh was found guilty and was removed from the post of prime minister and exiled from the Punjab.

Lal Singh's revolt convinced Hardinge that if matters carried on as they were, the gains the British had made from the First Sikh War would be lost. He called a meeting of 52 of the leading Sikh sardars and nobles in the town of Bhyrowal, situated on the west bank of Beas, and put his proposals to them. He gave them two options: one, that the British would quit Lahore leaving them to run their own government (knowing full well that they would not accept this option, which would amount to suicide); or two, that a British Protectorate would be established till Maharaja Duleep Singh came of age. The second option was unanimously agreed upon and was set down in the 'Treaty of Bhyrowal' on 18 December 1846. Under the treaty there would be a Council of Regency, comprising eight eminent individuals who would work under the British Resident, Colonel Henry Lawrence. Heading the list of eight were the two dubious characters, the C-in-C, Tej Singh and Ranjodh Singh Majithia. The others were Sher

Singh Attari, Dewan Deenanath, Fakir Nur-ud-din, Attar Singh, Shamsher Singh, and Bhai Nidhan Singh. The treaty stated that the 'power of the Resident would extend over every department and to any extent'. It was also agreed that the British would receive Rupees 20 lakh (£220,000) as an annual payment during the period of this protectorate and that British forces would occupy forts and posts considered essential within the Lahore territory as the governor general thought necessary. This gave the resident supreme powers within the Lahore territory, as well as those for external relations.

Lawrence now selected a team of British officers to help him govern the state. He brought in his two brothers, John and George, together with John Nicholson, Captain Abbot, Harry Lumsden, John Beecher, Reynel Taylor, and Herbert Edwards. In due course more were added. These chosen few were sent as divisional commissioners with full freedom of action. The only guiding advice Lawrence gave was to 'settle the country, make the people happy and take care there are no rows. [...] This was taken to mean less taxation, curbing the powers of the chiefs, dismantling all the fortifications that were not required by the British, and setting an example in honesty and orderly conduct.'[147]

The added responsibility given to Lawrence now required the strengthening of the military presence in the state. When General Sir John Littler set up headquarters at Lahore, after the Treaty of Lahore, he had under his command one British and eight Bengal Native Infantry battalions, two field batteries, one horse battery and a wing of irregular cavalry. His command was subsequently strengthened further by Hardinge, with an additional infantry brigade with 22 guns, formed as a mobile column. Similar mobile columns were also established at Jullundur and at Ferozepur. The total force now available to General Littler was close to 50,000 with 60 guns.

Hardinge was now ready to return home, but India, after the Afghan and Sikh wars, was hugely in debt. To balance his books before relinquishing his appointment as governor general, he instituted a series of economies and resorted to severe cost cutting. One of the economies he adopted, which was vehemently opposed by Gough, was to reduce the standing army by 50,000 men. Despite the C-in-C's opposition, he cut the strength of the NI battalions to 800 from the existing 1200, and the cavalry down from the existing 500 to 420 horse. Hardinge genuinely believed that India would now be at peace. Events, however, would soon prove him wrong.

A decision was also taken to raise regular Sikh regiments in the Indian Army. Initially two regiments, those of Ludhiana and Ferozepur were raised. Both were to play an honourable part in the history of the Indian Army and exist to this date. Both were raised on 31 July 1846 in the Malwa region, where over 10,000 'Malwai' soldiers of the Lahore Army who had been demobilized and sent home, were available for recruitment.

However, it is not clear whether any of these discharged soldiers were recruited into these two regiments. In December 1846, however, Lumsden raised his famous Regiment of Guides, and William Hodson, who would later raise Hodson's Horse, became his second-in-command. This was soon followed by the raising of a Frontier Brigade of three regiments, which later would form the famous Punjab Irregular Force. In February 1847 Lumsden did a successful drive through Hazara with 1,000 Sikhs, including two regiments which had fought in the field against Gilbert's division at Sobraon. It stands to reason, therefore, that if those regiments that had fought the British in the field, had been kept intact, there would have been no reason why a young trained soldier, discharged for no fault of his but for political reasons, would not form part of the new raisings. However, there is nothing on record to substantiate this.[148]

Despite such efforts, the mood in the Punjab countryside remained sullen. A plot had been discovered to assassinate Lawrence and the Council of Regency. The regent herself was reported to be involved in conspiracies and destabilizing acts. Because of this, she was removed from Lahore to an estate at Sheikhupura where she was confined. Reports were coming in that a seasoned Afghan intriguer, Sultan Mohammed, and Sardar Chattar Singh Attari, the governor at Hazara, were also plotting. The latter, the father of Sher Singh, who was a member of the Council of Regency, also had a daughter betrothed to the young maharaja, a marriage the British were subtly disapproving of. Lawrence felt that apart from these sporadic events, the situation was stable enough and that his commissioners had their respective areas under control. Major George Lawrence was at Peshawar, Captain Abbot at Hazara, whilst Lieutenant Herbert Edwards was at Dera Jat, attempting to stabilize the turbulent area situated between the two districts of Dera Ismail Khan and Dera Ghazi Khan on the west bank of the great Indus. Multan was separated by the river Chenab from Dera Jat by 35 miles.

After a rigorous year and a half in the Punjab, Henry Lawrence took sick leave at the end of 1847 and accompanied the returning governor general, Henry Hardinge, back to England. He was replaced by Sir Frederick Currie, who had been Hardinge's foreign secretary during the first war. The new governor general was the thirty-five-year-old James, the Earl of Dalhousie, who had been chairman of the Board of Trade in Robert Peel's government.

II. MULTAN – THE REVOLT

The second indication of widespread discontent was witnessed at Multan. This city had one of the strongest military forts in India and was at one time an outpost of the Afghan kingdom, one of the gateways to India with trade routes from Afghanistan and Central Asia passing through it. It was still a major trading city and had been captured from the Afghans by

Ranjit Singh in 1819. Being a commercial centre, the city was teeming with Hindu merchants and was controlled by a governor, Dewan Mulraj, appointed by the Lahore Durbar. Dewan Mulraj belonged to an illustrious Hindu family and his father had been governor of Multan before him.

Mulraj was considered loyal to the Lahore Durbar. However, towards the end of 1847, when Lawrence received reports of the pilfering of state revenue by him, Mulraj was asked to get his accounts in order and was questioned about certain expenses. He immediately responded by saying that he had had enough of being governor and wished to be relieved. When informed that his resignation had been accepted, and that his relief would arrive by March 1848, he condescendingly replied that he was prepared to remain in Lahore until that date. He also stated that he would hand over the governorship and the accounts for the past three years to the governor-designate when he arrived, a condition that Lawrence had insisted upon.

Sardar Kahn Singh, a Sikh, was appointed as the new governor. He left to take over his new assignment accompanied by two English officers, Van Agnew of the civil service and Lieutenant Anderson of the Bombay Army. Anderson commanded a strong escort of 3,000 – comprising two Sikh battalions of the Lahore Durbar, 1,500 in all, a battalion of the durbar Gurkhas, a cavalry regiment of 600 horses, and 100 gunners with 6 guns. The governor-designate and the British officers travelled to Multan by river while the escort marched overland, both reaching Multan on 18 April at the designated rendezvous point, the Eidgah outside the town.

The Eidgah was north of the Multan fort, at a distance of about 700 yards, but within range of its guns. It was also about three quarter of a mile distant from the Aam Khas, which was Mulraj's residence. The Aam Khas was about 400 yards to the east of the fort and located to its right when facing the Eidgah.

On their arrival, Mulraj paid a courtesy call on the governor-designate and early next morning, on 19 April, escorted Sardar Kahn Singh and the two British officers, accompanied by an escort of a company of Gurkhas, to the fort on a tour of inspection and to officially hand over the fort to him. After the inspection the keys of the fort were formally handed over to the new governor and Lieutenant Anderson replaced Mulraj's sentries with his Gurkha soldiers. Having done this, the governor and the two British officers left the fort accompanied by Mulraj. Along the way they passed through a mutinous looking group of Mulraj's soldiers who had gathered together after being relieved, and who now quite suddenly realized that they were without jobs. Lieutenant Anderson, noticing the sullenness and hostile expressions cast their way, stopped and spoke to them, assuring them that he would see to it that they are suitably reinstated in the Company's services. As they turned and approached the bridge over the moat, one of Mulraj's two soldiers present on duty at the bridge jabbed Van Agnew with his spear and unhorsed him. He then wounded him twice with his sword. One soldier of the British escort immediately knocked the attacker into the moat. Mulraj who was accompanying them made no effort to help. On the contrary, he left them to their fate and galloped off home accompanied by his mounted escort. Just as suddenly, a part of Mulraj's escort halted, turned around and attacked Lieutenant Anderson. Kahn Singh immediately picked up Van Agnew, lifted him onto his elephant and with the help of Mulraj's brother Rung Ram, left for the Eidgah. Anderson was rescued by his Gurkha escort who carried him back to the residence. After getting their wounds tended to by the Gurkha doctor, Van Agnew, at 11 a.m., wrote a letter to Sir Frederick Currie at Lahore giving him details of the incident. He also wrote to Mulraj, emphasizing the fact that he did not in any way link him with the incident and asked him to come to meet them at the Eidgah at 2 p.m. He also added that as a gesture of support and goodwill, Mulraj should apprehend the guilty soldiers and bring them with him.

Mulraj failed to appear at the appointed hour so Van Agnew wrote to General Van Courtland of the Lahore Durbar Army, who was located about 80 miles away. The letter was sent through Herbert Edwards, who was then at Dera Ismail Khan about 150 miles away, so that he too would be alerted to this event. At 4 p.m. Mulraj sent a message to say that he could neither send the guilty nor could he come himself because he was prevented from doing so by the Sikh, Muslim and Hindu soldiers who were now in open revolt. He advised Van Agnew to manage on his own as best as he could. Van Agnew then sent him a message to the effect that if he was to be thought innocent he had better arrive for a meeting. The messenger soon returned to report that by the time he reached the Aam Khas, Mulraj was presiding over a council of war. Pathan, Hindu, Muslim, and Sikh commanders were gathered there and were seen to be taking an oath of loyalty to him. That night all the British horses and animal transport were driven away. Kahn Singh and the two wounded British officers now realized that it was not just sullen anger, or a riot, but a mutiny had broken out and they were now on their own.

Next morning, in a last ditch effort to prevent the worst, Van Agnew sent Mulraj the decree signed by Maharaja Duleep Singh which he had brought with him. It was addressed to Mulraj ordering him to obey all orders given to him and to handover the fort to Sardar Kahn Singh. Those at the meeting at the Aam Khas responded that they regarded Mulraj as their chief, and it was he they would obey. By now, convinced that major trouble was brewing, Van Agnew sent another immediate dispatch to Peer Ibrahim Khan, the British agent at Bhawalpur, 80 miles away across the Sutlej, informing him of the situation and asking him to come to their aid without delay.

The commandant of Kahn Singh's Sikh cavalry escort was the first to defect to Mulraj. He was received by Mulraj and was presented with a gold necklace and bracelets. Sensing the mood among the British escort,

Mulraj sent messages to the remaining commanders offering them a big increase in pay if they came over to him. By that evening, all except the artillery detachment had transferred allegiance. That evening the Eidgah came under gunfire from the fort and Aam Khas. With Anderson seriously injured and in bed, Van Agnew ordered the gunners to lay their guns on the Aam Khas and to open fire on it. The gunners responded by firing one round and then stopped. Refusing to serve their guns, they abandoned Kahn Singh to join their comrades now in Mulraj's camp.

Van Agnew made a last ditch effort to ward off the crisis by sending a message to Mulraj asking for terms. Mulraj conferred with his chiefs and although he agreed that Kahn Singh and the British officers were to be allowed to leave Multan, events overtook this decision when a yelling, frenzied crowd surged on towards the Eidgah. Knowing that the end was near, Van Agnew sat on Anderson's bed to say goodbye to him when the crowd burst into the room. An old soldier, Gamdhur Singh, went straight to Van Agnew and cut his head off with three strikes of his sword before hacking his body to pieces. A similar fate befell the severely wounded Anderson. Kahn Singh and his son were taken prisoner. Later, when Multan was finally captured, the skeletal remains of Sardar Kahn Singh and his son were discovered in the dungeons, where they were deprived of food and water and kept chained till they died. Their personal servants, who were the only people who had not joined the mutineers and had stayed loyal, were beaten severely by rifle butts and pushed out of the Eidgah. The entire escort, comprising about 3,000 soldiers, mutinied and joined Mulraj, including the Gurkhas. Mulraj now sent couriers into the countryside raising the banner of revolt against the British who were holding the maharaja and their proper rulers prisoner at Lahore.

When Van Agnew's message reached Frederick Currie at Lahore, he responded by ordering General Whish, who was in command at Lahore, to march on Multan with the mobile column kept just for this purpose. General Van Courtland, at Dera Ismail Khan, had also received Van Agnew's message and was preparing to move on Multan to their aid when he received a further message from Frederick Currie to move without delay with two battalions of Muslim troops, a regiment of cavalry and a troop of horse artillery. News reached him a short while later of the massacre of the governor and the British officers, he therefore countermanded this order since now there was no urgent requirement to send troops. Instead he wrote to Lord Gough for instructions.

Gough knew Multan was a formidable fort, despite the fact that it originally had a weak garrison and only a few guns. Now, however, it had been reinforced by 3,000 mutineers. Though Mulraj was not liked in the area, his cause had struck an emotional chord, and therefore the possibility of the disbanded troops of the Lahore Army rallying to his call had also to be taken into account. Gough was opposed to an immediate largescale advance on Multan as he rightly felt it could provoke a full-scale war and he was not prepared for that. The weather was also becoming hot and Hardinge's reduction of 50,000 soldiers had substantially reduced the number of troops required to carry out a full-scale operation. He suggested waiting till winter, in the meantime bringing his army up to strength. He also suggested to the governor general that the troops who had been sent home when Hardinge had reduced the strength of the regiments should be recalled to prevent Mulraj employing them. Though Dalhousie readily agreed on postponing the Multan campaign until winter, he was however hesitant to change Hardinge's policy of reduction. Gough made it clear to Dalhousie that, in the event of another war in the Punjab, he thought a force of about 30,000 men with about 75 guns was essential, including the raising of the strength of the infantry and cavalry regiments to the pre-Hardinge cut-back levels.

III. CONTAINMENT

While these discussions were going on between the governor general and the C-in-C, unknown to them, Lieutenant Herbert Edwards had decided to march against Mulraj on his own initiative in response to Van Agnew's message, sent to him at Dera Fateh Khan for onward dispatch to General Van Courtland. He quickly assembled all the regular troops that he could muster, which amounted to 2 guns, 50 Zambooraks, 350 cavalry and 12 companies of infantry. Edwards requested Lieutenant Reynel Taylor, who was 65 miles north of Dera Fateh Khan at Dera Ismail Khan on the west bank of the Indus along with General Van Courtland, to send reinforcements. They were instructed to supply an infantry battalion and 4 guns to join him at Leia (today spelt as Layya), a town in the Punjab on the right bank of the Indus, directly opposite Lieutenant Edwards's location and 20 miles from him.

Edwards began to cross the Indus in such boats as he could lay his hands on, each crossing taking up to three hours. As soon as he had his little army across, one of Mulraj's chiefs holding Leia with 3,000 irregular troops fled. Leia was a trading city and was full of mercenary soldiers looking for jobs. Edwards began recruiting them, both for the defence of Leia and to increase the strength of his force. He had with him a Pathan chief, Faujdar Khan whose considerable military experience and prestige Edwards found invaluable. He knew all the soldiers available in the area and soon added 3,000 Pathan and Baluch mercenaries to Edwards's ranks.

On 29 April, Edwards received information that Mulraj had put together a force of 4,000 soldiers and 8 guns under his brother Rung Ram and that it was on its way to Leia. The force's task was to attack Edwards before 1 May. Edwards decided against meeting Mulraj's force at Leia and thought it better to move 10 miles north, opposite Dera Fateh Khan on the west bank, to await the reinforcements General Van Courtland was sending him. He left his cavalry with Faujdar Khan to cover his withdrawal, and with instructions to get first hand information on the size of Mulraj's force and the exact number of guns. He then marched north on 30 April.

Edwards sent his baggage across the Indus and, to await events, built a protective enclave at the ferry head with his infantry and guns. His cavalry returned next morning to inform him that Mulraj's force had reached Leia. Edwards immediately ferried his guns and cavalry across the river and at 8 a.m. the following morning he completed his withdrawal with his infantry. Edwards's main worry was the conduct of his Sikh troops. Information had reached him that Mulraj was offering 12,000 rupees for them to transfer allegiance to him and a further 12,000 if they brought Edwards's head along with them. His worries on that account eased when Van Courtland and his troops were ferried across and linked up with him the following morning. He brought with him the regiment of Surbhan Khan comprising 1,200 Muslim troops and 6 horse artillery 6-pounder guns.

Mulraj, already apprehensive at the fast unfolding of events, now responded to a rumour that a force from Lahore was marching to Multan. He sent an urgent message to his brother at Leia on 7 May, to abandon the city and to return posthaste to Multan in two forced marches. Learning of these developments, Edwards ferried over a 100 cavalry to reconnoitre Leia and to establish Rung Ram's whereabouts. When his cavalry reached the city, the governor appointed by Mulraj fled and followed the army back to Multan. Edwards then decided to re-cross the Indus and was on the verge of doing so, when a message arrived from Frederick Currie ordering him to stay on the west bank. Lahore had planned that no British troops would be part of the containing force. The task should be taken on by the Lahore Durbar Army. In the first instance five columns would move out to contain any such insurrection within a 50 miles radius of Multan. The main army would later deal with Multan.

Of the five columns selected for this purpose one would be Edwards's, with Van Courtland, and three Sikh columns. The main one comprising 5,000 troops under Raja Sher Singh Attari with Attar Singh and Shamsher Singh as his two second-in-commands. This column would advance along the Ravi from Lahore. The second column under Jawahar Mull would move to the west of Sher Singh, through the Sindh Sagar Doab beyond the Chenab. The third, under Sheikh Imam-ud-din, the former governor of Kashmir, would move to the east of Sher Singh along the Sutlej. The fifth column would be that of Nawab Bhawal Khan of Bhawalpur, who was south of the river Sutlej.

Sher Singh had begun to sense disaffection within his ranks. His Sikh troops could not be isolated from the general anti-British feeling which had by then permeated the Lahore territory so he decided to keep his columns intact but away from the troubled region. Sher Singh himself was still loyal to the durbar at this time but he was aware of open talk in his ranks and the fact that his soldiers wanted to go over to Mulraj. He took no notice of this until a plot to poison him was discovered. If the conspirators had succeeded in killing him the troops would have needed little persuasion to go over to Mulraj. The person who was to administer the poison was a Sikh soldier called Sujan Singh. Incriminating papers were found under his saddle. He was arrested, tried and found guilty by Sher Singh and the proceedings of the trial were sent to Currie in Lahore for confirmation. Currie gave the evidence to the Council of Regency, who decreed that Sujan Singh was guilty and was to be executed, the type of execution being left to Sher Singh and the other chiefs commanding the Sikh columns to decide. The troops were paraded and Sujan Singh was tied to the mouth of a gun and blown as an example to others, in the hope that this insurrection would die down.

What now remained with Edwards was his column and that of Bhawal Khan's, with which they were to occupy the lower Dera Jat, comprising two districts of Singhur and Dera Ghazi Khan. Singhur was dominated by the fort of Mungrota, occupied by Mulraj's troops. Edwards managed to take the fort without any opposition. He now decided to cross the Indus once again and occupy Leia, which was still being held by his small cavalry detachment of a 100 horse. In the meantime, Mulraj, taking heart at the fact that the Sikh columns of Sher Singh and Jawahar Mull were not involving themselves in the current operations, decided to occupy Leia himself. He hoped he might destroy General Van Courtland's column and then isolate and attack Edwards at Dera Fateh Khan.

On receiving this news Edwards sent a courier to Currie informing him of the developments and asking for Nawab Bhawal Khan's troops, who were still south of the Sutlej at Bhawalpur, to start without delay and to make a feint towards Multan. His cavalry at Leia, in the meantime sent him word that Mulraj's advance guard of 500 men were a day's march from Leia and were reported to be bringing up some guns. Edwards immediately reinforced his troops with 200 swordsmen. Mulraj's troops, who arrived in the early hours that morning, opened fire on Edwards's troops with their Zambooraks from across a shallow rivulet. Expecting Edwards's men to fight a defensive battle they were taken by surprise when instead they crossed the rivulet and attacked them. Taken aback by this move Mulraj's troops fled, leaving their Zambooraks and 12 dead men behind.

Edwards now joined forces with Van Courtland near the fort of Mungrota, 15 miles south of Dera Ghazi Khan. Their combined forces faced Mulraj who was deployed on the opposite bank of the Indus. Edwards also received some good news that his Baluch mercenaries had captured the fort at Dera Ghazi Khan. On 10 June, Currie, well aware that the Sikh columns were not moving, agreed to Edwards crossing the Indus to link up with Nawab Bhawal Khan's forces, the 'Daudputars' (Sons of David) as the people of Bhawalpur were called. Edwards was also given the authority to act as he thought fit but that his action was to be, as far as possible, restricted to the area of responsibility of his column. He was authorized by Currie to push Mulraj back into Multan, if he could do so, and to then lay siege to it if possible till further forces could reach him.

Bhawal Khan's troop of 10,000 soldiers, led by General Fateh Mohammed, had crossed the Sutlej in the first week of June. They crossed the river, and as ordered, moved north. Edwards now collected sufficient boats and transported his force of 2,500 Pathans across the 13-mile wide Indus at Dera Ghazi Khan on 10 June. The crossing took four days to complete. From here he marched southeast towards the Chenab, 40 miles away, intending to meet up with Bhawal Khan's troops at Kineyree on the east bank of the Chenab where there was a ferry.

The next day one of his scouts brought him information that Rung Ram was marching towards Bhawal Khan's troops in order to engage and destroy him before Edwards could link up with him. They were currently 3 miles south of Shujabad and intended to attack the Daudputars on 17 June. The full distance between Multan and Kineyree was 50 miles and Shujabad was exactly half way. Edwards immediately informed the British agent Ibrahim Khan, who was with the Bhawalpur troops, to dig trenches and fortifications and to avoid battle till he linked up with him. In the meantime, he sent every man he could spare to the Chenab ferry at Khangpur to build a floating platform of boats which could ferry his guns across. At dawn the next morning, as he neared the opposite bank, the sound of artillery fire indicated to Edwards that Rung Ram had arrived and battle had been joined. However, a message soon arrived to say that the Daudputars were firing their guns in delight to herald his arrival!

Peer Ibrahim Khan now informed Edwards that Rung Ram intended to camp on the night of 17 June at a village called Bukree, near the ferry where Edwards was to cross. He, therefore, had asked General Fateh Mohammed to secure his end of the ferry to prevent Rung Ram interfering with his crossing. Edwards launched his troops with a selected force of 3,000 men on 30 boats and sent them across in the early hours of 18 June under the command of Faujdar Khan. When the boats did not arrive back by 6 a.m. as promised, he commandeered two small boats and went across himself with his horse and servants. As he drew closer to the east bank the unmistakable sounds of battle reached him and when he reached the bank he was met by a guide sent by Faujdar Khan to escort him to the battlefield. He was told by the guide that Rung Ram had marched in the early hours to the ferry and had found it blocked by his Pathans and the Daudputars. He had then withdrawn to the nearby hill to engage them with his guns.

The opposing forces comprised Rung Ram's troops of 8,000 to 10,000 troops and 10 guns, while the Bhawalpur troops, led by General Fateh Mohammed Khan had around 8,500 cavalry and infantry, 11 ancient guns and 30 Zambooraks. Edwards had 5,000 irregulars, of whom 3,000 had crossed the Indus. This left 1,500 men and 10 guns under General Van Courtland who were yet to cross.

When Edwards arrived on the scene, he immediately realized that the Bhawalpur Army was in a completely disorganized state. When he asked to meet General Fateh Mohammed, he was directed to a very old man of around eighty years of age, with a skullcap on, sitting under a tree telling his beads oblivious to his officers gathered around him clamouring for orders. The old man was seemingly unconcerned by Rung Ram's shot breaking branches overhead and unaware that his reasonably equipped and brave army were deployed and awaiting his orders. When Edwards confronted him, it took him a while to realize who was speaking, as he came forward and looked blankly into his face. The Bhawalpur officers reported to Edwards who told them bluntly that,

> Nothing can be done with an army so disorganized as this. The enemy has taken up a strong position and will probably prefer to be attacked [...] I will write to General Courtland on the other side of the river to send us over some guns that are better than the enemy's, and not a move must be made till they come. In the meanwhile, occupy yourselves with recovering the order of your force; make the whole lie down in line in the jungle; keep them as much under cover as possible, and let your artillery play as hard as they can on the enemy guns. Above all stand fast, and be patient.[149]

Edwards then returned to his troops who were lying down in lines with their standards planted next to them. He dictated a letter to General Van Courtland and sent copies by two separate riders to make sure the message reached him. It was now 8 a.m. and Edwards expected General Van Courtland's relief to reach him by 3 p.m. He waited, with his troops, in the shade of the trees where the temperature was over 100 degrees Fahrenheit in the shade and with no water to drink. After six hours the old general of the Daudputars, without any prior warning, took his army and departed for the ferry, leaving Edwards and his 2,500 Pathans to fend for themselves.

Seeing this opportunity, Rung Ram commenced his advance and the Pathans responded by opening fire with their 30 Zambooraks. Edwards now took his faithful Faujdar Khan aside and told him to pick a force of loyal men and to charge the advancing Multani cavalry to disorient their advance, as it was essential to buy time till General Van Courtland's reinforcements arrived. Faujdar Khan led a charge that went through the enemy cavalry and returned back through them again, managing to buy a little time. Despite this, Rung Ram's steady advance continued. Suddenly Van Courtland's artillery bugle was heard sounding the gallop, and the first 6 pounder appeared followed closely by five more. They immediately unlimbered and the order 'action front' was given. Starting with round shot, the gunners quickly turned to grapeshot sending the Multanis to ground, until they eventually withdrew.

Seeing this, Edwards ordered his officers to their posts at the head of their troops. With banners streaming, the Pathans advanced on Rung

Ram. The horse artillery went forward once again at the gallop, unlimbered, and gave covering fire. The Multanis were completely routed. Rung Ram had disappeared on his elephant. His army was chased once again by the Daudputar cavalry, which had returned along with the Bhawalpur Army when Van Courtland's guns had reached Edwards. Rung Ram's troops retreated pell-mell to Noonar, and then to Shujabad, half way to Multan. The battle of Kineyree ended at 4.30 p.m. on 18 June 1848. Eight of the Multani's 10 guns were captured, and over 500 of them had been killed, and Edwards had lost 58 killed and had 89 wounded. The road to Multan now lay open.

Edwards let his men rest for three days and have their wounds attended to. On 22 June he moved north to Shujabad, 25 miles north on the road to Multan. His force now comprised 1,800 men, including General Van Courtland's men and the Daudputars, who were now under the command of a British officer, Lieutenant Edward Lake. The old Fateh Mohammed having been recalled by Bhawal Khan was on his way back to Bhawalpur.

Edwards now wrote to Currie at Lahore, suggesting an immediate attack on Multan and an attempt to occupy it, he felt that Mulraj after the defeat at Kineyree, would be less inclined to face a determine assault. He suggested that Major Napier, who was at Lahore with a battery of heavy guns, a mortar battery and engineers, should be sent by boat to Bhawalpur, from where they could join him. Currie consulted Napier who felt that the mobile brigade was sufficient for what Edwards had in mind, and that the venture may very well be a success. Though he had the power to make the decision himself, Currie decided to forward this request to Dalhousie and Gough. Gough promptly rejected it, for reasons he had already given earlier. To this he added,

> I have always understood from you that both the Sikh Army and the Sikh population are disaffected and should be guarded against. I take that these objections to weakening our force at Lahore and on the Frontier still exist. The movement of a siege train under these contingencies, with so insufficient an escort as a Brigade, would in my mind be a most hazardous measure.[150]

On 26 June, Edwards marched towards Multan, taking the fort at Secundrabad, 10 miles beyond Shujabad. He received information that Mulraj intended to intercept him at the junction of the road and the Wali Mohammed canal, just short of Multan. The bridge on the canal had been demolished. Edwards decided to bypass him, by crossing up-stream and making straight for Multan. He halted on a plain 4 miles from the city. When news of this reached Mulraj he withdrew his force to a point 3 miles out of Multan. His astrologers had told him that if he joined battle with Edwards on this day he would be victorious, and he was itching for a fight. On 30 June, Sheikh Imam-ud-din, the former governor of Kashmir and his Sikh column established contact with Mulraj. Edwards now

The Ruling Family of Lahore
1801-49

Maharaja Ranjit Singh Bahadur
1780-1839: Maharaja of Lahore from
1801 to 1839

Left to Right
Kanwar Kharak Singh
(later Maharaja),
Maharaja Ranjit Singh,
and Kanwar Naunihal Singh
(later Maharaja)

Maharaja Ranjit Singh Bahadur
1780-1839: Maharaja of Lahore from
1801-39

Maharaja Kharak Singh
1802-40:
Ruled for three months and was
deposed by his son Naunihal Singh

Maharaja Naunihal Singh
1821-40: Ruled for thirteen months
from 8 October 1839 to 5 November
1840 and was killed in an accident on
5 November 1840

Maharaja Ranjit Singh:
A sketch by Emily Eden

Left:
Maharaja Sher Singh: Ruled between
1841-43 and was assassinated on
15 September 1843. A painting by
August Shoefft

Maharaja Duleep Singh (1838-83):
Punjab was annexed on
21 March 1849 when he was eleven
years old. He ruled between the
years 1843-49

1. Maharaja Ranjit Singh: Founder and the most distinguished ruler of the kingdom of Lahore
2. Kr. Kharak Singh: Son of Maharaja Ranjit Singh succeeded him in 1839, died in 1841
3. Kr. Naunihal Singh: Grandson of Maharaja Ranjit Singh. Killed by the fall of an archway (Khuni Darwaza) while returning from the funeral of his father in 1841
4. Raja Makhdam Singh: (Mian Udham Singh) Son of Raja Gulab Singh of Jammu, killed alongwith Prince Naunihal Singh as a result of the fall of the archway (Khuni Darwaza) in 1841. Udhampur, near Jammu is named after him
5. Raja Gulab Singh: Holder of the fief of Jammu under Maharaja Ranjit Singh, eldest of the Dogra brothers who became Maharaja of Jammu & Kashmir in 1846, on the sale of the territory to him
6. Bhai Ram Singh: Notable Sikh divine, closely associated with the Lahore Durbar under Maharaja Ranjit Singh and his successors
7. Raja Suchet Singh: Third of the Dogra brothers killed in the fight against his nephew, Raja Hira Singh, wazir of Lahore, 1844
8. Raja Dhyan Singh: Prime Minister of Punjab under Maharaja Ranjit Singh, Kharak Singh and Sher Singh; murdered at Lahore by the Sandhanwalias along with Maharaja Sher Singh and his son in 1843
9. Hira Singh: Son of Raja Dhyan Singh, favourite of Maharaja Ranjit Singh, became wazir at Lahore after the murder of his father, 1843. Was himself killed by Sikh troops while fleeing from Lahore in 1844
10. Tej Singh: One of the prominent sardars of the Lahore Durbar, was commander-in-chief of the durbar troops at the time of the First Anglo-Sikh War, 1846

Ranjit Singh's Durbar, Lahore

11. Labh Singh: One of the sons of Raja Gulab Singh of Jammu
12. Lal Singh: A functionary of the Lahore Durbar in his early career, enjoyed the confidence of Maharani Jinda Kaur and became wazir of the Lahore Durbar in 1844. He was imprisoned and exiled for his role in Kashmir
13. Dewan Deenanath: A Kashmiri Brahmin, functioned as head of the department of finance under Maharaja Ranjit Singh and his successors
14. Fakir Aziz-ud-din: The most trusted of the advisers of Maharaja Ranjit Singh and his minister of foreign affairs
15. Hardit Singh: Son of Sardar Jawala Singh, a notable jagirdar of the Lahore Durbar
16. Budh Singh: A prominent sardar of the Lahore Durbar
17. Sultan Mohamed Khan: A Barakzai sardar who was granted Peshawar on contract, as a jagir.
18. Ali Mohammed Khan Khadkoh of Shikarpur, a Muslim chief in the service of Maharaja Ranjit Singh
19. Mohamed Khan: Vakil of the Amirs of Sindh at the court of Maharaja Ranjit Singh.
20. Nawab Sulfizar Khan: Nawab of Multan who was associated with the Lahore Durbar as a pensionary of Maharaja Ranjit Singh.
21. Ibrahim Khan: A Muslim dignitary.
22. Sher Singh: One of the sons of Maharaja Ranjit Singh, succeeded the throne in 1841 and was murdered in 1843 by the Sandhanwalia sardars
23. Partap Singh: Son of Maharaja Sher Singh who was murdered along with his father in 1843
24. Lehna Singh: Son of Desa Singh Majithia, a prominent sardar under Maharaja Ranjit Singh
25. Dr Honigberger: European medical officer
26. Colonel Mouton: French Cavalry officer
27. Henri Francois Stanislaus De La Roche: French Infantry officer
28. Colonel La Font: French Infantry officer
29. Fakir Chirag Din: A member of the Sayed family
30. General Allard: French Cavalry officer
31. General Avitabile: Italian Civil officer
32. General Ventura: Italian Infantry general
33. Colonel Foulkes: English Cavalry officer
34. Colonel Steinbach: Austrian Infantry officer
35. Colonel Court: English Infantry officer
36. Sham Singh: The celebrated Attariwala chief who distinguished himself in the service of the Lahore Durbar and died fighting in the First Anglo-Sikh War, 1845-46
37. Colonel Mehan Singh: Second-in-Command to Hari Singh Nalwa at the battle of Jamraud: Nazim of Kashmir
38. Fakir Nur-ud-din: Brother of Aziz-ud-din, a trusted civil functionary of Maharaja Ranjit Singh
39. Fakir Hari Dass: Hindu mendicant
40. Colonel C.A. Court: French Artillery officer
41. Meka Singh
42. Gurmukh Singh
43. Attar Singh: Sindhanwalia chief
44. Missar Beli Ram: Incharge of the Toshakhana of Maharaja Ranjit Singh
45. A jewel carrier
46. Bur Singh
47. Commandant Mehan Singh
48. Munshi: A mounshee, scribe
49. Commandant Lall Singh
50. Akalies
51. Irregular Cavalry
52. Regular Infantry
53. Bhai Nidhan Singh

From the Princess Bamba Collection.
The Lahore Fort. Painted by August Schoefft

Annotated Copy. Along with the copy of the painting by Lilian Morton, 1922. The Patiala Collection, Motibagh Palace.

All prominent generals and sardars of the Lahore state, present at the durbar, are named.

Personalities of the Lahore Durbar

Raja Suchet Singh of Sambha and Ramnagar

Raja Dhyan Singh of Poonch
Raja Kalan, Lahore Durbar
Prime Minister 1827-43

Raja Gulab Singh
Appointed Raja of Jammu
by Maharaja Ranjit Singh in 1822

Baba Sahib Singh Bedi

Fakir Syed Aziz-ud-din

Fakir Syed Nur-ud-din

Dewan Deenanath

Ajit Singh Sandhanwalia

Fateh Singh Kalianwala

Sardar Sham Singh Attari

Dr Johann Martin Honigberger

Alexander Burnes in his book *Travels into Bokhara* recorded the events at the court of Maharaja Ranjit Singh

Victor Jacquemont in *A Journey to India* records that 'the Sikh troops were unique in the world'

Baron Charles Van Hugel in *Travels in Cashmere and the Punjab* provides an insight into the Lahore Durbar

Raja Fateh Singh Ahluwalia of Kapurthala

The main entrance to the palace of the Lahore fort, the 'Alamgiri Darwaza', with the baradari in the Hazuri Bagh in the foreground

Maharaja Sher Singh entering Lahore in a procession of sardars and nobles of the durbar

The *samadh* of Maharaja Ranjit Singh outside the fort at Lahore on the banks of the Choti Ravi. To its left are the *samadhs* of Maharaja Kharak Singh and Maharaja Naunihal Singh

Prominent events during the reign of Maharaja Ranjit Singh

Akali Phula Singh: Killed in the battle of Theri (Naushera) in 1823

Hari Singh Nalwa: Killed in the battle of Jamraud in 1837. *(Photo courtesy: Imperial Hotel)*

Jamraud fort with the Khyber Pass in the background

Akali Phula Singh's *samadh* on the west bank (Yuzoofzie side) of the Kabul or Loonda river, at Naushera

Maharaja Ranjit Singh meeting the Governor General Lord William Bentinck at Ropar on 26 October 1831. The meeting continued till 1 November 1831

Afghan Adversaries of the Lahore Durbar

Dost Mohammad Khan, chief of the Barakzai. The Amir of Afghanistan 1836-40 and 1841-63, and his three sons: (*anti-clockwise from top left*) Haider Ali, governor of Ghazni, Mohammad Akram Khan and Abdul Ghani Khan. A painting by Emily Eden

Shah Shuja-ul-Mulk. Chief of the Sadozai, Amir of Afghanistan from 1802-09 and 1840-41

Maharaja Ranjit Singh's Persian horse Laili: The horse cost him 12,000 troops and 60 lakh rupees. The cost of his Peshawar campaign to procure it

Dost Mohammad Khan's Afghan warriors of the Barakzai tribe

The Kohinoor diamond of 108.93 carats. Presently in the Queen Mother's crown in the United Kingdom. Taken from Shah Shuja-ul-Mulk by Ranjit Singh in 1813

European officers in the service of the Lahore Durbar

General Jean-Francois Allard: General of Cavalry

General Paolo B. Avitabile: General of Artillery

General Jean-Baptiste Ventura: General of Infantry GOC, Fauj-e-Khas

General Claude August Court: General of Infantry

Colonels Mouton, de la Roche and La Font

General Jean-Francois Allard died on 23 January 1839 at Peshawar. He was buried at Lahore where his tomb stands to this day

Illustrations on this page are from The French and Lahore *by Jean-Marie Lafont*

The Lahore Durbar Army
Fauj-e-Ain Artillery

Darogha (later General) Illahi Bakhsh Darogha-e-Topkhana, 1821-46

The Zamzama or 'Bhangian di top' firing a 84-pound projectile on display at the Lahore fort

Topkhana 'Fili': Elephant-drawn heavy siege or field guns

Colonel Alexander Gardner, Lahore Durbar Artillery

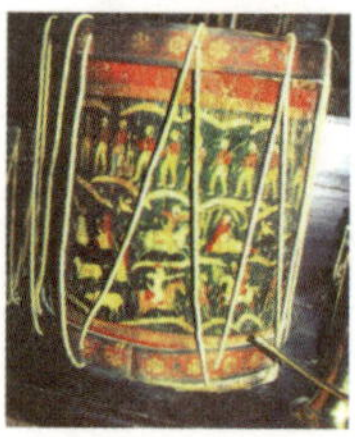

Tambur (drum) of Fauj-e-Khas

The siege gun 'Fateh Jung'

Topkhana 'Aspi': Horse artillery

Topkhana 'Gavi': Cattle-drawn field guns

A field gun and a bell mortar with the assorted ammunition available to them

The First Anglo-Sikh War, 1845-46

Maharaja Duleep Singh: Aged seven in 1845

Maharani Jinda Kaur: Regent of the Lahore Durbar 1843-49

Sardar Tej Singh, C-in-C in Lahore Durbar Army, with his two sons

Viscount Henry Hardinge, GCB Governor General of India, 1844-48

Raja Lal Singh, Wazir, Lahore Durbar

Sham Singh Attari
(Photo courtesy: Imperial Hotel)

General Lord Gough, GCB Commander-in-Chief, India, wearing his famous white 'fighting coat'

Major General Sir Harry Smith, Bart, GCB and Sardar Ranjodh Singh Majithia: The commanders of the only independent action at Aliwal on 28 January 1846

The Lahore Durbar Army, 1845-46
Fauj-e-Ain

Fauj-e-Khas (Avitabile's Brigade Group)
Officer — Cuirassier Rajman
Sipahi — Paltan Khas
Sowar — Lancia Rajman

Various Sikh Paltans – Summer Uniforms
Sipahi at rest — Rifle Protected
Naik — Kitted for battle — Bayonet Fixed
Sipahi — Kitted for battle

Topkhana Derah
Muslim 'Aspi Golandaz'
(Field Gun Crew)

Sikh Paltan — Winter Dress
Gorkha — Paltan
Purbiya — Paltan
Sikh Paltan — Summer Dress

Water colours by Ken Hunt

The Lahore Durbar Army, 1845-46
Fauj-e-Gair

Ghorcharra Sardar

Ghorcharra Sardars

Jagirdari Fauj

Sardar Akali Shock Troops

Misldari Fauj

Misldar Sardar Sipahi Jemadar

Water colours by Ken Hunt (except for the picture at the top right)

The Anglo-Sikh Wars of 1845-46 and 1848-49

British and East India Company Forces

Captain HM 24th Foot, 1846 (from *The History of the South Wales Borderers, 24th Foot, 1689-1937* by C.T. Atkinson)

An officer of HM 3rd Light Dragoons, 1846 (from *The Historical Record of the 3rd Light Dragoons 1847*)

Bengal Native Infantry Regiment, 1846
Courtesy: The Oberoi Collection, Wildflower Hall, Simla

An officer of the Bengal Irregular Cavalry, East India Company troops, 1845
Courtesy: The Oberoi Collection, Wildflower Hall, Simla

An officer of a Bengal Cavalry Regiment, East India Company troops, 1845
Courtesy: The Oberoi Collection, Wildflower Hall, Simla

Bengal Native Infantry Regiment at rest, 1846
Courtesy: The Oberoi Collection, Wildflower Hall, Simla

Bengal Irregular Horse (Skinners) in training, 1846

The Quarter Guard 2nd Bombay Grenadiers, Bombay Native Infantry, 1846
Courtesy: The Oberoi Collection, Wildflower Hall, Simla

The Battle of Mudki, 18 December 1845

HM 31st Foot charging the Sikh guns at Mudki, 18 December 1845

The charge of HM's 3rd Light Dragoons at the battle of Mudki

The Battle of Ferozshah, 22 December 1845

The charge of HM 3rd Light Dragoons at the battle of Ferozshah on 22 December 1845. A painting by Henry Martens

HM 62nd Foot storming a Sikh gun position at the battle of Ferozshah

Night bivouac at Ferozshah on 21 and 22 December 1845

Lord Gough resuming the attack on the morning of 22 December 1845 after the night bivouac on the field at Ferozshah

The Battle of Sobraon, 11 February 1846

The 31st Foot storming the Sikh lines at the battle of Sobraon: In the background Sergeant McCabe plants the Regimental Colour on the captured redan

British and East India Company troops crossing the river Sutlej by a bridge of boats after the battle of Sobraon

The Battle of Aliwal, 28 January 1846

A Sikh square repulsing the first charge of HM 16th Lancers while a troop of the Bengal European Artillery prepares to open fire. *Courtesy: Michael Perry*

HM 16th Queen's Lancers charging the Sikh infantry at the battle of Aliwal. Sergeant Newsome leads the front rank

HM 16th Queen's Lancers at the battle of Aliwal after breaking the Sikh squares

Multan, 1848-49

Lieutenant Herbert Edwards
Commissioner Dera Jat, Multan

Mulraj: The deposed governor of Multan, 1848
A calotype by Jethro McCosh, an army surgeon, taken in 1849. From *Victoria's Wars* by Saul David

The storming of Multan and its occupation on 2 January 1849

The Second Sikh War, 1848-49

James A.B. Ramsay, 10th Earl and 1st Marquess of Dalhousie Governor General, 1848-56

Sir Henry Lawrence

Lt Gen. Viscount Gough, GCB: Commander-in-Chief, India, during both the First and Second Anglo-Sikh wars

Sardar Chattar Singh Attari, Governor of Hazara

Raja Sher Singh Attari Commander Sikh forces

The Battle of Chillianwala, 13 January 1849

The battle of Chillianwala being fought at the foothills of the Himalayas; a scene from behind the British line

Captain Unnet leads the Grey Squadron of HM 3rd King's Own Light Dragoons in the charge against the Sikh line

The Battle of Gujrat, 21 February 1849

The battle of Gujrat in the Second Sikh War, 1849. A painting by Henry Martens

Raja Sher Singh Attari commanding the Sikh Army at the battle of Gujrat

The End of the Second Anglo-Sikh War

Major General Sir Walter Gilbert receiving the surrender of the Sikhs at Hammuck, on the left bank of the Swan river, near Rawalpindi on 12 March 1849

The eleven-year-old Maharaja Duleep Singh arrives at the British camp on 30 March 1849 when the terms of annexation were read out to him. He was to resign for himself, and his successors all rights, title and claim to the sovereignty of the Punjab

Maharaja Duleep Singh after the annexation of the Punjab with his family in exile

Maharaja Duleep Singh: Aged sixteen in 1854, in exile in England. A painting by Winterhalter

Dr Sir John Login

Maharani Jinda Kaur: In exile in England. A painting by George Richmond

Lady Lena Login

Maharani Bamba Duleep Singh, 1880

Maharaja Duleep Singh, 1885: Aged 47

Maharaja Duleep Singh, 1880: Aged 42

Maharani Bamba and the children at Elveden Hall, 1876: (Left to Right) Frederick, Sophia, Victor, Catherine and Bamba

Elveden Hall: A Georgian country house in Suffolk

A shooting party at Elveden: The Prince of Wales (later Edward the Seventh) seated third left and Maharaja Duleep Singh seated extreme right

Prince Victor Duleep Singh, 1896.
1866-1918

Prince Frederick Duleep Singh, 1903
1868-1926

The three princesses, 1892:
(Left to Right) Bamba, Catherine
and Sophia

The grave of Maharaja Duleep Singh (4 September 1838–22 October 1893) at Elveden

The grave of Princess Bamba Sutherland at Lahore, 1869-1957: The last of the Shukarchakia dynasty

Elveden churchyard, 1900: The grave of Maharaja Duleep Singh flanked by his wife Maharani Bamba and his young son Edward

received information that Mulraj had positioned his army to meet him at the 3-mile point, at a place called Suddoosam. Edwards deployed his troops to face Mulraj. On the right was Lieutenant Lake with the Daudputars. General Van Courtland was in the centre with his troops and guns, Edwards himself being to the left of centre with his Pathans, flanked by his Pathan cavalry. On the far left was Sheikh Imam-ud-din. Lieutenant Lake began the action by capturing a height, deploying his guns on it and opening fire on Mulraj's left. The remainder of the army then assaulted and the line advanced through villages and groves of date palms fighting hand to hand all the way. A well-aimed shot hit Mulraj's howdah and he was violently flung from his elephant to the ground. Scrambling to his feet he jumped on his horse and galloped off to the fort. This incident initiated a rout, his army took flight behind him being chased by Edwards's troops. Quin, a young civilian who had offered his services to Edwards, now led the charge of the Suraj Mukhi Regiment on Mulraj's guns, capturing most of them.

Edwards ordered the recall to be blown. He had lost 281 men, killed and wounded in the action, but had managed to bottle Mulraj up in the fort. For these incredible exploits, this young officer was later awarded the commander of the Bath, and the East India Company promoted him to Major and presented him with a gold medal.

IV. THE FIRST SIEGE

The news of the victory at Suddoosam, following that of Kineyree, reached Currie at Lahore on 10 July. He now decided to accept Edwards's advice, and that of Napier, and to disregard Dalhousie's and Gough's opposition to an immediate assault on Multan. Invoking the powers he had over the troops at Lahore, he ordered General Whish to 'take immediate measures for the dispatch of a siege train with its establishment and a competent escort and force, for the reduction of the fort at Multan.'[151] He then wrote to Dalhousie that he had taken this decision, 'from a conviction of its political necessity, and military practicability, at the present moment.' Dalhousie, though unhappy at this decision, replied,

> Since you have considered it necessary, in exercise of the powers conferred upon you, to assume this responsibility, and, in pursuance of it, have issued publicly the orders for carrying out your resolution into effect, the Government, being anxious to maintain your authority, do not withhold their confirmation of the orders you have issued.[152]

Gough too was most upset with this decision to take on a campaign in the worst possible season. The rivers would be in spate and heavy rain and mud would make overland movement difficult. Even worse would be the heat and accompanying diseases to which the British troops were susceptible. He wrote to Currie,

MULTAN, 1848-49

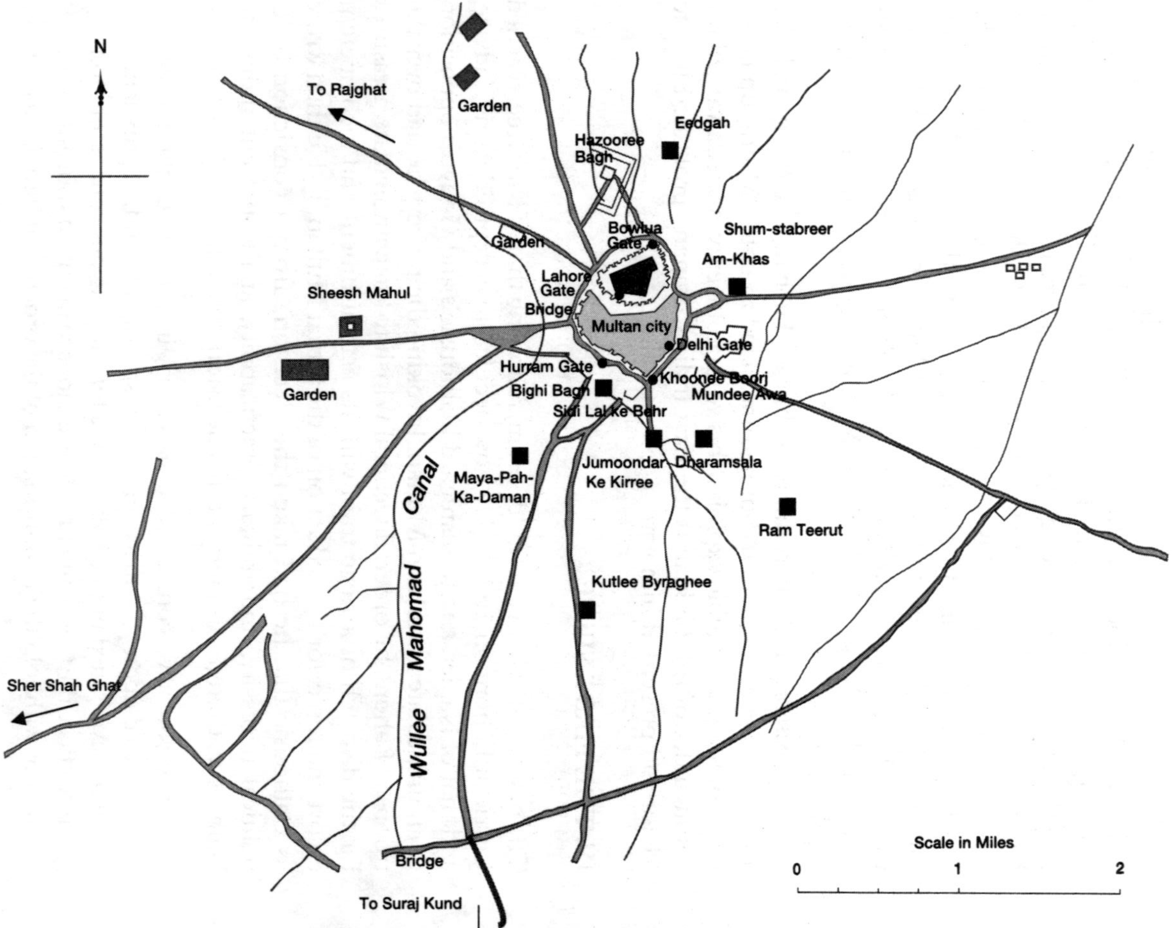

> [...] the troops have been ordered to move upon your responsibility. I have only to assure you that every facility and aid in my power shall be freely given, so as to carry out a successful result in the operations against Multan.[153]

A British force of divisional strength was assembled under General Whish comprising: the 1st Infantry Brigade under Brigadier Hervey, with HM 10th, the 8th and 52nd NI Battalions, the 2nd Infantry Brigade under Brigadier Markham, comprising HM 32nd, 49th, 52nd, and 72nd NI Battalions, the 1st Cavalry Brigade under Brigadier Slater with the 7th and 11th Irregular Cavalry Regiments and the 11th Light Cavalry, two troops of heavy artillery, four companies of Foot Artillery, two companies of Bengal Sappers and three companies of Pioneers. To this force would be added those troops currently with Lieutenant Edwards. This force left Lahore for Multan in the end of July.

George Bruce commented in his *Six Battles for India* that:

> It is worth notice that in the same way as Major George Broadfoot's actions largely brought about the First Sikh War, Sir Frederick Currie, by fanning the flames of a local rising, made the second one almost a certainty. Broadfoot and Currie were both appointed by Hardinge.

General Whish led his army part of the way down the Ravi on flat-bottomed barges and for the last week he marched it through the hot and arid countryside. A young NCO of HM 32nd, one of the few men of his regiment who knew how to read and write, and who during the march was suffering from malaria, later recorded his observations.

> I got worse, and it was as much as I could do to keep up; and I never should have done, had I not swallowed five drams of grog, about a pint in a bottle [...] We marched a long way that day [...] One man fell dead. I arrived in camp about nine o'clock. We lay in the tents panting for breath [...] The heat was above one hundred degrees, and the water was very bad, on account of the wells not being used, which caused the water to be stagnant and black, and smell very offensively, so that we were obliged to stop our noses while we drank. I began to get very low-spirited and given to fret; when all at once, I thought it would not do; so I rallied my feelings and walked about, and began to think I should soon feel better. This and the medicine the doctor administered soon began to revive me, and I felt a great deal better. The morning was hotter and closer than I ever felt it before, and the wind was awful – fairly piercing our flesh. We had not marched more than two miles upon the road before men began to fall dead in the ranks [...] Our line of march was strewed with dead, dying, and sick [...] Our doctors and apothecaries were all engaged in bleeding; but as the night was very dark, they could not find the vein, and they cut gashes across the arm anyway, so as to get blood. The cry for water

> was past all describing; the mouth and tongue were swollen and parched, the eyes looked wild and ghastly, and ready to start out of the head. How little do the people of England know the hardships of a poor soldier in India. Men lay upon the sand by the dozens, gasping for breath [...] All the skill of a physician could not restore them. I saw our old colonel looking at them, and he exclaimed, "Oh, my poor men, my fine regiment – what shall I do?" I felt very sorry for him, for he was in great trouble. As one man died he was carried out, and another came in his place. They were well and dead in an hour. The number who fell sick in the day was 175, and 14 dead. The heat in the tents was 130 degrees. All our dead were buried in a hole together, at sunset; and long before morning the wild beasts had torn up and dragged them to pieces. We made a junction with the army at Multan on the morning of the 25 of August, at about seven o'clock [...][154]

General Whish now decided to wait till his siege guns arrived before starting his attack. Edwards had wanted to attack while confusion still prevailed in Multan, but the situation had changed. Large ramparts had been built on the walls of the fort and the citizens were prepared to assist Mulraj, as they now believed that they were fighting for their homes against an invader. Unemployed and disaffected Sikh soldiers found their way to Multan and joined Mulraj. These same people had already begun to spread unrest amongst the Sikh troops, particularly amongst the men of Raja Sher Singh's column camped just behind Edwards.

The siege guns comprising: 24x18pdr, 10x8inch howitzers and 10 mortar's, 8 inch and 5½, inch arrived from Ferozepur on 4 September. Whish called a conference to decide how best to carry out the operations. The first suggestion, given to him by Napier, was to storm the fort by surprise, the second being to attack from the north by regular approaches. Whish turned both these options down. When all suggestions had been discussed, without adopting any of them, Lieutenant Lake in command of the Daudputars and one of the most junior officers present, suggested digging a forward trench. It would have to be about a mile long, from Ramtirath to a point opposite the Khooni Burj, about 1,600 yards from the fort walls and the Delhi Gate. In it would be placed the heavy guns to support the infantry that would then gradually drive the enemy from the houses and gardens outside the walls. The heavy guns could then be moved forward to breach the walls, through which the infantry would storm the fort. Whish readily accepted this suggestion and next day the trace marking the trench was laid.

This period of indecision had frustrated the younger officers a great deal. The buying of commissions and promotions was still a part of the system and colonels and majors, past the age of retirement, were feeling the strain of a summer campaign. Lieutenant Hodson wrote,

> They became after a fortnight's campaign, a burden to themselves, an annoyance to those under them and a terror to everyone but the enemy [...] I know of one infantry brigadier who could not see his regiment, when I led his horse by the bridle until his nose touched the bayonets; even then he said faintly, pray, which way are the men facing, Mr Hodson?[155]

The digging of the trench began on 7 September. The city itself was surrounded by high walls and bastioned towers while the fort, built on an old mound, towered above it. The houses and orchards outside the walls were occupied by the infantry; some were in British hands but most were with Mulraj. Both sides had dug entrenchments. On 12 September, Whish launched an attack to clear the Sikh infantry from the houses so that a trench could be dug. After a severe fight lasting all day, Whish moved his troops around 900 yards closer to the walls and Van Courtland pointed out a suitable position where the heavy British guns could be positioned to breach the walls. Whish lost: 5 British and 5 Indian officers killed; 32 other ranks were killed; 12 British, 1 Indian officer and 203 other ranks were wounded during this operation. A feeling of optimism now swept the British camp and people believed that victory was in sight. But soon came the news of Raja Sher Singh's defection to Mulraj.

This major setback forced General Whish to suspend operations until reinforcements arrived from Bombay. He ordered his troops back to Suraj Kund, 4 miles to the rear, at the site where Edwards had fought and defeated Mulraj. From here it was possible for him to cover the road south to Bhawalpur and west to the Raj Ghat ferry across the Chenab, which was the direct route to Dera Ghazi Khan and the Dera Jat. During the next three months the order of the day was aggressive patrolling and a further series of localized skirmishes. The Bombay Army reinforcements, due in mid-November, finally arrived on 10 December. The first effort to break the siege of Multan thus ended in a stalemate.

V. THE SECOND SIEGE

The Bombay Army was delayed because the general originally appointed to command the force was senior to General Whish, and General Whish's appointment had been approved by the governor general. When news of his appointment was received in the governor general's office in Calcutta, it was overruled, and Bombay was asked to find someone who was junior to General Whish. Brigadier Dundas, a British service officer, who had earlier served in the 60th Rifles, was finally appointed and took over his command, which comprised three Native Cavalry Regiments, the 1st Bombay Light Cavalry and the 1st and 2nd Scinde Irregular Horse; two British Infantry Regiments, the 60th Rifles and the 1st Bombay Fusiliers; four Native Infantry Regiments, the 3rd, 4th, 9th, and 19th Bombay Native Infantry. The artillery complement was 67 siege and 30 field guns.

George Bruce describes the Multan city and fort in *Six Battles for India* as below.

> It was built on a low hill, and was the gateway to India from central Asia, via the Punjab. It was hexagonal in shape with walls seventy-foot high and a moat forty-five feet wide and twenty-five feet deep. The highest part of the hill was closer to the northeast, at this point it dominated both the city and its approaches.
>
> Thirty strong towers rose from the fort walls; eighty guns of varying calibre poked their black muzzles out through the embrasures. A high and ancient wall, built on lofty ramparts from which many trees grew, also surrounded the town; immediately above this rose another wall, strengthened with corner towers and battlements. In and around the walls towered the high domes and minarets of mosques, temples and a Khan's palace.
>
> Multan, for those with the eye to see, was an ancient, fascinating and in parts beautiful city. To the English politicians, merchants and soldiers – the empire builders – it was at once immensely wealthy and strategically important.

With the arrival of the Bombay contingent, General Whish planned to resume his offensive operations without delay. To begin with, it would be the continuation of the operation of, 'containment' that had been suspended when Sher Singh had changed sides. The houses, village and other settlements to the northeast of the city had to be re-taken. This had partly been achieved before the suspension and it would now have to be resumed. Once this was achieved, Whish intended to bring up his heavy siege guns and breach the city walls so that the infantry could storm it. Mulraj's own house, the Aam Khas, his father's tomb and the surrounding garden, which was in the centre of his proposed area of deployment, became Whish's first objective.

General Whish deployed his force, with his Bengal troops, on the right facing the Delhi Gate and that part of the city wall nearest to the fort. The Bombay troops were positioned in the centre, reaching to the Wali Mohammed canal. Edwards and the Daudputars were on the left beyond the canal. The irregular forces and Sheikh Imam-ud-din's column were sent back on line-of-communication duties.

Whish launched his attack to secure this area using four columns, each containing about 1,000 soldiers. On the right, five companies of HM 10th and 52 NI, supported by four horse artillery guns and a squadron of the 11th Bengal Irregular Cavalry, were to take some brick kilns about a mile from the south-east part of the city wall. On the left, three companies of HM 32nd and six companies of the 72nd NI, also supported by four guns, were to clear the ground towards the Delhi Gate. Another column of five companies of the 60th Rifles and 3rd Bombay Infantry, supported by a squadron of the 1st Bombay Lancers, were to take a mound called the 'Mandi Awa'. The fourth column, on the left, would comprise five companies of the 1st Bombay Fusiliers and the 4th Bombay Rifles supported by the 7th Bombay Light Field Battery and a squadron of the Scinde Horse was to secure a small conical hill called 'Sidi Lal Ka Behr'. After about five hours of intense fighting, these objectives were secured, including the blue mosque of the Saint of Shams Tubrez. The position had been taken at a cost of 200 killed and wounded.

Whish was now able to bring up his guns to within 500 yards of the walls. He positioned three batteries comprising 18 mortars, including five high-calibre ones, two 24 pounders, six 18 pounders and four heavy howitzers. Mulraj, not to be outdone, continued to engage the British gun position throughout the deployment, causing considerable casualties amongst the gunners.

Early next morning the batteries opened fire, the howitzers and mortars engaged the town and the heavy guns the city walls, to secure a breach. Shelling continued throughout the night and some of the guns were moved further up towards the walls under the cover of darkness. The morale within the fort was obviously low as a number of people attempted to escape the city during the night. The men were stopped and taken prisoners while the women and children were allowed to leave.

By morning there were visible signs of damage to the walls. At 8 a.m. on 30 December, a chance hit by a mortar bomb fired by Lieutenant Newall of the Bengal artillery, hit Mulraj's main powder magazine, reported to hold around 800,000 lbs of powder. The terrific explosion killed over 800 people within its proximity and many thousands were injured. Mosques, houses and temples were also destroyed. It is to Mulraj's credit that his guns never stopped firing throughout this period. The British guns which had gone silent when the explosion took place, more in awe rather than for any other reason, now resumed their fire and continued, non-stop, for the next 24 hours. Some of the shots set fire to inflammables and houses, and soon entire streets within the city were on fire. On new year's eve, the British artillery fire increased in intensity and Whish let it be known that if a breach was effected that night, he would storm Multan in the morning.

Coincidentally, Mulraj had sent Whish a message on 31 to say that despite one of his magazines blowing up, he still had enough powder to hold out for another year. Whether this was bluster or not, only time would tell. Whish on the other hand expected that a breach would be effected that night and had made up his mind that if that did happen, he would launch his assault on the morning of 1 January, on the first day of the new year. Whish now sent a message to Mulraj giving him a chance to surrender before more slaughter took place. It was reported that when Whish's message arrived, Mulraj stuffed it into the barrel of his biggest gun and fired it in the direction of Whish's headquarters!

Early on the morning of 1 January, an inspection of the walls convinced the engineers that the breach was not sufficiently wide enough to enable a successful infantry assault. The attack was therefore postponed for another 24 hours and the cannonade of the walls continued in order to widen the breach. The intensity of fire was such that Corporal Ryder, one of the gunners, estimated that there were 'twenty shells in the air simultaneously.'[156]

On the night of 1-2 January, the engineers declared that there were two breaches sufficiently wide for the assault, the first in the region of the Khunee Burj and the second near the Delhi Gate. Early on 2 January, orders were issued for the storming of the city. There would be two columns: a column of Bengal Infantry under Brigadier Markham comprising HM 32nd and the 49th and 72nd NI battalions and the other, a Bombay column, under Brigadier Dundas comprising the 1st Fusiliers, the 4th Bombay Rifles and HM 19th. The assault on the Delhi Gate would be the responsibility of the Bengal troops and would be led by Captain Smyth and two companies of HM 32nd. The assaulting force formed up about 200 yards from their objective and at 3 p.m. the bugle sounded the advance. The infantry leading the engineers with ladders and other scaling equipment followed the assaulting companies as they advanced.

On reaching the wall the breaches were found to be too narrow, not even two soldiers could pass abreast of each other. In the meantime the ramparts were crowded by men, women and children throwing stones, beams and even cannon shots on the assaulting soldiers. It soon became apparent that without a wider breach the assault would fail. Smyth ordered the withdrawal and the companies fell back with a loss of 3 officers and 27 men killed or wounded. Smyth led them back at a brisk run to their left, straight to the trench called the 'Bloody bastion', which had just then been occupied by the three Bombay assault companies of the 1st Fusiliers, under the six-foot-five-inch tall Captain Leith.

The 1st Bombay Fusiliers advanced towards their breach, close to the Khooni Burj. On nearing the foot of the breach, Captain Leith shouted for his troops to charge and in a moment the lead elements, led by him, had entered the breach and scrambled up and over the rubble. Sergeant John Bennet carried the Colours to the top of the rubble and planted it right on top, standing with it to encourage the troops as they rushed past him. The Colour was riddled by bullets but miraculously Bennet remained unscathed. Having crossed the breach, the lead elements came face to face with Sikh soldiers. They received the first Sikh volley that once again miraculously missed all but Captain Leith, who was hit by a ball in his shoulder. Having fired their volley, Mulraj's Sikh infantry threw down their rifles and drew their swords. Leith, who wisely had not permitted his troops to fire their weapons in the assault, now ordered the firing of a volley followed by a bayonet charge straight into the soldiers. A ferocious melee ensued, swords clashing with the bayonets, till in the end the bayonets, as in all previous, hand-to-hand engagements with Sikh troops, finally prevailed. Mulraj's line broke and fell back, followed closely by the Fusiliers. Captain Leith lost a hand, cut clean off by the stroke of a sword.

Captain Smyth now followed the Bombay assault group with his own Bengal troops, led by his companies of HM 32nd, through the Fusiliers breach and into the city. Once inside, they fanned out into the narrow streets only to be met by fire from the houses and from other vantage points. Houses were entered and the incumbents shot or bayoneted. The severest opposition came from the premises of a temple where an officer and many withdrawing soldiers had decided to make a stand. A fierce hand-to-hand fight broke out and Corporal McGuire of the 32nd clashed with a Sikh officer holding his Regimental Colours in one hand and a sword in the other. The officer was finally killed by a bayonet thrust but not before McGuire had received a sword cut that laid open his upper arm from the shoulder to the elbow. The Colour was snatched by McGuire.

By the evening the town was in British hands and then both British and native infantry troops went on a spree of breaking into houses and wantonly killing innocent men, women and children, looting and raping. Before dawn on 3 January, British and Indian troops alike stole off to continue to loot the city's treasures before they could be seized by the prize agents, '[...] for the sale and distribution according to regulations.' George Bruce writes,

> [...] all the places were ransacked, and what could not be carried was destroyed by the ruthless barbarian troops, statuary, silks, jewels, gold, silver, fine swords, matchlocks, flintlocks, pistols inlaid with precious metals were fought over and seized. From the dead, rings, necklaces and bracelets were torn away [...] The city was a veritable treasure house, but much was lost. Most of the houses were nothing but heaps of ruins, beneath which were the bodies of those left to die after the shells struck.

General Whish had clearly lost control over his men for 24 hours. An official report however, sent subsequently by Brigadier Stalker of the Bombay Army to the C-in-C, reported that, 'I have the greatest pleasure in bearing testimony to the humanity and forbearance of the troops under my command. Not a single instance of wanton cruelty, or ill-treatment of the peaceable inhabitants of the town, has been brought to my notice.'[157] The British casualties were put at 400.

That night thousands of Multanis fled the city and the hundreds of bodies, mainly of dead Sikh soldiers, were disposed off. Major Edwards described the situation,

> Its streets were strewn with slain, chiefly Sikh's [...] There was scarce a roof or wall in the city which had not been penetrated by the English shells; and whole houses, scorched and blackened by the bombardment seemed about to fall over the corpses of their defenders.[158]

The city of Multan had been taken, now plans for the taking of the fort were put in motion. By 4 January the fort was completely surrounded, fresh gun positions were established about 500 yards from the fort and by first light on 4 January itself, the guns started an intense bombardment of the walls and the interiors of the fort. Gradually the guns were moved forward in freshly dug trenches towards the walls and the intended breaches. All this while, Mulraj's gunners and sharp shooters continued to engage targets causing some casualties. By 9 January, HM 32nd was occupying trenches within 20 yards of the fort, taking casualties during daylight hours as the soldiers on the ramparts were now shooting down at them.

Mulraj now sent a letter to Major Edwards, his opponent for the past year, asking if surrender terms could be discussed. Edwards responded by saying,

> This I cannot assent to, it is quite impossible. The time for that was April last. You then preferred war – now go through with it; or, if you are unable, surrender yourself to General Whish. After that you can represent anything you like.[159]

Mulraj then wrote a similar letter to General Whish, asking for an envoy to be sent to talk terms. General Whish responded by saying that an envoy could only be received to discuss nothing short of unconditional surrender. An elegantly clad envoy, one of Mulraj's confidential advisers, then arrived. When he began a speech starting with, 'The Dewan submits', followed by a list of conditions, his speech was cut short, and he was packed off to Mulraj with an emphatic statement that only an 'unconditional surrender' could and would be discussed.

That evening a fresh battery of 18 pounders was inducted and the intense bombardment of the walls began afresh. On 19 January, Whish toured the forward trenches to see the gaps in the walls for himself. It was now becoming necessary for him to end the Multan siege as soon as possible, as his troops were required by the C-in-C for the intended battle against Sher Singh and the Sikhs further north.

On 19 January, Mulraj once again wrote to Whish asking for permission to send a confidential agent for talks. A reply was sent to him that if he intended to surrender he could do so at 8 a.m. on the next day, 20 January. If, on the contrary, a messenger arrived from Mulraj, he would not be received and instead would be taken as a prisoner of war. No answer was received and orders were issued for the assault to begin on 22 January at 6 a.m. In the meanwhile, Mulraj was being advised by his army officers within the fort that he now had two options left – either to lead his men out of the fort to fight the British in the open, or to surrender. Mulraj decided to surrender and on 21 January wrote a letter to General Whish.

> I am now ready to come in, and for this purpose have sent my Vakil to arrange with you; your slave desires only protection for his own life, and the honour of his women. The whole of this disturbance was set on foot by my soldiers, and all my endeavours failed to quell it; now, however, I surrender myself. I ask only for my own life, and the honour of my women. You are an ocean of mercy – what more need be said? You are a sea of compassion; if you forgive me, I am fortunate; if you do not, I meet my fate with contentment.[160]

Whish answered,

> You write that you only ask for your life, and the honour of your women. This is my answer: that I have neither authority to give your life, nor take it, except in open war. The Governor General only can do this: and as to your women, the British government wars with men – not with women. I will protect your women and children to the best of my ability. Take notice, however, if you intend to come in at all, you had better do so before sunrise tomorrow, and come out by the Dowlat Gate. After sunrise you must take the fortune of war.[161]

On 22 January at 6 a.m., 10,000 troops formed up. The 18 and 24 pounders and the mortars continued their ceaseless fire and just as the assault was to begin, the Dowlat Gate opened and the Sikh and Multani troops streamed out. Orders were immediately given to cease fire. The army quickly formed a square and George Bruce describes the ceremony as, '[...] wretched and dirty but savage, determined and proud, with heads high, they laid down their arms and were received as prisoners.' Mulraj himself followed on a white horse, and the grenadier company of HM 32nd, were ordered to receive him and escort him to the generals' tent.

Thus ended the 27-day second siege of Multan. The British casualties were surprisingly low at 210 killed and 982 wounded. The artillery fired some 15,000 heavy shot, and 20,000 other assorted shots were fired into the walls and the city. Mulraj surrendered 54 guns and 4 mortars.

Dewan Mulraj was taken to Lahore and put on trial for his life before a bench of three British officers, two civilian and one military. He asked for Major Edwards to defend him, but Edwards declined saying that he considered Mulraj guilty. He was found guilty by the court and sentenced to death by hanging, but was recommended to mercy as 'a victim of circumstances.' Lord Dalhousie accepted this verdict and Mulraj was ordered to be banished across the seas to Penang.

On 27 January, General Whish, after leaving an occupying force composed of the 11th Bengal Light Cavalry, the 7th Bengal Irregular Cavalry, the 1st Bombay Light Cavalry, the 49th Bengal NI, the 4th Bombay Rifles, and the 9th Bombay NI with the necessary artillery troops to garrison Multan, marched his army north to link up with the C-in-C.

These forces were to play a part in what would in due course be known as the Second Sikh War.

Before leaving, the British ensured a decent burial for Lieutenant Anderson and Mr Van Agnew. They had been hurriedly buried by Mulraj, and were now reinterred with full military honours and a memorial was erected for them. The skeletal remains of Sardar Kahn Singh, the governor-designate, and his son whose remains were found, still chained next to each other in the dungeons, were cremated and the ashes sent home to their families.

The Second Sikh War 1848–49

I. THE PRELUDE

Despite the animosity that was felt towards the regent, Maharani Jinda, during the post-war period, the rebellion in Multan had shifted focus back to her and the people looked to her for leadership in this moment of crisis. Therefore, a decision was made to remove her from the Punjab.

Sir Frederick Currie had written to Governor General Dalhousie as early as 16 May 1848 that:

> There was no proof, though there is some ground for suspicion, that the Maharani was the instigator of the violence in Multan [...] It is certain that, at this moment, the eyes of Dewan Mulraj, of the whole Sikh Army and military population, are directed to the Maharani as a rallying point of the rebellion [...] Her removal from Punjab is called for by justice and policy, and there is no time for us to hesitate about doing what may appear necessary to punish State offenders, whatever may be their rank and station, and to vindicate the honour and position of the British government.[162]

On 15 May, the day before Currie's letter to Dalhousie, the maharani was separated from her young son and taken to Ferozepur by her own sardars. She went quite willingly as she was totally unaware that this was a British ploy and that the sardars had been assigned this duty with the approval of the Council of Regency. She actually believed that she was being taken to another location in the Punjab, and only realized that she was to be banished to Benaras when she reached Ferozepur and was told so. She then, as Cook describes it in *The Sikh Wars,* 'treated the Sikh Sardars to a flow of invective which would have done credit to any Khalsa barrack room'. Her destination was the fortress at Chunar.

It is not known whether she did have any influence over events leading up to the Multan crisis, or would have had any authority had she remained in Punjab. There's nothing on record to substantiate Currie's charge, other than the fact that a maid of hers, who had gone to Multan on personal business, once happened to meet Mulraj while she was there. However, it is true that by now she was completely hostile to the British. In her regular correspondence with the sardars and other nobles and chiefs of the state, rebellion was always a major subject. Most of these letters found their way into the hands of Currie's intelligence. The decision to banish her from Punjab added fuel to the fire and did more damage to British interest than leaving her under British guard, secluded in a house in Sheikupura.

The treatment meted out to the late Maharaja Ranjit Singh's wife and the mother of their current Maharaja Duleep Singh by the British gave rise to an increased anti-British sentiment. There was a deeply felt anger amongst the Lahore Durbar Sikhs that manifested itself throughout the Punjab, and perhaps did much to bring about the Second Sikh War. Another belief that became widespread was that, in the end, the British would not permit Duleep Singh to reign over his kingdom. The first repercussions of these fears were felt when discharged Sikh soldiers from all over the Punjab began to converge on Multan to join Mulraj.

Even as far north as Hazara, there was anger at the maharani's exile. British policy had always been one of divide and rule, and they used this tactic to create divisions in the powerful Attari family. Nanki, the daughter of the governor, Chattar Singh Attari, was engaged to be married to Maharaja Duleep Singh, and he rightly believed that the British would never permit this marriage to take place. Despite this they made his son, Sher Singh, a member of the Council of Regency.

Simultaneously, relations between Chattar Singh and the British commissioner, Captain Abbot, had soured to a point where Abbot became obsessed with getting Chattar Singh implicated with insurrection and removed from his post. What started as a clash of personalities now took a serious turn. In his *The Annexation of the Punjaub*, Major Evans Bell writes:

> Nothing whatever appears to prove that Sirdar Chuttar Singh promoted or approved the misconduct of the evil-disposed among the Sikh troops. Captain Abbot, however, had satisfied himself that Chuttar Singh was at the head of a vast conspiracy, and was about to march upon Lahore at the head of all the Durbar troops in Hazara. During the first week of August 1848, without any warning, without any communication with the governor of the province, Sirdar Chuttar Singh, without any intimation to his own official superiors, Captain Abbot roused the armed Mahomedan peasantry, over whom he had obtained great influence, and closed the passes through which the troops could move south to Lahore.

This was the last straw for Chattar Singh. With both these matters working on his mind, he wrote to his son Sher Singh, who was now serving with the British forces at the siege of Multan, of his intention to take up arms against the British and advised his son to do the same and to join Mulraj.

On 4 August, Chattar Singh gave a call to the Khalsa to rise and march on Lahore. Captain James Abbot knew that his regular brigade at Haripur and his feudal levy were prepared and ready to march south. Abbot had, in the meantime, mobilized all the Muslim irregulars in his area to check Chattar Singh when his move south became imminent. On 6 August, the Pakli Brigade, comprising 800 bayonets, 2 squadrons of cavalry, 4 field guns, and 20 Zambooraks, rebelled and prepared to march on Lahore. Lieutenant John Nicholson was dispatched from Peshawar to Attock with an escort of 60 Jagirdari Horse and 150 Pathans. At Hasan Abdal, he raised a further levy of 1,000 men and concentrated at Margala to prevent the Sikh regiments from marching north to join Chattar Singh. Meanwhile, Chattar Singh moved his entire force from Haripur to Hasan Abdal.

Nicholson had led a force of Pathans and captured the fort at Attock, provisioning it for a period of three months and placing it under the command of Lieutenant Herbert. Nicholson himself blocked the mountainous tract close to Taxila, over which the road passed south to the Jhelum. The fort at Attock covered the crossing from Peshawar. On 23 October the Peshawar brigade rebelled. As long as Attock was held by the British, the Peshawar brigade could not cross the river to link up with Chattar Singh. He, in turn, was bottled up in the Sind Sagar Doab – the territory between the Jhelum and the Indus. The link up and march south to establish a junction with the Sikh Army, which Sher Singh was putting together on the Chenab close to Ramnagar, had been temporarily blocked.

By now, Chattar Singh had sent envoys throughout the Punjab asking the sardars and chiefs to rise up against the British. He had also sent emissaries to Dost Mohammad Khan in Afghanistan, who had been deposed by the British when Shah Shuja had been put on the throne by them. Chattar Singh asked for his assistance and offered him Sikh support to regain his throne once the British had been defeated. He also offered him Peshawar, which had been the bone of contention between the Afghans and the Lahore Durbar ever since Ranjit Singh had captured the city from the Afghans on 6 May 1834. A message for his assistance was also sent to the ruler of Kashmir, Maharaja Gulab Singh.

Sher Singh never considered Mulraj a confidante or a person to be respected. He was compelled to take a decision due to pressures from his father and his own soldiers, some of whom had already deserted because he had allied himself with the British. His father had been insulted by Abbot and had openly revolted against the British at Hazara. It was now impossible for him to remain with the British as he and his father would be on opposing sides in the ensuing conflict. He would also have found it impossible to exercise control over his Sikh soldiers, who were already extremely restless. Consequently, he sent a message to Mulraj on 12 September stating his intention of joining him, which he did on 14 September, along with his entire column, comprising 3,400 infantry, 900 cavalry and 7 guns. Sher Singh went to the north of the city and joined Mulraj. General Whish, as has been seen, was greatly perturbed by Sher Singh's change of loyalty, and the consequent alteration in the balance of strength. He now decided to suspend further operations in Multan until his reinforcements arrived from Bombay.

During this period, Edwards, who had got to know Sher Singh and his views of Mulraj over the past months, played on Mulraj's existing suspicion of Sher Singh. A letter was written by him to Sher Singh and was allowed to fall into Mulraj's hands. It appeared to confirm Mulraj's suspicion that Sher Singh's offer of support was part of a British plan to enter the fort and seize it from within. Therefore, he refused him permission to enter the fort, and instead told him to establish his camp outside the walls. Sher Singh was then summoned by Mulraj and confronted with the letter. An angry and highly indignant Sher Singh vehemently denied the charge. He informed Mulraj that in view of this charge and the consequent lack of faith between them, he intended to leave as soon as he was ready to march to join his father at Hazara. Mulraj agreed to this.

Sher Singh seethed with anger at Mulraj's charge and the news that his father had been insulted by Abbot. As Major Evans Bells records, 'When Sirdar Chuttar Singh was fully committed beyond all possibility of retreat or redemption – when redress was refused, and he was sentenced without judgment – his sons threw in their lot with their father, and the second Sikh war began.'

Having also received information of a reasonable response from the chiefs and sardars to his father's message of revolt, Sher Singh struck camp. In the early hours of 9 October, he marched north along the Chenab, expecting to join his father, who he presumed was on the march down to the Chenab, but who was in fact still at Hazara.

Sher Singh had decided to move up the Chenab to Ramnagar. He has been accused by some critics of not confronting the British at Gujranwala, where Raja Lal Singh had arrived with his newly raised brigade, but there are good reasons for this. First, Lal Singh's reputation was one of treachery, and he was not trusted by the chiefs and sardars. Second, his reason for moving far north was tactically sound. He intended to engage the British Army at Ramnagar, where there was a ferry across the river, and then draw them across the Chenab to his main defensive position on ground of his choosing. This would be further back on relatively high ground at the edge of a forest, south of the river Jhelum, on the line Rasul, Tupai, Lullianee, Lucknawala, Kote, Mung, Fatteh Shah Ka Chuck, and Shadewala, forming a semicircle short of the Jhelum. Chillianwala was south of this defensive line and would be the forward-most village in the event of a British attack on their position.

His decision was sound and guided by well thought-out principles. First, Ramnagar, Chillianwala and the villages mentioned above were in the middle of Sikh territory, hostile to the British. Second, the Sikh Army always lived off the land and surplus food could be found in this region. Third, to the east of this area lay Bhimber, Gulab Singh's domain. Gough had openly expressed his concern that Gulab Singh would support the Sikhs in the event of an initial setback to the British, and a Dogra force under Dewan Hari Chand and Lieutenant Colonel Steinbach was already stationed at Bhimbur. However, Gulab Singh was pursuing a policy of 'friendly neutrality' towards the British. Contrary to Gough's views, an early British victory could very well bring Gulab Singh out on their side. If that happened, Sher Singh felt that he was in a position to intervene more effectively from this location. Fourth, to the north lay the Jhelum and beyond it the Salt range, and beyond that territory that could be dominated by the Afghans. As Peshawar had been offered to Dost Mohammad for his support, it was taken for granted that Dost Mohammad would give support to the Sikh Army while protecting its rear. Fifth, this location would be closer for the Sikh brigades in the northern areas, Peshawar and Bannu, to establish a smooth link up, including his father's brigade, from Hazara. Finally, the further the British were drawn from Lahore, the more tenuous would be their line of communication, which would require strong protection as it passed through hostile country, reducing the troops available to the British in the field.

The Sikh revolt was now at its peak. On 23 October, the Peshawar brigade mutinied, attacking the residency with artillery. The commissioner, Major George Lawrence, his wife and an aide, Lieutenant Bowie, escaped by riding south to Kohat, where the Afghan governor, Sultan Mohammed Khan, offered him sanctuary. On his arrival there, however, the governor promptly handed him over to Chattar Singh. The troops at Bannu revolted on 21 October and shot dead their governor, Malik Fatteh Khan Tiwana and Colonel John Holmes, a British officer of their own Lahore Durbar Army. They then crossed the Indus linking up with Sher Singh at Ramnagar. Raja Lal Singh, the former prime minister who had been exiled from the Punjab after the Kashmir episode, had quietly reentered Punjab and raised a brigade. He now marched from Wazirabad to within 9 miles of Gujranwala, 60 miles north of Lahore. Two more chiefs, Arjan Singh and Jowahar Singh, also raised their levies and moved to join Sher Singh. British intelligence reports indicated that thousands of demobilized soldiers, made redundant after the Treaty of Lahore, were flocking to Sher Singh's standard at Ramnagar.

Dalhousie was in Calcutta and in a belligerent mood. In a confrontational after-dinner speech, he laid down his policy.

> To the last, I have sought honestly to give effect to a policy which I approved. I have sought to avoid war or conquest, I seek no longer to

> pursue a policy which I am satisfied can never be successful, and I have resolved to prosecute with vigour a war, which on the part of the Government of India, I had hoped to have avoided. The Sikhs have forced me, for this Government, again to draw the sword, and I beg you to interpret my words in the clearest and most emphatic meaning when I say that being compelled to it I have drawn the sword, and have thrown away the scabbard [...] The Sikh Nation has called for war and on my word, Sirs, they will have it with a vengeance.[163]

Attempts to convince the people of the Lahore state that the new administration was for their betterment or that their government was actually that of the young maharaja, though run by others until he came of age, had failed. An experienced Lawrence made no effort whatsoever to set right this feeling. On the contrary, steps were taken to further accentuate it. The Council of Regency was made up of those who were considered traitors by most people in the state. No effort was made to understand the growing sullenness and bitterness that increased daily, or to do anything about the 70,000 trained soldiers of the Fauj-e-Ain and the 100,000 men of the Fauj-e-Gair who had been flung out on the streets for no fault of theirs. Lawrence, almost apologetically, writes in April 1847:

> I see around me, and hear of, so many men, who, having been generals and colonels in the Sikh Army, are now struggling for existence; and at the same time, know that so little justice has been done in recent reductions, that my great wonder has been the good conduct of the Sikh Army during the last 12 months.[164]

Though Lawrence realized that the situation was deteriorating and bitterness was growing, he was either incapable of redressing it on his own or Dalhousie's mind was closed to his entreaties. The situation was difficult and it is hard to understand Lawrence's insistence on initiating reforms that he knew would give an impression of the permanency of British rule in the state. The powder keg was waiting to explode and all that was required was a catalyst to set it off. It came in the form of the indifferent and cruel treatment meted out to Maharani Jinda Kaur, the maharani of their late and much-loved Maharaja Ranjit Singh, and the mother of their young maharaja.

Lord Gough now informed Dalhousie that he would require a force of 24,000 men and 78 guns, in addition to a force of 5,000 men and additional guns from Sind. At present, he had just 10,000 men and 48 guns available to him at Lahore. He also, once again, asked for the re-enlistment of all the discharged soldiers. At the end of September, while agreeing for the army to be mobilized, Dalhousie very reluctantly permitted Gough to re-enlist the discharged soldiers, 'for the duration of this war establishment'.[165]

The sepoy regiments were now brought up to strength and some supplies were also available. This gave Gough some flexibility to make a preliminary move. He ordered Brigadier Cureton to take a divisional level force comprising HM 3rd and 14th Light Dragoons, 8th Bengal Native Cavalry, 12th Irregular Cavalry, three troops of horse artillery and one light field battery, Brigadier Godby's infantry brigade – 2nd European Regiment, 31st and 70th NI's; and Brigadier Eckford's brigade – HM 29th, 31st and 56th NI's to march north on 2 November to occupy the fort at Gujranwala, 60 miles north of Lahore and 30 miles south-east of Ramnagar. The object was to counter Lal Singh's possible advance to Lahore, with elements from the Sikh Army presently on the Chenab.

Gough reached Ferozepur on 6 November 1848. He was then informed that Sher Singh had a screening force across the Chenab at Ramnagar, but had kept the bulk of his army north of the Chenab. Gough decided to try and entice the Sikhs south of the Chenab at Ramnagar into battle. There he would try to beat them if possible and, if not, to dash across the Chenab by one of the fords to cut Sher Singh's rear. This would have prevented Chattar Singh from linking up with the Bannu and Peshawar brigades. He intended to destroy them all in piecemeal battle. Gough now sent Brigadier Colin Campbell with 2 NI battalions to support Cureton at Gujranwala, and to take over command of the entire force there.

As far as Currie was concerned, the situation had become impossible. He was, for all intents and purposes, governing the Lahore state with a Council of Regency, but Dalhousie was preparing for war against the Lahore state. He had informed Currie in a letter written on 3 October that the state of Lahore was 'considered to be directly at war with the British government'.[166] By now thoroughly alarmed, Currie wrote to Gough at Ferozepur asking for him to come quickly and strengthen the British position in the capital. He also emphasized that the garrison was there by treaty to aid, advise and protect the Lahore state. He rightly pointed out the ridiculous state of affairs by telling Gough, 'We cannot continue to protect and maintain a state which we declare to be at war with us'.[167]

Gough crossed the Sutlej with General Sir Walter Gilbert's division and hurried on to Lahore, still unaware of whether he would be fighting for or against the Lahore state. Gough complained on 15 November at Lahore, 'I do not know whether we are at peace or war, or who it is we are fighting for'.[168] In the meantime, generals Thackwell and Gilbert's divisions had crossed the river Ravi to join brigadiers Campbell and Cureton. It was only then that Dalhousie thought it fit to make the position clear to Gough, that they were fighting to defeat the Lahore Durbar and not to defend it against Sher Singh and the rebel Khalsa.

As early as 5 October 1848, Dalhousie had made his intentions clear to annex Punjab in a letter to Sir John Hobhouse, president of the Board of Control.

> There remains no longer any alternative for the British government. The die is cast. Regard for the preservation of our own power [...] and

> the necessity of maintaining its reputation in order to secure our position in India, compel us to declare war, and to prosecute it to the entire submission of the Sikh Dynasty and the absolute subjugation of the whole people. There will be no peace for India, no security for our frontier – no release from anxiety – no guarantee for the tranquillity and improvement of our own provinces until it shall have been done. The Government of India, after anxious and grave deliberation, have without hesitation resolved, that the Punjab can no longer be allowed to exist as a power and must be destroyed [...] The extension of our limits by the subjection of the Punjab is no longer a question of expediency, but a matter of necessity and self preservation [...].[169]

As a sop to the directors of the Company, who were always wary of such matters and concerned about the expenditure involved in any such undertaking, he said, 'the defection of so many chiefs will be followed by extensive confiscation; and the available revenue of the Punjab greatly increased'.

In response to a section of public opinion and the press in England casting doubts on this policy, the question asked was, 'Did England intend to seize and hold the territory of the Sikh boy maharaja, the nobles and the people, when the Khalsa was defeated?' Dalhousie responded by saying, 'Our acts require no explanation. The army has, with others, taken up arms with the published and proclaimed intention of expelling us from the Punjab.'[170] Regarding the eleven-year-old maharaja, he was more direct and insulting when he added, 'A child notoriously surreptitious – a brat begotten of a Bhistie – and no more the child of old Ranjeet than Queen Victoria.'[171]

Even though Dalhousie was by now blind with the passion of empire building and had forgotten that the events in the Punjab were very much attributable to a failure of British policy in Lahore, he added in the same letter, 'It is odd that, at this moment, a Sikh regiment furnishes my guard and a Sikh is walking sentry at my door.'[172]

Dalhousie was clearly guilty of perpetrating fraud. On the one hand, he was pretending that he was still bound by a treaty to protect the Lahore state, while on the other he was secretly telling his officials and generals that British India was at war with the Sikhs, but that there would be no declaration of policy until the Sikhs had been defeated. Once the Sikhs were defeated, independent Punjab would be encompassed into the British Empire.

Meanwhile, Gough was on the march up to Ramnagar. On the way, he got news of the Bannu brigade linking up with Sher Singh, who was still positioned on the north bank of the Chenab, opposite Ramnagar. Although he was still holding the fort at Attock, Herbert was under intense pressure from Chattar Singh and was now likely to buckle in at anytime. This would clear the way for the Peshawar Brigade and for

THEATRE OF OPERATIONS DURING THE SECOND ANGLO-SIKH WAR 1848-49

Map published in 1848

Chattar Singh to join Sher Singh in the Jetch Doab – the land between the Chenab and the Jhelum. His intention of destroying the Sikhs in piecemeal battle was fast receding.

The Order of Battle, Army of the Punjab, November 1848[173]

Commander-in-Chief
Lord Gough

Second-in-Command
General Sir Joseph Thackwell
(In addition to command of the 3rd Infantry Division)

1st Infantry Division (Links up with the army on its return from Multan, on 18 February 1849, before the battle of Gujrat)
Major General Whish

1st Brigade	2nd Brigade	3rd Brigade (Bom)
Brigadier Markham	Brigadier Harvey	Brigadier Dundas
HM 32nd Foot	HM 10th Foot	HM 60th Rifles
51st NI	8th NI	1st Bombay Fusiliers
72nd NI	52nd NI	3rd Bom NI
		19th Bom NI

2nd Infantry Division
Major General Sir Walter Gilbert

1st Brigade	2nd Brigade
Brigadier Mountain	Brigadier Godby
HM 29th Foot	2nd Bengal Europeans
30th NI	31st NI
56th NI	70th NI

3rd Infantry Division
General Sir Joseph Thackwell

1st Brigade	2nd Brigade	3rd Brigade
Brigadier Pennicuick	Brigadier Hoggan	Brigadier Penny
HM 24th Foot	HM 61st Foot	15th NI
25th NI	36th NI	20th NI
45th NI	46th NI	69th NI

1st Cavalry Division
Brigadier Cureton

1st Brigade	2nd Brigade	3rd Brigade
Brigadier Michael White	Brigadier Pope	Brigadier Salter
HM 3rd Lt Dragoons	HM 9th Lancers	11th Bengal Lt Cavalry
HM 14th Lt Dragoons	1st Bengal Lt Cavalry	7th Irregular Cavalry
5th Bengal Lt Cavalry	6th Bengal Lt Cavalry	11th Irregular Cavalry
8th Bengal Lt Cavalry		

Bengal Artillery
Brigadier Tennant

Horse Artillery	Foot Artillery	Heavy Batteries
Brigadier Brooke	Brigadier Hathwaite	Major Horsford
Colonel Brind	3 Fd Batteries under	2 Batteries under
Colonel Grant	Major Dawes &	Majors Shakespear
6 Troops under	Capts Kinleside &	& Ludlow
Lt Col Lane,	Austin	
Majors Christie,	1 Bombay Fd Battery	
Huish, Warner,		
Duncan & Fordyce		
(on strength from		
18 February 1849)		

II. THE SKIRMISH AT RAMNAGAR

Gough joined Campbell and Cureton on 21 November at a little village called Noewalla, about 10 miles from the walled city of Ramnagar. Other than the 24-in guns presently on their way up from Lahore and the 1st Infantry Division under General Whish on its way up from Multan, his army was now concentrated on the Chenab.

On his way from Multan, Sher Singh had decided to deploy his army on the north bank of the Chenab, opposite Ramnagar, situated two miles from the river on the opposite bank. The location was well chosen. Firstly, he was close to his father Chattar Singh at Hazara, and was in constant communication with him. When the moment arose, Chattar Singh could link up with him without delay. Secondly, Gulab Singh of Kashmir had, as always, stayed aloof, but information had been received that he was preparing to move. Sher Singh was in the right position to intervene in case he was intending to link up with the British. Finally, he had ensured food supplies from the productive upper districts of the Chenab.

Sher Singh had a screen on the Chenab opposite Ramnagar. Some Ghorcharras and infantry were on the south bank, while the larger part of his screen was dug in on the opposite bank. His guns were well sited, concealed with only their muzzles visible, and were well within range of the forward elements of his screen. In this position, they could ensure support or give covering fire in the event of a withdrawal. The forward elements of the screen were interspaced and well hidden in the uneven and broken ground, where a number of dry rivulets joined the Chenab. One of Punjab's major rivers, the Chenab could be up to 400-yards wide at this point, but in this dry season consisted of only one main channel near the north bank and streams interspersed with sandbanks. In the middle of the river bed, there was an elevated island which had crops growing on it. The northern bank was much higher than the southern bank and overlooked it. The riverbed was around 250-yards wide from the main channel to the southern bank, and though appearing dry to the eye, was actually wet, soft and deep sand, with patches of quicksand in it.

Gough now ordered Colin Campbell to take an infantry brigade, the cavalry division, three troops of horse artillery, and one light field battery to clear the forward elements of Sher Singh's screen on the night of 21 November. His objective was to push him across the river and take possession of the entire southern bank. While Campbell prepared for his night attack, without taking anyone in his headquarters into confidence other than his army chaplain, Gough rode out in the early hours of 21 November and joined Campbell's force as it advanced on Ramnagar. At first light, Gough was within the walled town on the high mound on which the town stood, 2 miles from the Chenab. From here, as the sun rose, he got a grandstand view of Sher Singh's screen deployed on the further bank. While most of the Sikh Army appeared to be across the river, sizeable groups of Ghorcharras were visible on the south bank.

Gough climbed onto the roof of one of late Maharaja Ranjit Singh's palaces, which gave him an excellent view of the entire battlefield which lay before him. The first sight that caught his eye were the Ghorcharras, who were moving towards the ford in order to withdraw to the north bank. It appeared that the task given to Campbell had been achieved without a shot being fired. Ready for a fight at all times, Gough became overconfident. His inherent urge at times like this to 'close with the inimy', as he put it, occasionally overcame caution. He now gave an order for two troops of horse artillery, under Majors Lane and Warner, with five regiments of cavalry to pursue the Sikh cavalry, 'inflicting as much punishment as possible, to then advance as rapidly as the ground permitted and to punish the enemy as it crossed the river'.[174]

The two horse artillery troops galloped forward and unlimbered, firing at the withdrawing Sikh cavalry with grape then moving forward again. Suddenly they found themselves in deep sand and their guns began to sink, all the time being under fire from the Sikh heavy guns which were waiting for just such an opportunity. Seeing this, the Sikh cavalry rode across from the north bank to the aid of the Ghorcharras, who were withdrawing but had come under fire from the horse artillery. A squadron of the 3rd Dragoons, under Captain Ouvry, was now ordered to cover the gunners by keeping the Sikh horse at bay. Ouvry led his squadron in a charge at a body of Sikh horse, which was now close to the river on the

BATTLE LOCATIONS DURING THE SECOND ANGLO-SIKH WAR, 1848-49

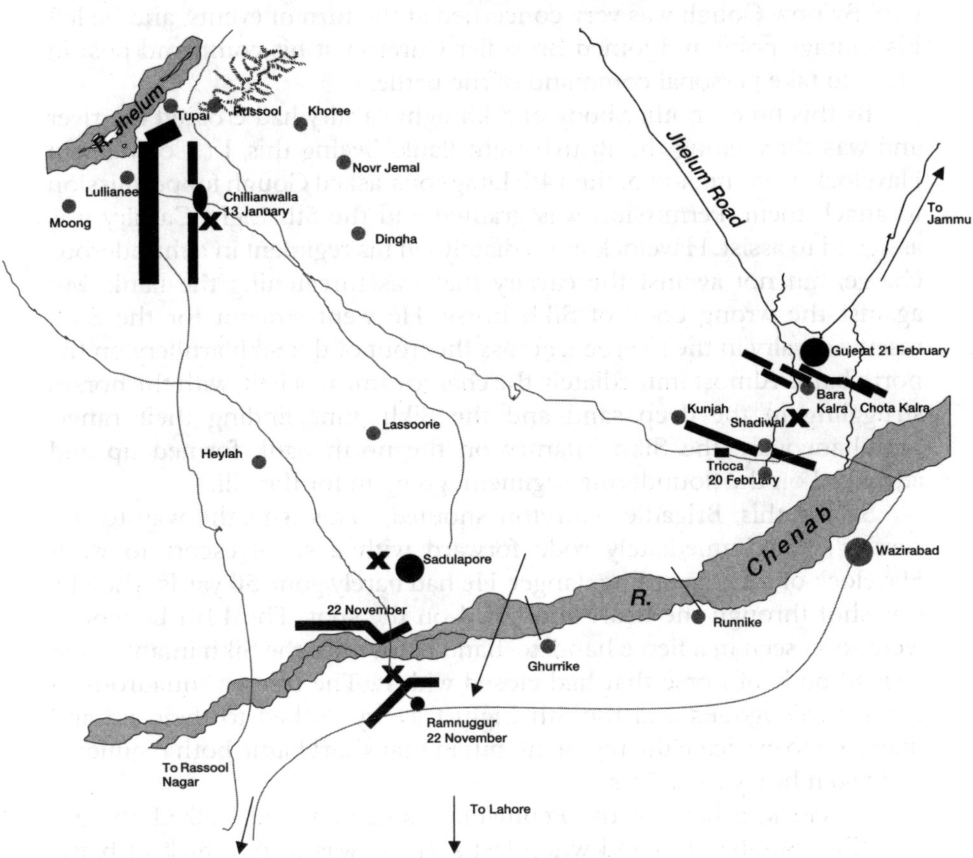

north bank intent on reaching the gunners who were desperately trying to recover their sunken guns. Ouvry managed to disperse them, but then strangely swept right across the front of the Sikh artillery and on to the wet sand. Luckily, the squadron sustained minimal damage from the guns, but 17 horses got stuck in the sand.

Brigadier White watched the Sikh cavalry until it reached dry ground, and then ordered the 3rd Dragoons and the 8th Light Cavalry to charge those Sikhs who were attempting to interfere with Ouvry's squadron and the still struggling horse gunners. The Sikh cavalry withdrew in the face of this charge, reformed on the north bank and then advanced again from another direction. Their aim was to draw the British cavalry into a patch of wet sand that lay between them, which was also part of the Sikh artillery's killing ground. Brigadier White didn't take the bait. Under constant fire from the Sikh gunners, the two majors finally managed to recover all of their guns except one of Lane's troop. Despite the British cavalry's interference, the Sikhs held their ground and nothing substantial was achieved. Once the British cavalry had withdrawn, the Sikh infantry, supported by the Ghorcharras, moved out and recovered the abandoned gun. By now Gough was very concerned at the turn of events, and he left his vantage point and joined Brigadier Cureton at his command post in order to take personal command of the battle.

By this time, another body of Sikh light cavalry had crossed the river and was threatening the British right flank. Seeing this, Lt Col William Havelock, in command of the 14th Dragoons, asked Gough for permission to attack them. Permission was granted and the 5th Light Cavalry was assigned to assist. Havelock immediately led his regiment in a thunderous charge, but not against the cavalry that was threatening the flank, but against the wrong body of Sikh horse. He went straight for the Sikh reserve cavalry in the riverbed, across the front of the Sikh artillery on the north bank. Almost immediately the charge came to a halt, with the horses struggling in the deep sand and the Sikh guns finding their range. Simultaneously, the Sikh infantry on the north bank formed up and advanced on the floundering regiment, going in for the kill.

Seeing this, Brigadier Cureton shouted, 'This isn't the way to use cavalry', and immediately rode forward with a small escort to warn Havelock of the impending danger. He had barely gone 50 yards when he was shot through the heart and killed on the spot. The 14th Dragoons were soon seen in a fierce hand-to-hand battle with the Sikh infantry and a small body of horse that had closed with it. The reserve squadrons of the 14th Dragoons and the 5th Light Cavalry dashed to their aid and managed to extricate the regiment, but in that short battle both regiments had taken heavy casualties.

Havelock, a hero of the Peninsular campaign, had walked straight into Sher Singh's trap and when last seen he was in the thick of battle with his left arm dangling, virtually cut off by a sword stroke. His badly wounded torso was recovered a few days later. The Dragoons finally managed to withdraw, but lost their commanding officer, another 6 officers and 43 troopers as casualties. Of these, 3 officers – captains Fitzgerald, McMahon and Coronet Chetwynd – and 12 troopers were killed and 4 officers and 31 troopers were wounded.

In total, 26 men were killed and 59 wounded on the British troops engaged in this skirmish in Ramnagar. Besides Brigadier Cureton, considered by all as the best cavalry commander then in India, the British also lost the commanding officer of the 14th Dragoons. The commanding officer of the 5th Bengal Light Cavalry, Lt Col Alexander, was severely wounded.

The skirmish at Ramnagar on 22 November had ended and while most of the Sikhs had withdrawn to the north bank, groups of Ghorcharras were still around, which kept the British on their toes. Gough established camp at Ramnagar and waited for the supply train to catch up. Records show that on the first night, the supply position was completely disorganized. HM 61st recorded that 'the men had no blankets or greatcoats in the freezing weather'. The 3rd Dragoons had no food or fodder for their horses. However, as always, the troops made the best of the situation. Lentils, horse meat and elephant 'lugs' made of chaffed straw (*bhusa*) were on the menu that evening!

General Thackwell was now appointed general officer commanding of the Cavalry Division to replace Brigadier Cureton, and Brigadier Campbell took over Thackwell's 3rd Infantry Division.

Plans were drawn up to follow the Sikhs, who were still on the north bank opposite Ramnagar. The distance between Ramnagar and Wazirabad was 22 miles, linked by a road that ran south of the Chenab. In this 22-mile stretch, there were five fords across the river, the first being at Ramnagar. The other four were at Garhi-ki-Pattan, 8 miles from Ramnagar, at Ranni-Khan-ki-Pattan, 5 miles further at Ali-Sher-ka-Chak, and finally at Wazirabad on the Grand Trunk Road linking Lahore to Peshawar.

Gough decided to cross the river and turn left, downstream, to attack Sher Singh from the east. General Thackwell was given command of this river crossing and the turning movement. He was allotted White's Cavalry Brigade consisting of five regiments. The 14th Dragoons were replaced by the 3rd and 12th Bengal Irregular Cavalry. While its original three – the 3rd Dragoons, the 5th and 8th Bengal Light Cavalry – remained on its strength, raising the brigade strength to five regiments. Campbell's 3rd Infantry Division, comprising three infantry brigades and three horse artillery troops, was commanded by majors Christie, Huish and Warner, and two Bengal field batteries were commanded by Austin and Kinleside. Thackwell was to take along a pontoon train and two days' supplies.

Thackwell's move was to start at midnight on 30 November. However, there was no moon and it was 2 a.m. before he managed to get started. By dawn, he had reached Garhi-Khan-ki-Pattan and found that the opposite end of the ford was held by about 4,000 Sikhs. Moving on, he reached Ranni-Khan-ki-Pattan at about 11 a.m., but found the crossing point unsuitable for wheeled transport. Once again, Sikhs were holding the far bank, which would have made it an opposed crossing without artillery support. Ali-Sher-ka-Chak was also found unsuitable for wheeled transport, as the current of the river was very strong. Much time had been lost in starting out, primarily due to the slow movement of the pontoons, that a conference was held to decide the future course of action. Campbell seriously suggested returning to Ramnagar, but Thackwell decided to move on to the ford at Wazirabad. John Nicholson, who had returned to the army at Ramnagar after leaving a holding force on the Taxila Heights, was sent on ahead, along with lieutenants Baird, Smith and Yule and his Pathans, to arrange boats at the Wazirabad crossing. The aim was to have the troops cross without delay once they arrived.

By the time Thackwell reached Wazirabad, it was 6 p.m. and dark, but Nicholson had arranged around 20 boats. By morning, Brigadier

Pennicuick's brigade, comprising HM 24th Foot and the 25th and 45th NI, had crossed the river and established a bridgehead on the north bank. Brigadier Hoggan's brigade, comprising the HM 61st Foot and the 36th and 46th NI, attempted to wade across, but only made it as far as a large sandbank where, thoroughly drenched, it bivouacked in the freezing cold night. Three risalas of the 3rd Irregular Cavalry also managed to cross, but all the troops spent the night wet and hungry. Once again, the commissariat department had failed in its arrangements, and the men finally got their meal the next day, after waiting 36 hours.

Early the next morning, on 2 December, the crossing resumed and by midday, Thackwell's entire force, comprising 14,000 troops, 66 guns and his supplies were on the north bank. Thackwell began his move down the north bank at 2 p.m. and reached the village of Durawal, 12 miles downstream by dusk. By now Thackwell was within 9 miles of the Sikh encampment of Ramnagar, where he established camp. Sher Singh drew back his troops guarding the fords at Garhi-ki-Pattan, Ranni-Khan-ki-Pattan and Ali-Sher-ka-Chak. Communication was now established with Gough through the Garhi-ki-Pattan ford. Gough informed Thackwell that he was to be reinforced by Godby's brigade through the Garhi-ki-Pattan ford, and that no movement towards the Sikhs was to be made until Godby linked up with him.

III. THE CANNONADE AT SADULPUR

On both 1 and 2 December, Gough opened a continuous heavy cannonade in order to keep Sher Singh's attention on him. Meanwhile, Thackwell waited for Godby to cross at Garhi-ki-Pattan and link up with him. Godby found the ford impossible to cross with his equipment and remained on the south bank until an alternative arrangement could be found. Acting on Gough's orders to wait for the reinforcing brigade before taking any further action, or fresh orders to the contrary from the C-in-C, Thackwell stayed at his location at Durawal. These orders finally arrived in the late evening of 2 December, by which time it was too late to make a move towards the Sikhs. Gough now delegated powers to Thackwell to decide his own course of action. Meanwhile, Thackwell had reached a village called Sadulpur, about 2 miles from the river and around 9 miles from the former Sikh defensive position opposite Ramnagar. Here he camped, having dispatched an NI battalion to guard the ford at Garhi-ki-Pattan.

During this time, Sher Singh had moved from Ramnagar to meet Thackwell at Sadulpur on the morning of 3 December. There he established his defensive position in sugarcane fields, just north of the village. This was the type of ground the Sikhs liked for battle, as it was heavily covered in crops for cover.

Thackwell began his advance at 6 a.m. on 3 December and halted when he reached the village of Sadulpur. Nicholson's Pathan horse was sent forward to reconnoitre. The three villages to the front – Tarwala, Ratti and Kamukhel – were each occupied by a company of infantry. Between these villages and Sadulpur lay an open stretch of land about half a mile wide, on which the line halted. At about 2 p.m., Sikh guns opened fire on a patrol of the 5th Light Cavalry, and a large body of Sikh cavalry and infantry was seen to advance. The infantry companies in the villages abandoned their positions, the troops falling back to the main force. Startled by this fire and withdrawal of his forward elements, Thackwell fell back 200 yards to reorganize. The Sikhs, who had been occupying dense cover, now moved out to attack. Thackwell's response was to throw a defensive line forward of Sadulpur. According to Gough and Innes, Sher Singh 'had shown the customary skill of the Sikhs in choosing a strong defensive position which his men might be relied on to hold with their wonted stubbornness. But also, as usual, neither leaders nor followers understood how to attack'.[175] The Sikhs opened a heavy cannonade lasting two hours. Thackwell countered this by making the troops lie down, avoiding heavy casualties.

On the morning of 4 December Gough reinforced Thackwell with the 9th Lancers and the 14th Dragoons. Later that morning by 9 a.m., Godby had managed his crossing, putting his brigade under Thackwell's command.

Gough had made it clear to Thackwell, before he had left Ramnagar, that no offensive operation must be attempted, unless his reinforcements had reached him, and that there should be plenty of time for any operation to be concluded in daylight. As Thackwell chose to follow Gough's orders religiously, an opportunity had been lost. That night, the night of the 3 and 4 December, under the cover of darkness, Sher Singh withdrew from Sadulpur to his prepared position on the Jhelum. When morning arrived, Thackwell found the Sikh Army gone. He immediately sent out patrols to establish their whereabouts. No contact was made until they reached a village called Helan on the Jalalpur road, where a small skirmish took place between Thackwell's patrols and the Sikh rear guard. Meanwhile, the Sikh Army had by now reached their prepared defensive position short of the Jhelum, from the village of Rasul in the east to a village called Shadewala in the west, with the river Jhelum (also known as Hydespes in Greek) behind them to the north. This was also the battlefield where the Indian King Porus had engaged Alexander the Great over 2,000 years earlier.

Gough now realized that the actions at Ramnagar and Sadulpur had been covering troop actions. Sher Singh had cleverly lured Gough forward across the Chenab to the ground of his choosing and his prepared position, short of the Jhelum.

The cannonade had cost the British 21 dead and 51 wounded. Gough and Innes attempted to justify the result by stating that 'Sher Singh had been driven back from the Chenab to the Jhelum; from a rich country, where supplies were readily obtainable, to jungle; his opportunities of intriguing with the durbar were cut off by the increased stretch of territory lying between him and Lahore'. Had Thackwell not followed Gough's orders to the letter and insisted upon waiting for reinforcements he knew were not likely to arrive, he could have joined battle by the early afternoon that day. The engagement at Sadulpur, therefore, ended in an exchange between the guns of the two forces, with no infantry or cavalry intervention.

The distance between the Sikh defensive line, Rasul-Shadewala, was just 20 miles from the Sikh position opposite Ramnagar. This was too near for communication between Sher Singh and Lahore to have been in any way disrupted, as claimed by Gough and Innes. The Sikh defence line on the Jhelum was chosen by Sher Singh during the weeks he was in this region prior to the skirmish at Ramnagar, on which defensive preparations had already begun. If that were the case, Sher Singh would have definitely taken care of his supply factor and other details of his logistics. Therefore, this justification lacks conviction. Ramnagar and Sadulpur were obviously covering troop actions. Sher Singh was cleverly drawing Gough in onto the ground of his choosing, where he hoped to fight a decisive pitched battle. Less than 10,000 troops were committed by him in these actions. The major portion of his army was on the main Sikh defence line short of the Jhelum.

On 4 December, Thackwell camped with his army at Helan, which was about 14 miles north-west of Sadulpur and 8 miles directly north of the enemy position on the north bank of the Chenab opposite Ramnagar. Chillianwala was 12 miles from Helan, with the river Jhelum 4 miles behind Chillianwala. Gough, who joined him there on 8 December, intended waiting there until General Whish arrived with his 1st Infantry Division from Multan.

On 18 December, Sher Singh began to move 10,000 men towards Dingha, 8 miles from Chillianwala, in the direction of Wazirabad, his objective being to interfere with the British line of communication forcing Gough to dispatch troops to hold the ford at Wazirabad. While this was taking place, news arrived of the fall of the Attock fort on 2 January. The road was now clear for the Peshawar brigade to cross the Indus and link up with Chattar Singh, and then for the combined force to link up with Sher Singh at Chillianwala.

Gough had intended to attack Sher Singh once Whish arrived from Multan with his division. On 19 December, a 51-gun salute in the Sikh camp announced the fall of Attock and the decision of the Amir of Kabul, Dost Mohammad Khan, to ally himself with the Sikhs. The possibility of Sher Singh's army now receiving a major reinforcement of the Haripur and Peshawar brigades of the Fauj-e-Ain, and of the Afghan contingent, forced Gough into deciding to launch his attack before this dramatic increase in the enemy's strength took place. Gough's strength (as claimed by him) stood at 12,000 troops* and 66 guns and he had remained at Helan for 40 days since the Sadulpur engagement.

IV. CHILLIANWALA

> There was a desperate drawn battle deep within the province at Chillianwala, in which three British regiments lost their colours [...] "Remember Chillianwala!" became a battle cry and a blood-stained slogan in the upheaval (1857) which was to come.
>
> Winston Churchill[176]

At first light on 12 January 1849, Gough moved from Loah Tibba, adjacent to Helan, in the direction of Dingha which was 12 miles away. His intelligence was that Sher Singh's right extended to the villages of Lakhniwala and Fateh-Shah-ka-Chak. The main force was at Lullianee, with the left extending to Rasul on the Jhelum, occupying the southern extremity of a low range of hills intersected by ravines. Gough now decided to move on Chillianwala for a personal reconnaissance. On 12 December, Colonel Patrick Grant, the adjutant general, put the Sikh force as under:

The Sikh Right at Lakhniwala – The Bannu Brigade under Ram Singh with 1 regiment of cavalry, 4 infantry battalions and 17 guns.
The Sikh Centre Right at Fateh-Shah-ka-Chak – Sardars Attar Singh and Lal Singh with 2 regiments of cavalry, 6 old and 4 new battalions of infantry and 17 guns.
The Sikh Centre Left at Lullianee – Sher Singh with 1 regiment of cavalry, 5 old and 4 new battalions of infantry, around 4,000 Ghorcharras, and 20 guns.
The Sikh Left at Rasul with 2 new infantry battalions, 5 guns and an unspecified number of Ghorcharras.
The Sikh reserve at Mung – Surat Singh with an unspecified number of Fauj-e-Gair troops and 3 guns.

In *The Sikh Wars,* Cook estimated the total Sikh strength to be about 30,000 troops and 66 guns. Assuming all the units were up to their war establishment, 14,000 troops (15 infantry battalions, the 4 cavalry regiments and the artillery units manning the 66 guns) belonged to the erstwhile Lahore Durbar Army, the Fauj-e-Ain. The remaining 10 infantry battalions were newly raised, which means 8,000 additional troops. This puts the Fauj-e-Ain figure at 22,000 troops and 66 guns. The feudal forces of the Fauj-e-Gair, primarily Ghorcharras, have been put at 4,000 with Sher Singh at Lullianee. One must assume that additional feudal forces would also be with the other sardars – Raja Lal Singh, Attar Singh and Ram Singh. This confirms Cook's figure of around 30,000.

The location and terrain at Chillianwala is described by Sir George Macmunn in his *Vignettes from the Indian Wars*:

> Chillianwala lies three or four miles south of Rasul on the Jhelum, and is best reached from Rasul itself, or from the Chillianwala road between Lala Musa and the Malakwal bridge over the Jhelum [...] The Sikh Army was, we know, posted and entrenched on the heights near Rasul across one of the roads from Peshawar to Lahore. The Kharian ridge dies away to a low rolling down, just by Rasul, and on the southern extremity of the ridge and on the downs, the Sikh Army was posted, the village of Rasul being near their centre, their right stretching round to Mung. Behind the ridge, between it and the Jhelum and on the ridge itself, lay their camps. Their position covering the ford was provided with a perfect glacis of sloping grass.

This range of hills sloped down to the plain, but ravines and fissures crossed it towards the Jhelum, where it ended in sudden precipices above sandy flats and channels. A broad and dense jungle of thorny bushes, up to 2,000-yards wide and 8-ft high, ran from a plain at the foot of the hills near the river for several miles in a south-easterly direction.

The Sikh front was covered by a jungle with thorny bushes (*ber*), about 7-8 ft feet high, a number of thickets of stocky but short broad-leaved trees (*dhak*) and taller trees of sheeshum, mango and the thorny *kikar* (tamarisk), which were also growing in sporadic clumps within the forest.

Sher Singh's deployment gave Gough little option but to commit himself to a frontal attack against the entrenched Sikh position.

In the British camp, reveille was sounded well before first light on 13 January. Camp was struck and loaded on bellowing camels, and the heavy guns were harnessed to the patient elephants. While the troops, led by their NCOs, set about packing their camp and equipment in an excited and visibly charged atmosphere, the officers of the 2nd Bengal Europeans met to drink a glass of wine to their survival. At 7 a.m., on a cloudless yet crisp and cold morning, Thackwell moved his division forward in brigade columns of cavalry, artillery and infantry towards the Sikh position. Each column formed its own advance guard and the heads of columns were positioned 100 yards from each other, directed by the heavy artillery, in front of which was the C-in-C.

Towards midday, the column approached the dense jungle that extended south of the river for several miles, indicating they were nearing the Jhelum and the Sikh position.

A strong body of Sikh horse and infantry were now visible occupying a low hill, upon which was the village of Chillianwala. The 24th Foot was sent against them. The Sikh force, positioned there as a light screen, fell back to a position at the forward edge of the jungle before 24 January could make contact. Gough rode up the hill to get a proper look at the battlefield. He could see the nearest part of Sher Singh's entrenched position and also his forward elements on the edge of the jungle about a mile away.

Having satisfied himself with his reconnaissance, he decided to postpone the attack until the following morning and gave orders to his staff accordingly. The Sikh gunners, who had been ordered to lie low, could not resist opening fire when they saw the British C-in-C in front of them. With ball whistling past his ears, Gough and his reconnaissance group took note of the position of the Sikh battery and rode off the hill, ordering his heavy 24-pounders to engage the Sikh gun positions and silence their fire. Guns on both sides answered shot for shot, and as Lieutenant Sandford of the artillery wrote later, 'The guns rent the air, but instead the Sikhs answered this thunderous salvo with the whole of their field artillery. Bang, bang, went the guns, one after the other, in one continued stunning roar, and our hearts beat and our pulses quickened in anticipation'.[177] Gough now decided to attack immediately rather than waiting until the following morning. Once more the sound of guns, the smell of cordite and the impatience of closing with the 'inimy' had got the better of him.

As the army deployed, the guns kept up a steady fire on the Sikh positions. On the extreme left was White's cavalry brigade, comprising HM's 3rd Light Dragoons and the Bengal 5th and 8th Light Cavalry, along with Warner's Horse Artillery battery to their right. Next came Campbell's division with Hoggan's brigade on the left, comprising the 46th NI, HM 61st Foot and the 36th NI. Pennicuick's brigade was to their right, comprising the 45th NI, HM 24th Foot and the 25th NI. Robertson's field battery was positioned to the left of Hoggan's brigade and Mowatt's field battery lay between the two brigades. Penny's brigade, the third brigade of Campbell's division, was in reserve. The heavy guns were positioned in front of Chillianwala, and then came Gilbert's division, with Mountain's brigade to the left comprising the 30th NI, the 56th NI and HM 29th. To their right was Dawes's field battery and then Godby's brigade, comprising the 31st NI, 2nd Bengal Europeans and the 70th NI. Next came Christie's horse battery followed by Pope's cavalry brigade, which they supported. Pope's brigade comprised HM 14th Light Dragoons, the 9th Bengal Lancers less a wing and the 1st and 6th Bengal Light Cavalry, less a wing of both regiments. These three detached wings under Colonel Lane, along with Huish's horse battery, were detached to keep in check a force of Ghorcharras on the slopes leading to Rasul. Penny's brigade, comprising the 15th, 20th and 69th NI regiments, were in reserve and positioned just north of the Chillianwala hill and was tasked with exploiting success.

The British line was around 3 miles long, but was still outflanked at each end by Sher Singh's army. The forward elements of the Sikh Army were a mile away and the main defence line, which was 6 miles long, was behind the thick jungle.

The artillery bombardment continued for an hour while the army, by now fully deployed, lay down and waited for it to stop. At 3 p.m., Gough

THE BATTLE OF CHILLIANWALA, 13 JANUARY 1849

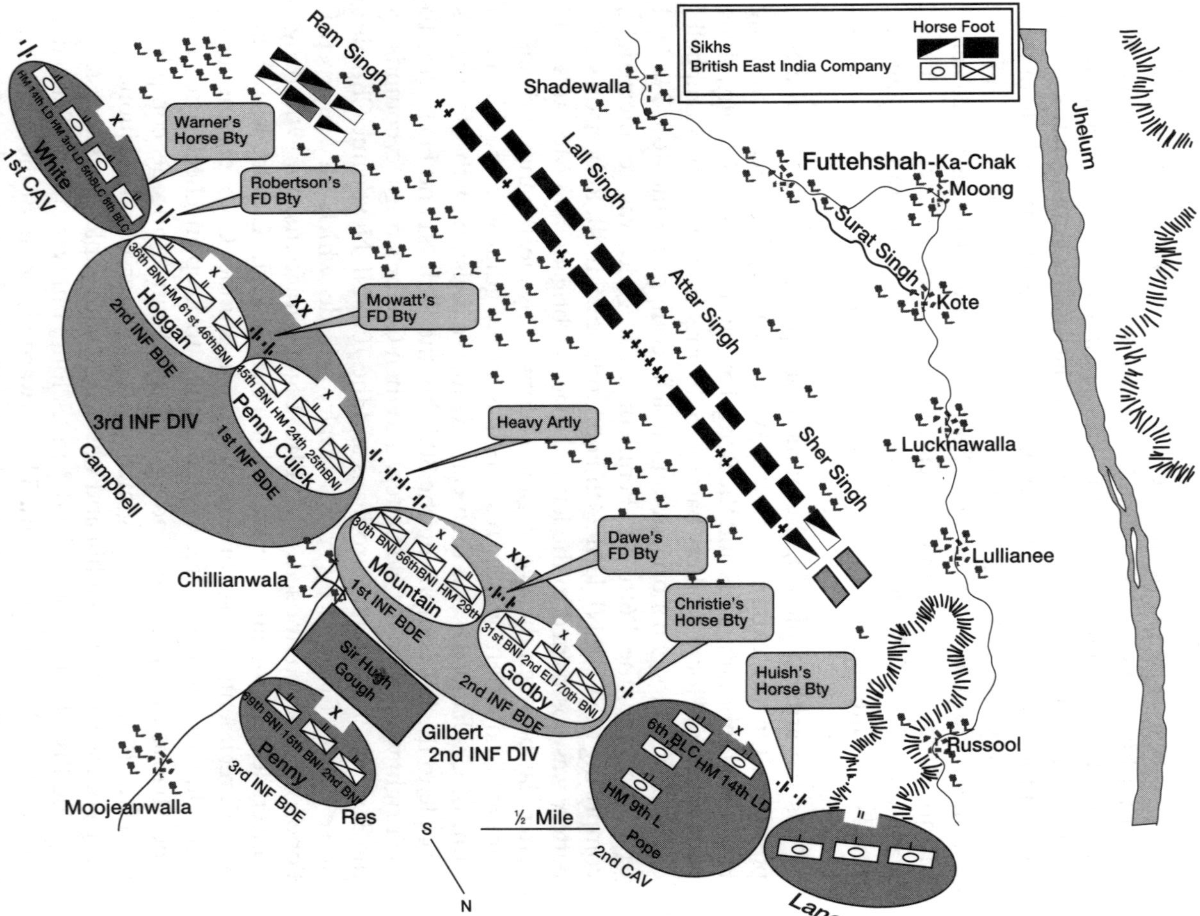

ordered his line to advance and to assault the Sikh gun positions on the various brigade fronts 'with musketry and the bayonet'.

The battle is best described by George Bruce in *Six Battles for India*.

> A confused, indecisive but bloody battle. It was nearly hidden in the jungle. It is hard to know the exact relationship of events, for there are really no coherent accounts; all are more or less defused and obscured by vague abstract detail. Neither the divisional nor brigade commanders – nor even Gough himself – knew precisely where the various other brigades were in relation to the rest of the army, or what they were doing [...] Flickering movements of the red coats in the green thickets – confusion and uncertainty – the metallic bellow of the guns – the frequent clatter of muskets – the constant clash of bayonets and the talwar – the shouts and screams of men locked in hand-to-hand fighting: these were all that Gough could know of the battle, except for the little news his staff officers, groping their way back through the thorns, were able to bring him.

According to Gough's dispatch, his sole act during the fighting was to order Brigadier Penny's brigade forward to support Brigadier Pennicuick's brigade on the left, which the Sikhs had badly cut up and flung back.

Both divisional commanders had lost sight of their troops and, as a consequence, control of their brigades. Therefore, Campbell attached himself to Hoggan's brigade and left Pennicuick to act independently. Before doing so, he rode up to the brigade, assembled the troops in an open patch and addressed them saying, 'There must be no firing, the bayonet must do the work!'[178] and then galloped off to Hoggan's brigade to direct its advance. Gilbert advanced his division against the Sikh left, as the visibility through sparse jungle in the direction of the village of Lullianee was much better, which permitted him to retain control of his division.

Out of touch with his divisions, Gough remained with the heavy guns between the jungle and Chillianwala, unable to see how the battle was progressing but available to his generals, who knew his whereabouts.

To the left of Chillianwala, Pennicuick advanced his brigade into the jungle opposite Attar Singh. However, the jungle was so thick that keeping the line intact became impossible and companies broke up into little groups and sections while desperately trying to maintain their direction. Officers and men of the 24th Foot, who were wearing the regiment's tall Albert Shakos, had them ripped off or torn to shreds by the thick *kikar* and *ber* thorns. All the while, the Sikh guns kept up their fire, directed at the sound of advancing troops or in the direction and distance provided by the Colour party holding their Colours high. The 24th, which bore the brunt of this fire, increased its pace to cover the half mile from its start line to its objective, in order to get to grips with the Sikh guns. In the process, they outdistanced the 25th and 46th NI on either flank and soon came to the end of the forest beyond which lay the Sikh guns. These were positioned on a 300-yard deep grassy upward slope ending in a network of pools. The guns were manned by the yellow-turbaned black-and-white uniformed gunners and were backed up by red-coated Sikh infantry.

The 24th Foot now faced the Sikh guns, which were firing grape at point-blank range. The men dashed forward onto the guns. Being first, the Grenadier Company was mowed down in droves. When they finally reached the guns, they were met by the gunners who refused to yield, until once again the bayonet prevailed and the guns were finally taken. At this point, Brigadier Pennicuick was shot and mortally wounded. His son, an ensign with the 24th Foot who had recently graduated from Sandhurst, ran forward and stood over his father's body, sword in hand, when he too was killed. The 24th Foot now made a fatal error in concentrating on spiking the guns before consolidating its position. Seeing its chance, the Sikh infantry counter-attacked with musket and sword, and retook the guns. During this severe hand-to-hand fighting, the entire Colour party of the 24th was killed, including their commanding officer, Colonel Brooks, and a number of other officers. The two NI battalions, of which the 25th NI had launched its attack resolutely soon after the 24th had launched its own, were also halted and withdrawn into the jungle. The 45th also reached the Sikh gun position just as the brigade was withdrawing and fell back. Being unable to achieve its objective, the combined brigade withdrew to Chillianwala. The regimental Colour of the 24th Foot was brought out by a private soldier but the Queen's Colour was never found. The 25th lost both its Colours and the 45th, two of its three Colours – one of which was honorary.

In this short period of perhaps 20 minutes, from the time they crossed the edge of the forest until they were counter-attacked and pushed back, the 24th Foot lost 13 officers and 225 men killed and 9 officers and 278 men wounded, out of a total strength of 31 officers and 1,065 men who went into battle that afternoon. The 25th took 3 officers and 201 other ranks as casualties, and the 45th took 4 officers and 75 other ranks.

News of this disaster did not reach Campbell or the neighbouring brigade commanded by Hoggan until later. In the meantime, Hoggan led his brigade through 800 yards of sparser jungle until he reached the end of it, opposite Raja Lal Singh's defended sector. He broke out of the trees about 80 yards from the Sikh guns and immediately saw massed Sikh cavalry to his front. The 61st Foot fired volley after volley, scattered the cavalry and assaulted the guns, which they took and managed to spike. The 36th met Sikh infantry and was beaten back into the jungle, losing its Colours in the confusion. On the left, the 46th reached the gun positions and was attacked by cavalry, which it successfully repulsed. Brigadier Godby's son, a teenaged ensign, was severely wounded by a sabre but was rescued alive along with Ensign Conoly, who exhibited extreme courage and managed to extricate himself with only a few cuts and bruises. General Campbell sabered a Sikh gunner, but was wounded by a sword cut.

As the 36th fell back, the Sikh infantry attacked the exposed flank. Campbell changed the front of two companies of the 61st to the left, who successfully halted the attack. The 61st then turned right to face a second infantry attack launched by a combination of Lal Singh and Attar Singh's forces, and then faced up to and stopped a cavalry charge. The 46th joined the 61st and the brigade then reversed its direction, changed front to the right, and rolled up Attar Singh's position, taking 13 guns, including the gun position that had earlier repulsed the 24th Foot. Mention is made once again of the Sikh gunners manning their guns to the last man. In one case, a gun crew limbered up its gun and pulled out as the assault reached its position.

During this action, Ram Singh's cavalry galloped forward in an attempt to turn the British flank. General Thackwell, who was then with Brigadier White's cavalry brigade, ordered Captain Unett's squadron of the 3rd Light Dragoons and the 5th Bengal Light Cavalry forward. As George Bruce puts it,

> The Dragoons violently charged and scattered the Sikh horse, then swept on furiously into the heart of a mass of Sikh infantry, who bravely closed on their flanks. Led by Unett, the Dragoons cut their way through at great cost, galloped on for half a mile then charged back, driving the opposing horse and foot out of the field.

Out of 106 dragoons, including three officers in this squadron, 23 dragoons were killed and 17 wounded, including two of the officers. Of the horses, 18 were killed and 8 wounded. On re-forming, there were just 48 dragoons left in their saddles. The 5th Light Cavalry failed in its task but later rallied on the 8th Light Cavalry, which was following.

While the 24th was facing its ordeal, on the British right Brigadier Pope, who was protecting Gilbert's flank, lost control of his brigade. Bruce describes this incident.

> Seeing a large body of [Sher Singh's] Sikh horse sweeping in towards Godby's flank from the direction of Rasul, Pope detached [as earlier described] two squadrons of the 9th Lancers and the 1st and 6th Bengal Light Cavalry with some 9-pounders under Colonel Lane to protect it [...] Observing more Sikh cavalry on his front, he formed into a line and advanced on the same front as General Gilbert's two infantry brigades. Pope, who in his younger days had been a dashing Lieutenant Colonel of Indian Cavalry, was now an elderly gentleman so stiff and corpulent that he needed the help of two men to mount his horse. Even worse, he knew almost nothing of handling large bodies of cavalry. While bringing his brigade forward for the action he had unsteadied them by giving contradictory orders that faced them in several directions, partly owing to the jungle and partly because his eyesight was so bad.

Having got his brigade into line, he now moved forward at a slow trot with no scouts out and, in his myopic way, led his men at an angle instead of straight ahead. In doing so, he masked the fire of his own horse artillery battery and then of Brigadier Godby's infantry brigade. Compounding this astonishing blunder, he slowed his brigade first to a walk and then to a halt, while he presumably wondered how on earth he could extricate himself from the approaching Sikh cavalry without too much danger. It seems he meant to give the order, 'Three's right!' to clear the artillery and the infantry front, but somehow this came out as 'Three's about!' This order was passed on and obeyed, just as a mass of brilliantly garbed Sikh cavalry began its charge. It started as a gallop, then a panic-stricken rout, until the whole brigade of some 3,000 men tore from the field, through the horse artillery, upsetting horses, carriages and guns, past the astonished Gough and on until they reached the tents of the field hospital. There they were rallied by the Chaplin, Mr Whiting, who, pistol in hand, threatened to shoot anyone who passed him. Gough later said he regretted that he could not promote him to a Brevet Bishop! The Sikh Ghorcharras saw their opportunity and attacked the guns, cut down Major Christie and several men, spiking the guns they could not recover. They then seized and drove away another 4 guns and ammunition wagons with 50 horses harnessed to them. The commanding officer of the 14th Light Dragoons shot himself some months later, upset over a slur cast on his personal courage.

With Pope's cavalry brigade having fled the field, the left flank of Godby's brigade (opposed by Sher Singh's brigade) became dangerously exposed, as there was now a considerable distance between him and Lane's ad-hoc force covering Rasul. To protect it, he threw back his right wing. Meanwhile, the remainder of the brigade continued its advance at a fast pace and soon made contact with Sher Singh's defences. The order to charge was given and, as Lieutenant Sandford recorded,

> [...] the men bounded forward like angry bulldogs, pouring in a murderous fire. The enemy's bullets whizzed above our heads; the very air teeming with them; man after man was struck down, and rolled in the dust. But a passing glance was all that we could give them. And onward we went, bearing on their line with a steadiness that nothing could resist. They [Sikhs] fired a last volley and [withdrew] into the jungle, leaving the ground covered in dead and wounded. Pursuit in the jungle like that was useless, where we could not see 20 yards before us; so we halted and began to collect our wounded, when all of a sudden fire was opened on us from the rear. A large body of the enemy [Sher Singh's troops] had turned our flank in the jungle, and got between us and the rest of the troops; another party was on our left, and we found ourselves with one field-battery, completely surrounded and alone in the field.[179]

Godby's situation was now very much like that of Pennicuick, but he was alive and in command. He gave the order to 'right about face' to meet a Sikh cavalry threat from behind and the troops moved forward firing and loading on the march. The 2nd Bengal Europeans in the centre had attacked the Sikh guns as ordered. The 70th NI formed square and remained that way, while the 31st somehow got detached and, as mentioned earlier, had linked up with Mountain's brigade way out on the left.

Sandford of the 2nd Europeans recalls the events thus.

> At last General Gilbert rode up, and said to Steel [their commanding officer], "Well Major, how are you? Do you think you are near enough to charge?" "By all means," said Steel. "Well then, let's see how you can do it. Men of the 2nd Europeans, prepare to charge – Charge!" [...] The Sikhs fought like devils. They charged down on us, singly, sword in hand, and strove to break through our line. But it was no-go and, after a short struggle, we swept them before us [...] The enemy lay in heaps around – some dead, some dying – but fierce and untamed even in their dying struggle; numbers of them were bayoneted by our men in the act of rearing themselves up and taking aim at the officers [...][180]

Meanwhile, Brigadier Mountain's brigade had advanced with HM 29th on its right, the 56th NI in the centre and the 30th on the left, ably supported by Dawes's battery. They suddenly found themselves in the open, opposite a Sikh gun position – at the junction of Attar Singh and Sher Singh's brigades. The Sikhs opened fire with grape and the first casualties were the colour party, with the regimental colour of the 29th being shot out. The 29th fired a volley, charged and carried a Sikh battery to its front at the point of the bayonet, although with heavy casualties. The Sikh infantry were now seen throwing away their rifles and drawing their talwars. In some cases, the gunners were seen to grab hold of the bayonets and use their swords to dispatch their opponents. However, the position was taken and the 29th claimed to have captured 12 guns. The 56th lost its colonel and a number of officers, and was now charged by Sikh cavalry and overrun. However, their Grenadier Company stood fast and then wheeled to the right to link up with Godby's brigade.

The 29th was attacked in the rear by Sikh cavalry and about faced to meet this threat. Having repulsed the attack, it then moved left to join up with the 30th NI and the Grenadier Company of the 56th, and moved along the Sikh position. It was joined by the 31st NI, which had somehow detached itself from Godby's brigade on the extreme right and joined Hoggan's brigade on the extreme left. On their way, they lapped Mountain's and Penny's brigades, which were between them. This should never have happened. They had advanced to the left through the jungle, and misjudged Hoggan's brigade to be that of Mountain's. They had moved along the entire front of the Sikh position all the while. Both brigades finally faced their original front.

As darkness descended, Mountain and Hoggan's brigades, supported by White's cavalry brigade, were well established on the Sikh position. The main body of Sikh troops facing them now fell back on its camps on the Jhelum at Tupai and then moved to its new position at Rasul. Those facing Godby and Penny soon followed suit by withdrawing towards the Rasul heights, pursued by Colonel Lane's artillery, which fired salvo after salvo of grape until they disappeared into the ravines of Rasul.

Mountain's brigade had taken heavy casualties. The 29th suffered 241 casualties in officers and men, with the 56th losing 330 officers and men, and the 30th under 300. The 56th lost both its Colours and the 30th lost one.

The battle was over and the sun had set. Gough decided to hold the Sikh line overnight in case Sher Singh, who had withdrawn to Rasul, should try to reoccupy it during the night. The Sikhs had taken heavy casualties, but the army was intact and was now positioned on the extreme left defences of its original line, on the Jhelum at Tupai and on the Rasul heights. However, both Gough's divisional commanders objected to his decision on the grounds that their men were parched with thirst and there was no water except at Chillianwala. Therefore, they advised a withdrawal to Chillianwala to which Gough reluctantly agreed, saying gruffly while conceding, 'I'll be damned if I move until my wounded are safe.'[181] Once all the wounded were taken back, he ordered the withdrawal to Chillianwala. That night Sher Singh carried off his guns that had been left behind and had not been spiked.

In the battle lasting three-and-a-half hours, Gough had taken 2,357 casualties – 706 were killed and 1,651 were wounded. Those killed included 22 British officers, 16 Indian officers, 57 NCO's, 5 trumpeters and drummers, 597 rank and file, 1 lascar, 8 syces, and 132 horses. The wounded included 67 British officers, 27 Indian officers, 1 warrant officer, 90 NCOs, 17 trumpeters and drummers, 1,439 rank and file, 8 lascars, 2 syces, and 44 horses. The Sikhs had also taken heavy casualties but unfortunately there is no record of what they were. They had withdrawn from the field, but Gough had failed in his objective of either defeating them, or pushing them back into or across the Jhelum. Thirteen Sikh guns had been captured.

Gough was cheered by his troops the next morning, as he rode down the line in a heavy drizzle. Dalhousie, then at Ferozepur, viewed the battle differently. Pope had panicked, Campbell had failed to co-ordinate the attack of his two brigades and Pennicuick had rushed the 24th Foot unaided into the attack. He became convinced that Gough had failed because he relied more on the bayonet rather than on his heavy guns and mortars. He now wrote to Sir John Hobhouse, president of the Board of Control, 'If he [Gough], disregards in his obstinacy these means again, if he again fights an incomplete action with terrible carnage as before, you must expect to hear of my taking a strong step; he shall not remain in command of that army in the field.'[182]

In England, the outcry was far worse. 'A British Army had been fought to a draw by "A wild Indian people".'[183] A number of regimental and Queen's Colours had been lost and also four British guns. Casualties were exceedingly high. The government was pressurized into sacking Gough and Sir Charles Napier was announced as his successor. Even the eighty-five-year-old Lord Wellington said he was willing to go out to fight the Sikhs if Napier was not. 'If you do not go, I must,' he told Napier.

As news took time to arrive, Gough was ignorant of his sacking as he rode forward to see the Sikh defences early on 14 January, the day after the battle. He was accompanied by his brigadier of artillery, Brigadier Tennant, Brigadier White, the commander of 1st Cavalry Brigade whose patrols were already well out in front, and Major Mackeson, the representative of the governor general. The Sikh guns he expected to recover had been removed by Sher Singh that night, so he contented himself by viewing the dead and the debris of war.

He had intended to defeat Sher Singh decisively, failing which to push him into the Jhelum or beyond it, to the less productive Sind Sagar Doab. Sher Singh could now be seen at Tupai on the Jhelum and on the Rasul heights. Gough waited the next three days, mulling over his options while the countryside was inundated with torrential rain. Gough's indecision stemmed from whether or not he should attack Sher Singh in Rasul straight away, or whether he should wait for the Multan force to reach him before he attacked. As a protective measure, he ordered the engineers to dig a deep entrenchment around his camp, in case Sher Singh attacked him from his secure position. As was his nature, he was inclined to attack without delay. Sher Singh's reinforcements from the north, which were moving rapidly, led by his father Chattar Singh, could link up with him any day, which Gough wished to avoid.

On the third day a tall imposing person in Afghan dress descended on Gough's camp. He was General Elahu Bakhsh, a Sikh artillery general from the Peshawar brigade who had deserted Sher Singh and decided to surrender to Gough. He told Gough that Sher Singh was in a well-entrenched position and it was defended in strength. Therefore, he advised against an attack on Rasul. Gough agreed to wait for the Multan reinforcements in the form of General Whish's 1st Division to reach him. Two days later, the Sikh guns gave a 21-gun salute as Chattar Singh marched into their camp with a force of 6,000 soldiers.

For Gough, the position was now clear – he needed the four British regiments with Whish and his Multan force to augment his current British regiments, which had taken severe casualties at Chillianwala. He was still not satisfied that the NI regiments would be steady enough during the next battle, though their performance at Chillianwala had been relatively satisfactory.

Gough's assessment was that the Sikhs at Rasul occupied a very strong natural fortress. With its perfect artillery positions among the hills and ravines, Sher Singh would make a stand there. The negative aspect for Sher Singh was that the Sikh Army traditionally lived off the land and this hill region could not supply the quantity of food needed for both man and horse. Gough rightly believed that Sher Singh would find it difficult to hold Rasul indefinitely without additional grain and fodder. He would then have two options: either to watch his horses and animal transport grow weak, or to come off the hill to find a suitable grazing ground and source of food for his troops. Gough's patience prevailed and, towards the end of January, Sher Singh made a move to draw Gough into attacking him at Rasul. Gough refused to move. Two days later, on 2 February, Sher Singh marched out of Rasul at night, through a hill pass to Khoree, 4 miles south in a wooded plain, leaving a holding force of 12,000 infantry and 27 guns.

As Gough had anticipated, Sher Singh had indeed become very concerned about his precarious supply position, particularly as news had reached him that the Multan forces were about to link up with Gough. He rightly felt that a combined force would be too much for him to face. Therefore, he tried his utmost to bring Gough to battle before Whish and his force arrived. If he could engage Gough, he intended to retire to Rasul and to lure him there. Gough refused the bait, despite his being pushed in that direction by an impatient governor general and those of his own generals, who sided with Dalhousie.

At first Sher Singh moved his army south towards Dingha, threatening to cut off Gough's line of communication. But Gough stood firm. On 11 February, he therefore advanced his whole force north again to Khoree in an attempt to draw him out of his entrenched camp. Once again, Gough refused to oblige him. On 13 February, Sher Singh's fears were confirmed when the advance party of Whish's 1st Division, led by Brigadier Cheape, with a few squadrons of cavalry arrived with news that Whish was marching 20 miles a day and would arrive soon. Hearing this news, Sher Singh immediately withdrew his army and the garrison at Rasul into a defensive position around the walled city of Gujrat, 25 miles to the east on the banks of the Chenab.

Sher Singh now publicly declared his intention of marching on Lahore. As a demonstration of his intent, he sent a force of 6,000 soldiers to take and hold the Sudra ford at Wazirabad, held by a small force of two Bengal cavalry regiments and a few guns under Lieutenant Hodson. With Gough having anticipated this move, and Whish anticipating Gough's order, he swiftly moved Colonel Byrne with HM 53rd Foot and the 13th NI with four guns and two regiments of irregular cavalry to oppose the crossing. The force was in position when the Sikh force arrived on the

Chenab. Seeing that the British had deployed to meet them, the Sikhs withdrew. Sher Singh then prepared his position at Gujrat. By now, Whish's division had also arrived at Ramnagar.

Once again, Gough turned down suggestions by his staff to attack Sher Singh at Gujrat. He sent all his administrative staff, his non-combatants and surplus baggage to his supply depot at Ramnagar. On 15 February, he broke camp located between Chillianwala and Mujianwala and marched to Lassoorie, via Dingha. This swift move south secured his communications with Whish, who was just 12 miles south across the Chenab at Ramnagar. On the next day, he moved on to Pakka Masjid and on 17 February to Kunjah, from where the Sikh position at Gujrat was visible. On 18 February, he moved to Trakhur, then on to Shadiwal on 20 February.

Gough had held a council of war on the morning of 16 February and, as George Bruce puts it,

> Here he finalized plans for linking with Whish's force and confronting Sher Singh. He then set his army in motion. He marched in battle order – ready always – nine miles south-east to Sadulpur, near the Chenab, where Sher Singh had lost his chance in December of crushing Thackwell's smaller force [This is incorrectly stated – at that time Sher Singh's strength was less than 10,000 troops], four miles to Ishera, next day, where he was joined by one brigade of Whish's force; three miles to Tricca, on the 18th, where Whish's second brigade joined him, the smoke of the Sikh campfires darkening the sky only five miles away. On the 20th, Brigadier Dundas arrived with Whish's third brigade after a forced march of 45 miles. Gough advanced through the rich and fertile farmlands to Shadiwala, only three miles from the Sikh battle line. "For miles and miles around, there is nothing but luxuriant corn fields," Lieutenant Sandford remarked in his journal. "I am pitched right in the centre of one, and have a verdant carpet under my feet. Just imagine the damage an army like this must do to the crops."

V. GUJRAT

Gough had a force of 33,300 men and 106 guns of the regular army. Of these, 4,000 troops were left for his line of communication protection, leaving him 30,000 troops with which to fight his battle. The 33,300 included 3,292 gunners, 8,166 cavalry, 21,146 infantry, and 633 engineers.[184]

Order of Battle of the Army of the Punjab on 21 February 1849[185]

Commander-in-Chief
General Sir Hugh Gough

Brigadier Tennant's Heavy artillery
12 x 18 pounder guns
10 x 8in Howitzers

Cavalry Division
Lt Gen Sir J. Thackwell

2nd Cavalry Brigade	4th Cavalry Brigade	1st Cavalry Brigade
Colonel Lockwood	Colonel Hearsey	Brigadier White
HM 14th Light Dragoons	3rd Irr Cavalry	HM 3rd Light Dragoons
1st Bengal Lt Cavalry	9th Irr Cavalry	HM 9th Lancers
11th Irr Cavalry (part)		8th Bengal Lt Cavalry
14th Irr Cavalry (part)		The Scinde Horse
		Two Troops horse Artillery

1st Infantry Division
Major General Whish

1st Brigade	2nd Brigade	3rd Brigade
Brigadier Hervey	Brigadier Markham	Brigadier Hoggan
HM 10th Foot	HM 32nd Foot	5th Bengal Lt Cav
8th NI	51st NI	6th Bengal Lt Cav
52nd NI	72nd NI	45th NI
Tp horse Arty	2 Tp's Horse Arty	69th NI
Coy Pioneers	Dawes Lt Fd Bty	Bom Lt Field Bty
2Tp's horse arty	(reserve)	

2nd Infantry Division
Major General W.R. Gilbert

4th Brigade	5th Brigade
Brigadier Mountain	Brigadier Penny
HM 29th Foot	2nd Bengal Europeans
30th NI	31st NI
56th NI	70th NI

3rd Infantry Division
Brigadier Colin Campbell

7th Brigade	8th Brigade	9th Brigade (Bombay)
Brigadier Carnegie	Brigadier McLeod	Brigadier Dundas
HM 24th Foot	HM 61st Foot	HM 60th Rifles
25th NI	36th NI	1st Bombay Europeans
46th NI	3rd Bombay NI	
2 Lt Fd Battery's	19th Bombay NI	Bombay Lt Fd Battery

The Sikh Army strength is not known. The figure of 60,000 men under Sher Singh at Gujrat, quoted by Gough in his dispatch to Dalhousie, is highly exaggerated. Sher Singh surrendered 16,000 troops after the battle of Gujrat. Therefore, we are expected to assume that about 44,000 Sikh troops were either killed at Gujrat, or had left the field after the battle. This figure is totally incorrect.

The figure of the Sikh Army at Chillianwala, as accepted by Cook in *The Sikh Wars* to be around 30,000 troops, seems to be correct. To this, we add 6,000 troops brought into the Sikh Army by Chattar Singh Attari before the battle of Gujrat, and 1,500 Afghan Horse led by Akram Khan, son of Dost Mohammad Khan. This adds up to around 37,000 troops, less the casualties taken at Chillianwala, and puts the total strength of the Sikh Army before the battle of Gujrat at around 35,000 troops – 25,000 of these being regulars and 10,000 feudal levies, including the Afghan horse. The Sikhs had 59 guns. If 16,000 surrendered at Gujrat and the British heavily outnumbered the Sikhs in both the calibre and numbers of guns by 106 guns to 59, it is possible that Sikh casualties were somewhat higher at Gujrat than at earlier battles. It is also possible that the levies of the Fauj-e-Gair left the field once the battle was over, as they had done at Ferozshah. The figure of 35,000 Sikh troops, both regular and irregular taking part in the battle of Gujrat, is a more likely number.

Gujrat lies 6 miles north of river Chenab and a road from Sadulpur to the north of the river and Ramnagar to the south of it cross at a ford a mile west of Wazirabad on the south bank. The road then moves north, 6 miles to Gujrat and then further north to the town of Jhelum.

River Katela flows as a wide, wet *nullah* into the Chenab 3 miles upstream of the Wazirabad ford in a north-south direction. Flowing in the same north-south direction is a second dry *nullah*, the river Dwara, which joins the Chenab about 5 miles downstream of the ford. As mentioned earlier, the city of Gujrat lies 6 miles north of the river between the two *nullahs*. One-and-a-half miles south of Gujrat lies the village of Kalra, which is located on the east bank of the Dwara, while another village, Chota Kalra, lies parallel to it on the west bank of the Katela. A mile south of Kalra is another small village called Hariawalla, also on the east bank of the Dwara. On the west bank of the Dwara, opposite Kalra, is a cluster of three villages – Loonpur, Jumna and Narowal.

Further south, once again on the west bank of the Dwara and due north of the Wazirabad ford, are three large villages – Shadiwal adjoining the west bank of the Dwara and 4 miles from the Chenab, Kunjah another 4 miles to the west of Shadiwal and Tricca, one-and-a-half miles south of Shadiwal, once again adjoining the west bank of the Dwara.

Reconnaissance had shown that the Sikh position at Gujrat was a mile and a quarter south of the city, facing south, just short of Kalra. The Sikh line stretched 3 miles from the river Dwara to the river Katela. Both nullahs provided reasonably effective obstacles on both flanks. The Sikh cavalry was on either flank beyond both *nullahs*, with the Afghan horse on

THE BATTLE OF GUJRAT, 21 FEBRUARY 1849

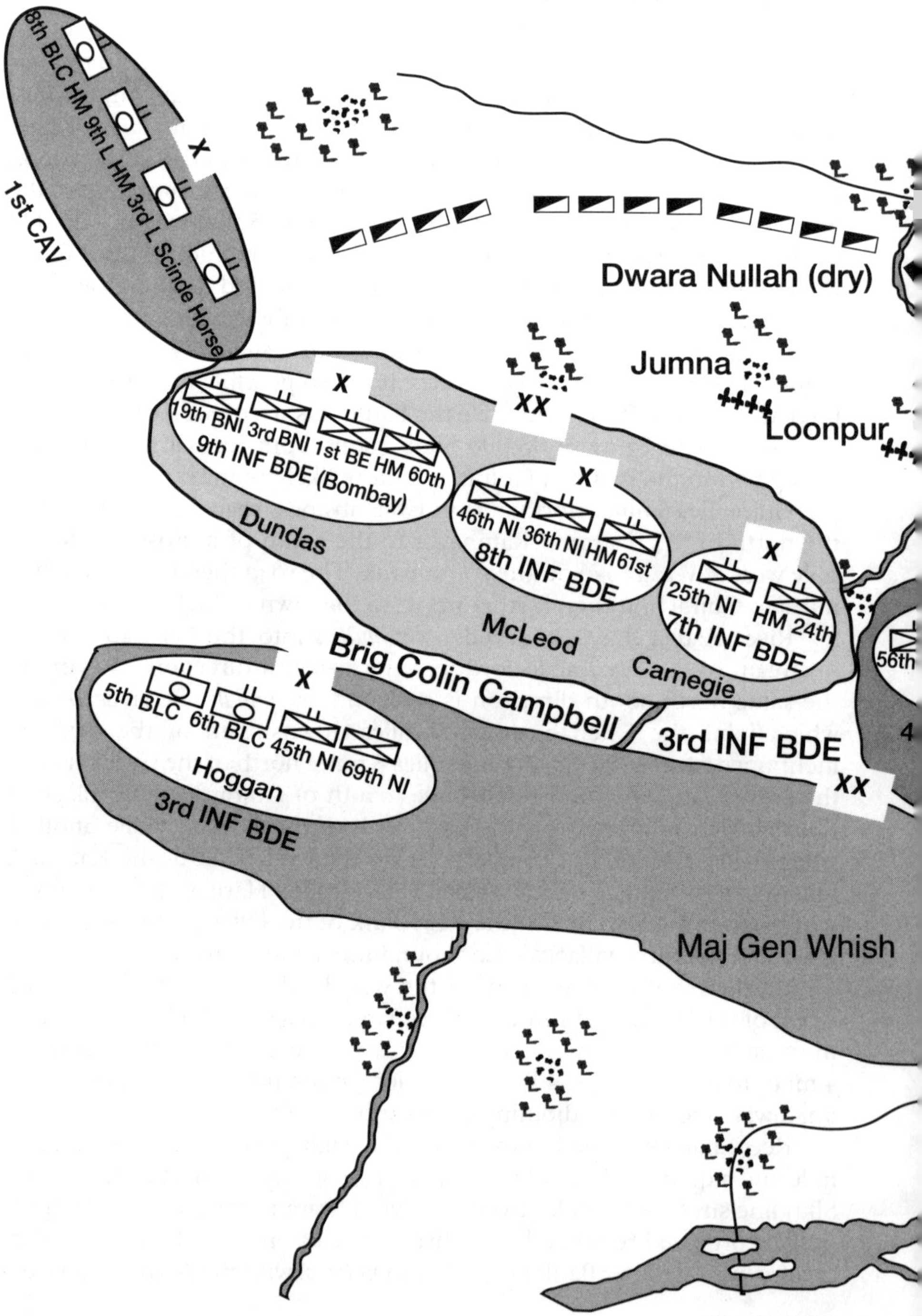

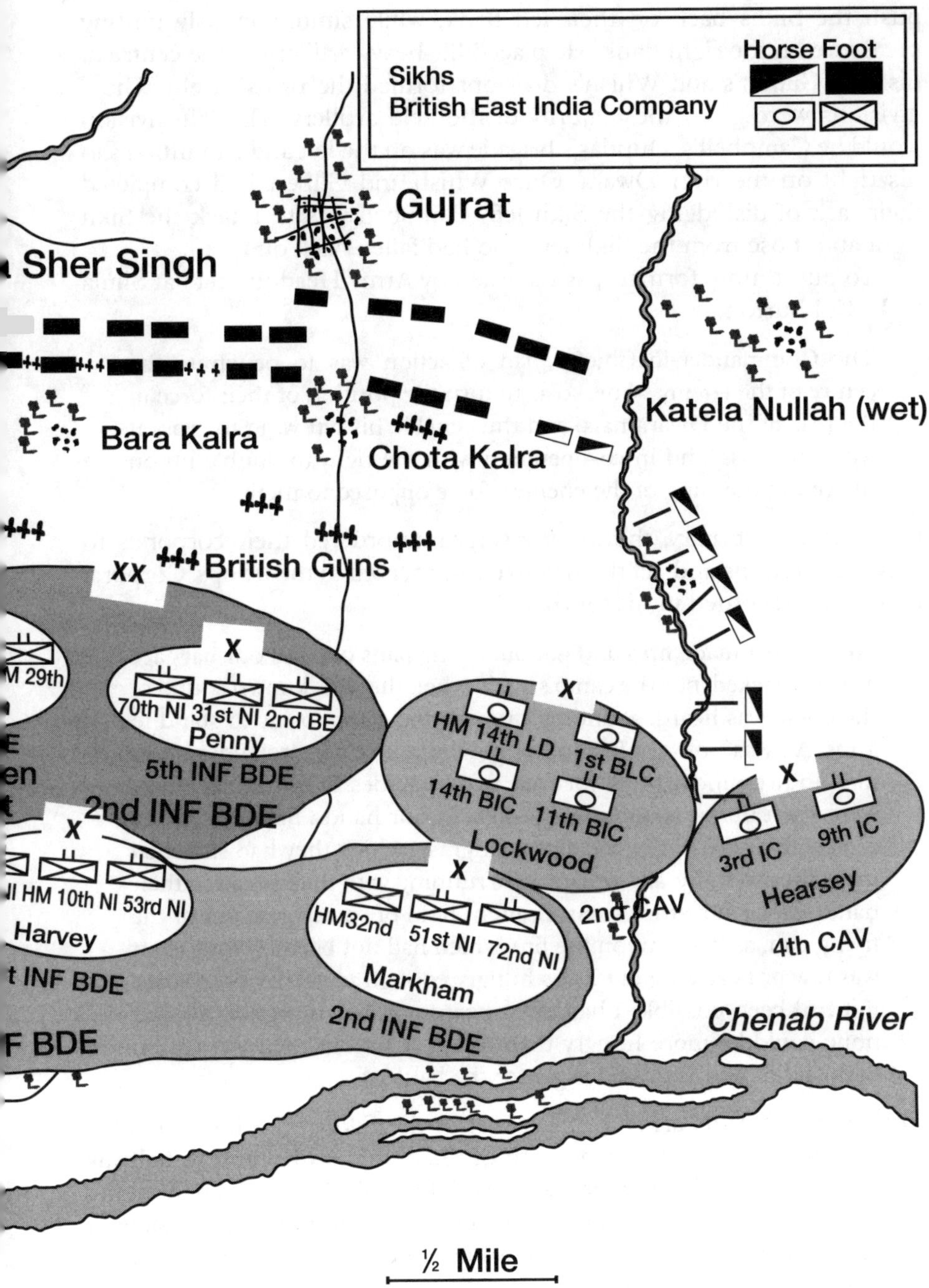

Horse Foot
Sikhs
British East India Company
Gujrat
Sher Singh
Bara Kalra
Chota Kalra
Katela Nullah (wet)
British Guns
XX
X
M 29th
70th NI 31st NI 2nd BE
Penny
5th INF BDE
2nd INF BDE
HM 14th LD
1st BLC
14th BIC
11th BIC
Lockwood
3rd IC
9th IC
Hearsey
4th CAV
2nd CAV
HM 10th NI 53rd NI
Harvey
t INF BDE
HM32nd 51st NI 72nd NI
Markham
2nd INF BDE
F BDE
Chenab River
½ Mile

the right. Sher Singh had placed his guns between his deployed regiments and in the two fortified villages of Kalra and Chota Kalra.

Gough had decided to launch his attack against the Sikh right and centre – Kalra being in the middle of his line of advance. His plan was to push the Sikhs back on their left flank, while simultaneously putting preassure on the right flank. He placed his heavy artillery in the centre of his line. Gilbert's and Whish's divisions formed the British right. These divisions were given the majority of the field artillery. The left division would be Campbell's. Dundas's brigade was on the left and Mountain's to his right on the river Dwara. Once Whish and Gilbert had completed their task of dislodging the Sikh left, Campbell was to attack the Sikh right and those from the Sikh left who had fallen back on them.

To put it more formally, as recorded by Army Headquarters at Simla by Lt Col Burton,

> The Commander-in-Chief's plan of action was to penetrate the centre of the enemy's line, so as to turn the position of their force in the rear of the Dwara nala, and thus enable his left wing to cross it with little loss, and in co-operation with the right to double up on the centre the wing of the enemy's force opposed to them.[186]

Early on 21 February, the orderly sergeants ordered their corporals to draw their rations and get them cooked and served to the troops. Corporal Ryder later recorded in his journal:

> We had just made fires and got our frying pans on, and our baggage was not packed, nor the camp struck, when the well-known sound of the bugle was heard, sounding through the camp for us to stand to arms. All was now confusion: we got a dram of grog served out per man and a pound of bread for every two comrades. Our accoutrements were soon upon us and our muskets in our hands. Some might be seen with a slice of raw meat in their grasp, which they had snatched up as they went by, and others were running with their bread in their hands eating it as they went. I caught hold of some meat out of the frying pan, as it was upon the fire, which had not been on long, so it was raw or nearly so; but I was hungry enough to eat my boot soles, if it had been possible. I had often heard talk of a hungry army, but none could be more hungry than this [...] Yet our men were all in high spirits, and appeared eager for the battle.[187]

Gough lined up his army 3 miles west of the Sikhs. The line extended from Kunjah on the left, then south of Shadiwal and beyond to halfway between the two nullahs, which was his right flank. Tricca was behind the line. The walled city of Gujrat, with its tall minarets, was clearly visible in the early morning sun behind the Sikhs, who were now also manning their line. Gough rode down the front of his army to a wild cheering from his troops. Thackwell was on the extreme left flank with White's cavalry brigade, and next came Campbell's division with all three brigades forward – Dundas on the left, McLeod in the centre and then Carnegie. Gilbert's division came next, with Mountain and Penny on the left. Then Whish came with Harvey's brigade and Markham's forward with Hoggan in reserve. The field gun troops and horse artillery were positioned between the brigades. Lockwood's cavalry brigade, along with Hearsey's, were on the right, with their flank resting on the Katela.

At 7.30 a.m., the bugles sounded the advance and the line moved forward to cover the 3 miles between them and the Sikhs. The Sikh guns opened fire first, but the shot fell well short of the advancing British. This was a grave error, as it gave away the Sikh battery positions. Gough halted his line at about 9 a.m. The artillery was ordered forward, covered by skirmishers, and Gough's guns, except for 12 guns of his reserve batteries, opened fire with round shot and shrapnel. Appropriately, the first shot was fired by Dawes, considered the hero of Chillianwala. Far to the left, Blood's Bombay Battery, in battle for the first time, drew particular praise. Not to be outdone, the Sikh guns responded with equal ferocity, moving forward to get into range. As Cook states, 'The [British] gunners suffered heavy casualties and indeed, in this battle, the proportion of losses among the artillery was higher than amongst the infantry.'

Lieutenant Sandford of the 2nd Europeans later recorded his impressions:

> The round shot flew about us, and ploughed up the ground in all directions. Five or six men were knocked down in as many seconds, when we were ordered to lie down [...] At the end of an hour we were ordered to advance another hundred yards and then lie down again. A company from each regiment in the brigade was sent up to the front to support the troop of horse artillery attached to us; and poor fellows, they suffered dreadfully, being brought in one after another wounded – some with legs shot off, some cut in half, some torn with grape – scarcely half of our rifle company was left. All this time, the fire was very hot on us, carrying off three men at a time, shells bursting over us, or burying themselves in front, scattering the earth in our faces [...] The troop in front [Fordyce's] suffered dreadfully – every shot pitched right into them, and the gallant manner in which they worked their guns is beyond all praise. Twice had they to retire to the rear for fresh horses and men, and each time as they came up again and passed through our line, we gave them a hearty cheer, and the fine fellows waved their caps and dashed on again as if death was a joke to them.

Gough positioned himself near his heavy 24-pounder guns. The artillery continued to fire on the Sikh position for three hours. The Sikh guns also took their toll, but finally numbers prevailed and the 109 British guns proved superior over the 59 of the Sikhs. Battery after battery of Sikh guns were shot out and silenced. While the gun duel was taking place, the Sikh cavalry crossed the Katela and attempted to scatter Lockwood and Hearsey's cavalry on the British right. Hearsey, commanding the irregular cavalry – the 3rd and the 9th – used his artillery troop to keep them away.

At 11 a.m., Gough ordered a general advance and simultaneously ordered Gilbert to send forward light troops to draw out fire from any hidden guns. They had barely advanced 200 yards when two Sikh batteries, hidden near Kalra, opened fire with grape at 300 yards. Sikhs manning the mud walls of the village fired a strong volley at the advancing troops. Gilbert now ordered Penny to storm Kalra and the 2nd Bengal Europeans, followed by the 31st and 70th NI, moved forward.

The fire was so intense, with the men falling all around, that the order went out, 'Officers to the front – lead on your men'. The brigade stormed Kalra, with the Sikh infantry and guns standing their ground until the British numbers finally prevailed and those holding out fell to the bayonet. The storming of Kalra cost Gough an extremely high casualty figure of 321 – 6 officers and 143 men of the 2nd Europeans, 128 men of the 31st NI and 44 of the 70th NI killed and wounded.

Next, Brigadier Hervey was ordered forward. Supported by Fordyce's troop of horse artillery, his 10th Foot and 8th NI attacked Chota Kalra. The Sikhs had some protection from the village walls, in which they had cut loopholes to fire through. The horse artillery troop galloped forward and fired at point-blank range, while the infantry stormed the village. Once again, a fierce hand-to-hand battle raged, until numbers prevailed and those Sikhs who had survived fell back. The horse troop also took heavy casualties and Captain Anderson was killed. The assaulting forces took 94 casualties between them.

At one stage, the 3rd Light Dragoons 'presented a front' to a body of Sikhs escorting a battery of six guns, and drew them to where the 60th Rifles were lying in wait. When in range, the rifleman opened fire, killing the gunners and escort to a man. The dragoons then trotted forward and spiked the guns.

Supported by the Afghan horse, the Sikh cavalry on the right now attempted to turn the British flank. Captain Duncan moved his horse artillery troop and opened fire at 500 yards. However, Akram Khan continued his charge and Thackwell ordered the Scinde Horse and two squadrons of HM 9th Lancers to intercept it. The charge crashed into a mass of Afghan horse, considerably superior to the attackers in number. For a few minutes, there was a fierce melee and then the Afghans broke. With the main body of the cavalry on their flank, they galloped back through the Sikh camp, hotly pursued by the Scinde Horse, which had captured two standards in its charge. Thackwell recorded later:

> These troops made a most brilliant charge. At the same time I advanced the guns [...] The fire of the guns soon put the ghorcharras

> in retreat, and the glorious charge of the troops on their left caused their whole force to seek safety in retreat by the Baradari [...] But as we were then considerably in advance of the left of the infantry [...] and ignorant of the force the enemy might have [...] it became necessary to proceed with caution. Yet I was able to open fire upon the enemy, both on the right and left of the former place, which caused them considerable loss, and hastened their retreat.[188]

A small body of the Afghan cavalry, around 30 horsemen, now charged past the British guns and swept on towards Gough in the time-honoured Afghan tradition of going for the leader of the enemy force. Lieutenant Stannus, commanding the 5th Bengal Light Cavalry of the commander-in-chief's personal escort, recognized them and led a counter charge. After a short but sharp fight, in which he was wounded, the Afghans scattered.

Kalra having fallen, the British line on the left advanced along the Dwara, the 24th leading astride the dry bed. They were now confronted by stiff resistance from the red-coated Sikh regular infantry. As a result, a dangerous gap opened between Gilbert and Whish's division in the centre and Campbell's on the left. Seeing this, the Sikhs pushed a combined force of infantry and cavalry into the gap in an attempt to penetrate and split the British line. At that moment, Gough was receiving the congratulations of his staff on the success that seemed imminent, when the Sikhs launched a 'do or die' bid for victory.

As George Bruce puts it,

> Holding high their great yellow banners, marching in a closely held line with a few surviving guns between regiments, the red-breasted Sikhs, black-bearded and turbaned, strode through the British gap before wheeling to right and left for a massed flank attack. The danger worsened when two troops of horse artillery Gough had sent up, at the last moment ran out of shell and shot – they had to await a fresh supply from the rear. Forward companies of the Sikhs, shouting their sacred war cry, began to charge the isolated British gunners.

The situation seemed critical when Campbell, watching from the flank, ordered Captain Ludlow to unlimber his 18-pounders and engage the enemy. Ludlow opened fire at a distance of 600 yards and his accurate fire brought the Sikh advance to a halt. With their casualties mounting, the advancing Sikhs began to withdraw, covered by their cavalry.

On the right, Whish followed the retreating Sikhs after taking Chota Kalra. Once again, the gap in the British lines widened, causing Gough to send a message to slow down. George Bruce quotes Corporal Ryder of the 32nd describing that moment:

> The enemy formed several squares to keep us in check whilst they got their guns away, but our field artillery galloped to the front and opened a most destructive fire of grape and canister, which swept

> them down by whole battalions. On we rushed, bearing down all before us, charging and cheering. We took every gun we came up to, but their artillery fought desperately: they stood and defended their guns to the last. They threw their arms around them, kissed them and died. Others would spit at us when the bayonet was through their bodies. An aide-de-camp now rode up with orders from Lord Gough to say that the right of the line was too far forward, and that we were to halt [...]
>
> This was a very trying time for the right of the line. While we were standing waiting for orders to advance, the enemy were boldly reforming their line in our front and keeping up a fire on us; although it was nearly harmless, as they (as usual) fired high. Our men were, with the greatest difficulty in the world, kept in check by the officers. Lord Gough sent a second order for the right to keep back, as the left could not keep up; and the Brigadier [Markham] told the aide-de-camp that he could not keep the men back, nor did he, until he rode at all hazard in front of the line, telling the men to cease firing and to halt. The enemy had now brought some guns to bear upon us with grape. The first round they fired fell just in front of us, and as the ground was fresh ploughed, the shots buried themselves in it, but the second round came [...] slightly wounding one of our men and severely wounding another. They also made a gap in the 51st Regiment of Native Infantry [...]
>
> One of the Sikh cavalry regiments, bearing a black flag, then deliberately formed line in front of us, as if about to charge us, when our men could stand it no longer. We opened fire upon them, and whether any word "forward" was given or not, I do not know, but forward we went, and when near to them, and just as they were about to spring forward upon us, we opened such a well-directed fire, and poured it into them with such deadly effect, that it fetched down man and horse by scores to the ground, while numbers of saddles were emptied and the horses went off, leaving their lifeless riders behind. On we went, charging and cheering, bearing all down before us and the black flag fell into our hands [...]

General Campbell had turned the Sikh right, forcing the Sikh line to withdraw towards Bhimbur. Every now and then, they made a stand in the hamlets they passed or in some tactically suitable position. On each attempt to hold a position, they were attacked, overrun and bayoneted.

By 1 p.m., Gough had managed to overthrow the remainder of Sher Singh's army, which was now rapidly withdrawing. By 2 p.m., with thousands of rider-less horses careering on the field, Gough had stormed the city of Gujrat with Whish's 2nd Brigade, during which 80 soldiers surrendered to the 30th NI. He then advanced beyond it. The British cavalry and infantry were now in pursuit of Sher Singh and his army.

Those who abandoned their uniforms were caught and killed with the sword, pistol and grapeshot. No quarter was given. The chase ended when darkness descended.

During the pursuit, Thackwell personally led his cavalry and took no prisoners. On the other flank, the 14th Light Dragoons captured a standard and the 1st Bengal Light Cavalry overran a battery of nine guns that were withdrawing. The irregular cavalry continued the chase for 15 miles.

At dawn the next day, General Gilbert set out in hot pursuit to demand unconditional surrender, strengthened by the 14th Dragoons – a regiment of irregular cavalry – and two batteries of field artillery. Gilbert covered 50 miles in 72 hours and then halted for three days on the Jhelum. He crossed it on 28 February. He was joined there by Brigadier Hearsey, with his 3rd and 9th Irregulars. On 8 March, he was 31 miles away from Rawalpindi – a day's march. Sher Singh had halted at Rawalpindi with 16,000 troops.

Sher Singh and Lal Singh surrendered to Gilbert and brought with them the British prisoners, Major George Lawrence and his family, Lieutenant Herbert, and others who had been taken prisoner at Peshawar and Attock. On 10 March, Gilbert had reached Manikyala, where Sardar Khan Singh Majithia surrendered with 1,000 of his feudal levy and some guns. On 12 at Hammuk, on the left bank of the Swan river, Sher Singh, Chattar Singh and other sardars and officers of the Sikh Army surrendered formally and gave up their swords and 17 guns. On 14 March, Gilbert reached Rawalpindi and moved his division close to the Sikh camp on the outskirts. There, a large square was formed through which Sher Singh's troops marched by regiments, each laying down their weapons. In all, some 20,000 muskets and 41 guns were surrendered to the British. 'Those who watched the surrender ceremony greatly admired the bearing of the Sikh soldiers, who still carried themselves with pride. They were tired and hungry, but their spirit was by no means broken.'[189]

Captain Thackwell, who was present, recorded that, 'the reluctance of some of the old Khalsa veterans to surrender their arms was evident. Some could not restrain their tears, while on the faces of others, rage and hatred was visibly depicted'. Yet others were heard saying, 'Today died Ranjit Singh,' as they laid down their weapons.

Dost Mohammad's Afghan horse, led by his son Akram Khan, crossed the Khyber into Afghanistan on 19 March and Gilbert entered Peshawar on 21 March 1849.

For six hours of battle, British casualties were relatively low. The main reason for this was the destruction of the Sikh artillery batteries by the overwhelming superiority, both in calibre and numbers, of Gough's guns. Five officers and 91 other ranks were killed and 24 officers and 646 other ranks were wounded – 83 of these casualties were gunners, 53 guns were taken on the field and 3 guns were found later. 'The victory was Brigadier

Tennant's,' Gough was reported to have said later about his artillery commander. It was at Gujrat that the artillery really came into its own. For the first time, it had shown itself superior to the Sikh artillery and it was the gunners who had the major share in the decisive victory.

Corporal Ryder wrote,

> When we asked some of the prisoners if they had had enough of fighting, and if they were tired of it, they said they were not – they should fight yet again; and if we fought fair, they should beat us. They asked us what our officers gave us to make us drunk with, for we must be drunk, they said, when we shouted and ran up to the batteries, in the face of their fire, and to the mouth of their guns. They called us, "beardless boys," and said we must be mad, or fools, to go up to their fire in the way we did [...] They were fine-looking men as ever drew swords. We seemed like children by the side of them. They were well-made and bold looking, and I wonder how such boys as we beat them [...]

All the sardars and officers were taken as prisoners of war, the men being given a rupee each and allowed to return to their villages. Chattar Singh and Sher Singh, along with the others, were sent to Futehgarh in north-central India and held in captivity. Both were released on parole a short while later, but on their return they fed Brahmins in their village on the occasion of the solar eclipse, which was taken by the Lahore administration to be a violation of their parole, and they were once again arrested and exiled. Both died in the same year, in 1858, while still in exile.

* As per the order of battle of his army given on pages 194-195, Gough had with him at Helan 2 infantry divisions, the 2nd and 3rd, comprising 5 infantry brigades. These brigades had 15 infantry battalions, of which 3 were HMs and 12 NIs. He also had 1 cavalry division of 3 brigades comprising 10 cavalry regiments, 3 HMs and 7 Bengal. The actual strength was 14,000 infantry, 6,000 cavalry and 1,400 gunners, which was 21,400 in all, plus engineers, pioneers etc., and not 12,000 troops. This unit strength, recorded by the then Adjutant General Lt Col Pat Grant for the battle of Chillianwala, is in Appendix D, page 134, in Archer's, *Commentaries on the Punjab Campaign 1848-49*.

Epilogue

ANNEXATION OF THE PUNJAB

Punjab was annexed on 30 March 1849, twenty days after the Sikh Army surrendered on 10 March at Rawalpindi. The formal annexation ceremony was held at Lahore in a full durbar on 30 March, and the governor general's proclamation was read out. It was attended by the eleven-year-old Maharaja Duleep Singh, and all the nobles of the state who had not taken part in the rebellion. Thus, Dalhousie's oft-repeated policy of encompassing the Punjab into the Indian empire was announced to those who never took part in the war. As Major Evans Bell puts it, 'It was Lord Dalhousie who converted our protective occupation into a so called conquest'.

The situation in Multan and the Second Sikh War were used as an excuse by the British to conquer the Punjab. The former was at most a law and order problem, a rebellion by the governor of the district on being asked to clarify some aspects of governance, including financial irregularity. The governor, Mulraj, had rebelled and killed the Sikh governor-designate and the two accompanying British officers. The durbar troops, of which Raja Sher Singh, a member of the Council of Regency was a part, were sent to Multan to tame the rogue governor.

What would have happened if subsequent events had taken a different course? We should first try to ascertain why Chattar Singh Attari and Raja Sher Singh Attari had rebelled. At that point in time, their rebellion had been an isolated incident. The word of Captain Abbot, a British district commissioner, was taken against that of a Sikh governor who stood accused of disaffection, despite the fact that the resident, Henry Lawrence, had already reported to the governor general on Abbot's conduct. Lawrence had stated that,

> His Lordship will have observed a very ready disposition on the part of Captain Abbot to believe the reports that are brought to him of conspiracies, treasons, and plots, suspicion of everybody, far and near, even of his own servants, and a conviction of the infallibility of his own conclusions, which is not shaken by finding time after time that they are not verified.[190]

In this case too, subsequent enquiry proved Abbot's accusation to be unsubstantiated. Nevertheless, Chattar Singh felt utterly humiliated. Abbot's conduct and the fact that Sir Frederick Currie was non-committal on the wedding of his daughter Nanki to Maharaja Duleep Singh, to whom she was engaged, was the last straw. It was only then that the seeds of revolt were sown.

Raja Lal Singh who took up arms against the state was already exiled from the Punjab. The other three who took part in the Second Sikh War – Attar Singh, Ram Singh and Kahn Singh Majithia – were soldiers. If these few sardars took up arms it was at most a localized revolt, not a rebellion.

> There is a list of thirty-four Sirdars, or leading Chieftains, in the Blue Book, who, with their relatives and dependents took no part in the rebellion. Twenty-eight of these are Sikhs, two are Mahomedan, and four are Hindoos. Of the sixteen who signed the Treaties and Articles of Agreement of 1846, only five joined in the rebellion, and one, Ranjodh Singh Majithia who was a member of the Council of Regency, was imprisoned at Lahore on suspicion of carrying out a treasonable correspondence.

The resident had also reported that,

> [...] up to 4 October no Sirdar had joined Chuttar Singh, who had failed utterly to induce any of the Regular troops, except those who had been with him at Hazara to join him [...] He had marched towards the camp of his son, Rajah Shere Singh and the other insurgents, in despair at the refusals he had received from the Sikh officers at Peshawar. It was not until October that the troops at Bunnoo [21 October] and Peshawar [23 October] broke into mutiny.[191]

Of the eight members of the Council of Regency, six had remained loyal to their positions. If discharged soldiers flocked to the standards of the rebels, the blame must again be found elsewhere. Those who ran the state and who were responsible for day-to-day governance were the ones answerable. They remained oblivious to the deteriorating situation which gradually slipped out of their control.

After the First Sikh War, the Treaty of Bhyrowal entered into on 22 December 1846, had constituted a Council of Regency to create policy and to manage the day-to-day affairs of the state during Maharaja Duleep Singh's minority. Colonel Henry Lawrence was appointed commissioner and presided over the council. His mandate was:

> A Council of Regency, composed of leading chiefs, will act under the control and guidance of the British Resident.
>
> The power of the Resident extends over every department, and to any extent.
>
> Those terms give the British Resident unlimited authority in all matters of internal administration, and external relations, during the Maharaja's minority.

In a letter dated 3 July, the governor general reminds the resident that the articles of agreement:

> [...] give to the Government of India, represented at Lahore by its Resident, full power to direct and control all matters in every department of the State.
>
> It is politic that the Resident should carry the Native Council with him, the members of which are, however, entirely under his control and guidance; he can change them and appoint others, and in military affairs his power is as unlimited as in the civil administration; he can withdraw Sikh garrisons, replacing them by British troops, in any and every part of Punjab.[192]

What further authority was required? Lawrence was the supreme power. The council was for all practical purposes his council of advisors. Select British officers were appointed commissioners to manage the administration of the far-flung districts. Durbar governors were also appointed to those districts, but effective control once again remained in the hands of the resident's chosen few. For Dalhousie to state 'that the Sikhs had risen in rebellion against a benevolent Government'[193] smacks of hypocrisy. If anything, it was the failure of the resident at Lahore, and those of his appointees in the districts, to identify the escalating events and to then exercise control over a situation which encompassed only a miniscule few of the chiefs of the Lahore state.

The first Council of Regency comprised eight eminent people. These were – Raja Deenanath, Raja Tej Singh, Bhai Nidhan Singh, Fakir Nur-ud-din, Shamsher Singh Sandhanwalia, Uttur Singh Kaleewala, Raja Sher Singh Attari and Sirdar Ranjodh Singh Majithia – who at that point of time were perfectly blameless in their public conduct. Frederic Currie, former foreign secretary of the Government of India told them that,

> [...] if they refused to accept the Terms which the Governor General offered, the Maharaja and themselves would be entirely at his mercy, and would not be entitled to receive any allowance whatever. If they signed the Terms, and continued to give their advice and assistance

> whenever they were called upon to do so, their jagheers would not be confiscated.

He used blackmail to achieve what he wanted.

Mulraj's revolt was symptomatic of the situation that then existed in the Punjab. Over 150,000 soldiers had been demobilized and left unemployed by the treaty. Old customs which had governed the lives of the people for centuries were done away with. Land reforms were introduced, which affected the feudal landowners who ruled their fiefdoms with an iron hand with large levies and exercised judicial powers over them. It would be naive to expect them to gladly accept a radically new way of life overnight. Maharani Jinda Kaur, the mother of their maharaja and wife of their beloved sovereign, Ranjit Singh, was exiled from the Punjab. In short, all aspects of the historical and traditional day-to-day existence of the people of Punjab were interfered with. No matter how positively history may view these reforms, there was bound to be an immediate reaction which would take its toll on the thought process of the people. Major changes such as these, thrust on the people within days of the defeat of their army in the first war, definitely crystallized views. A belief which also became widespread was that Maharaja Duleep Singh would eventually be done away with and the British would encompass the Punjab into their Indian Empire.

When Dalhousie made known his imperious decision on 3 October 1848, that the State of Lahore was considered to be directly at war with the British government, Currie, who was standing in as the resident for Lawrence who was on leave in England, quite rightly pointed out that the Treaty of Bhyrowal was still in force and that 'they could not continue to protect and maintain a state which they had declared to be at war with them'. Dalhousie did not even take his commander-in-chief into confidence, for Lord Gough complained in a letter written to his son when in Lahore, on 15 November, that he did not know whether they were at peace or war, or who it is they were fighting for.

Dalhousie was waiting for the right opportunity, his mind was made up. He had made his position clear to the president of the Board of Trade, Sir John Hobhouse, on 5 October, that,

> Regards for the preservation of power [...] compel us to declare war, and to prosecute it to the entire submission of the Sikh Dynasty [...] The Government of India [...] have without hesitation resolved, that the Punjab can no longer be allowed to exist as a power and must be destroyed.

That he intended to do away with the Lahore State before the Second Sikh War had even begun, is abundantly clear. The proclamation itself is filled with disinformation to justify the annexation. One obvious example being, 'Of their annual tribute no portion has at any time been paid; and large loans, advanced to them by the Government of India, have never been repaid'. The Blue Book contradicts the assertion that 'not one rupee', 'that no portion', had ever been paid. On 23 February 1848, the resident reports as follows to the governor general: 'The Durbar have paid into this treasury gold to the value of Rupees 1,356,837. By this payment they have reduced their debt to the British government from upwards of forty lakh of rupees to less than twenty-seven.'

George Bruce adds that in early November,

> He [Dalhousie] had not yet told the Lahore Government, the Council of Regency, that he was at war with them, nor would he do so until the job was done. "The subsequent destiny of the Sikh dynasty and Sikh nation will be pronounced upon when the objects above mentioned [defeating, disarming and crushing all forces of the Sikhs] are accomplished," he informed Currie in November. Whether or not they realized what was in the wind, the Council of Regency meanwhile continued to fulfil loyally those of their treaty obligations that they could.

Dalhousie was here guilty of something near to fraud. Pretending he was still bound by treaty to protect the Lahore State, while he secretly advised his officials and generals that British India was at war with it, but that there would be no declaration of policy until the Sikh armed forces were defeated. By such means, aided by violence, was independent Punjab to be added to the Indian Empire.

Dalhousie's passion for empire building, his ambition to leave his mark on British-Indian history, forced the use of such unethical methods. Ambition seemed to come to him before truth and honour. The revolt of a dismissed governor and less than half a dozen chiefs and nobles was used as an excuse to encompass Punjab into the British Empire while the government in the Punjab was run by his nominees. What could be more hypocritical.

In *The Annexation of the Punjaub*, Major Evans Bell says,

> The State of Lahore at war with the British government while the Sovereign of the Punjaub was at Lahore, the Ward and Pupil of the Resident! The State of Lahore at war with the British Government, while the administration of the Panjaub was carried on at Lahore by the British Resident, in the name of the infant Sovereign, by virtue of a treaty with him, and in unaltered accordance with the arrangements of that treaty! Where was the State of Lahore with which the British government was at war, to be found?

In his six years as the governor general in India, Dalhousie, more than the others, laid the foundation of the trouble to come in the not too distant future; the Indian revolt of 1857. This he achieved within eight years of the end of the Second Sikh War. He deposed Nawab Wajid Ali Shah and annexed Awadh. Awadh as he should have been aware, contributed the most to the Bengal Regiments of the East India Company. When the revolt came in 1857, out of the 8 regiments of Bengal Light Cavalry that fought in the Sikh wars, only the Governor General's Bodyguard remained loyal – 5 mutinied and 3 were disarmed. Of the Irregular Cavalry, 5 remained loyal while 3 mutinied and 4 were disarmed. A total of 14 of the 20 cavalry regiments that took part in the Sikh wars of 1845-46 and 1848-49 were disaffected. Of the Bengal Infantry that took part in both these wars, 23 mutinied, 11 were disarmed and disbanded, 5 partially mutinied, their loyal portions going to form new regiments. Three were disarmed but remained in service. Just 2 battalions remained completely loyal out of the 53 that took part. Almost all of them were recruited from the erstwhile Kingdom of Awadh. Of the 31 stations where troops mutinied in that year, 14 were in north-central India, engulfing Awadh territory. So much for Dalhousie's foresight (*see* Annexure XIV).

Not content with Punjab and Awadh, Dalhousie brought in his Doctrine of Lapse, creating bitterness and unrest in a number of princely states, many of whom later took an active part in the events of 1857. He introduced reforms that no matter how laudable, impinged upon thousands of years of Indian history. It was not Mangal Pandey or a greased cartridge that created a national rebellion, they simply became the catalyst which set off events. India, suffocated by these acts of British arrogance, was by then ready to throw off the mantel of domination and all that was required was an excuse.

Similarly Currie's bad judgement in sending Maharani Jinda Kaur into exile became that catalyst in Punjab in 1848, causing thousands of Sikhs, both demobilized soldiers and others, to flock to the few sardars who had raised the banner of revolt. Had Lawrence been the resident, it is most unlikely that he would have taken this step.

For the maharani, those who considered her a traitor at the end of the first war, saw in her a rallying point at the start of the second, because of her incarceration by the British and their hostile attitude towards her. In 1846, the situation could not have been worse. She had conspired along with Raja Lal Singh and Raja Tej Singh to get her belligerent army cut to size. The British played their part to perfection in this conspiracy and helped her in achieving her goal which fitted in with their own. Three years later in 1849, the same British sent her into exile, from which she would never return. On her death, her ashes too had to be immersed in the river Godavari at Nasik in central India. Ironically, one of her intimate confidants in the conspiracy of 1846, her former commander-in-chief during the First Sikh War, Raja Tej Singh, who was now a member of the Council of Regency, was one of the three signatories of the existing six, then in the council, who signed the order exiling her to Benaras. Adherence to the various articles of the treaty were also on a selective basis. For the maharani, Article 10 of the Treaty of Bhyrowal provided for her to receive an allowance of Rupees 150,000 per year (15,000 pounds sterling). When she was first moved to Sheikhupura from Lahore in 1847, it was reduced, despite the treaty, to Rupees 48,000. After her deportation to Benaras, it was further reduced to Rupees 12,000. At Benaras she was deprived of her jewellery and other valuables.

Though the reason given for exiling the maharani first to Sheikhupura on 20 August 1847, and then to Benaras on 16 May 1848, was her continuing role in enticing revolt and attempts to get the resident and others poisoned at Lahore, the more compelling reason however, was the refusal of the nine-year-old Duleep Singh in putting the 'Raj Tilak' on the forehead of Raja Tej Singh in full durbar, whom Henry Lawrence had decided to appoint as the Raja of Sialkot for services rendered during the First Sikh War. His consistency in refusing to do as asked, was attributed to the instructions he had received from his mother. The maharani was under a strict military guard at Sheikhupura and visitors to her were regulated as was her correspondence. Nevertheless, in view of her influence over her son, she was exiled to Benaras. Mother and son would now meet in 1861, fourteen years later.

Maharani Jinda arrived at Benaras on 2 August 1848 and her escort handed her over to her warder Major MacGregor, who kept her and her twelve servants confined to her apartment. They were under heavy guard and could not cross the sentry posts. Four of her man servants, including her munshi Ram Kishan, were allowed access to her as they carried in food and other items ordered by her. The guard was composed of one subedar and sixty men. Most of her jewellery was taken from her on arrival at Benaras, and her allowance reduced, on the pretext that she could save money to engineer her escape. Her current attitude and the fact that an escape route had been tested by her, by sending one of her maids through, convinced Major MacGregor that the maharani intended to escape. He immediately transferred her under heavy escort, provided by an entire battalion, the 65th NI, a company of the 48th NI, and a troop of the 8th Irregular Cavalry, to the fortress of Chunar, where he handed her over to the Commandant, Captain Rees and his adjutant, Lt Nelson. Major MacGregor stayed on as her personal warder.

Each day, both in the morning and evening, the duty officer called on her, and because she was in *parda* spoke to her to ensure her presence. She had a lilt in her voice which made it easily distinguishable. On 15 April it was reported that her voice was hoarse due to a bad cold. On the 16 and 17 her cold got worse and on 19 April 1849 she was found missing from her apartment. A massive search was launched but there was no trace of her.

The resourceful maharani had requested for a woman tailor, and one had been chosen for her by Major MacGregor. This seamstress came daily, and eventually, the sentries quite used to her, let her go by without checking her identity. On 15 April, the maharani changed clothes with her seamstress and walked out of the fortress. She then dressed as a *sanyasin* in saffron clothes and carrying on her person whatever jewellery she could, walked for thirty-four days to Nepal. At night she would stay at temples, where she would be fed and given a bed to sleep on.

On reaching Nepal on 21 May 1849, and disclosing her identity, the Prime Minister Rana Jung Bahadur gave her sanctuary, a house next to his own to live in and an allowance of a thousand rupees a month. She would live in Nepal for the next twelve years.

Raja Sher Singh's manifest, written when he was imprisoned at Lahore, sums up the feeling.

> It is well known to all the inhabitants of the Punjab, to the whole of the Sikhs, and in fact to the world at large, [with] what oppression, tyranny and undue violence, the Feringhees have treated the widow of the great Maharaja Runjeet Singh, now in bliss. They have broken the treaty by imprisoning, and sending away to Hindustan, the Maharanee, the Mother of her people.

Even the Amir of Kabul, Dost Mohammad, an avowed enemy of the late Maharaja Ranjit Singh, in a letter to Abbot writes,

> There can be no doubt that the Sikhs are daily becoming more and more discontented. Some have been dismissed from service, while others have been banished to Hindustan, in particular the mother of Maharaja Duleep Singh, who has been imprisoned and ill-treated. Such treatment is considered objectionable by all creeds, and both high and low prefer death.

Cook adds,

> Lord Dalhousie took the view that the Sikhs had risen in rebellion against a benevolent Government, which had treated them leniently after their first offence, and that it would be unsafe to trust them again. He considered that the Sikhs had asked for trouble and deserved all that they could get. In particular he thought it essential that the Sikh Sardars should be stripped of all power, so that they would not in the future have the resources to cause trouble. He regarded annexation as a thoroughly sound plan.

Lawrence took a diametrically opposite view. He would have liked to avoid complete annexation and regarded it at the best as a regrettable necessity. He considered that many of the Sikh sardars had been forced into active or passive support for Sher Singh and his associates by the weakness of the durbar, the strength of the Khalsa and to some degree by the tactlessness of the British. He thought that British ineptitude in the handling of the Mulraj affair had to some extent led to the late conflict. He therefore felt that it would be unwise to be too hard on the leaders of the Sikh community and that it would pay a far greater dividend in the long run if they were treated leniently. Whereas Dalhousie believed that the time had come to crush the Sikhs completely, Lawrence considered that, having beaten them in the field, the best British policy was to treat them with fairness and justice and to convert them into firm friends as a bulwark for British authority in the future.

Henry Lawrence was an experienced administrator. Having joined the Bengal artillery in 1823, he soon moved to the civil service and came into contact with the Sikhs for the first time in 1839, during the First Afghan War. Dalhousie was a thirty-five-year-old aristocrat and politician, and now governor general whose sum total in administrative experience had been as president of the Board of Trade in Sir Robert Peel's government. He had no military experience, which did not, however, prevent him, in his intimidating way, from dictating to the genial and highly experienced Commander-in-Chief Lord Gough on military matters. Lawrence had been an administrator in India and knew and respected the Sikhs and the people of the Punjab. With no previous knowledge of the Punjab and the Sikhs, Dalhousie once again in his arrogant manner, contrived to advise him on each occasion about what should be done, instead of listening to his views and then accepting or rejecting his advice.

Lawrence had returned to Lahore on 18 January and was present at the Battle of Chillianwala. He had been promptly asked by Dalhousie to prepare a proclamation of annexation, to be implemented as soon as the war was over. He accordingly drew up a document which he forwarded to the governor general. Dalhousie, just as promptly shot it down as it held out hopes of leniency which he had no intention of allowing. His remarks on the document sent back to Lawrence simply stated that the contents were 'objectionable both in matter and manner'. He then in an acrimonious way added, 'I can allow nothing to be said or done which would raise the notion that the policy of the Government of India depends on your presence in the Punjab'.[194] Relations between the two continued to deteriorate and when complete annexation was decided upon, Henry Lawrence offered to resign. However, Lawrence was held in high esteem and even Dalhousie could not afford to let him go. He eventually persuaded him to stay on by using the argument that he was better placed to look after the interests of the Sikhs by remaining at Lahore.

Once annexation was complete, he publicly indicated his lack of confidence in him when, instead of appointing Henry Lawrence as governor, which was the obvious thing to do, considering Lawrence's vast experience in the Punjab, Dalhousie instead set up a 'Board of Control' of which Henry Lawrence would be president and would look after political matters. His brother John Lawrence, whose views were more akin to Dalhousie's, would look after financial matters, and a third member, Mansell, would look after judicial and legal questions. For a while things worked, but soon differences cropped up between the members on various issues.

The rift finally came over the question of treatment to be meted out to the jagirdars. Lawrence was anxious to make things easy for them and to leave them with the resources which would enable them to continue as men of authority. Dalhousie wanted to strip them of all power. When Montgomery took over from Mansell, he agreed with John Lawrence, who in turn shared Dalhousie's views on this subject and, thus, they adopted a hard line approach towards this issue. Henry Lawrence then decided to resign and applied for the post of resident in the State of Hyderabad for which he was selected. He left Punjab in 1852. Before he could join, however, Dalhousie sent him as resident to Rajputana. His brother John Lawrence now took over Punjab and pursued Dalhousie's policy.

Cook remarks, 'For Punjab these changes did not auger well'. Sir Charles Napier had replaced the good-natured Gough as commander-in-chief.

> He was a blunt soldier who loathed committees and had the average soldier's dislike for politicians and civil servants. He would have preferred Punjab to be put under military rule, as Sind had been when he conquered it in the war of 1843 "to introduce the blessings of courts martial", as he put it. He had no use at all for Lord Dalhousie, whom he referred to as "the laird of Cockpen" and went on to describe him as "a young Scotch lord with no head for governing an empire."

He was soon to find the general situation too frustrating for him. Fortunately, Dalhousie for once thought otherwise, and a year later in 1850 Napier resigned and went home.

Major Evans Bell sums up his book on the annexation, with the following paragraph.

> According to Oriental ideas the greatest Sovereign is he who can make Princes, and who has the largest number of Princes under his command and protection. Lord Dalhousie might have gained the hearts of Princes and people by a plain statement of what had been done, and what it was he intended to do in the Punjaub. Instead of doing so, he violated treaties, abused a sacred trust, threw away the grandest opportunity ever offered to the British government of planting solid and vital reform up to the Northern limits of India, and by an accusation as unjust as it was imprudent, weakened our frontier, scattered our military strength, and entailed a heavy burden upon the Empire. That, I believe, will be the verdict of posterity and history upon the transactions which have just passed under our review.

NOTIFICATION

Foreign Department, Camp Ferozpore, 30 March

The Governor General is pleased to direct that the accompanying proclamation, by which the Punjaub is declared to be a portion of the British Empire in India, be published for general information, and that a royal salute be fired at every principal station of the army on the receipt thereof. By order of the Right Honourable the Governor General of India.

(Signed) P. Melvill
Under-Secretary to the Government of India,
with the Governor General.

PROCLAMATION

For many years during the time of Maharaja Ranjit Singh, peace and friendship prevailed between the British nation and the Sikhs. When Ranjit Singh was dead and his wisdom no longer guided the Councils of the State, the Sirdars and the Khalsa Army, without provocation and without cause, suddenly invaded the British territories. Their army was again and again defeated. They were driven with slaughter and in shame from the country they had invaded, and, at the gates of Lahore, the Maharaja Dulip Singh tendered to the Governor General the submission of himself and his chiefs, and solicited the clemency of the British government.

The Governor General extended the clemency of his Government to the State of Lahore, he generously spared the kingdom which he had acquired a just right to subvert, and, the Maharaja having been replaced on the throne, treaties of friendship were formed between the States.

The British have faithfully kept their word, and have scrupulously observed every obligation which the treaties imposed upon them.

But the Sikh people and their chiefs have, on their part, grossly and faithlessly violated the promises by which they were bound.

Of their annual tribute no portion whatever has at any time been paid, and large loans advanced to them by the Government of India have never been repaid.

The control of the British government to which they voluntarily submitted themselves, has been resisted by arms.

Peace has been cast aside. British officers have been murdered when acting for the State; others engaged in a like employment have been thrown into captivity. Finally, the whole of the State and the whole Sikh people, joined by many of the Sirdars in the Punjab, who signed the treaties, and led by a member of the Regency itself, have risen in arms against us and have waged a fierce and bloody war for the proclaimed purpose of destroying the British and their power.

The Government of India formerly declared that it required no further conquest, and it proved by its acts the sincerity of its professions.

The Government of India has no desire for conquest now, but it is bound in its duty to provide fully for its own security and to guard the interests of those committed to its charge.

To that end, and as the only sure mode of protecting the State from the perpetual recurrence of unprovoked and wasting wars, the Governor General is compelled to resolve upon the entire subjugation of a people whom their own Government has long been unable to control, and whom (as events have now shown) no punishment can deter from violence, no acts of friendship can conciliate to peace.

Wherefore, the Governor General of India has declared,

And hereby proclaims, that the Kingdom of the Punjab is at an end: and that all the territories of Maharaja Ranjit Singh are now and henceforth a portion of the British Empire in India.

His Highness the Maharaja shall be treated with consideration and with honour.

The few chiefs who have not engaged in hostilities against the British shall retain their property and their rank.

The British government will leave to all the people, whether Mussulmen or Hindoo or Sikh, the free exercise of their own religion: but it will not permit any man to interfere with others in the observance of such forms and customs as their respective religions may either enjoin or permit.

The jagheers and all the property of Sirdars or others who have been in arms against the British, shall be confiscated to the State.

The defence of every fortified place in the Punjab which is not occupied by British troops shall be totally destroyed: and effectual measures shall be taken to deprive the people of the means of renewing either tumult or war.

The Governor General calls upon all the inhabitants of the Punjab – Sirdars and people – to submit themselves peaceably to the authority of the British government which has hereby been proclaimed.

Over those who shall live as obedient and peaceful subjects of the State, the British government will rule with mildness and beneficence.

But if resistance to constituted authority shall again be attempted; if violence and turbulence be renewed; the Governor General warns the people of the Panjaub that the time for leniency will then have passed away, and that their offence will be punished with prompt and most rigorous severity.

By order of the Right Honourable the Governor General of India
(Signed) H.M. Elliott
Secretary to the Government of India,
with the Governor General.
Head-Quarters, Camp Ferozepore, 29 March 1849.

EXILE OF MAHARAJA DULEEP SINGH

After the proclamation, the ten-and-a-half-year-old Duleep Singh was informed of his future:

1. His Highness the Maharaja Duleep Singh shall resign for himself, his heirs, and successors all right, title and claim to the sovereignty of the Punjab, or to any sovereign power whatever.
2. All the property of the State, of whatever description and wheresoever found, shall be confiscated to the Honourable East India Company, in part payment of the debt due by the State of Lahore to the British government and of expenses of the war.
3. The Gem called the Koh-i-noor, which was taken from Shah Sooja-ul-moolk by Maharaja Ranjit Singh, shall be surrendered by the maharaja of Lahore to the queen of England.
4. His Highness Duleep Singh shall receive from the Honourable East India Company, for the support of himself and his relatives, and the servants of the State, a pension of not less than four, and not exceeding five, lakhs of the company's rupees per annum.*
5. His Highness shall be treated with respect and honour. He shall retain the title of Maharaja Duleep Singh Bahadoor, and he shall continue to receive during his life such portion of the above named pension as may be allotted to him personally, provided he shall remain obedient to the British government, and shall reside at such place as the governor general of India may select.[195]

The process of segregating Duleep Singh from his people had begun even before the formalities of the annexation were complete. Within a week of the event, on 6 April 1849, a doctor, John Spencer Login of the Bengal Army Medical Service, was appointed as his guardian.

> Dalhousie had little sympathy for the boy who was supposedly his protégé and who had now been relieved of his throne and his fortune. He did not see why a person he had earlier referred to as a "child notoriously surreptitious, a brat begotten of a Bhisti, and no more the son of old Runjit Singh than Queen Victoria", should be treated with more than cursory justice. He thought it necessary however to justify his action to his critics in London and wrote to Sir John Hobhouse, chairman of the East India Company, explaining the reasons for the confiscation of property that might be considered by some the rightful heritage of their juvenile charge:
>
> "Whatever my 'affectionate friends' at Leadenhall Street should, or may, think, you at least will find no fault with my having regarded the Koh-i-noor a thing by itself, and with my having caused the Maharaja of Lahore, in token of submission, to surrender it to the Queen of England. The Koh-i-noor had become in the lapse of ages

> a sort of historical emblem of conquest in India. It has now found its resting place.
>
> "The pension of the Maharaja is fixed at no less than four lakhs. His own stipend, I mean, and (was) always meant to be 1,200,000 rupees like the Raja of Sattarah. He has a large territory but he is a boy..."[196]

Having annexed the Punjab with a full treasury which in any case had been under their own control since 1846, and personal jewellery and other precious items in the maharaja's *Toshakhanna* (from where condescendingly Duleep Singh was to be allowed to 'choose a few pieces' before the jewellery was annexed, as were to be his personal estates built by his forefathers in Gujranwala and other places), and with the state producing extensive revenue, which he had promised the directors of the East India Company before the Second Sikh War would be available to them after the annexation, Dalhousie was now turning vindictive, perhaps because of the criticism in London that events did not justify annexation.

As per Dalhousie's own admission, in his provision post-annexation, Duleep Singh was to receive an allowance of Rupees 12 lakh, as he indicates in his letter to Sir John Hobhouse. However, he had now decided to deprive Duleep Singh of his income because he was a boy! Dalhousie, throughout his handling of the Punjab situation, had consistently let personal prejudice override his sense of fair play and justice. He seemed to conveniently forget that when he had planned the allowance prior to the war, the maharaja had been a year younger or that in a few years he would be an adult and that such treaties were always in perpetuity.

Eleven months later, on 19 February 1850, Duleep Singh arrived at the small town of Fatehgarh on the river Ganges, in what is today the district of Farukhabad in Uttar Pradesh where he would spend the next four years. The excuse used by Dalhousie was that information had reached the government that an attempt would be made to abduct him from Lahore and take him to the hills, from where a fresh attempt would be made to rally the Sikhs in the Punjab in another attempt at insurrection. This story was planted, knowing full well that it was pure fiction, in order to remove him from the Punjab. With no Sikh Army left at Lahore and with the sardars and hill chiefs by now subservient to British authority, and with the British Army now at Lahore in full force, Dalhousie's conspiracy theory seemed if anything childish, nevertheless it was used to effect and Duleep Singh was exiled from Lahore eleven months after the annexation.

Assuming that the news of his transportation would leak out and that there would be a reaction of sorts to his removal from the state, appropriate military precautions were taken to thwart such an eventuality: 'the removal of the ex-king of the Punjaub from his ancestral lands was a minor military operation involving an escort of infantry, horse artillery and several squadrons of cavalry.'

The overall plan behind his removal from Punjab, however, seemed to be to isolate the eleven-year-old Duleep Singh from the people and events of the state, and to then convert him to Christianity, after which he was to be sent to England. Of the family, only the late Maharaja Sher Singh's Rajput lady of his harem, Rani Dukhnoo of Kangra,[197] and her son Sheo Deo Singh, who was then six years old, but who could also be a claimant to the throne, were sent into exile along with him.

Suitable accommodation was found in Fatehgarh. A property which lay on the Ganges, surrounded by a park with a number of out-houses was bought for him out of his own allowance and was renovated. This had once belonged to a local nawab and was now with the East India Company. The accommodation was sumptuous. It was partly damaged during the revolt of 1857 and today forms part of the Rajput Regiment's Centre at Fatehgarh. Life in Duleep Singh's new surroundings was forged into a set routine. A ride early in the morning 'escorted by a retinue of fierce looking Sikhs jostling behind, followed by a detachment of the Body Guard in scarlet uniforms and troopers of the famous regiment Skinners Horse, otherwise known as "Canaries" in saffron'.[198] This was followed by studies under his new tutor Walter Guise, which included English, history, general knowledge, and the sciences. He was an average student as Dr Login had assessed him to be. In a letter to Login who was in Calcutta on holiday, Duleep Singh wrote, 'We are all well here, Captain Campbell presided at our examination, and I got twenty marks; but Shahzada [his nephew] got only ten'.[199] The afternoons were spent in play and his favourite sport hawking, and hunting out in the country. At six o'clock, he routinely met with those of his retinue who had accompanied him into exile, and spent an hour or so with them. These included Dewan Ajodhia Prasad his scribe, his Persian tutor Zahoor-el-Deen, Hakim Jaikishan his doctor, and his *purohit,* Golab Rai, amongst others. All of them were soon to be sent back to Lahore, including his old faithful personal servant Mian Kheema who was replaced by Bhajan Lal who had been engaged by Dr Login.

Bhajan Lal was the son of a wealthy merchant of Farukhabad, and though a Brahmin, had studied in the American Presbyterian Mission, while still observing the rules of Hinduism he had acquired more than a toleration of Christianity. Why he should accept to be a servant when he was from a well-to-do family is fairly obvious: to educate Duleep Singh, as he put it, in the beliefs of the *Firanghees*. Bhajan Lal now began to read the Bible to the twelve-year-old Duleep Singh. In a second letter to Dr Login during the same holiday, he writes, 'You will be surprised to learn of my determination to embrace the Christian religion. I have long doubted the truth of the one I was brought up in, and convinced of the truth of the religion of the Bible which I have made Bhajan Lal read portion of it to me.'[200]

Dalhousie pretended to be outraged as it would be assumed in India that the government had brought about this conversion. He ordered an enquiry to find out if Duleep Singh had been coerced into this decision by someone at Fatehgarh, or whether it truly was a calling from his 'Inner self'. The enquiry duly over, and Dalhousie duly convinced that it was indeed a decision of Duleep Singh's 'inner self' permission was given for him to be converted. He now wrote to Duleep Singh:

> My dear Maharaja,
> I have received with the most lively satisfaction the letter in which you express your desire to be at once baptized, and to be admitted as a member of the Church of Christ. When you at first showed an inclination to believe in the truths which you found declared in the word of God, I advised you not to act hastily, to continue in your study of the Bible, and to test by time the strength and sincerity of your belief.
>
> You have followed my advice, and I have learnt with real pleasure from the statement of the Archdeacon and Mr Jay that they have found you quite fit to receive the baptism you desire to obtain. I, on my part, most readily assent to your wish, and I thank God and Saviour of us all, who had put into your heart a knowledge of, and a belief in, the truth of our holy religion, and that you may show to your countrymen in India an example of a pure and blameless life, such as befits a Christian prince.
>
> I beg Your Highness to believe in the strength and sincerity of the regard in which I shall ever feel towards you, and to remain, now and always, Your Highness's sincere and affectionate friend.[201]

From 'a Brat begotten of a Bhisti', to a 'sincere and affectionate friend', were typical of Dalhousie's inconsistencies that marked the eight years of his governor generalship of India. Dalhousie was now delighted and put in motion the third step, which was to send Duleep Singh to England. As part of his over-all plan, which he had confided to Login at the very beginning, and which Login in turn had confided to his wife in a letter from Lahore, 'I cannot put the Bible in his hands yet' after receiving a letter from Dalhousie which stated that, 'If Duleep Singh is to go to England, let him be quietly baptized before he goes and by his own name of Duleep Singh'.[202]

Winters were spent in Fatehgarh and summers in Mussoorie, where he had an opportunity of mixing with other children. In Fatehgarh he had a small circle of friends, children of the officers of the station. The one who would become his good friend, was Tommy Scott, who later became Colonel Tommy Scott and transferred to the Indian Civil Service. He would always stand by Duleep Singh, even during his troubled period in later years.

Lady Login in her *Recollections* says that the relationship between her husband and Duleep Singh was always warm and affectionate. They were the only 'parents' he knew and both were to remain close to him till the end of their days. Just once she remembers a 'childish' incident between the two.

> There had been a thunder shower and Duleep Singh fully clothed went out to play in the pouring rain. Dr Login ordered him up to his room to change, to which he responded that he would only do so as he did each evening at six o'clock. He was ordered up again and once again he refused. He was now threatened with punishment. Duleep Singh then burst into tears and pleaded the "Treaty of Lahore" which stipulated that he was to be allowed to do as he liked!

Duleep Singh was baptized on 8 March 1853 by the Reverend William Jay, the Station Chaplin, in the Fatehgarh Church, in the presence of about twenty officers of the station and an equal number of his own staff from the Punjab.

At the beginning of 1854 Duleep Singh was given the requisite approval to visit England, and Dalhousie personally wrote to him,

> I am very happy to tell you that I have this moment received permission of the Court of Directors [of the East India Company] that you should visit England. In the belief that this intelligence will give you pleasure, I hasten to convey it to you with my own hand.[203]

In April 1854 Duleep Singh set off for Calcutta, halting en-route at Lucknow and Benaras where a Pandit, Nilkanth Goreh, (Christianized as Nehemiah), one of the first Brahmins to have been converted to Christianity, and who was now working as a missionary amongst the people, was added to the party. Bhajan Lal had been held back by his family and Pandit Goreh was to be his replacement. In Calcutta, Duleep Singh was met fondly by Dalhousie, who gave him a parting gift of a beautifully bound Bible, and wrote to him a farewell letter:

> My dear Maharaja,
> Before you quit India, I have been desirous of offering you a parting gift which in future years might sometimes remind you of me.
>
> Since that day when the course of Public events placed you a little boy in my hands, I have regarded you in some sort as my son. I therefore ask you, before we part, to accept from me the volume which I should offer to my own child, as the best of all gifts, since in it alone is to be found the secret of real happiness either in this world or that which is to come.
>
> I bid you farewell, my dear Maharaja, and beg you to believe me always, with sincere regard,
> Your Highness's faithful friend,
> Dalhousie[204]

Duleep Singh sailed for England on 19 April 1854. He was fifteen years of age. He reached England in the mid-summer of 1854. On the way they had passed Malta and Gibraltar where he was given a twenty-one gun salute. On reaching Southampton, he was taken straight to London and put up in Mrs Claridge's Hotel, The Mivart, in Brook Street.

A summons then arrived from Buckingham Palace for him to meet the queen. This meeting between the thirty-five-year old Victoria and the fifteen-year-old Duleep Singh took place on 1 July as the queen recorded in her journal:

> After luncheon, to which Mama came, we received the young Maharaja Duleep Singh, the son of Runjeet Singh, who was deposed by us after the annexation of the Punjaub. He has been carefully brought up, chiefly in the hills, and was baptized last year, so that he is a Christian. He is extremely handsome and speaks English perfectly, and has a pretty graceful and dignified manner. He was beautifully dressed and covered with diamonds. The "Koh-i-noor" belonged to, and was once worn by him. I always feel so much for these poor deposed Indian Princes.

The queen was so impressed with him that she there and then commissioned Winterhalter, her favourite artist, to paint his portrait. This relationship between the two would weather many storms, but the queen remained his friend and supporter to his very last day. She also became the godmother of his oldest son. She also ordered, despite local rumblings, that in protocol, in the order of precedence, his would be the same as that of a European prince and would be addressed as 'Your Serene Highness'. To this there were murmurs in certain quarters in England, but the queen refused to budge.

She then wrote to Lord Dalhousie.

> The Queen wishes to tell Lord Dalhousie how much interested and pleased we have been in making the acquaintance of the young Maharaja Duleep Singh. It is not without pain and sympathy that the Queen sees this young Prince once destined to so high and powerful a position and now reduced to so dependent one by our arms; his youth, amiable character, and striking good looks; as well as being a Christian, the first of his high rank who has embraced our faith, must incline every one favourably towards him, and it will be a pleasure to us to do all we can to help him and to befriend and protect him.

On 21 August the queen went to her estate 'Osborne' on the Isle of Wight, and Duleep Singh was invited to stay for a week. Prince Albert and the royal children too became just as fond of him during this visit and from then on he became an integral part of the royal family's social calendar. The queen now tried her hand at match-making and suggested that he marry the exiled Raja of Coorg's daughter, who was also her goddaughter,

Princess Gouramma. Duleep Singh politely declined saying that not only was Gouramma a friend, he did not wish to marry till he was twenty-one or two and he had seen the world!

Duleep Singh was now a regular invitee to royal social events, and on one such occasion with Lady Login present, when he and the queen were together, as winter had set in, the queen, concerned about the fact that he had never been in such cold weather before and that it could make Duleep Singh ill, suggested that he wear woollen underclothes, to which Duleep Singh replied, 'Indeed Ma'am, I cannot bear the feel of flannel next to my skin. It makes me long to scratch and you would not like to see me scratching myself in your presence'.

Duleep Singh was now sixteen and he decided that he wished to manage his own affairs. It was suggested that he wait till he was twenty-one, as was the case in Britain. He was, however, unmoved and pointed out that the Treaty of Lahore had stated that he would no longer be a minor and would manage his own affairs at sixteen. The queen backed him on this, and while he was awaiting a response from the East India Company, he and a few friends were sent on a tour of the Continent. On his return, by which time the revolt of 1857 had taken place, and the Indian administration was still far from stable, the East India Company not wishing to generate any further bitterness, particularly so since Sikh troops in India had sided with the British during the revolt, agreed on 29 December 1857 to give him full powers as a major, to manage his own affairs.

Being befriended by various people in England and with the queen's warm support, Duleep Singh took a liking to England and decided that for the present he would like to live there for some time. Dr Login was able to get him Mulgrave Castle in Yorkshire, which was to be his first rented home and which got him involved in English country life and shooting. He next rented the estate of Lord Breadalbane at Auchlyne on Loch Tay. By now he had also decided that despite his closeness to Sir John and Lady Login, he should break free of their influence over him and accepted the advice of Dr Login, who was surprisingly of the same opinion, to meet a Colonel Oliphant, an ex-chairman of the Court of Directors of the East India Company, who was prepared to look after Duleep Singh's affairs.

Duleep Singh had also by now decided that he would bring his mother back from Nepal to a suitable place in India and towards that end he sent Pandit Goreh to Kathmandu. In England, he gave out that he intended to go to India to shoot tiger. This was against the queen's advice as she did not want him to go. In early February 1861 he reached Calcutta where he was received with a twenty-one gun salute and Lord Canning, the viceroy sent his ADC aboard to receive him. He was looked after in Calcutta extremely well but was not permitted to visit the Punjab.

In view of the Government of India's continued animosity towards his mother, Duleep Singh decided to cut short his trip to India and to take her back with him to England. To this request the government readily agreed. Mother and son met for the first time since 1848 on 16 January 1861, after a period of thirteen years, at the Spence's Hotel in Calcutta.

The Indian government was delighted with Duleep Singh's decision to take his mother to England, and offered to return her jewellery which had been confiscated at Benaras and Chunar. In addition, she was offered an allowance of 3,000 pounds sterling as an annuity for her in England. Mother and son arrived in England in early summer 1861 and Dr Login in the meanwhile had found accommodation for her, close to his own at Lancaster Gate. On their arrival, Login used all his influence to get her jewellery and other valuables cleared by Customs. The maharani was quite overwhelmed by his kindness and, as recorded by Lady Login, told him 'that had she known what he really was like, and how extremely kind and useful he would prove to be, she would never have arranged to have him poisoned, as she had at one time contemplated.'

Over the next few months, mother and son were ensconced together for hours on end each day while she filled him in on events of the past. She told him of a prophecy which had been written in a Sikh book called *Sakhians*, which clearly stated that he would return in glory to rule Punjab. The queen receiving reports of the negative influence his mother was having on him decided that she would speak to him about it.

He now wrote to Mrs Login saying 'you will be glad to hear that my mother has given me leave to marry an English lady and I think I have found one who will make me a good wife'. 'Unfortunately the Maharaja failed to propose to the lady promptly, and lost her to another, but consoled himself with an invitation to shoot over her husband's moors.'[204]

Perhaps because of the queen's conversation with him regarding his mother, or because of the wishes of the maharani herself, who was not really happy in England, about which she was quite vocal, referring to the British as 'Firanghees' and 'Malaech', that all of a sudden in June 1862 Duleep Singh informed Login that 'I have decided to arrange for my mother's return to India, and will see Sir Charles Wood on the subject at once, to have a place of residence fixed for her.'[205] Everyone in London was delighted at this development but that was not the case in Calcutta. Sir John Lawrence who was now a member of the Indian Council vehemently opposed her return. While objections and counter-objections flew between London and Calcutta, Maharani Jinda Kaur, partially blind by then, suddenly died on 1 August 1863 at the age of forty-four, at her residence, at Abingdon House in Kensington. Duleep Singh, who was at Loch Kennard Lodge in Perthshire, up in Scotland, hurried down to London. Her body was held in an un-consecrated vault in the Kensal Green Cemetery, until she could, as per her wishes, be taken to India for her last rites.

In 1862, Duleep Singh bought Hatherop Castle in Gloustershire. But a year later, when Elveden in Suffolk, near Thetford, on which he had set his mind, came on the market, he immediately decided to buy it. By now he was well into British country life and Elveden was in the middle of England's finest sporting estates.

Two months after his mother's death, on 18 October, Dr John Login died. On hearing the news his first reaction was, 'I have lost my father' and later asserted solemnly, 'If that man is not in heaven, then there's not a word of truth in the Bible!'[206] Duleep Singh wanted him to be buried in a family vault at Elveden but Lady Login wanted him at Felixstowe and Duleep Singh made all the arrangements for his funeral as well as a memorial to him.

> It had been a sad year for the Maharaja. He had lost his mother and his "father"; his faithful valet Thornton had died as well as his secretary Cawood. In addition, Gouramma, who had lately given birth to a daughter, his goddaughter, was dying of consumption. His love affairs with English ladies had all gone wrong, and in his present sanctimonious mood, he had come to the conclusion that even if he found a lady of society to marry he would only be led into a life of idleness. He told Lady Login that what he really wanted was a very young Eastern girl, "a good Christian wife", he could train up to be what he called "an help-meet".[207]

On 16 February, Duleep Singh left England for India with his mother's body safely in the hold. On his last visit to Cairo, during his initial journey to England, as a fifteen-year-old boy, he had been taken to the American Presbyterian School to give away prizes. He had then observed some 'charming girls' there. Before leaving he had written to the head of the mission asking him to find him a suitable 'good Christian wife' from amongst his charges. On reaching the Suez, taking advantage of the delay in the passing of his ship, he rushed ahead to Cairo to the Mission school where on arrival 'he observed a small fifteen-year-old student teacher giving lessons to a large, but disciplined class, and decided she was just the girl for him.'[208] Her name was Bamba Muller, she was the illegitimate daughter of an Abyssinian slave, a Copt and thus a Christian, and Ludwig Muller a partner in the German firm of merchant bankers, Todd Muller and Co. The maharaja proposed to her through an interpreter, as she knew no English and received her consent. Then after giving the mission the task of preparing her as a suitable bride saying 'I think it desirable that she should learn English and music, and to give her own orders',[209] he informed the mission that he would be back from India in six months when he would marry her and take her back to England. Having given these instructions he hurried back to his ship and departed for Bombay.

Maharani Jinda Kaur's cremation took place at Nasik on the west bank of the river Godavari, as Duleep Singh was not permitted to perform the last rites in the Punjab. A part of her ashes were immersed in the river and others were buried in an urn, in a small brick memorial and cenotaph which was erected on the site. The maharani wanted her ashes to be interred at the memorial erected to Maharaja Ranjit Singh at Lahore. They were therefore kept at Nasik till the time arrived for that to be possible. This was finally done on 17 March 1924, when her granddaughter, Princess Bamba Sutherland, brought the ashes from Nasik and interred them in the memorial of Maharaja Ranjit Singh, after Sardar Harbans Singh, a descendent of the late brave and loyal Sardar Sham Singh Attari, offered prayers and performed the *ardas*.[210]

Shortly after the cremation, Duleep Singh returned to Cairo and called on the British Consul, Robert Colquhoun on 28 April, to inform him that he intended to get married and he requested him to publish the banns. This was the first that the news of his intended marriage was made public and the Consul immediately informed Lord Palmerston at the Foreign Office. The queen, when she heard the news wondered why the maharaja had not taken her into confidence.

Duleep Singh was married on 7 June 1864 but before the event he wrote to Sir Charles Phipps, who the queen in her concern had sent to meet Lady Login, to find out whether she knew more about this marriage than she herself had been informed.

> I have hitherto hesitated not knowing whether I ought to write but fearing lest I should be considered negligent by the queen who has been gracious and kind to me that I take this opportunity of writing privately to you and explaining what has prevented me from acquainting Her Majesty of my approaching marriage. The young lady is an illegitimate daughter (though adopted by her father) [...] and it is her birth that has prevented me from telling you of this sooner knowing that there is such an objection to it in England. Therefore should the queen hear of my marriage and be offended with me for not having told her of it be so good as to explain why I did not do so [...][211]

Though there were objections in certain quarters, the fact of his fiancée's illegitimacy seemed not to worry the queen. She seemed more concerned as to whether Bamba was suitable in other respects and when Duleep Singh arrived in London with his bride, it was Colonel Oliphant who wrote to her setting her mind to rest.

> I am truly happy to say that I can send you a very favourable report. In person she is small and delicately made, has a sweet smile, winning expression, a soft black eye, and her complexion is like the late Princess Gouramma. She is unable to speak English as yet beyond a very little [...] but she is quite self possessed and has a natural dignity of manner which has struck all those introduced to her. Lady Login has just come in, and I am happy to report that her son Roland, who was here last night, went home and told her that the Maharanee was

> such a nice little thing, so beautiful an eye and so pretty a hand, and such good manners and in short his heart was quite relieved.[212]

As the renovation of Elveden was being delayed, at the beginning of August Duleep Singh took his heavily pregnant wife to Auchlyne on Loch Tay. No sooner had they arrived that Bamba gave birth to a boy who lived for just two days and was buried under a block of polished granite opposite the church at Taymouth. As the completion of Elveden was further delayed, Duleep Singh took his wife on holiday to Egypt after the trauma of losing her newborn son. On his return they settled down at Elveden.[213]

Elveden was in the centre of England's sporting country and over the next few years, apart from living in a beautifully renovated home, the interiors done up in Mughal and Indian decor, Duleep Singh turned the estate into one of the country's finest sporting venues, where 'In an average season the bag might be ten thousand pheasant, ditto partridges, three thousand hares and 70,000 rabbits'. In that period he himself held the British record of '440 grouse over his own gun in a day at Grandtully, the estate he rented in Perthshire, and 780 partridge for a thousand cartridges at Elveden'.[214]

They had been a year at Elveden when an invitation came from the queen, who had discretely given Maharani Bamba time to learn some English to avoid her feeling self-conscious, to 'dine and sleep' at Windsor. On their arrival, the queen kissed her, as an acknowledgement of her rank....The two Princesses made her sit between them all evening, cross-questioning her about Egypt and her life there. In her journal for 30 November, the queen wrote: 'The good Maharaja (in his Indian dress) & his lovely little wife, beautifully dressed in Indian stuffs, covered with splendid jewels & pearls, like a princess in a fairy tale, dinned. He is so amiable & agreeable, but gets too fat.' At about the same time, 'An anonymous writer, who called himself, 'one of the Old Brigade' described him as follows: 'It was only when His Highness assumed evening dress that visions of Mooltan, Chillianwala, and Goojerat faded from one's brain, and a podgy little man seemed to stand before one, divested of the physique and martial bearing one associates with other warriors or Sikhs, and only requiring, as it were, a chutnee-pot peeping out of his pocket to complete the illusion.'[215]

Bamba's second son was born in June 1886 and a small Christening ceremony was held at Elveden. Eight months later, the queen commanded them to Windsor for a second christening, at which she would be the godmother. The baby was christened Victor Albert by Victoria. Victor Albert was followed by Frederick Victor born in 1868, Bamba Sophia Jinda in 1869, Catherine Hilda in 1871, Sophia Alexandra 1876, and Edward Albert Alexander in 1879.

By now Duleep Singh, with growing responsibilities, started a long drawn out dispute with the India Office about more money and possession of his private estates in India. A little money was conceded, but the Indian government refused to concede to what he wanted, including the private property owned by his forefathers. Though the queen took up his issue on a number of occasions with successive governments, nothing was forthcoming in cash or kind, which drove Duleep Singh to despair and bitterness. It was now that the thought of the prophecy regarding him, told to him by his mother, came to mind.

He also wrote a series of letters to the *Times* and other papers staking his claim and bringing out the injustice done to him, hoping that the papers, as well as the people, would support him. As no assistance seemed forthcoming from any quarter, Duleep Singh, by now frustrated and embittered, decided to become a Sikh again and to follow the prophecy. He now wrote to the queen's secretary Sir Henry Ponsonby, declaring his intention of returning 'to the faith of his ancestors'.

Duleep Singh then wrote to the queen,

> [...] as Your Majesty is the only true and disinterested friend I possess in the world I did not like that you my Sovereign should hear from any other source in the first instance but myself of the possibility of my re-embracing the faith of my ancestors, though I mentioned it to Sir Henry Ponsonby.
>
> I have sent for a Bhaee or Brother to come with a copy of the Holy Book of the Sikhs to teach me to read it.
>
> [...] Shortly after I ascended the throne of the Punjab it was found written in a book of Sikh prophecies called *Sakheean* that a man of my name would be born who, after becoming entirely dispossessed of all he inherited and residing alone for a long period in a foreign country, would return to be the eleventh gooroo or teacher of the Khalsa or the Pure and that his prosperity then would exceed that of his ancestors. He would also establish a new faith.
>
> [...] While discussing the prophecy with my mother I jeeringly remarked "but mother, how can all this come to pass if I do not return to India at all". She replied, "Mark my words my child, perhaps I may not live to see the day but whenever the right moment arrives circumstances will so shape themselves that thou wilt be compelled to quit England against thy will."
>
> Under all these circumstances my Sovereign I do not believe and indeed my Sovereign I do not now particularly care that justice will ever be done to me, but I do believe that my destiny whatever that may be will be fulfilled.[216]

On 15 August 1885, Ponsonby wrote to Randolph Churchill, yet another Secretary of State for India.

> The Queen commands me to inform you that she fears the financial difficulties of the Maharaja Duleep Singh are rendering him desperate,

> that he is consequently susceptible to intrigues of evil counsellors in India, who are calling upon him to come to Punjab, and that she fears if not relieved from his pressing necessities he may take some step which may lead to serious consequences.

Randolph Churchill replied that 'after careful consideration of the facts of the case, he could not assume any responsibility to increase the ample, liberal and generous allowance in any degree'.[217]

> The Government, whatever it gave out in its lengthy correspondence with him, were by now convinced that Duleep Singh was living beyond his means, for reasons other than the maintenance of his position and estate. He was a popular member of the Alhambra. He soon concentrated his attentions on one of the chorus girls Polly Ash, whom he set up in Covent Garden with an annuity. Like the Prince of Wales he enjoyed his visits to Paris and was often seen at the tables there. One of the attractions in Paris was the courtesan Leonide le Blanc, whom he shared for a time with an unlikely pair, the Duc d'Aumale and the young Clemenceau. The gossip was that he was particularly attached to a young actress. His attentions were said to be "ardent" – he had her send him a telegram twice a day – "just to know if you are alright". If her manner was patrician her accent was not. Her name was Ada Wetherill.[218]

Meanwhile, the viceroy, Lord Dufferin had made it clear that in the event of Duleep Singh reaching India, he would be forced to live at Ottacamund or any other place of his choosing within the Madras Presidency. To this Duleep Singh replied,

> His Excellency the Viceroy has only to put me under arrest and send to any part of India that he may think proper to do so. For I am quite prepared to suffer any prosecution from the most immoral and unjust British government which, because it is incapable of doing justice, prefers to bully the weak, rather than disgorge what it had acquired in a most unscrupulous manner.[219]

On 25 March 1886, Duleep Singh released to the press the text of an open letter to be published in their columns.

> My dear countrymen, It was not my intention ever to return to India, but Sutgooroo, who governs all destiny, and is more powerful than I, his erring creature, has caused circumstances to be so brought about, that against my will, I am compelled to quit England, in order to occupy a humble sphere in India. I submit to his will, being persuaded that whatever is for the best will happen.
>
> I now, therefore, beg forgiveness of you, Khalsajee, or the Pure, for having forsaken the faith of my ancestors for a foreign religion; but I was very young when I embraced Christianity.

> It is my fond desire on reaching Bombay to take the Pahul again, and I sincerely hope for your prayers to the Sutgooroo on that solemn occasion. But in returning to the faith of my ancestors, you must clearly understand, Khalsajee, that I have no intention of conforming to the errors introduced into Sikhism by those who were not true Sikhs – such, for instance, as wretched caste observations or abstinence from meats and drinks, which Sutgooroo has ordained should be received with thankfulness by all mankind – but to worship the pure and beautiful tenets of Baba Nanak and obey the commands of Gooroo Govind Singh.
>
> I am compelled to write this to you because I am not permitted to visit you in the Punjab, as I had much hoped to do. Truly a noble reward for my unwavering loyalty to the Empress of India. But Satgooroo's will be done.
>
> With Wah Gooroojee de Fateh, I remain, my beloved Countrymen. Your own flesh and blood. Duleep Singh.[220]

The Pioneer, a widely circulated English daily in India, chose in response to play his letter down and to be sarcastic when it wrote,

> In brief it means that His Highness has no intention of giving up either his beef steak or brandy pawnee. What effect the manifesto will produce remains to be seen. If Duleep Singh makes himself troublesome he will have to face the consequences. He may have reason to conclude before long that the position of a well-to-do English country gentleman is more comfortable than an Oriental pretender.[221]

The Government of India on the other hand seemed worried. In England that day the queen in a routine audience with her foreign secretary at Windsor, raised the

> issue of the poor M. DS, who is becoming very violent & threatens open defiance, & his going to India to raise the Sikhs! All this is perfect madness, & Ld Rosebery thinks he had not been well managed & that money should be given him, to prevent him going to India.[222]

The following morning on 31 March 1886, the maharaja's party comprising the reluctant maharani, his six children, a Sikh attendant, a native servant, a European nurse and an ayah embarked on the *P&O Verona* bound for Bombay. His last letter written on board ship, before sailing was to the queen in which he thanked her for all that she had done for him and his family, and then bid her goodbye.

In India rumours of Duleep Singh's return were rife and the government soon entered into consultations at all levels to assess the reaction amongst the Sikhs to his arrival, particularly so after his open letter. Colonel Hennessy of the 15th Sikhs, when asked by the Government House for his opinion, reported back,

> In regard to Duleep Singh's influence over the Sikhs he would indeed be a bold man who could say he had no fear of it in his own regiment. I most devoutly trust the subject will not be put to the test in my day. The spirit of the Sikhs is not dead. And they are full of national fire. I should tremble in my shoes were the gentleman to arrive at our borders with the Russians! The British government should hold him fast and secure in England in my opinion.[223]

With similar views coming in from all sources, the Viceroy decided that Duleep Singh should be detained enroute. He was to be arrested under Regulation 111 of 1818. On 15 April the order went out from Simla to Aden.

> Maharajah Duleep Singh with Maharanee, six children and servants is passenger by Peninsular and Oriental Verona from London. Please require the whole party to land and detain under surveillance at Aden till further orders. You can inform Maharajah that the address which has been issued by His Highness renders his return to India undesirable. Should His Highness on this announcement express a desire to go back to England, he may be allowed to do so on an English ship, on giving you a solemn pledge in writing that, in consideration of his release from his present detention, he will not renew his attempt to return to India and will abstain from all treasonable practices.[224]

On 16, the viceroy, Lord Dufferin reported his questionable action to London. The queen was 'rather startled' when she heard the news, but did not exactly disapprove, she scribbled on the message, 'but better than if he went to India. He brought it on himself.'[225]

Delayed by head winds, the *Verona* reached Aden on 21 April. Brigadier Hogg, the resident, went on board and informed the maharaja that by the order of the Government of India he could go no further. Duleep Singh, however, refused to leave the ship till he was arrested. This the resident did by tapping him symbolically on the shoulder. Passengers and crew then gave a loud and sympathetic cheer as he and his family filed down the gangplank into captivity.

Now followed a flurry of telegrams between Aden, Simla and London and finally Duleep Singh, by now highly frustrated, wired the viceroy, 'I desire to take advantage of my cousin's presence here to be re-initiated into Sikhism. Kindly telegraph the resident saying I may go through the ceremony in his presence.'[226] After due consultations with the lieutenant-governor in the Punjab, whose opinion was that 'refusal might be misunderstood', permission was given but the resident was told to stay away. Duleep Singh returned to the Sikh faith by taking 'Pahul' on 25 May.

The 'Panj Piaras', mandatory on such an occasion were composed of Sikhs brought in for the ceremony from the neighbouring ships in harbour.

Having sent his family back to England and by now fed up with a never ending game of double speak with the Government in India and the India Office, Duleep Singh had reached the end of his tether and was all set to take on the establishment. To start with he wrote to Ponsonby, 'I return to Paris being unable to get justice. Resigned stipend, thus ending Annexation Treaty and getting rid of all dealings with the most tyrannical government in the world, Indian administration.'[227]

On 3 June he boarded the *SS Natal* bound for Marseilles. In England, the queen, then at Balmoral, 'was angry with Lord Kimberely for his apparently hard-hearted treatment and annoyed that her expressed wish should have such little effect'.[228]

To Sir Robert Montgomery at the India Office he wrote that [...] he wished to receive no further communication from them saying that:

> I neither respect such a tyrannical and unjust administration, nor am I any longer loyal to the British Crown (having offered my services to Russia). I seek nothing from you gentlemen as I have only one prayer now, that God may, before I die, enable me to have revenge on the Indian administration and humiliate that government, and to cause the expenditure of many more millions of poor John Bull's money than the three million pounds I should have asked, for the loss of my private property, out of which I have been so piously swindled by the Christian British nation.[229]

He signed as 'a rebel now in earnest'.

In another letter to the Russian ambassador in Paris he wrote offering his services to the emperor and requested a passport which 'as soon as I receive I shall go to St Petersburg'.[230] He confided this to Grafton in a letter and then added, 'If I am received well by the Emperor I shall go to the border of India. If not I shall go to Pondicherry and be a thorn in the side of Lord Dufferin'.[231]

On hearing of this from Grafton and Ponsonby, the queen wrote to him,

> I hear extraordinary reports of your resigning your allowance & of your intending to transfer your allegiance to Russia. I cannot believe this of you who professed such loyalty & devotion towards me – who you know has always been your true friend & who I may say took a maternal interest in you from the time when now 32 years ago you came to England as a beautiful & charming boy [...][232]

She then spoke to Lord Cross 'about the unfortunate M. DS's wife and sons, who will have to be provided for if he throws up everything & goes quite wrong in his passionate excitement & irritation, having been misled by wrong-headed Indians and relations.'[233]

Duleep Singh responded by saying,

> Gracious Sovereign, [...] It greatly pains me to inform Your Majesty that it is no longer in my power either to contradict the current reports or to give the assurance which you so graciously demand. For Your Majesty's Government having branded me disloyal when God knows I was most loyal and devoted to Your Majesty. I had no other course open to me except either to turn traitor or continue to submit to the insults repeatedly offered to me by the Administration of India [...] I am not responsible most Gracious Sovereign but it is the Council of India and Lord Dufferin together who are responsible for driving me away from my allegiance to Your Majesty. I have most Gracious Sovereign not only resigned my stipend but have also set aside and annulled that wicked Treaty of the Annexation of the Punjab which was extorted from me and my ministers by the late Marquis of Dalhousie when I was of tender age and the ward of your Majesty's Government [...] Neither friend nor foe has put these notions into my head and heart. It is the study of the records of the wicked deeds of my guardians as preserved in the Blue Books of 1848-49 and the subsequent refusal both on the part of the Council of India and the Home Government to render me some measure of justice added to that very recent degradation inflicted on me at Aden that has embittered my feelings [...] I am deeply sensible and to the day of my death will never forget Your Majesty's boundless graciousness to me and to mine but history teaches us that it is the sense of injustice and suffered wrong, the cruel coercion, and infliction of tyrannical oppression that has driven many men to desperate deeds and I also am human [...][234]

Duleep Singh believed that with the Great Game between Russia and Britain in progress in central Asia, and more so in Afghanistan on the borders of India, he would be welcomed by the Russians with open arms. Russia on the other hand had a different priority and it found itself currently occupied fully by events in the Mediterranean. Besides the Russian government was not sure of Duleep Singh's commitment. The Russian Foreign Minister de Giers, therefore, on receipt of his ambassador, Kotzbue's letter to him informing him of Duleep Singh's correspondence with him and also of their subsequent meeting, told him to make a non-committal reply, worded such that it would be innocuous if read by other eyes, which Kotzbue did.

> Highness, The Imperial Government protects peace. It wants it and maintains it in its own vast possessions; it desires it in those of the other powers and feels that the Governments are jointly responsible in their efforts of guaranteeing among the peoples the benefactions of security and stability of institutions. Far from it, hence, the thought

> of favouring or provoking troubles in India. No reason impels it and Your Highness would not find the means necessary to realize plans of insurrection or of vengeance. I am authorised to affirm this to you in consequence of what you were good enough to say to me in the course of our interview. Kindly accept etc. Kotzbue.

Duleep Singh now wrote another letter and unknown to him it was sent again to the foreign minister, who in turn sent this and the earlier letter to the Czar, who wrote on it 'maybe sometime it will be useful'.

Unfazed, but disappointed by the ambassador's reply, Duleep Singh now entered into discussions with a number of revolutionary groups then active in Paris. The venue of these meetings was at the Reynolds Bar on rue Royale. The diverse groups included the Irish Finians, whose leaders were the Casey brothers, Patrick and James. They took him under their wing and printed his manifestos and proclamations etc. There were also their fraternal Irish-Americans, English detectives, journalists, spies, and Russian agents.

One of these conspirators was Elie de Cayon, who was the Paris correspondent of *The Moscow Gazette*, whose editor was the powerful Mikhail Katkoff. His *Gazette* was pan-Slavist in policy and expansionist in the direction of India. He met often with Duleep Singh and when convinced that his views were consistent, and that he was determined to push matters to a head, he wrote to Katkoff recommending that he meet with him. Katkoff invited Duleep Singh to Moscow.

During his Paris sojourn, his proclamations and letters to newspapers were signed by him, initially as 'Maharaja of the Sikhs under the Treaty of Bhyrowal'. As his enthusiasm grew, his signature became more grandiose, to 'The Lawful Sovereign of the Sikh Nation under the Treaty of Bhyrowal with Great Britian, 1846.' And finally, to 'Both Sovereign and Guru of the Sikh nation.'[235]

The maharaja now summoned the nineteen-year-old Ada Wetherill to Paris to accompany him to Russia and left Paris by train on 21 March accompanied by Ada, who was by now expecting a child, his ADC Aroor Singh, a great deal of sporting equipment and a couple of cocker spaniels. Katkoff urgently wired General Bogdanovitch, a leading member of the military faction favouring territorial expansion, to order the frontier police to let him through. In Moscow he was put up at the Hotel Dussaux.

On receiving the news that Duleep Singh had reached Moscow, Lord Salisbury, the foreign secretary, wrote an angry letter to his ambassador in Moscow to ask the Russian foreign minister how Duleep Singh was let into Russia when he had earlier declined to give him permission. The British ambassador Sir Robert Morier, registered his protest, and when de Giers reported the matter to Czar Alexander III, that he had been informed of the maharaja's arrival in Moscow by the British ambassador, the Czar answered: 'It is passing strange that the British ambassador should have at his disposal at St Petersburg a better police than I have'.[236]

As talks between Katkoff, General Bogdanovich and Duleep Singh dragged on with no solution in sight, he made a request for an audience with the Czar. This was politely turned down with the reply that under the circumstances such a meeting could not be considered 'desirable'. He then decided to write to the Czar.

His long and rambling letter was that of self-delusion and smacked of desperation. Some of the salient points were,

> [...] I wish to become your loyal subject [...] I only desire the freedom of the 250 million of my people from the British tyrants[...] I have been deputed by most of the powerful Princes of India to come to Russia and pray the Imperial Government to take their cause in hand. These Princes posses altogether some 300,000 soldiers in their service and are prepared to revolt should the Imperial Government think proper to make an advance upon the British [...] The Princes of India when free, and if allowed to manage their own affairs, would join together and pay a large annual tribute of three million pounds Sterling which could go up to ten million, to be paid to the Russian treasury [...] At the moment the whole of India is with me and as soon as the People of Hindustan are assured of my arrival in Russia their joy will know no bounds [...] should the invasion of India be entertained in the Imperial Council, an army of not less than 200,000 and 2000 cannons be provided for the purpose [...] I would suggest that 2 or 3 English speaking gentleman be appointed to discuss the matter further.[237]

What is incredible, however, is that the Czar took the letter seriously, and in his own hand wrote notes in the margin, against Duleep Singh wanting to become his loyal subject he noted 'it is desirable'. On his claim that all the Princes of India were behind him he wrote, 'It would be desirable to verify this fact' and to two or three English speaking gentleman being deputed to discuss this matter further he added, 'It can be done'.[238]

To his son Prince Victor, Duleep Singh wrote,

> I cannot tell you how happy I am to be in Russia. There is plenty of Grouse shooting and fine salmon fishing in the north. I mean to indulge myself. The woodcock shooting on the coast of the Black Sea is very good and so is snipe and wild fowl shooting in Crimea. So you see my dear old man I am in a sportsman's paradise. Besides money from India will flow to me like water now that I am in Russia.[239]

On 18 September, Maharani Bamba died following renal complications. On hearing the news he wired Victor 'Heart-broken – can't realize – will write next week'.[240]

All the letters of condolence were forwarded to him in Moscow. To the Prince of Wales's letter Duleep Singh answered,

> Your Royal Highness's sympathy in my late bereavement has been forwarded to me from England – Under other circumstances I should have felt most grateful for Your Royal Highness's condescension's, but in the present circumstances, while your illustrious mother proclaims Herself the Sovereign of a throne and an Empire both of which have been acquired by fraud by pious Christian England, and of which Your Royal Highness also hopes one day to become the Emperor, these empty conventional words addressed to me amount to an insult. For Your Royal Highness's sympathy can only be expressed by one friend towards another – but which cannot ever exist between enemies. Signed Duleep Singh, Sovereign of the Sikh Nation and proud implacable foe of England.[241]

The queen who was doing all she could for Maharani Bamba and the children, was infuriated by this letter of Duleep Singh's:

> [...] the unfortunate M. DS has published a most violent, crazy letter, speaking of being "The lawful Sovereign of the Sikhs" and "England's implacable foe"! Heard this evening that his poor wife, the M'ee Bamba, had died quite suddenly yesterday. How terrible for the poor children, who are quite fatherless & motherless.[242]

In July 1887, Katkoff fell ill, and Duleep Singh wrote to his Russian friend Count Cheremetoff. 'M. Katkoff's serious and dangerous illness is causing me great uneasiness, for were he to die, I would be left without anyone to protect me and might be turned out of Russia through some intrigue at the High Quarters'.[243] Katkoff died in August. On 26 December, Ada gave birth to a daughter Paulina Alexandra. His hope now lay with Aroor Singh who had been sent to India with a letter to the princes to bring money from them, and if possible, letters of support to Russia. Unknown to him Aroor Singh was arrested by the secret police the day after he landed in India.

With no support now in Moscow and the government being consistently indifferent to him, Duleep Singh first moved to a cheaper hotel, and then left Moscow to live in Kiev at the Hotel de France for a while, till money arrived from India. While in Kiev, he toyed with the idea of joining the Russian Orthodox Church which he thought may endear him to the Russian Establishment. He wrote to his cousin Gurbachan Singh, who was initially horrified and hastened to write back to say:

> As to Your Majesty's joining the Russian faith we beg to say that it would produce a very bad effect among the Indians and more particularly with Sikhs who believe in you as their Guroo. [...] According to their idea, you became Christian in accordance with the prophecy [...] and not on your own accord. Already the English papers of the Punjab are giving out that you are not a Sikh. If you ever take Russian Orthodox baptism they will spread the news at once and the people will not trust us.

In his next letter softening his stand a little Gurbachan Singh adds,

> In our humble opinion Your Majesty must remain Sikh unless the Russian Government binds itself to help Your Majesty at once and gets you back to the country. In that event you must remain Sikh outwardly up to the time that Your Majesty is firmly on the throne.[244]

Duleep Singh returned to Paris at the beginning of November 1888. The purpose of his return was to sell his jewellery left with his agent in Paris before leaving for Russia, to raise money to live on, as there was nothing so far forthcoming from India. From Paris he once again wrote to the queen a condescending letter. Giving her the benefit of the doubt for his personal matters being held up by various governments 'as she was a constitutional Monarch', he then went on to say,

> My diamond, the Kohinoor, I understand, is entirely at your own personal disposal. Therefore, believing your Majesty to be "the most religious lady" that your subjects pray for every Sunday, I do not hesitate to ask that this gem be restored to me, or else that a fair price be paid for it to me out of your privy purse.[245]

On 21 May Duleep Singh married the four-month-pregnant Ada Douglas Wetherill. Ada's second child, a girl, was born on 25 October 1889 and was christened Princess Ada Irene Helen Beryl Duleep Singh. At the beginning of 1890 Duleep Singh had a stroke in his hotel room in Paris which affected his left leg and side, and the left half of his face which were paralysed.

Prince Victor visited him on two occasions in Paris and during the second visit found that Duleep Singh, by now lonely and depressed after his stroke, had mellowed considerably. He now wrote a letter to the queen,

> May it please Your Majesty, My son Victor is writing this letter from my dictation – I have been struck down by the hand of God and am in consequence quite unable to write myself – I have been disappointed in everyone in whom I have been led to believe and now my one desire is to die at peace with all men – I therefore pray Your Majesty to pardon me for all I have done against You and Your Government and I throw myself entirely on Your clemency.[246]

Lord Salisbury was vehemently opposed to his returning, but the queen did not see why she should not have the maharaja back. 'I cannot agree with Ld S's objection to this poor unfortunate Maharaja's return to England as he wd. be far safer here' she cyphered Lord Cross. 'I believe many feel with me that the former Govt. are very gtly to blame for what has happened & therefore we shd. Be merciful.'[247]

Lord Cross wrote to Duleep Singh to say:

> I am now commanded to inform you that, on the understanding that henceforward Your Highness will remain obedient to the Queen-

> Empress of India, and will regulate your movements in conformity with instructions that may be issued to you by Her Majesty's Government, Her Majesty, on the advice of Her Ministers, has been graciously pleased to accord you the pardon you have sought.[248]

The maharaja arrived in England on 26 August and settled down at No. 6 Clifton Gardens, Folkestone which Victor had rented for him. After a month he returned to France for a cure, to Aix-la-Chapelle for curative baths and then decided to stay the winter in Paris.

The queen on a private visit to France in March 1891 received a request from Duleep Singh who was close by at Nice, that he wished to pay his respects to her. The queen was staying close by at Grasse, at the Grand Hotel. She described her meeting to her daughter Vicky who was then the Empress of Prussia in a letter.

> The poor Maharajah Duleep Singh came to see me yesterday having driven down from Nice with his second son Fredric [...] When I came in I gave him my hand wh. he kissed, and said: "Pardon my not kneeling" for his left arm and leg are paralysed tho he can stand and walk a little. I asked him to sit down – & almost directly he burst out into a most terrible & violent fit of crying almost screaming – and I stroked & held his hand, & he became calm and said: "Pray excuse me & forgive my faults" & I answered "They are forgotten & forgiven [...]"[249]

On 24 April, though ill and weak Duleep Singh crossed over to England to visit his youngest son Edward who was seriously ill. He stayed in England a week and then returned to France. The very next day, the thirteen-year-old Edward, suffering from pleuro-pneumonia died. Six months later, on 22 October, the last maharaja of Lahore, Duleep Singh, died in his small hotel room in Paris. He was fifty-five years old.

The funeral took place on 29 October at Elveden. The queen sent her Lord in Waiting Lord Camoys to stand in for her. Wreaths from old friends lay all around: Ada's was a star of lilies and camellias, with 'ADA' worked in the middle with violets. Many friends from France and England attended. The Prince of Wales sent a wreath inscribed 'For Auld Lang Syne'. Another simply said 'From Queen Victoria'. On the plate on the coffin was engraved 'Duleep Singh, Maharaja of Lahore, GCSI. Born 4 September 1838. Died 22 October 1893.'

Of Duleep Singh becoming a born again Christian, there is no record, but his last rites were performed as a practicing Protestant and he was buried close to the Elveden Chapel. All his children remained Christians till the day of their death.

After Duleep Singh's death, Maharani Ada Irene Helen Beryl Duleep Singh (born on 15 January 1869) lived in France and during the First World War, drove an ambulance at the battle of Verdun. She returned to England heavily in debt where she died in 1930. She was cremated as per her wish at the Golders Green Crematorium.

Prince Victor Duleep Singh (born on 10 July 1866) was educated at Eton and later at Trinity College Cambridge. He then joined the Royal Military Academy at Sandhurst from where he was commissioned into the Royal Dragoon Guards, the Royals. He married Lady Anne Coventry, the daughter of the 9th Earl of Coventry. He then settled in Paris with his wife Princess Anne Duleep Singh. During the First World War he was ordered to remain in Paris where he died on 7 June 1918 at the age of fifty-two. He was buried on 11 June at the Cimetiere de Monaco, high up on the hill behind Monte Carlo. Princess Anne died on 2 July 1956 and as per her wish was buried next to her husband at Monaco. They had no children.

Prince Frederick Jay Duleep Singh (born on 23 January 1868) was educated at Eton and later at Magdalene College, Cambridge. He settled at Blo Norton in Norfolk. He joined the Loyal Suffolk Hussars (Suffolk Yeomanry) and later as a Major transferred to the King's Own Royal Regiment Norfolk Imperial Yeomanry and served from 1917-19 in France during the First World War. He returned to live in Blo Norton where he died on 15 August 1926 at the age of fifty-eight, following a stroke. He never married.

Princess Catherine Hilda Duleep Singh (born on 27 October 1871) studied at Somerville Hall, Oxford. In 1903 she was permitted to tour India extensively, inclusive of a visit to Lahore and Amritsar. She then lived for a while with her former governess and friend Lina Schafer at Kassel, but left Germany in 1937 when the Nazis came to power. She died on 8 November 1942 at her home in Penn, at the age of seventy-one. She was cremated as per her wish in the Golders Green Crematorium. She never married.

Princess Sophia Jindan Alexdrowna Duleep Singh (born on 8 August 1876) lived at Blo Norton in Thachford Cottage bought by her brother Frederick for his sisters. She joined the Suffragette movement demanding the right of vote for women in Britain. During the First World War she organized patriotic flag days and visited wounded Indian soldiers regularly at Brighton. She died in her sleep on 22 August 1948, at the age of seventy-two and was cremated at the Golders Green Crematorium. She never married.

Prince Edward Albert Alexander Duleep Singh was born in 1879 and died at the age of thirteen in 1893, of pleuro-pneumonia. He was buried at Elveden next to his mother.

Princess Pauline Alexandra Duleep Singh (born on 26 December 1887) married Lieutenant J.S.A Torry of the 12th Battalion the Rifle

Brigade. He was killed during the battle of Loos on 19 September 1915. There is no existing record of her death. She had no children.

Princess Ada Irene Helen Beryl (born on 25 October 1889) married a Frenchman, Pierre Marie Villament, in 1910. Her body was fished out of the sea on 8 October 1926 by some fisherman and a note was found on her saying that 'she was tired of life'. She had no children.

Princess Bamba, the oldest of Duleep Singh's daughters, (born on 29 September 1869) studied at Somerville Hall, Oxford. She married Lt Col David Walters Sutherland in 1915. He was a doctor in the Indian Army who later became the principal at the King Edwards' Medical College, Lahore, from 1909 to 1921. She continued to live at Lahore after the Partition of India in 1947. Her home was 'The Gulzar', at No. 16, Jail Road. She died on 10 March 1957 at Lahore and is buried in the cemetery attached to the Church of Mary Magdelane, also called the 'Goreon ka Kabristan', behind the famous Lahore Gymkhana Club. Her head stone was erected by her secretary Pir Karim Bakhsh Supra, to whom she left her house and worldly possessions. Her collection of 89 paintings, of the Sikh period, were sold by him to the Lahore Fort museum and are display there as the 'Princess Bamba Collection'. She had no children.

Of Duleep Singh's nine children, four sons, of whom two died young and five daughters, Prince Victor and Princesses Bamba, Pauline and Irene were married. There were no children between them.

Elveden was sold by the Duleep Singh's trustees to the Guinness family in 1894 for 159,000 pounds sterling. It remains today as part of the same trust.

The kingdom of Lahore which was created by the Great Ranjit Singh of which he became the maharaja in 1801, ended in 1849 with the annexation of the Punjab. With the death of his nine grandchildren, the last of whom died in 1957, ended the Sikh Shukarchakia dynasty of the Lahore Durbar. Many dynasties over the centuries have faded out of history, but the tragedy of the lapse of this one could perhaps be equated with that of the ending of the great Moghul dynasty which ruled India for 400 years.

After the revolt of 1857, the last Moghul Emperor Bahadur Shah Zafar was transported to Burma and lived in a bamboo hut with two companions. When he died, he was buried in an unmarked grave. At Lahore too, the last of the great Shukarchakia dynasty of the Sikhs, was buried in a two square yard piece of ground in the 'Gorean ka Kabristan', with no family or friends from the former Lahore Durbar present. It brings to mind Bahadur Shah Zafar's lament, written during the last years of his life, while incarcerated in Burma:

Kitna hai budnaseeb Zafar Dufn ke liye
do gaz Zameen bhi na mili kue yar mei.

(How unfortunate is Zafar that he does not possess even two yards of land to be buried in, when he dies.)

Was it a coincidence that none of Duleep Singh's children had any children of their own, resulting in the lineage fading out of history, or was it the *Hukum* of Sri Guru Gobind Singhji, the tenth Guru, who said that if any one built a memorial to him, his dynasty and his family would end? This speculation will go on forever, but the name of Ranjit Singh, the great maharaja of Lahore, will continue to inspire generations. Ranjit Singh, an illiterate man, who built and ruled a kingdom larger than what is today Pakistan, before he had reached the age of twenty-one.

Annexures

ANNEXURE I
THE TREATY WITH LAHORE OF 1809

Treaty between the British Government and the Raja of Lahore (Dated 25 April 1809)

WHEREAS certain differences which had arisen between the British government and the Raja of Lahore have been happily and amicably adjusted; and both parties being anxious to maintain relations of perfect amity and concord, the following articles of treaty, which shall be binding on the heirs and successors of the two parties, have been concluded by the Raja Ranjit Singh in person, and by the agency of C.T. Metcalfe, Esquire, on the part of the British government.

Article I: Perpetual friendship shall subsist between the British government and the State of Lahore: the latter shall be considered, with respect to the former, to be on the footing of the most favoured powers, and the British government will have no concern with the territories and subjects of the Raja to the northward of the river Sutlej.

Article 2: The Raja will never maintain in the territory which he occupies on the left bank of the river Sutlej more troops than are necessary for the internal duties of that territory, nor commit or suffer any encroachments on the possessions or rights of the Chiefs in its vicinity.

Article 3: In the event of a violation of any of the preceding articles, or of a departure from the rules of friendship, this treaty shall be considered null and void.

Article 4: This treaty, consisting of four articles, having been settled and concluded at Amritsar, on the 25th day of April 1809, Mr C.T. Metcalfe has delivered to the Raja of Lahore a copy of the same in English and Persian, under his seal and signature; and the Raja has delivered another copy of the same under his seal and signature, and Mr C.T. Metcalfe engages to procure within the space of two months a copy of the same, duly ratified by the Right Honourable the Governor General in Council, on the receipt of which by the Raja, the present treaty shall be deemed complete and binding on both parties, and the copy of it now delivered to the Raja shall be returned.

ANNEXURE II

THE PROCLAMATION OF PROTECTION TO CIS-SUTLEJ STATES AGAINST LAHORE

(1809)

Translation of an 'Ittila Nama', addressed to the Chiefs of the Country of Malwa and Sirhind, on this Side of the River Sutlej (3 May 1809)

IT is clearer than the sun, and better proved than the existence of yesterday, that the marching of a detachment of British troops to this side of the river Sutlej was entirely at the application and earnest entreaty of the several chiefs, and originated solely from friendly considerations in the British government, to preserve them in their possessions and independence. A treaty having been concluded, on 25 April 1809, between Mr. Metcalfe on the part of the British government, and Maharaja Ranjit Singh, agreeably to the orders of the Right Honourable the Governor General in Council, I have the pleasure of publishing, for the satisfaction of the Chiefs of the country of Malwa and Sirhind, the pleasure and resolutions of the British government, as contained in the seven following articles:

Article 1: The country of the Chiefs of Malwa and Sirhind having entered under the British protection, they shall in future be secured from the authority and influence of Maharaja Ranjit Singh, conformably to the terms of the treaty.

Article 2: All the country of the Chiefs thus taken under protection shall be exempted from all pecuniary tribute to the British government.

Article 3: The Chiefs shall remain in the full exercise of the same rights and authority in their own possessions which they enjoyed before they were received under the British protection.

Article 4: Should a British force, on purposes of general welfare, be required to march through the country of the said chiefs, it is necessary and incumbent that every chief shall, within his own possessions, assist and furnish, to the full of his power, such force with supplies of grain and other necessaries which may be demanded.

Article 5: Should an enemy approach from any quarter, for the purpose of conquering this country, friendship and mutual interest require that the chiefs join the British Army with all their force, and, exerting themselves in expelling the enemy, act under discipline and proper obedience.

Article 6: All European articles brought by merchants from the eastern districts, for the use of the army, shall be allowed to pass, by the thanedars and sardars of the several chiefs, without molestation or the demand of duty.

Article 7: All horse purchased for the use of cavalry regiments, whether in the district of Sirhind or elsewhere the bringers of which being provided with sealed 'Rahdaris'* from the Resident at Delhi, or officer commanding at Sirhind, shall be allowed to pass through the country of the said Chiefs without molestation or the demand of duty.

* A 'Rahdari' is a movement order or a permit to carry.

ANNEXURE III

PROCLAMATION OF PROTECTION TO CIS-SUTLEJ STATES AGAINST ONE ANOTHER
(1811)

For the Information and Assurance of the Protected Chiefs of the Plains between the Sutlej and Jumna
(22 August 1811)

ON 3 May 1809 an 'Ittila Nama' comprised of seven articles was issued by the orders of the British government, purporting that the country of the Sardars of Sirhind and Malwa having come under their protection, Raja Ranjit Singh, agreeable to treaty, had no concern with the possessions of the above Sardars. That the British government had no intention of claiming Peshkashs or Nazarana, and that they should continue in the full control and enjoyment of their respective possessions. The publication of the 'Ittila Nama' (*see* Anexxure II) was intended to afford every confidence to the Sardars, that the protection of the country was the sole object, that they had no intention of control, and that those having possessions should remain in full and complete enjoyment thereof.

Whereas several Zamindars and other subjects of the Chiefs of this country have preferred complaints to the officers of the British government, who, having in view the tenor of the 'Ittila Nama' have not attended, and will not in future pay attention to them; for instance, on 15 June 1811, Dilawar Ali Khan of Samana complained to the Resident of Delhi against the officers of Raja Sahib Singh for jewels and other property said to have been seized by them, who, in reply, observed that the 'Kasba of Samana being in the Amaldari of Raja Sahib Singh, his complaint should be made to him'; and also, on 12 July 1811, Dasaundha Singh and Gurmukh Singh complained to Colonel Ochterlony, Agent to the governor general, against Sardar Charat Singh, for their shares of property, &c.; and, in reply, it was written on the back of their arzi, 'that since, during the period of three years, no claim was preferred against Charat Singh by any of his brothers, nor even the name of any co-partner mentioned; and since it was advertised in the 'Ittila Nama' delivered to the Sardars, that every Chief should remain in the quiet and full enjoyment of his domains, the petition could not be attended to,' – the insertion of these answers to complaints is intended as examples, and also that it may be impressed on the minds of every Zamindar and other subject, that the attainment of justice is to be expected from their respective chiefs only, that they may not, in the smallest degree, swerve from the observation of subordination. It is, therefore, highly incumbent upon the Rajas and other Sardars of this side of the river Sutlej, that they explain this to their respective subjects, and court their confidence, that it may be clear to them, that complaints to the officers of the British government will be of no avail, and that they consider their respective Sardars as the source of justice, and that, of their free will and accord, they observe uniform obedience.

And whereas, according to the first proclamation, it is not the intention of the British government to interfere in the possessions of the Sardars of this country, it is nevertheless, for the purpose of meliorating the condition of the community, particularly necessary to give general information, that several sardars have, since the last incursion of Raja Ranjit Singh, wrested the estates of others, and deprived them of their lawful possessions, and that in the restoration, they have used delays until detachments of the British Army have been sent to effect restitution, as in the case of the Rani of Tirah, the Sikhs of Chulian, the Talukas of Karauli and Chehloundy, and the village of Chiba; and the reason of such delays and evasions can only be attributed to the temporary enjoyment of the revenues, and subjecting the owners to irremediable losses. It is, therefore, by order of the British government, hereby proclaimed – that if any one of the Sardars or others has forcibly taken possession of the estates of others, or otherwise injured the lawful owners, it is necessary that, before the occurrence of any complaint, the proprietor should be satisfied, and by no means to defer the restoration of the property – in which, however, should delays be made, and the interference of the British authority become requisite, the revenues of the estate from the date of ejection of the lawful proprietor, together with whatever other losses the inhabitants of that place may sustain from the march of troops, shall without scruple be demanded from the offending party; and for disobedience of the present orders, a penalty, according to the circumstances of the case and of the offender, shall be levied, agreeably to the decision of the British government.

ANNEXURE IV

THE INDUS NAVIGATION TREATY OF 1832

Articles of a Convention established between the Honourable East India Company, and His Highness the Maharaja Ranjit Singh, the Ruler of the Punjab, for the opening of the Navigation of the Rivers Indus and Sutlej
(Originally drafted 26 December 1832)

BY the grace of God, the relations of firm alliance and indissoluble ties of friendship existing between the Honourable the East India Company and His Highness the Maharaja Ranjit Singh, founded on the auspicious treaty formerly concluded by Sir C.T. Metcalfe, Bart., and since confirmed in the written pledge of sincere amity presented by the Right Honourable Lord W.G. Bentinck, G.C.B. and G.C.H., Governor General of British India, at the meeting at Rupar, are, like the sun, clear and manifest to the whole world, and will continue unimpaired, and increasing in strength from generation to generation. By virtue of these firmly established bonds of friendship, since the opening of the navigation of the rivers Indus proper (i.e., Indus below the confluence of the Panjnad) and Sutlej (a measure deemed expedient by both States, with a view to promote the general interests of commerce), – has lately been effected through the agency of Captain C.M. Wade, Political Agent at Ludhiana, deputed by the Right Honourable the Governor General for that purpose. The following Articles, explanatory of the conditions by which the said navigation is to be regulated, as concerns the nomination of officers, the mode of collecting the duties, and the protection of the trade by that route, have been framed, in order that the officers of the two States employed in their execution may act accordingly:

Article 1: The provisions of the existing treaty relative to the right bank of the river Sutlej and all its stipulations, together with the contents of the friendly pledge already mentioned, shall remain binding, and a strict regard to preserve the relations of friendship between the two States shall be the ruling principle of action. In accordance with that treaty, the Honourable Company has not, nor will have any concern with the right bank of the river Sutlej.

Article 2: The tariff which is to be established for the line of navigation in question is intended to apply exclusively to the passage of merchandise by that route, and not to interfere with the transit duties levied on goods proceeding from one bank of the river to the other, nor with the places fixed for their collection: they are to remain as heretofore.

Article 3: Merchants frequenting the same route, while within the limits of the Maharaja's government, are required to show a due regard to his authority, as is done by merchants generally, and not to commit any acts offensive to the civil and religious institutions of the Sikhs.

Article 4: Any one purposing to go the said route will intimate his intention to the agent of either State, and apply for a passport, agreeable to a form to be laid down: having obtained which, he may proceed on his journey. The merchants coming from Amritsar, and other parts on the right bank of the river Sutlej, are to intimate their intentions to the agent of the Maharaja, at Harike, or other appointed places, and obtain a passport through him; and merchants coming from Hindustan, or other parts on the left bank of the river Sutlej, will intimate their intentions to the Honourable Company's agent, and obtain a passport through him. As foreigners, and Hindustanis, and Sardars of the protected Sikh states and elsewhere, are not in the habit of crossing the Sutlej without a passport from the Maharaja's officers, it is expected that such persons will hereafter also conform to the same rule, and not cross without the usual passports.

Article 5: A tariff shall be established exhibiting the rate of duties liveable on each description of merchandise, which, after having been approved by both governments, is to be the standard by which the superintendents and collectors of customs are to be guided.

Article 6: Merchants are invited to adopt the new route with perfect confidence: no one shall be suffered to molest them or unnecessarily impede their progress, care being taken that they are only detained for the collection of the duties, in the manner stipulated, at the established stations.

Article 7: The officers who are to be entrusted with the collection of the duties and examination of the goods on the right bank of the river shall be stationed at Mithankot and Harike; at no other places but these two shall boats in transit on the river be liable to examination or stoppage. When the persons in charge of boats stop of their own accord to take in or give out cargo, the goods will be liable to the local transit duty of the Maharaja's government previously to their being landed, as provided in Article 2. The superintendent stationed at Mithankot, having examined the cargo, will levy the established duty, and grant a passport, with a written account of the cargo and freight. On the arrival of the boat at Karike, the superintendent of that station will compare the passport with the cargo; and whatever goods are found in excess will be liable to the payment of the established duty, while the rest, having already paid duty at Mithankot, will pass on free. The same rule shall be observed in respect to merchandise conveyed from Harike by the way of the rivers towards Sind, that whatever may be fixed as the share of duties on the right bank of the river Sutlej, in right of the Maharaja's own dominions and of those in allegiance to him, the Maharaja's officers will collect it at the places appointed. With regard to the security and safety of merchants who may adopt this route, the Maharaja's officers shall afford them every protection in their power; and merchants, on halting for the night on either bank of the Sutlej, are required, with reference to the treaty of friendship which exists between the two States, to give notice, and to show their passport to the Thanedar, or officers in authority at the place, and request protection for themselves. If, notwithstanding this precaution, loss should at any time occur, a strict inquiry will be made, and reclamation sought from those who are blameable. The articles of the present treaty for opening the navigation of the rivers above mentioned, having, agreeably to subsisting relations, been approved by the Right Honourable the Governor General, shall be carried into execution accordingly.

Dated at Lahore 26 December 1832.
[Seal and signature at the top.]

ANNEXURE V

THE DECLARATION OF WAR OF 1845

Proclamation by the Governor General of India.
Camp, Lashkari Khan ki Sarai,
13 December 1845

THE British government has ever been on terms of friendship with that of the Punjab.

In the year 1809, a treaty of amity and concord was concluded between the British government and the late Maharaja Ranjit Singh, the conditions of which have always been faithfully observed by the British government, and were scrupulously fulfilled by the late Maharaja.

The same friendly relations have been maintained with the successors of Maharaja Ranjit Singh by the British government up to the present time.

Since the death of the late Maharaja Sher Singh, the disorganized state of the Lahore Government has made it incumbent on the Governor General in Council to adopt precautionary measures for the protection of the British frontier: the nature of these measures and the cause of their adoption, were, at the time, fully explained to the Lahore Durbar.

Notwithstanding the disorganized state of the Lahore Government during the last two years, and many most unfriendly proceedings on the part of the durbar, the Governor General in Council has continued to evince his desire to maintain the relations of amity and concord which had so long existed between the two states, for the mutual interests and happiness of both. He has shown, on every occasion, the utmost forbearance, from consideration to the helpless state of the infant Maharaja Dalip Singh, whom the British government had recognized as the successor to the late Maharaja Sher Singh.

The Governor General in Council sincerely desired to see a strong Sikh Government re-established in the Punjab, able to control its army, and to protect its subjects; he had not, up to the present moment, abandoned the hope of seeing that important object effected by the patriotic efforts of the chiefs and people of that country.

The Sikh Army recently marched from Lahore towards the British frontier, as it was alleged, by the orders of the durbar, for the purpose of invading the British territory.

The Governor General's agent, by direction of the Governor General, demanded an explanation of this movement, and no reply being returned within a reasonable time, the demand was repeated. The Governor General, unwilling to believe in the hostile intentions of the Sikh Government, to which no provocation had been given, refrained from taking any measures which might have a tendency to embarrass the Government of the Maharaja, or to induce collision between the two states.

When no reply was given to the repeated demand for explanation, while active military preparations were continued at Lahore, the Governor General considered it necessary to order the advance of troops towards the frontier, to reinforce the frontier posts.

The Sikh Army has now, without a shadow of provocation, invaded the British territories.

The Governor General must therefore take measures for effectually protecting the British provinces, for vindicating the authority of the British government, and for punishing the violators of treaties and the disturbers of the public peace.

The Governor General hereby declares the possessions of Maharaja Dalip Singh, on the left or British bank of the Sutlej, confiscated and annexed to the British territories.

The Governor General will respect the existing rights of all Jagirdars, Zamindars, and tenants in the said possessions, who, by the course they now pursue, evince their fidelity to the British government.

The Governor General hereby calls upon all the chiefs and sardars in the protected territories to co-operate cordially with the British government for the punishment of the common enemy, and for the maintenance of order in these states. Those of the chiefs who show alacrity and fidelity in the discharge of this duty, which they owe to the protecting power, will find their interests promoted thereby; and those who take a contrary course will be treated as enemies to the British government, and will be punished accordingly.

The inhabitants of all the territories on the left bank of the Sutlej are hereby directed to abide peaceably in their respective villages, where they will receive efficient protection by the British government. All parties of men found in armed bands, who can give no satisfactory account of their proceedings, will be treated as disturbers of the public peace.

All subjects of the British government, and those who possess estates on both sides the river Sutlej, who, by their faithful adherence to the British government, may be liable to sustain loss, shall be indemnified and secured in all their just rights and privileges.

On the other hand, all subjects of the British government who shall continue in the service of the Lahore State, and who disobey the proclamation by not immediately returning to their allegiance, will be liable to have their property on this side the Sutlej confiscated, and themselves declared to be aliens and enemies of the British government.

ANNEXURE VI

GENERAL ORDER BY THE RIGHT HON. THE GOVERNOR GENERAL OF INDIA
FOREIGN DEPARTMENT, CAMP OF LAHORE, 20 February 1846

THE Right Hon. the Governor General requests that the Commander-in-Chief will cause the following arrangements to be made for escorting His Highness the Maharajah Dhuleep Singh to his palace in the citadel of Lahore, this afternoon. The escort will consist of two regiments of European cavalry, two regiments of native cavalry – the body guard to be one; one regiment of irregular horse, two troops of horse artillery, one European and one native.

The secretary to the Government of India, F. Currie, Esq., will take charge of His Highness and his suite, and will be accompanied by the Political Agent, Major Lawrence, the Governor General's Private Secretary, Charles Hardinge, Esq., the Aide-de-Camp of the Governor General: two Aides-de-Camp of the Commander-in-Chief, one Aide-de-Camp from each General officer of division, in uniform.

The escort will be formed at the nearest convenient spot to the Governor General's camp, at two o'clock, and proceed to His Highness's camp, and thence to his palace.

On alighting from his elephant, a salute of twenty-one guns will be fired by the horse artillery.

His Highness the Maharajah of the Sikh nation, selected by the chiefs as their sovereign, having on the 18th instant, intimated his intention to proceed to the Governor General's camp at Lulleeanee, attended by His Highness's Wuzeer, the Rajah Gholab Singh, and other chiefs, was received in durbar on the afternoon and the staff being present. His Highness's ministers and chiefs there tendered his submission, and solicited the clemency of the British government.

The Governor General extended the clemency of the British government to a prince the descendant of the Maharajah, the late Runjeet Singh, for so many years the faithful ally and friend of the British government, as the representative of the Sikh nation selected by the chiefs and the people to be their ruler, on the condition that all the terms imposed by the British government, and previously explained to His Highness's ministers and chiefs, should be faithfully executed.

On withdrawing from the durbar, the Maharajah received the usual salutes due to His Highness's exalted rank.

His Highness has since remained near the Governor General's camp, and as it will be conducive to His Highness's comfort, that he should rejoin his family, the Governor General desires that he may, with all honour and in safety, be conducted by the British troops to the gates of his palace this day.

The following Proclamation was issued on the 18th instant, by the Governor General, promising protection to all persons at Lahore and elsewhere who peaceably continue in their usual employment of trade and industry.

The Governor General is satisfied, after the experience of this campaign, that he can rely on the discipline of this invincible army, as fully and securely as he has always been, confident that the day of battle, under their distinguished Commander, would be one of victory.

He trusts at present that no officers or soldiers will pass the advanced sentries of their encampment to enter the town of Lahore, and he requests His Excellency the Commander-in-Chief to give the necessary instruction to carry this order strictly into effect, as well as to protect all persons bringing provisions into the camp.

By order, & c. F. Currie,
Secretary to the Government of India,
with the Governor General

To the Right Hon. Sir Henry Hardinge, G.C.B.
Governor General of India

RIGHT HONOURABLE SIR,
I have the honour to state, for the information of Your Excellency, that, in accordance with the instructions contained in the order of the Governor General of yesterday's date, I proceeded in the afternoon with the escort ordered, and accompanied by the officers mentioned below, on elephants, to conduct the Maharajah Dhuleep Singh to his palace in the citadel of Lahore.

Major Lawrence, the Governor General's Political Agent
Captain Gilbert, Aide-de-Camp to General Gilbert
W. Edwards, Esq., Under Secretary of the Foreign Department
Capt. Tottenham, Aide-de-Camp to General Smith
R. Cust, Esq., Assistant Secretary to the Foreign Department
Lt Col Irvine, Engineers
Lt Col Smith, ditto
C. Hardinge, Esq., Private Secretary to the Governor General
Captain Napier, ditto
Captain Smith, ditto
Lt Col Wood, Military Secretary to the Governor General
Captain Cunningham
Captain Hardinge, Aide-de-Camp to the Governor General
Captain Grant, ditto
Lord Arthur Hay, ditto
Captain Bagot, Aide-de-Camp to the Commander-in-Chief
Captain Edwards, ditto

The procession was arranged in the following order :-
9th Irregular Cavalry
3rd Light Cavalry
Her Majesty's 16th Lancers
Troop Horse Artillery, Europeans
Troop Horse Artillery, natives
Her Majesty's 9th Lancers
The Secretary with the Maharajah and Suite,
The Governor General's Body Guard

The escort was formed in open column of troops left in front, commanded by Brigadier Cureton, C.B.

We proceeded in this order to the encampment of the Maharajah's camp, about one and a half miles from our piquets, and nearly the same distance from the citadel gate of the city.

At about three-quarters of a mile from the Maharajah's camp, I was met by the minister, Rajah Gholab Singh, and some of the chiefs.

Intimation of our approach was then sent on to the Maharajah, that he might be ready on his elephant upon our arrival.

On reaching the Maharajah's camp, the troops of our escort drew up, and the Maharajah, with Bhaee Ram Singh on the same elephant, came forward from his tent, accompanied by several chiefs.

After the usual salutation, and complimentary questions and replies, I placed the Maharajah's elephant next to mine, and the troops having fallen in, as at first, proceeded round the walls of the city to the gate of the citadel.

On arriving, Brigadier Cureton drew up the escort in line in front of the gateway, and I took the Maharajah, accompanied by the officers enumerated in the former part of this letter, with Rajah Gholab Singh and the other chiefs, into the interior of the citadel, and to the inner door of his palace.

I then observed to the Maharajah and chiefs that, by order of the Right Hon. The Governor General, I had thus brought the Maharajah, conducted by the British Army, to his palace, which His Highness had left for the purpose to tendering submission to the British government, and for placing himself, his capital, and his country, at the mercy of the Governor General, and requesting pardon for the insult that had been offered; and that the Governor General had thus restored him to his palace as a mark of the favour which he desired to show to the descendant of the late Maharajah Runjeet Singh.

A salute of twenty-one guns was then fired by the horse artillery.

We then took leave of the Maharajah at the gate of his palace, and returning to the outside of the city, we, continuing our progress round Lahore, thus returned to our camp.

As our camp is situated opposite to the south-east end of the city-face, and the citadel is immediately within the city walls at the north-west angle, we made the entire circuit of Lahore. I considered this preferable to going through the city, the streets of which are narrow, and would have much impeded the progress of our large escort.

We did not see one gun upon any part of the walls: all the embrasures were empty.

I have the honour to be, & c.,

F. CURRIE,
Secretary to the Government of India,
with the Governor General.

ANNEXURE VII

FROM HIS EXCELLENCY THE COMMANDER-IN-CHIEF TO THE RIGHT HON. SIR HENRY HARDINGE, GCB, GOVERNOR GENERAL OF INDIA, & C.

Headquarters, Army of the Sutlej, in front of Lahore,
22 February 1846

RIGHT HONOURABLE SIR,
I have now to offer my congratulations on some of the earliest fruits of our victory of the 10th instant. About noon on the 20th, a day henceforth very memorable in our Indian annals, the army under my command pitched its tents on the plain of Myan Meer, under the walls of the Sikh capital. The entire submission of the Maharajah and his advisers to the will of the British government had been before personally tendered to you, and graciously accepted; and this morning, in fulfillment of one of the conditions which your wisdom had dictated for the real interests of the ruler and people of the Punjab, I had the honour to conduct a brigade of troops to the city, which took formal possession of the Badshahee Musjid and Hoozooree Bagh, forming a part of the palace and citadel of Lahore. I trust the observance of a strict discipline, to preserve unshaken that confidence which the people of the city and county around it evidently repose in the generosity, clemency, and good faith of their conquerors. Supplies of all sorts are willingly brought to our camp and punctually paid for; and I believe that by every class of persons in this vicinity the presence of our troops is felt to be a national benefit, none certainly, have had real cause to lament it as a calamity.

I have, & c.,
HUGH GOUGH, General,
Commander-in-Chief, East Indies

General Order by the Right Hon. The Governor General of India.
Foreign Department, Camp Lahore, 22 February 1846

The British Army has this day occupied the gateway of the citadel of Lahore, the Badshahee Mosque, and the Hoozooree Bagh.

The remaining part of the citadel is the residence of His Highness the Maharaja, and also that of the families of the late Maharajah Runjeet Singh, for so many years the faithful ally of the British government. In consideration of these circumstances, no troops will be posted within the precincts of the palace gate.

The army of the Sutlej has now brought its operations in the field to a close, by the dispersion of the Sikh Army and the military occupation of Lahore, preceded by a series of the most triumphant successes ever recorded in the military history of India. The British government, trusting to the faith of treaties and to the long subsisting friendship between the two states, had limited military preparations to the defence of its own frontier.

Compelled suddenly to assume the offensive by the unprovoked invasion of its territories, the British Army, under the command of its distinguished leader, has, in sixty days, defeated the Sikh forces in four general actions, has captured 220 pieces of field artillery, and is now at the capital, dictating to the Lahore Durbar the terms of a treaty, the conditions of which will tend to secure the British Provinces from the repetition of a similar outrage.

The Governor General being determined, however, to mark with reprobation the perfidious character of the war, has required and will exact, that every remaining piece of Sikh artillery which has been pointed against the British Army during this campaign shall be surrendered.

The Sikh Army, whose insubordinate conduct is one of the chief causes of the anarchy and misrule which have brought the Sikh state to the brink of destruction, is about to be disbanded.

The soldiers of the army of the Sutlej have not only proved their superior prowess in battle, but have on every occasion, with subordination and patience, endured the fatigues and privations inseparable from a state of active operations in the field. The native trips of this army have also proved that a faithful attachment to their colours and to the Company's service is an honorable feature in the character of the British sepoy.

The Governor General has repeatedly expressed, on his own part, and that of the Government of India, admiration and gratitude for the important services which the army has rendered.

The Governor General is now pleased to resolve, as a testimony of the approbation of the Government of India of the bravery, discipline, and soldier-like bearing of the army of the Sutlej, that all the generals, officers, non-commissioned officers, and privates, shall receive a gratuity of twelve months' batta.

Every regiment which, in obedience to its orders, may have remained in posts and forts between Loodiana and Ferozepore, and was not present in action, as in the case of the troops ordered to remain at Moodkee to protect the wounded, and those left in the forts of Ferozepore and Loodiana, shall receive the gratuity of twelve months' batta.

Obedience to orders is the first duty of a soldier, and the Governor General, in affirming this principle, can never admit that absence, caused by the performance of indispensable duties, on which the success of the operations in the field greatly depended, ought to disqualify any soldier placed in these circumstances from participating in the gratuity given for the general good conduct of the army in the field.

All regiments and individuals ordered to the frontier and forming part of the army of the Sutlej, which may have reached Loodiana or Busseean before the date of this order, will be included as entitled to the gratuity.

By order of the Right Hon. the Governor General of India,

F. CURRIE
Secretary to the Government of India
with the Governor General

Arrangements were fast being made for the occupation of the conquered country, which is exceedingly fertile, and will yield annual revenue of £ 400,000. The chief town is Jullinder, with 40,000 inhabitants; Phulloor, Pugwarra, and Sultanpore are also of note. The cantonments of the British will not be far distant from Lahore, so as to be able to keep down all attempts at insurrection.

ANNEXURE VIII

FIRST TREATY WITH LAHORE OF 1846

Treaty between the British Government and the State of Lahore, concluded at Lahore, on 9 March 1846

WHEREAS the treaty of amity and concord, which was concluded between the British government and the late Maharaja Ranjit Singh, the ruler of Lahore, in 1809, was broken by the unprovoked aggression on the British provinces of the Sikh Army in December last. And whereas, on that occasion, by the proclamation dated the 13 December, the territories then in the occupation of the Maharaja of Lahore, on the left or British bank of the river Sutlej, were confiscated and annexed to the British provinces; and, since that time, hostile operations have been prosecuted by the two governments, the one against the other, which have resulted in the occupation of Lahore by the British troops. And whereas it has been determined that, upon certain conditions, peace shall be re-established between the two governments, the following treaty of peace between the Honourable English East India Company, and Maharaja Dalip Singh Bahadur, and his children, heirs, and successors, has been concluded, on the part of the Honourable Company, by Frederick Currie, Esq., and Brevet-Major Henry Montgomery Lawrence, by virtue of full powers to that effect vested in them by the Right Honourable Sir Henry Hardinge. G.C.B., one of Her Britannic Majesty's most Honourable Privy Council, Governor General, appointed by the Honourable Company to direct and control all their affairs in the East Indies; and, on the part of His Highness the Maharaja Dalip Singh, by Bhai Ram Singh, Raja Lal Singh, Sardar Tej Singh, Sardar Chattar Singh Atariwala, Sardar Ranjodh Singh Majithia, Dewan Deenanath, and Fakir Nur-ud-din, vested with full powers and authority on the part of His Highness.

Article I: There shall be perpetual peace and friendship between the British government, on the one part, and Maharaja Dalip Singh, his heirs and successors, on the other.

Article 2: The Maharaja of Lahore renounces for himself, his heirs and successors, all claim to, or connection with, the territories lying to the south of the river Sutlej, and engages never to have any concern with those territories, or the inhabitants thereof.

Article 3: The Maharaja cedes to the Honourable Company, in perpetual sovereignty, all his forts, territories, and rights, in the Doab, or country, hill and plain, situated between the rivers Beas and Sutlej.

Article 4: The British government having demanded from the Lahore State, as indemnification for the expenses of the war, in addition to the cession of territory described in Article 3, payment of one and a half crores of rupees; and the Lahore Government being unable to pay the whole of this sum at this time, or to give security satisfactory to the

British government for its eventual payment; the Maharaja cedes to the Honourable Company, in perpetual sovereignty, as equivalent for one crore of rupees, all his forts, territories, rights, and interests, in the hill countries which are situated between the rivers Beas and Indus, including the provinces of Kashmir and Hazara.

Article 5: The Maharaja will pay to the British government the sum of fifty lacs of rupees, on or before the ratification of this treaty.

Article 6: The Maharaja engages to disband the mutinous troops of the Lahore Army, taking from them their arms; and His Highness agrees to reorganize the regular, or Ain, regiments of infantry, upon the system, and according to the regulations as to pay and allowances, observed in the time of the late Maharaja Ranjit Singh. The Maharaja further engages to pay up all arrears to the soldiers that are discharged under the provisions of this article.

Article 7: The regular army of the Lahore State shall henceforth be limited to 25 battalions of infantry, consisting of 800 bayonets each, with 12,000 cavalry: this number at no time to be exceeded without the concurrence of the British government. Should it be necessary at any time, for any special cause, that this force should be increased, the cause shall be fully explained to the British government; and, when the special necessity shall have passed, the regular troops shall be again reduced to the standard specified in the former clause – of this article.

Article 8: The Maharaja will surrender to the British government all the guns, thirty-six in number, which have been pointed against the British troops, and which, having been placed on the right bank of the river Sutlej, were not captured at the battle of Sobraon.

Article 9: The control of the rivers Beas and Sutlej, with the continuations of the latter river, commonly called the Ghara and Panjnad, to the confluence of the Indus at Mithankot, and the control of the Indus from Mithankot to the borders of Baluchistan, shall, in respect to tolls and ferries, rest with the British government. The provisions of this article shall not interfere with the passage of boats belonging to the Lahore Government on the said rivers, for the purposes of traffic, or the conveyance of passengers up and down their course. Regarding the ferries between the two countries respectively, at the several ghats of the said rivers, it is agreed that the British government, after defraying all the expenses of management and establishments, shall account to the Lahore Government for one-half of the net profits of the ferry collections. The provisions of this article have no reference to the ferries on that part of the river Sutlej which forms the boundary of Bahawalpur and Lahore respectively.

Article 10: If the British government should, at any time, desire to pass troops through the territories of His Highness the Maharaja for the protection of the British territories, or those of their allies, the British troops shall, on such special occasions, due notice being given, be allowed to pass through the Lahore territories. In such case, the officers of the Lahore State will afford facilities in providing supplies and boats for the passage of rivers; and the British government will pay the full price of all such provisions and boats, and will make fair compensation for all private property that may be damaged. The British government will moreover observe all due consideration to the religious feelings of the inhabitants of those tracts through which the army may pass.

Article 11: The Maharaja engages never to take, or retain, in his service, any British subject, nor the subject of any European or American State, without the consent of the British government.

Article 12: In consideration of the services rendered by Raja Gulab Singh of Jammu to the Lahore State, towards procuring the restoration of the relations of amity between the Lahore and British governments, the Maharaja hereby agrees to recognize the independent sovereignty of Raja Gulab Singh, in such territories and districts in the hills as may be made over to the said Raja Gulab Singh by separate agreement between himself and the British government, with the dependencies thereof, which may have been in the Raja's possession since the time of the late Maharaja Karak Singh: and the British government, in consideration of the good conduct of Raja Gulab Singh, also agrees to recognize his independence in such territories, and to admit him to the privileges of a separate treaty with the British government.

Article 13: In the event of any dispute or difference arising between the Lahore State and Raja Gulab Singh, the same shall be referred to the arbitration of the British government; and by its decision the Maharaja engages to abide.

Article 14: The limits of the Lahore territories shall not be, at any time, changed, without the concurrence of the British government.

Article 15: The British government will not exercise any interference in the internal administration of the Lahore State; but in all cases or questions which may be referred to the British government, the Governor General will give the aid of his advice and good offices for the furtherance of the interests of the Lahore Government.

Article 16: The subjects of either State shall, on visiting the territories of the other, be on the footing of the subjects of the most favoured nation.

This treaty, consisting of sixteen articles, has been this day settled by Frederick Currie, Esq., and Brevet-Major Henry Montgomery Lawrence, acting under the directions of the Right Honourable Sir Henry Hardinge, G.C.B., Governor General, on the part of the British government; and by Bhai Ram Singh, Raja Lal Singh, Sardar Tej Singh, Sardar Chattar Singh Atariwala, Sardar Ranjor Singh Majithia, Dewan Deenanath, and Fakir Nur-ud-din, on the part of the Maharaja Dalip Singh; and the said treaty has been this day ratified by the seal of the Right Honourable Sir Henry Hardinge, G.C.B., Governor General, and by that of His Highness Maharaja Dalip Singh.

Done at Lahore, this 9th day of March, in the year of our Lord 1846, corresponding with the 10th day of Rabi-ul-awal 1262, Hijri, and ratified on the same day.

SUPPLEMENTARY ARTICLES TO FIRST TREATY WITH LAHORE OF 1846

Articles of Agreement concluded between the British Government and the Lahore Durbar, 11 March 1846

WHEREAS the Lahore Government has solicited the Governor General to leave a British force at Lahore, for the protection of the Maharaja's person and of the capital, till the reorganization of the Lahore Army, according to the provisions of Article 6 of the treaty of Lahore, dated the 9th instant: And whereas the Governor General has, on certain conditions, consented to the measure: And whereas it is expedient that certain matters concerning the territories ceded by Articles 3 and 4 of the aforesaid treaty should be specifically determined; the following eight articles of agreement have this day been concluded between the afore-mentioned contracting parties.

Article I: The British government shall leave at Lahore, till the close of the current year, A.D. 1846, such force as shall seem to the Governor General adequate for the purpose of protecting the person of the Maharaja, and the inhabitants of the city of Lahore, during the reorganization of the Sikh Army, in accordance with the provisions of Article 6 of the treaty of Lahore; that force to be withdrawn at any convenient time before the expiration of the year, if the object to be fulfilled shall, in the opinion of the durbar, have been obtained; but the force shall not be detained at Lahore beyond the expiration of the current year.

Article 2: The Lahore Government agrees that the force left at Lahore, for the purpose specified in the foregoing article, shall be placed in full possession of the fort and the city of Lahore, and that the Lahore troops shall be removed from within the city. The Lahore Government engages to furnish convenient quarters for the officers and men of the said force, and to pay to the British government all the extra expenses, with regard to the said force, which may be incurred by the British government, in consequence of their troops being employed away from their own cantonments, and in a foreign territory.

Article 3: The Lahore Government engages to apply itself immediately and earnestly to the reorganization of its army, according to the prescribed conditions, and to communicate fully with the British authorities left at Lahore, as to the progress of such reorganization, and as to the location of the troops.

Article 4: If the Lahore Government fails in the performance of the conditions of the foregoing article, the British government shall be at liberty to withdraw the force from Lahore, at any time before the expiration of the period specified in Article 1.

Article 5: The British government agrees to respect the bona fide rights of those Jagirdars within the territories ceded by Articles 3 and 4 of the treaty of Lahore, dated 9th instant, who were attached to the families of the late Maharaja Ranjit Singh, Kharak Singh, and Sher Singh; and the British government will maintain those Jagirdars in their bona fide possessions, during their lives.

Article 6: The Lahore government shall receive the assistance of the British local authorities in recovering the arrears of revenue justly due to the Lahore government from their Kardars and managers in the territories ceded by the provisions of Articles 3 and 4 of the treaty of Lahore, to the close of the Kharif harvest of the current year, viz. 1902, of the Sambat Bikarmajit.

Article 7: The Lahore government shall be at liberty to remove from the forts in the territories specified in the foregoing article, all treasure and state property, with the exception of guns. Should, however, the British government desire to retain any part of the said property, they shall be at liberty to do so, paying for the same at a fair valuation; and the British officers shall give their assistance to the Lahore Government, in disposing on the spot of such part of the aforesaid property as the Lahore Government may not wish to remove, and the British officers may not desire to retain.

Article 8: Commissioners shall be immediately appointed by the two governments, to settle and lay down the boundary between the two states, as defined by Article 4 of the treaty of Lahore, dated 9 March 1846.

GOVERNMENT NOTIFICATION.

Foreign Department, Camp, Umritsir, 16 March 1846

The Right Hon. the Governor General of India has been pleased to direct the publication, for general information, of the subjoined extracts from the proceedings of the Government of India, relative to the re-establishment of amicable relations between the British Government and the State of Lahore, and the recognition of the independence of Maharajah Gholab Singh.

No: 1

Note of Conference between F. Currie, Esq., and Major H.M. Lawrence, on the one part, and the ministers and chiefs of the Lahore Durbar on the other, 8 March 1846.

The ministers and chiefs having assembled at the tent of the Governor General's agent, for the purpose of signing the treaty the conditions of which had been previously discussed and determined, produced, on the part of the Maharajah, a letter addressed to Major Lawrence, the Governor General's agent, of which the following is a translation:-

'The feelings of consideration, kindness, and generosity which have been evinced towards the Lahore State by the Right Hon. the Governor General, and His Excellency's respect for the former friendship of the British government with the late Maharajah Runjeet Singh, have been communicated to me through Mr Secretary Currie and yourself, and have caused me to feel most grateful.

'Certain important matters will now be represented to you by the following confidential personages: Bhaee Ram Singh, Rajah Lal Singh, Sirdar Tej Singh, Dewan Deena Nath, Fakeer Noor-ood-Deen, and you, who are the guardian of the perpetual friendship of the two governments, will represent these matters to the Governor General, and will, doubtless, use your endeavours to procure a favourable decision regarding them.

'The Lahore Government, it is known, is endeavouring to arrange its affairs, and it is necessary that effectual measures should be taken to prevent the recurrence of any disturbances. With this view it is very desirable that some British regiments, with artillery and officers, should be directed to remain at Lahore for a few months, for the protection of the State. After affairs have been satisfactorily settled, and the period which may be fixed upon expired, the British troops will then return.'

To the above paper the following reply was made verbally, and was, at the request of the minister and chiefs, written down and given to them:

'The letter from the Maharajah to Major Lawrence, expressing gratitude to the Governor General, has been read in presence of the minister and chiefs of the darbar. At the close of that letter, it is requested that a British force may be left at Lahore for a limited period.

'Upon this, it is to be observed, that from the wording of the letter, it is not evident that the retention of a British force at Lahore is sincerely and urgently desired by the Lahore Government, and the nature of the disturbances which are to be provided against are not specifically described. In so important a matter, general expressions are out of place. The British government desires to exercise no interference with the Government of Lahore after the treaty of peace is concluded, and the Governor General is not willing to have any concern with the Lahore Government, or to accede to any measure not provided for by the treaty. This has been repeatedly explained to the Lahore Durbar. If, therefore, for any special reason, and on any particular account, the assistance and intervention of the British government are desired by the Lahore Durbar, the fact should have been more distinctly stated in the Khurreeta, and the causes which render such aid indispensable should have been given in detail. However, as the Maharajah has authorized the chiefs named in the Khurreeta, and who are present, to make known all the particulars of the case, they should now state all the circumstances in full.'

The minister and chiefs, after consultation, read aloud the substance of the paper, of which the following is a translation, but requested that it might be put in the form of a Khurreeta from the Maharajah, and sent in the evening. A communication was then made to the Governor General who, determined that a British force should, under certain conditions, to be entered in a separate engagement, occupy Lahore for a limited time; the treaty was then sighed by the commissioners, and the meeting broke up.

Translation of Document alluded to in preceding paragraph afterwards sent from the Durbar as a Formal Khurreeta, with the seal of the Maharajah.

'All the circumstances regarding the disorganization of the Government of Lahore since the demise of the late Maharajah Runjeet Singh until the present time are well known to the British government.

'The satisfactory settlement of affairs, the discharge of the disturbers of public peace, and the reorganization of the army under the stipulations of the new treaty, are now engaging consideration. But lest, after the departure of the British forces, the evil disposed of should create fresh disturbances, and endeavour to ruin the State, it is the earnest and sincere desire and hope of the Lahore Durbar that British troops with intelligent officers should, for some months, as circumstances may seem to require, be left at Lahore for the protection of the Government and the Maharajah and the inhabitants of the city. When affairs have been satisfactorily settled, and the period prescribed for the stay of the British force shall have expired, the troops may then be withdrawn.'

True note and translation
F. CURRIE,
Secretary to the Government of India,
with the Governor General

No: 2

General Order by the Right Hon. the Governor General of India.
Foreign Department, Camp, Lahore, 8 March.

The treaty of peace between the British government and that of His Highness the Maharajah Dhuleep Singh has been signed.

The treaty will be ratified by the Governor General, in presence of the Maharajah and the Sikh chiefs tomorrow afternoon, the 9th instant, at four o'clock, in the Governor General's tent.

The Governor General invites His Excellency the Commander-in-Chief, His Excellency the Governor of Scinde, with their present staff, to attend on this occasion, also the Generals of division, the Brigadiers, the head of each department, and all officers commanding corps, with one native officer from every regiment.

His Highness the Maharajah Dhuleep Singh will be received by a salute of twenty-one guns. The street leading to the Governor General's tent will be lined by detachments of regiments according to the orders which His Excellency the Commander-in-Chief will be pleased to issue.

The following day the Governor General will pay His Highness the Maharajah a visit of congratulation on the restoration of peace between the two governments, and will leave the camp for that purpose at three o'clock. The escort will be fixed in the General Order of His Excellency the Commander-in-Chief.

The thirty-six pieces of Sikh artillery which were pointed against the British Army have been surrendered and brought into camp. The disbandment of the Sikh Army, its reorganization, on the same rate of pay as in the time of the late Maharajah Runjeet Singh, and the limitations of its numbers, have been settled by the treaty.

At the earnest solicitation of the Government of the Maharajah Dhuleep Singh, the Governor General has consented to occupy the citadel and town of Lahore by British troops for a limited period, that opportunity may be afforded the Lahore Government of completing the reorganization of its army, according to the stipulations of the treaty.

If by the good offices of the British government peace and order can take the place of the military anarchy and misrule by which the Sikh nation has been brought to the verge of dissolution, the Governor General will rejoice that the co-operation of the British government, by the aid of its faithful army, shall have been successful in effecting that object. It is the strongest proof which the British government can give of the sincerity of its desire to see a Sikh Government re-established. The British government having afforded the protection desired, the troops will be withdrawn before the end of the year. The details of the force will be determined between the Governor General and His Excellency the native troops will continue to receive Scinde pay and allowances.

It is by the valour and discipline of the British troops, led by their distinguished commander, that these important and complete successes have been gained, and the Governor General is confident that, during the temporary occupation of the fortified town of Lahore, the troops will prove, by their good conduct, that they are as generous and humane after victory, as they are brave and invincible in the field of battle.

By order of the Right Hon. the Governor General of India.

F. CURRIE,
Secretary to the Government of India,
With the Governor General

No: 3

Memorandum of Proceedings of a Durbar held at Lahore, on 9 March 1846.

At 4 p.m., of 9 March, a public Durbar was held in the state tent of the Right Honourable the Governor General, at which His Excellency the

Commander-in-Chief and Staff, His Excellency the Governor of Scinde and Staff, with the British and native officers invited in the Governor General's order, dated 8 March instant, attended.

The young Maharajah of Lahore, attended by the Minister Rajah Lal Singh, Rajah Gholab Singh, the Commander-in-Chief of the Lahore Army, Sirdar Tej Singh, and about thirty other Sirdars and civil officers, with their suites, were present.

After the treaty of peace was ratified and exchanged with the usual ceremonies, the Governor General addressed the chiefs in the following terms, the address being translated, sentence by sentence, by the Secretary to the Government of India, Mr F. Currie:

'On this occasion of ratifying the treaty of peace between the British government and the Maharajah Dhuleep Singh, in the presence of His Excellency the Commander-in-Chief, His Excellency the Governor of Scinde, and the officers of the British Army on the one hand, and of the Sikh chiefs on the other, I have to repeat the assurances which have so often been given by me and by my predecessors of our desire that peace and friendship may always subsist between the two governments.

'The British government desires to see a Sikh Government re-established which may be able to control its army, protect its subjects, and willing to respect the rights of its neighbours.

'By this treaty the Lahore Government has sufficient strength to resist and punish any native poser which may venture to assail it, and to put down all internal commotions.

'Wisdom in council and good faith in fulfilling its engagements will cause the Sikh Government to be respected, and enable it to preserve its national independence.

'For forty years it was the policy, in Runjeet Singh's time, to cultivate friendly relations between the two governments, and during the whole of that period the Sikh nation was independent and happy. Let the policy of that able man towards the British government be the model for your future imitation.

'The British government in no respect provoked the late war. It had no objects of aggrandizement to obtain by hostilities. The proof of its sincerity is to be found in its moderation in the hour of victory.

'A just quarrel, followed by a successful war, has not changed the policy of the British government. The British government does not desire to interfere in your internal affairs. I am ready and anxious to withdraw every British soldier from Lahore. At the earnest solicitation of the Sikh Government, I have reluctantly consented to leave a British force in garrison at Lahore, until time shall have been afforded for the reorganization of the Sikh Army, by which assistance the stipulations of the treaty may be more easily carried into effect.

'In no case can I consent that the British troops shall remain in garrison for a longer period than the end of this year.

'I state this publicly, that the entire world may know the truth, and the motives by which I am actuated in this matter.

'The Sikh Army must, according to the treaty, be immediately reorganized by reverting to the same system and rate of pay as in Runjeet Singh's time.

'If the friendly assistance now afforded by the British government be wisely followed up, and honest exertions made by the chiefs without delay, you will become an independent and prosperous state.

'The success or failure is in your own hands; my co-operation shall not be wanting: but, if you neglect this opportunity, no aid on the part of the British government can save the state.

'I leave my political agent, Major Lawrence, assisted by Major M'Gregor, and a most able General officer, Sir John Littler, to command the British troops. These officers possess my entire confidence.

'Again I repeat, my anxious desire is to see a Sikh Government strong and respected, an obedient army, patriotic chiefs, and a happy people.

'I trust the reign of the Maharajah will be long and prosperous, and celebrated for the happiness of his people under a just and pacific Government.'

At the close of this address the Sirdars expressed in warm terms their gratitude to the Governor General, and their resolution to follow the advice His Excellency had given them.

The usual presents were then given, after which the Durbar broke up.

F. CURRIE,
Secretary to the Government of India,
with the Governor General

No: 4
Treaty between the British government and the State of Lahore

Whereas the treaty of amity and concord, which was concluded between the British government and the late Maharajah Runjeet Singh, the ruler of Lahore, in 1809, was broken by the unprovoked aggression, on the British Provinces, of the Sikh Army in December last, and whereas, on occasion, by the Proclamation dated 13 December, the territories then in the occupation of the Maharajah of Lahore on that, the left or British bank of the river Sutlej, were confiscated and annexed to the British Provinces, and since that time hostile operations have been prosecuted by the two governments, the one against the other, which have resulted in the occupation of Lahore by the British troops; and whereas it has been determined that, upon certain conditions, peace shall be re-established between the two governments, the following treaty of peace between the Hon. English East India Company and Maharajah Dhuleep Singh Bahadoor and his children, heirs, and successors, has been concluded on the part of the Honourable Company by Frederick Currie, Esq., and Brevet-Major Henry Montgomery Lawrence, by virtue of full posers to that effect, vested in them by the Right Honourable Sir Henry Hardinge, GCB., one of Her Britannic Majesty's Most Honourable Privy Council, Governor General, appointed by the Honourable Company to direct and control all their affairs in the East Indies, and on the part of His Highness the Maharajah Dhuleep Singh by Bhaee Ram Singh, Rajah Lal Singh, Sirdar Tej Singh, Sirdar Chuttur Singh Attareewalla, Sirdar Runjoor Singh Majethea, Dewan Deena Nath, and Fakeer Noor-ood-Deen, vested with full powers and authority on the part of His Highness.

Article 1: There shall be perpetual peace and friendship between the British government on the one part, and Maharajah Dhuleep Singh, his heirs and successors, on the other.

Article 2: The Maharajah of Lahore renounces for himself, his heirs and successors, all claim to, or connection with, the territories lying to the south of the river Sutlej, and engages never to have any concern with those territories or the inhabitants thereof.

Article 3: The Maharajah cedes to the Honourable Company in perpetual sovereignty, all his forts, territories, and rights, in the doab or county, hill and plain, situate between the rivers Beas and Sutlej.

Article 4: The British government having demanded from the Lahore State, as indemnification for the expenses of the war, in addition to the cession of territory described in Article 3, payment of one and a half crores of rupees, and the Lahore Government being unable to pay the whole of this sum at this time, or to give security satisfactory to the British government for its eventual payment, the Maharajah cedes to the Honourable Company, in perpetual sovereignty, as equivalent for one crore of rupees, all his forts, territories, rights, and interests, in the hill countries which are situate between the rivers Beas and Indus, including the provinces of Cashmere and Hazarah.

Article 5: The Maharajah will pay to the British government the sum of fifty lac of rupees on or before the ratification of this treaty.

Article 6: The Maharajah engages to disband the mutinous troops of the Lahore army, taking from them their arms; and His Highness agrees to reorganize the regular, or Aeen regiments of infantry, upon the system and according to the regularization as to pay and allowances observed in the time of the late Maharajah Runjeet Singh. The Maharjah further engages to pay up all arrears to the soldiers that are discharged under the provisions of this article.

Article 7: The regular army of the Lahore State shall henceforth be limited to twenty-five battalions of infantry, consisting of 800 bayonets each, with 12,000 cavalry: this number at no time to be exceeded without the concurrence of the British government. Should it be necessary at any time, for any special cause, that this force should be increased, the cause shall be fully explained to the British government, and when the special necessity shall have passed, the regular troops shall be again reduced to the standard specified in the former clause of this article.

Article 8: The Maharajah will surrender to the British government all the guns, thirty-six in number, which have been pointed against the British troops, and which, having been placed on the right bank of the river Sutlej, were not captured at the battle of Sobraon.

Article 9: The Control of the rivers Beas and Sutlej, with the continuation of the latter river, commonly called the Gurrah and the Punjnud, to the confluence of the Indus at Mithakote, and the control of the Indus from Mithakote to the borders of Beloochistan, shall, in respect to tolls and ferries, rest with the British government. The provisions of this article shall not interfere with the passage of boats belonging to the Lahore Government on the said rivers for the purposes of traffic or the conveyance of passengers up and down their course. Regarding the ferries between the two countries respectively, at the several ghats, of the said rivers, it is agreed that the British government, after defraying all the expenses of management and establishments, shall account to the Lahore Government for one-half of the net profits of the ferry collections. The provisions of this article have no reference to the ferries on that part of the river Sutlej which forms the boundary of Bahawalpur and Lahore respectively.

Article 10: If the British government should, at any time, desire to pass troops through the territories of His Highness the Maharajah for the protection of the British territories, or those of their allies, the British troops shall, on such special occasion, due notice given, be allowed to pass through the Lahore territories. In such case the officers of the Lahore State will afford facilities in providing supplies and boats for the passage of the rivers, and the British government will pay the full price of all such provisions and boats, and will make fair compensation for all private property, that may be damaged. The British government will moreover observe all due consideration to the religious feelings of the inhabitants of those tracts through which the army may pass.

Article 11: The Maharajah engages never to take, or retain in his service, any British subject nor the subject of any European or American state, without the consent of the British government.

Article 12: In consideration of the services rendered by Rajah Gholab Singh, of Jummoo, to the Lahore State, towards procuring the restoration of the relations of amity between the Lahore and British governments, the Maharajah hereby agrees to recognize the independent sovereignty of Rajah Gholab Singh in such territories and districts in the hills as may be made over to the said Rajah Gholab Singh by separate agreement between himself and the British government, with the dependencies thereof, which may have been in the Rajah's possession since the time of the late Maharajah Kurruk Singh, and the British government, in consideration of the good conduct of Rajah Gholab Singh, also agrees to recognize his independence in such territories, and to admit him to the privileges of a separate treaty with the British government.

Article 13: In the event of any dispute or difference arising between the Lahore State and Rajah Gholab Singh, the same shall be referred to the arbitration of the British government, and by its decision the Maharajah engages to abide.

Article 14: The limits of the Lahore territories shall not be, at any time, changed without the concurrence of the British government.

Article 15: The British government will not exercise any interference in the internal administration of the Lahore State, but in all cases or questions which may be referred to the British government, the Governor General will give the aid of his advice and good offices for the furtherance of the interests of the Lahore Government.

Article 16: The subjects of either state shall, on visiting the territories of the other, be on the footing of the subjects of the most favoured nation.

This treaty, consisting of sixteen articles, has been this day settled by Frederick Currie, Esq., and Brevet-Major Henry Montgomery Lawrence, acting under the directions of the Right Honourable Sir Henry Hardinge, GCB, Governor General, on the part of the British government, and by Bhaee Ram Singh, Rajah Lal Singh, Sirdar Tej Singh, Sirdar Chuttur Singh Attareewalla, Sirdar Runjoor Singh Majethea, Dewan Deena Nath, and Fakeer Noor-ood-Deen, on the part of the Maharajah Dhuleep Singh, and the said treaty has been this day ratified by the seal of the Right Honourable Sir Henry Hardinge, GCB, Governor General, and by that of His Highness Maharajah Dhuleep Singh.

Done at Lahore, this 9th day of March, in the year of our Lord 1846, corresponding with the tenth day of Rubbeeoolawul: 1262, Hijree, and ratified on the same date.

MAHARAJA DHULEEP SINGH, (L.S.)
BHAEE RAM SINGH, (L.S.)
RAJAH LAL SINGH, (L.S.)
SIRDAR TEJ SINGH, (L.S.)
SIRDAR CHUTTUR SINGH ATTAREEWALLA, (L.S.)
SIRDAR RUNJOOR SINGH MAJETHEA, (L.S.)
DEWAN DEENA NATH, (L.S.)
FAKER NOOR-OOD-DEEN, (L.S.)
H. HARDINGE, (L.S.)
F. CURRIE.
H.M. LAWRENCE

By order of the Right Honourable the Governor General of India,

F. CURRIE,
Secretary to the Government of India,
with the Governor General

No: 5

Memorandum of a State Visit paid by the Governor General to the Maharajah of Lahore in His Highness's Palace on 10 March 1846.

On the afternoon of 10 March, the Governor General, attended by His Excellency the Commander-in-Chief, His Excellency the Governor of Scinde, and the British officers who were present at the ratification of the treaty on the 9th instant, paid a visit of congratulating to the Maharajah Dhuleep Singh at the Palace in Lahore, on this occasion Dewan Deena Nath, by direction of the minister and assembled chiefs, read from a written paper an address, of which the following is a translation:

'It is impossible for us adequately to express the gratitude which we feel to the Governor General, for his having determined to continue the ancient relations which existed with the late Maharajah Runjeet Singh, and for his generosity, kindness, and mercy in maintaining this Government.

'For the excellent advice which was given yesterday, through kindness and friendship, to the assembled Sirdars, exhorting them to unanimity, prudence, and good government, we are also most grateful. We consider this good advice as having a direct tendency to effect the re-establishment of the Government of the country. We have further to express our gratitude for arrangements having generously been made, in compliance with our solicitations, for leaving a garrison in Lahore of British troops, with Major Lawrence and other trustworthy officers, for our protection and that of the city.

'These troops will assuredly be honourably dismissed towards the Sutlej, upon a satisfactory settlement of affairs being affected within the period prescribed for their stay.

'The various acts of generosity shown by the Governor General on the present occasion entirely satisfy us that His Excellency will ever maintain the same magnanimous and generous policy towards this State, and that, taking compassion on the extreme youth of the Maharajah, His Excellency will maintain all those friendly relations which existed in the time of the late Maharajah Runjeet Singh.'

After the presentation by the Maharajah of the usual offerings, the Governor General and suite returned to camp.

True memorandum and translation,

F. CURRIE,
Secretary to the Government of India,
with the Governor General

No. 6

Note of the proceedings of a meeting of the minister and chief of the Lahore Durbar and the British commissioners, held at the tent of the Governor General's Agent, on 11 March 1846.

On the forenoon of the 11th instant, the minister and chiefs of the durbar attended at the tent of the Governor General's agent, when the following agreement was concluded, and subsequently confirmed by the Right Hon. the Governor General:

Articles of Agreement concluded between the British government and the Lahore Durbar, on 11 March, 1846.

Whereas the Lahore Government has solicited the Governor General to leave a British force at Lahore for the protection of the Maharajah's person, and of the capital, till the reorganization of the Lahore Army, according to the provisions of Article 6 of the treaty of Lahore, dated the 9th instant; and whereas the Governor General has, on certain conditions, consented to this measure; and whereas it is expedient that certain matters concerning the territories ceded by Articles 3 and 4 of the aforesaid treaty should be specifically determined, the following eight articles of agreement have this day been concluded between the aforementioned contracting parties:-

Article 1: The British government shall leave at Lahore, till the close of the current year AD 1846, such force as shall seem to the Governor General adequate for the purpose of protecting the person of the Maharajah and the inhabitants of the city of Lahore during the reorganization of the Sikh Army, in accordance with the provisions of Article 6 of the treaty of Lahore. That force to be withdrawn at any convenient time before the expiration of the year, of the object to be fulfilled shall, in the opinion of the Durbar, have been attained; but the force shall not be detained at Lahore beyond the expiration of the current year.

Article 2: The Lahore Government agrees that the force left at Lahore for the purpose specified in the foregoing article shall be placed in full possession of the fort and city of Lahore, and that the Lahore troops shall be removed from within the city. The Lahore Government engages to furnish convenient quarters for the officers and men of the said force, and to pay the British government all the extra expenses with regard to the said force which may be incurred by the British government in consequence of their troops being employed away from their own cantonments, and in a foreign territory.

Article 3: The Lahore Government engages to apply itself immediately and earnestly to the reorganization of its army according to the prescribed condition, and to communicate fully with the British authorities left at Lahore as to the progress of such reorganization, and as to the location of the troops.

Article 4: If the Lahore Government fails in the performance of the conditions of the foregoing article, the British government shall be at liberty to withdraw the force from Lahore at any time before the expiration of the period specified in Article 1.

Article 5: The British government agrees to respect the bona fide rights of those Jaghirdars within the territories ceded by Articles 3 and

4 of the Treaty of Lahore, dated 9th instant, who were attached to the families of the late Maharajah Runjeet Singh, Kurruck Singh, and Shere Singh, and the British government will maintain those Jaghirdars in their bona fide possessions during their lives.

Article 6: The Lahore Government shall receive the assistances of the British local authorities in recovering the arrears of revenue justly due to the Lahore Government from their Kardars and managers in the territories ended by the provisions of Articles 3 and 4 of the Treaty of Lahore, to the close of the Khurreef harvest of the current year, viz., 1902 of the Sumbut Bikramajeet.

Article 7: The Lahore Government shall be at liberty to remove from the forts in the territories specified in the foregoing article all treasure and state property, with the exception of guns. Should, however, the British government desire to retain any part of the said property, they shall be at liberty to do so, paying for the same at a fair valuation, and the British officers shall give their assistance to the Lahore Government in disposing on the spot of such part of the aforesaid property as the Lahore Government may not wish to remove, and the British officers may not desire to retain.

Article 8: Commissioners shall be immediately appointed by the two Governments to settle and lay down the boundary between the two states, as defined by Article 4 of the Treaty of Lahore, dated 9 March 1846.

MAHARAJA DHULEEP SINGH, (L.S.)
BHAEE RAM SINGH, (L.S.)
RAJAH LAL SINGH, (L.S.)
SIRDAR TEJ SINGH, (L.S.)
SIRDAR CHUTTUR SINGH ATTAREEWALLA, (L.S.)
SIRDAR RUNJOOR SINGH MAJETHEA, (L.S.)
DEWAN DEENA NATH, (L.S.)
FAKER NOOR-OOD-DEEN, (L.S.)
H. HARDINGE, (L.S.)
F. CURRIE.
H.M. LAWRENCE

By order of the Right Honourable the Governor General of India,

F. CURRIE,
Secretary to the Government of India,
with the Governor General

ANNEXURE IX

TREATY BETWEEN THE BRITISH GOVERNMENT AND MAHARAJAH GHOLAB SINGH, CONCLUDED AT UMRITSIR ON 16 MARCH 1846

TREATY between the British government on the one part, and Maharajah Gholab Singh, of Jummoo, on the other, concluded on the part of the British government by Frederick Currie, Esq., and Brevet-Major Henry Montgomery Lawrence, acting under the orders of the Right Honourable Sir Henry Hardinge, GCB, one of Her Britannic Majesty's Most Honourable Privy Council, Governor General, appointed by the Honourable Company to direct and control all their affairs in the East Indies, and by Maharajah Golab Singh in person.

Article 1: The British government transfers and makes over, for ever, in independent possession, to Maharajah Gholab Singh, and the heirs male of his body, all the hilly or mountainous country, with its dependencies, situate to the eastward of the river Indus, and westward of the river Ravee, including Chumba and excluding Lahool, being part of the territory ceded to the British government by the Lahore State, according to the provisions of Article 4 of the Treaty of Lahore, dated 9 March 1846.

Article 2: The eastern boundary of the tract transferred by the foregoing article to Maharajah Gholab Singh shall be laid down by commissioners appointed by the British government and Maharajah Gholab Singh respectively for that purpose, and shall be defined in a separate engagement after survey.

Article 3: In consideration of the transfer made to him and his heirs, by the provisions of the foregoing articles, Maharajah Gholab Singh will pay to the British government the sum of 75 lac of rupees (Nanuckshahee), 50 lac to be paid on ratification of this treaty, and 25 lac on or before 1 October of the current year, 1846.

Article 4: The limits of the territories of Maharajah Gholab Singh Shall not be at any time changed without the concurrence of the British government.

Article 5: Maharajah Gholab Singh will refer to the arbitration of the British government any disputes or questions that may arise between himself and the Government of Lahore, or any other neighbouring state, and will abide by the decision of the British government.

Article 6: Maharajah Gholab Singh engages for himself and heirs to join with the whole of his military force the British troops when employed within the hills, or in the territories adjoining his possessions.

Article 7: Maharajah Gholar Singh engages never to take or retain in his service any British subject, nor the subject of any European or American state, without the consent of the British government.

Article 8: Maharajah Gholab Singh engages to respect, in regard to the territory transferred to him, the provisions of Articles 5, 6, and 7, of the separate engagement between the British government and the Lahore Durbar, dated 11 March 1846.

Article 9: The British government will give its aid to Maharajah Gholab Singh in protecting his territories from external enemies.

Article 10: Maharajah Gholab Singh acknowledges the supremacy of the British government, and will, in token of such supremacy, present annually to the British government, one horse, twelve perfect shawl goats of approved breed (six male and six female), and three pairs of Cashmere Shawls.

This treaty consisting to ten articles, has been this day settled by Frederick Currie, Esq., and Brevet-Major Henry Montgomery Lawrence, acting under the directions of the Right Honourable Sir Henry Hardinge, GCB, Governor General, on the part of the British government, and by Maharajah Gholab Singh in person, and the said treaty has been this day ratified by the seal of the Right Honourable Sir Henry Hardinge, GCB, Governor General.

Done at Umritsir, this 16th day of March, in the year of our Lord 1846, corresponding with the 17th day of Rubbeeoolawul 1262, Hijree.

GHOLAB SINGH, (L.S.)
H. HARDINGE (L.S.)
F. CURRIE.
H.M. LAWRENCE.

By order of the Right Honourable the Governor General of India,

F. CURRIE,
Secretary to the Government of India,
with the Governor General

(True extracts)

ANNEXURE X

SECOND TREATY WITH LAHORE OF 1846
(Also known as The Treaty of Bhyrowal)

Foreign Department, Camp, Bhyrowal Ghat, on the left Bank of the Beas, 22 December 1846

THE late Governor of Kashmir, on the part of the Lahore State, Sheikh Imam-ud-din, having resisted by force of arms the occupation of the province of Kashmir by Maharaja Gulab Singh, the Lahore Government was called upon to coerce their subject, and to make over the province to the representative of the British government, in fulfilment of the conditions of the treaty of Lahore, dated 9 March 1846.

A British force was employed to support and aid, if necessary, the combined forces of the Lahore State and Maharaja Gulab Singh in the above operations.

Sheikh Imam-ud-din intimated to the British government that he was acting under orders received from the Lahore Durbar in the course he was pursuing; and stated that the insurrection had been instigated by written instructions received by him from the Wazir Raja Lal Singh.

Sheikh Imam-ud-din surrendered to the British agent on a guarantee from that officer, that if the Sheikh could, as he asserted, prove that his acts were in accordance with his instructions, and that the opposition was instigated by the Lahore minister, the durbar should not be permitted to inflict upon him, either in his person or his property, any penalty on account of his conduct on this occasion. The British agent pledged his Government to a full and impartial investigation of the matter.

A public inquiry was instituted into the facts adduced by Sheikh Imam-ud-din, and it was fully established that Raja Lal Singh did secretly instigate the Sheikh to oppose the occupation by Maharaja Gulab Singh of the province of Kashmir.

The Governor General immediately demanded that the ministers and chiefs of the Lahore state should depose and exile to the British provinces of the Wazir Raja Lal Singh.

His Lordship consented to accept the deposition of Raja Lal Singh as an atonement for the attempt to infringe the treaty by the secret intrigues and machinations of the Wazir. It was not proved that the other members of the durbar had cognizance of the Wazir's proceedings; and the conduct of the sardars, and of the Sikh Army in the late operations for quelling the Kashmir insurrection, and removing the obstacles to the fulfilment of the treaty, proved that the criminality of the Wazir was not participated in by the Sikh nation.

The ministers and chiefs unanimously decreed, and carried into immediate effect, the deposition of the Wazir.

After a few days' deliberations, relative to the means of forming a government at Lahore, the remaining members of the durbar, in concert with all the sardars and chiefs of the state, solicited the interference and aid of the British government for the maintenance of an administration, and the protection of the Maharaja Dalip Singh during the minority of His Highness.

This solicitation by the durbar and chiefs has led to the temporary modification of the relations between the British government and that of Lahore, established by the treaty of 9 March of the present year.

The terms and conditions of this modification are set forth in the following articles of agreement.

Articles of Agreement concluded between the British Government and the Lahore Durbar on 16 December 1846

Whereas the Lahore Durbar and the principal chiefs and sardars of the State have, in express terms, communicated to the British government their anxious desire that the Governor General should give his aid and his assistance to maintain the administration of the Lahore State during the minority of Maharaja Dalip Singh, and have declared this measure to be indispensable for the maintenance of the government: And whereas the Governor General has, under certain conditions, consented to give the aid and assistance solicited, the following articles of agreement, in modification of the articles of agreement executed at Lahore on 11 March last, have been concluded, on the part of the British government, by Frederick Currie, Esq., Secretary to the Government of India, and Lt Col Henry Montgomery Lawrence, C.B., Agent to the Governor General, North-West Frontier, by virtue of full powers to that effect vested in them by the Right Honourable Viscount Hardinge, G.C.B., Governor General, and on the part of His Highness Maharaja Dalip Singh, by Sardar Tej Singh, Sardar Sher Singh, Dewan Deenanath, Fakir Nur-ud-din, Rai Kishan Chand, Sardar Ranjor Singh Majithia, Sardar Atar Singh Kaliwala, Bhai Nidhan Singh, Sardar Khan Singh Majithia, Sardar Shamsher Singh, Sardar Lal Singh Muraria, Sardar Kehar Singh Sindhianwala, Sardar Arjun Singh Rangranglia, acting with the unanimous consent and concurrence of the chiefs and sardars of the state assembled at Lahore.

Article 1: All and every part of the treaty of peace between the British government and the State of Lahore, bearing date 9 March 1846, except in so far as it may be temporarily modified in respect to clause 15 of the said treaty by this engagement, shall remain binding upon the two governments.

Article 2: A British officer, with an efficient establishment of assistants, shall be appointed by the Governor General to remain at Lahore, which officer shall have full authority to direct and control all matters in every department of the State.

Article 3: Every attention shall be paid, in conducting the administration, to the feelings of the people, to preserving the national institutions and customs, and to maintain the just rights of all classes.

Article 4: Changes in the mode and details of administration shall not be made, except when found necessary for affecting the objects set forth in the foregoing clause, and for securing the just dues of the Lahore Government. These details shall be conducted by native officers as at present, who shall be appointed and superintended by a Council of Regency, composed of leading chiefs and sardars, acting under the control and guidance of the British Resident.

Article 5: The following persons shall in the first instance constitute the Council of Regency, viz., Sardar Tej Singh, Sardar Sher Singh Atariwala, Dewan Deenanath, Fakir Nur-ud-din, Sardar Ranjor Singh Majithia, Bhai Nidhan Singh, Sardar Attar Singh Kaliwala, Sardar Shamsher Singh Sindhianwala; and no change shall be made in the persons thus nominated, without the consent of the British Resident, acting under the orders of the Governor General.

Article 6: The administration of the country shall be conducted by this Council of Regency in such manner as may be determined on by themselves in consultation with the British Resident, who shall have full authority to direct and control the duties of every department.

Article 7: A British force, of such strength and numbers, and in such positions, as the Governor General may think fit, shall remain at Lahore for the protection of the Maharaja, and the preservation of the peace of the country.

Article 8: The Governor General shall be at liberty to occupy with British soldiers any fort or military post in the Lahore territories, the occupation of which may be deemed necessary by the British government for the security of the capital, or for maintaining the peace of the country.

Article 9: The Lahore State shall pay to the British government twenty-two lac of new Nanakshahi rupees of full tale and weight per annum, for the maintenance of this force, and to meet the expenses incurred by the British government; such sum to be paid in two instalments, of 13 lac and 20,000 in May or June, and 8 lac and 80,000 in November or December of each year.

Article 10: Inasmuch as it is fitting that Her Highness the Maharani, the mother of Maharaja Dalip Singh, should have a proper provision made for the maintenance of herself and dependents, the sum of 1 lac and 50,000 rupees shall be set apart annually for that purpose, and shall be at Her Highness's disposal.

Article 11: The provisions of this engagement shall have effect during the minority of His Highness Maharaja Dalip Singh, and shall cease and terminate on His Highness attaining the full age of 16 years, or on 4 September of the year 1854; but it shall be competent to the Governor

General to cause the arrangement to cease, at any period prior to the coming of age of His Highness, at which the Governor General and the Lahore Durbar may be satisfied that the interposition of the British government is no longer necessary for maintaining the government of His Highness the Maharaja.

This agreement, consisting of eleven articles, was settled and executed at Lahore, by the officers and chiefs and sardars above named, on 16 December 1846.

ANNEXURE XI

PROCLAMATION

Lahore, 22 July 1848

THE crimes and offences of Diwan Mulraj, the former nazim of Multan, his rebellion against the Government of the Maharaja Dhalip Singh, his treacherous murder of the British officers, and his schemes and plots for the subversion of the Khalsa Government are matters of notoriety.

Diwan Mulraj and his force have been twice beaten in two general actions by the troops of the Maharaja under the command of Lieutenant Edwardes and General Cortlandt and the army of the Nawab of Bahawalpur; and the rebel has betaken himself to the city and fort of Multan.

A large British force of all arms with an efficient siege train is now moving on Multan for the reduction of the fort and city, and the full and complete punishment of the rebel and his associates. This army will not return to its cantonments till these objects are fully accomplished and such condign punishment has been inflicted on the rebels to the Maharaja's Government and the insulters of the British power as will be a warning to all people.

But while the British government will take ample and awful vengeance on the guilty in this rebellion, it is desirous that the innocent should not be involved in the ruin which awaits the rebel and his followers, and that those who have only joined the rebel standard as mercenaries should have an opportunity of escaping the vengeance which will be visited on all those found in arms, aiding and abetting the rebel when the British force arrives in Multan.

Notice is therefore now given to the people in arms at Multan and the inhabitants of the city. The former are warned to lay down their arms and depart to their homes. Those who are not the actual perpetrators and abettors of the outrage committed on the British officers, or servants and soldiers of the Maharaja who have deserted their colours or His Highness's service, and joined the rebellion against the Khalsa Government will be permitted if they depart at once to go away unmolested.

When the British Army arrives before Multan, it will be too late; the hour or grace will have passed away. The inhabitants of the city and those who possess property therein are warned that if, on account of armed opposition, it becomes necessary to take forcible possession of the city by storm, it will be impossible to save their lives, or those of their families, or protect their property. The city will, of necessity, it is to be feared, be involved in bloodshed, plunder, and ruin.

On the arrival of the British Army before Multan, if the city has been peaceably surrendered the fort only will be attacked. If the fort be not unconditionally surrendered with those therein to the British power it will be besieged, and on being captured by storm the garrison will be put to the sword.

This proclamation is issued now with a view to save unnecessary bloodshed, and that all concerned may be fully informed of what will assuredly take place and that they may act accordingly.

ANNEXURE XII

PROCLAMATION BY THE RESIDENT AT LAHORE

18 November 1848

TO the subjects, servants, and dependents of the Lahore State, and the residents of all classes and castes, whether Sikh, Musalman, or other, within the territories of Maharaja Dhalip Singh, from the Beas to the mountains beyond Peshawar. Whereas certain evil-disposed persons and traitors have excited rebellion and insurrection and have seduced portions of the population of the Punjab from their allegiance, and have raised an armed opposition to the British authority; and whereas the condign punishment of the insurgents is necessary; therefore the British Army under the Command of the Right Hon'ble the Commander-in-Chief has entered the Punjab districts. The army will not return to its cantonments until the full punishment of all insurgents has been effected, all armed opposition to constituted authority put down, and obedience and order have been re-established.

And whereas it is not the desire of the British government that those who are innocent of the above offences, have taken no part, secretly or openly, in the disturbances, and who have remained faithful in obedience to the Government of Maharaja Dhalip Singh, be they Sikh or be they of any other class, should suffer with the guilty; therefore all persons who are not concerned directly or indirectly in the present disturbances, are assured that they have nothing to fear from the coming of the British Army. Such persons are exhorted to remain without apprehension in their villages and homes, and, as loyal subjects of the Maharaja, to give every aid by providing carriage, supplies and the like, to the army which has entered the Lahore territories, not as an enemy to the constituted government, but to restore order and obedience.

Furthermore all classes of the community, be they Sikh or be they of any other caste or tribe, who merely through ignorance may have been led away by the false statements of the evil-disposed and insurgent Sirdars and other and have left their homes and assembled themselves under the standard of rebellion, are hereby admonished instantly to separate themselves from the insurgents and to return to their villages. If they do so now without hesitation or delay, no injury will happen to them; if they neglect this warning and advice, certain destruction will come upon them in common with the other insurgents and rebels, and disturbers of the public peace.

ANNEXURE XIII

DETAILED STATEMENT OF THE NUMERICAL STRENGTH OF CORPS ENGAGED IN THE SEVERAL ACTIONS DURING THE PUNJAB CAMPAIGN

P.S. Lumsden, Major General. Adjutant General in India.
(Commentaries on the Punjab Campaign 1848-49 L. Archer)

BESIEGING FORCE BEFORE MOOLTAN, 1848-49
ARTILLERY

Officers and Men	Guns.*
H.A. - -	
Other Artillery -	
Sappers and Miners	
Pioneers (no returns obtainable in England)	

CAVALRY.
No Returns in England.

INFANTRY.
H.M. 10th Foot, 1088
H.M. 32nd Foot. No Returns at Horse Guards or War Office.

The expenditure of ammunition or guns during the siege of Mooltan was 42,347 rounds.

All Ranks		**Authority**
I-RAMNUGGUR		
1st Troop 2nd Brigade Horse Artillery	125	Monthly Return
3rd ditto ditto	148	Do
1st Troop 3rd ditto 2nd ditto ditto	330	General Quarterly Return, dated 1 October 1848
No. 5 Lt Field Battery and 3rd Co. 7th Bn. Foot Artillery.	157	Monthly Return
No. 10 ditto and 1st Co. 1st ditto	172	Do
Her Majesty's 3rd Light Dragoons.	693	General Quarterly Return, dated 1 October 1848
Ditto 14th ditto	648	Do
5th Light Cavalry - -	514	Do
8th ditto - -	513	Do
Her Majesty's 24th Foot -	1190	Do

Ditto 61st Foot -	1046	Do
2nd European Bengal Fusiliers -	818	Do
22nd Native Infantry - -	952	Monthly Return
25th ditto - -	905	Do
31st ditto - -	949	Do
36th ditto - -	1051	Do
46th ditto - -	905	Do
56th ditto - -	1008	Do

II.-SADOOLAPORE.

1st Troop 2nd Brigade Horse Artillery	114	Chillianwala Figures plus the casualties at Sadoolapore
2nd ditto ditto -	154	Do
3rd ditto ditto	143	Do
No. 10 Light Field Battery -	184	Do
No. 5 ditto -	92	Do
Her Majesty's 3rd Light Dragoons -	710	Do
5th Light Cavalry - -	511	Do
8th ditto - -	509	Do
3rd Irregular Cavalry - -	610	Do
Her Majesty's 24th Regiment	*1006	*Bayonets
Ditto 61st Regiment	813	Do
25th Native Infantry	610	Do
31st ditto	756	Do
36th ditto	768	Do
46th ditto	599	Do
56th ditto	838	Do
2 Companies Pioneers - -		Do

III. – CHILLANWALA.

1st Troop 2nd Brigade Horse Artillery.	109	Monthly Return
2nd ditto ditto	154	Do
3rd ditto ditto	143	Do
4th ditto ditto	147	Do
1st Troop 2nd Brigade Horse Artillery.	300	
2nd ditto ditto		
No. 1 Co. 1st Bn. and No. 10 Battery Foot Artillery.	181	Do
No. 3 Co. 1st Bn. and No. 17 Light Field Battery.	178	Do
No. 3 Co. 7th Bn. and No. 5		

Battery Foot Artillery - -	92	Do
-	158	Do
No. 1 Co. 4th Bn. Foot Artillery	118	Do
No. 2 Co. 4th Bn. Ditto	69	Do
No. 4 Co. 4th Bn. ditto	709	Quarterly General Return,
Her Majesty's 3rd Light Dragoons		dated 1 January 1849
Ditto 9th Lancers -	768	Do
Ditto 14th Light Dragoons	673	Do
1st Light Cavalry - -	517	Do
5th ditto - -	510	Do
6th ditto - -	516	Do
8th ditto - -	508	Do
3rd Irregular Cavalry - -	604	Do
9th ditto - -	607	Do
Her Majesty's 24th Foot -	1176	Do
Ditto 29th Foot -	1134	Do
Ditto 61st Foot -	1136	Do
2nd European Bengal Fusiliers -	976	Do
15th Native Infantry - -	1026	Monthly Return
20th Native Infantry - -	1008	Quarterly General Return 1 January 1849
25th ditto - -	920	Monthly Return
30th ditto - -	972	Do
31st ditto - -	983	Do
25th ditto - -	963	Do
36th ditto - -	976	Do
45th ditto - -	908	Do
46th ditto - -	1040	Quarterly General
56th ditto - -	-	Return, 1 January 1849
69th ditto - -	1008	Monthly Return
70th ditto - -	1081	Quarter General Return 1 January 1849
6 Companies Pioneer - -	336	Do

IV. – GOOJERAT.*

4th Troop 1st Brigade Horse Artillery		145	Monthly Return
1st Troop 2nd	ditto	118	Do
2nd ditto	ditto	118	Do
3rd ditto	ditto	145	Do
4th ditto	ditto	148	Do
1st Troop 3rd	ditto	470	Quarter General Return
2nd ditto	ditto		1 January 1849
4th ditto	ditto		
1st Co. 1st Bn. Foot Artillery with No. 10 Lt Field Battery		185	Monthly Return

3rd ditto ditto No. 17 ditto	172	Do
2nd Co. 2nd Bn. Foot Artillery -		
3rd Co. 3rd Bn. ditto -	97	Do
4th ditto ditto -	92	Do
1st Co. 4th Bn. Foot Artillery -	400	Quarter General Return
2nd ditto ditto -	including	1 January 1849
4th ditto ditto (Dett.)	absent dett 4th Co. 166 full strength	
3rd Co. 7th Bn. Foot Artillery (Dett.)		Do
3rd Co. 7th Bn. Foot Artillery, with No. 5 Lt Field Battery.	98	Monthly Return
6th ditto ditto	102	Quarter General Return t January 1849

*In this return of the force at Goojerat it will be observed that the following European Regiments are omitted, viz., the 24th Foot and 1st Bn. 60th, the King's Royal Rifle Regiment. These two corps may be estimated at about a total of 1500 rank and file and 44 officers.

3rd Troop Bomb. Horse Artil. –	167	Monthly Return
Her Majesty's 3rd Light Dragoons.	669	Quarter General Return 1 January 1849 deducting casualties at Chillianwallah
Ditto 9th Lancers -	756	Do
Ditto 14th Light Dragoons	654	Do
1st Light Cavalry - -	510	Do
5th ditto -	488	Do
6th ditto - -	499	Do
8th ditto - -	505	Do
3rd Irregular Cavalry - -	604	Do
9th ditto - -	607	Do
11th ditto (2 Ressallahs)	-	-
12th ditto - -	592	Quarter General Return 1 January 1849
13th ditto - -	551	Do
14th ditto (2 Ressallahs)	-	-
Guide Corps - - -	-	-
Scinde Horse - - -	-	-
Her Majesty's 10th Foot -	1106	Monthly Return
Ditto 29th Foot - -	893	Quarter General Return 1 January 1849, deducting casualties at Chillianwala

Ditto 32nd Foot - -	1139	Quarter General Return 1 January 1849
Ditto 61st Foot - -	958	Monthly Return
2nd European Bengal Fusiliers -	909	Quarter General Return 1 January 1849, deducting casualties at Chillianwallah
8th Native Infantry - -	917	Monthly Casualties
13th ditto - -	993	Quarter General Return 1 January 1849
15th ditto - -	970	Ditto, deducting casualties at Chillianwallah
20th ditto - -	1008	Quarter General Return 1 January 1849
25th ditto - -	661	Monthly Return
30th ditto - -	567	Do
31st ditto - -	804	Do
36th ditto - -	833	Do
45th ditto - -	897	Quarter General Return 1 January 1849, deducting casualties at Chillianwallah
46th ditto - -	854	Do
51st ditto - -	955	Monthly Return
52nd ditto - -	822	Do
56th ditto - -	894	Do
69th ditto - -	941	Quarter General Return 1 January 1849, deducting casualties at Chillianwallah
70th ditto - -	1056	Do
72nd ditto - -	1019	Quarter General Return 1 January 1849
2nd Co. and detachment 3rd Co. Sappers.	300	Do
6 Companies Pioneers - -	333	Do

[Total of all ranks imperfect for the reason explained in note.]

P.S. LUMSDEN, Major-General.
Adjutant-General in India.

ANNEXURE XIV

REGIMENTS INVOLVED IN THE SIKH WARS

QUEEN'S REGIMENTS

(Designations - From 'Regiments of the British Army' by Victor Sutcliffe)

Designation in 1845	**Subsequent History**
The 3rd (King's Own) Light Dragoons	3rd (King's Own) Hussars 1861. 3rd The King's Own Hussars 1921. Amalgamated with the 7th Queen's Own Hussars as The Queen's Own Hussars 1958. Part of *The Queen's Royal Hussars (Queen's Own and Royal Irish) 2009.*
9th (Queen's) Royal Lancers	9th Queen's Royal Lancers 1921. Amalgamated with 12th Royal Lancers as the 9th/12th Royal Lancers (The Prince of Wales's) 1960. Part of *The 9th/12th Royal Lancers 2009.*
14th (The King's) Regiment of (Light) Dragoons	14th (King's) Hussars 1861. 14th King's Hussars 1921. Amalgamated with The 20th Hussars as 14th/20th Hussars 1922. 14th/20th King's Hussars 1936. Part of *The King's Royal Hussars 2009.*
16th (The Queen's) Regiment of (Light) Dragoons (Lancers)	16th The Queen's Lancers 1921. Amalgamated with The 5th (Royal Irish) Lancers as The 16th/5th Lancers 1922. Part of *The Queen's Royal Lancers 2009.*
HM 9th (East Norfolk) Regiment of Foot	The Norfolk Regiment 1881. The Royal Norfolk Regiment 1935. Amalgamated with The Suffolk Regiment to form The East Anglian Regiment (Royal Norfolk and Suffolk) 1959. Part of *The Royal Anglian Regiment 2009.*
HM 10th (North Lincoln) Regiment of Foot	Lincolnshire Regiment 1881. The Royal Lincolnshire Regiment 1946. Amalgamated with The Northamptonshire Regiment as The 2nd East Anglian Regiment (Royal 10th/48th Foot) 1959. Part of *The Royal Anglian Regiment 2009.*
HM 24th (2nd Warwickshire) Regiment of Foot	South Wales Borderers 1881. Amalgamated with The Welsh Regiment as The Royal Regiment of Wales 1969. Part of *The Royal Welsh 2009.*
HM 29th (Worcestershire) Regiment of Foot	1st Battalion The Worcestershire Regiment 1881. Amalgamated with The Sherwood Foresters (Nottinghamshire and Derbyshire Regiment) as The Worcestershire and Sherwood Foresters Regiment (29th/45th Foot) 1970. 2nd Battalion *The Mercian Regiment 2009.*
HM 31st (Huntingdonshire)	The East Surrey Regiment 1881.

Regiment of Foot	Amalgamated with The Queen's Royal Regiment (West Surrey) as The Queen's Royal Surrey Regiment 1959. Part of The Queen's Regiment 1966. Part of *The Princess of Wales's Royal Regiment 2009.*
HM 32nd (Cornwall) Regiment of Foot	The 32nd (Cornwall) Light Infantry 1858. The 1st Battalion The Duke of Cornwall's Light Infantry 1881. Amalgamated with The Somerset Light Infantry as The Somerset and Cornwall Light Infantry 1959. Absorbed into The Light Infantry 1966. Part of *The Rifles 2009.*
HM 50th (Queen's Own) Regiment of Foot	1st Battalion The Queen's Own (Royal West Kent) Regiment 1881. The Royal West Kent Regiment (Queen's Own) 1921. Amalgamated with The Buffs (Royal East Kent Regiment) as The Queen's Own Buffs 1961. Absorbed into the Queen's Regiment 1966. Part of *The Princess of Wales's Royal Regiment 2009.*
HM 53rd (Shropshire) Regiment of Foot	The King's Light Infantry (Shropshire Regiment) 1881. The King's (Shropshire Light Infantry) 1882. Absorbed into The Light Infantry as The King's Shropshire Light Infantry1921. Part of The Light Infantry 1968. Part of *The Rifles 2009.*
HM The 60th (King's Royal Rifle Corps)	The King's Royal Rifle Corps 1881. Absorbed into the Royal Green Jackets as The Royal Green Jackets 1966. Part of *The Rifles 2009.*
HM 61st (South Gloucestershire) Regiment of Foot	2nd Battalion The Gloucestershire Regiment 1881. Part of The Royal Gloucestershire, Berkshire and Wiltshire Regiment 1994. Part of *The Rifles 2009.*
HM 62nd (Wiltshire) Regiment of Foot	The Duke of Edinburgh's (Wiltshire Regiment) 1881. The Wiltshire Regiment (The Duke of Edinburgh's) 1920. Amalgamated with the Royal Berkshire Regiment as The Duke of Edinburgh's Royal Regiment (Berkshire and Wiltshire) 1959. Part of The Royal Gloucestershire, Berkshire and Wiltshire Regiment 1994. Part of *The Rifles 2009.*
HM 80th (Staffordshire Volunteers) Regiment of Foot	2nd Battalion The South Staffordshire Regiment 1881. Amalgamated with The North Staffordshire Regiment as The Staffordshire Regiment (The Prince of Wales's) 1959. Part of *The Mercian Regiment 2009.*
HM 98th (Prince of Wales) Regiment of Foot	The Prince of Wales's (North Staffordshire) Regiment 1881. The North Staffordshire Regiment (Prince of Wales's) 1921. Part of The Staffordshire Regiment (The Prince of Wales's) 1959. Part of *The Mercian Regiment 2009.*

EAST INDIA COMPANY EUROPEAN REGIMENTS
(From *The Sikh Wars* by H.C.B. Cook – updated)

1st Bengal European Light Infantry	1st Bengal European Fusiliers 1846. 1st Bengal Fusiliers 1858. 101st (Royal Bengal) Fusiliers 1861. 1st Battalion Royal Munster Fusiliers 1881. Disbanded 1922.
2nd Bengal European Regiment	2nd Bengal European Fusiliers 1850. 2nd Bengal Fusiliers 1858. 104th (Bengal) Fusiliers 1861. 2nd Battalion Royal Munster Fusiliers 1881. Disbanded 1922.
1st Bombay European Fusiliers	1st Bombay Fusiliers 1858. 103rd (Royal Bombay) Fusiliers 1861. 2nd Battalion Royal Dublin Fusiliers 1881. Disbanded 1922.

EAST INDIA COMPANY INDIAN REGIMENTS
(From *The Sikh Wars* by H.C.B. Cook – updated)

The Governor General's Bodyguard	To India as The President's Bodyguard in 1947. *The President's Bodyguard 2009.*
1st Bengal Light Cavalry	Mutinied at Lucknow 1857.
3rd Bengal Light Cavalry	Mutinied at Meerut 1857.
4th Bengal Light Cavalry	Disarmed in 1857.
5th Bengal Light Cavalry	Disarmed at Peshawar in 1857. Later disbanded.
6th Bengal Light Cavalry	Mutinied at Jullundur 1857.
7th Bengal Light Cavalry	Mutinied at Lucknow 1857.
8th Bengal Light Cavalry	Disarmed at Meean Mir 1857.
11th Bengal Light Cavalry	2nd Bengal Light Cavalry 1850. Mutinied at Cawnpore 1857.
2nd Bengal Irregular Cavalry	2nd Bengal Cavalry 1861. 2nd Bengal Lancers 1890. 2nd Lancers (Gardener's Horse) 1903. Amalgamated with the 4th Cavalry 1922, retaining its title The 2nd Royal Lancers (Gardener's Horse) 1935. To India 1947. *2nd Lancers (Gardener's Horse) 2009.*
3rd Bengal Irregular Cavalry	3rd Bengal Cavalry 1861. 3rd Bengal Cavalry (Skinner's Horse) 1901. 3rd Skinner's Horse 1903. Amalgamated with the 1st Duke of York's Own Lancers (Skinner's Horse) as the 1st Duke of York's Own Skinner's Horse 1922. Skinner's Horse (1st Duke of York's Own Cavalry) 1927. To India 1947. *1st Horse (Skinner's Horse) 2009.*
7th Bengal Irregular Cavalry	5th Bengal Cavalry 1861. 5th Cavalry 1901. Amalgamated with the 8th Cavalry as the 3rd Cavalry 1922. To India 1947. *3rd Cavalry 2009.*
8th Bengal Irregular Cavalry	Mostly mutinied at Bareilly 1857, but loyal part became the 6th Bengal Cavalry in 1861. 6th (Prince of Wales's) Bengal Cavalry in 1863. 6th Prince

	of Wales's Cavalry 1903. 6th King Edward's Own Cavalry 1906. Amalgamated with the 7th Hariana Lancers to form the 18th King Edward's Own Cavalry 1922. To India 1947. *18th Cavalry 2009.*
9th Bengal Irregular Cavalry	Partly mutinied in 1857 and the remainder disbanded in 1861.
11th Bengal Irregular Cavalry	Disarmed at Behrampore and then mutinied in 1857.
12th Bengal Irregular Cavalry	Partly mutinied at Segowli. Loyal portion disbanded in 1861.
13th Bengal Irregular Cavalry	Mutinied at Benares in 1857.
14th Bengal Irregular Cavalry	Mutinied at Nowgong and Jhansi in 1857.
15th Bengal Irregular Cavalry	Mutinied at Sultanpore in 1857.
16th Bengal Irregular Cavalry	Disarmed at Rawalpindi in 1857.
17th Bengal Irregular Cavalry	7th Bengal Cavalry 1861. 7th Bengal Lancers 1900. 7th Lancers 1903. 7th Hariana Lancers 1904. Amalgamated with 6th King Edward's Own Cavalry to form the 18th King George's Own Lancers in 1906. Further amalgamated with The 19th Lancers (Fanes Horse) 1922. To Pakistan 1947. *19th Lancers (Fanes Horse) 2009.*
Corps of Guides (Cavalry)	Queen's Own Corps of Guides, Punjab Frontier Force 1875. Queen's Own Corps of Guides (Lumsden's) 1901. Queen Victoria's Own Corps of Guides, Frontier Force (Lumsden's) 1911. 10th Queen Victoria's Own Corps of Guides Cavalry, Frontier Force 1922. To Pakistan 1947. *10th (Guides) Cavalry (Frontier Force) 2009.*
1st Bombay Light Cavalry	1st Bombay Lancers 1880. 1st (Duke of Connaught's Own) Bombay Lancers 1890. 31st Duke of Connaught's Own Lancers 1903. Amalgamated with the 32nd Lancers to form the 13th Duke of Connaught's Own Lancers 1922. 13th Duke of Connaught's Own Bombay Lancers 1923. 13th Duke of Connaught's Own Lancers 1927. To Pakistan 1947. *6th Lancers (Watson's Horse) 2009.*
1st Scinde Irregular Horse	1st Scinde Horse 1860. 5th Bombay Cavalry (Jacob-Ka-Risalla) 1885. 5th Bombay Cavalry (Scinde Horse) 1888. 35th Scinde Horse 1903. Amalgamated with The 36th Jacob's Horse to form the 14th Prince of Wales's Own Scinde Horse 1922. Scinde Horse (14th Prince of Wales's Own Cavalry) 1927. To India 1947. Part of *14th Horse (Scinde Horse) 2009.*
2nd Scinde Irregular Horse	2nd Scinde Horse 1860. 6th Bombay Cavalry (Jacob-Ka-Risalla) 1885. 6th Bombay Cavalry (Jacob's Horse) 1888. 36th Jacob's Horse 1903. Amalgamated with the 35th Scinde Horse (see above) 1922. Part of *14th Horse (Scinde Horse) 2009.*
Bengal Sappers and Minders	Bengal Sappers and Pioneers 1847. Bengal Sappers

	and Miners 1851. A number of companies mutinied in 1857. 1st Sappers and Miners 1903. 1st Prince of Wales's Own Sappers and Miners 1906. 1st King George's Own Sappers and Miners 1923. King George Vs Own Bengal Sappers and Miners 1927. Mainly to Pakistan in 1947.
Bombay Sappers and Miners	3rd Sappers and Miners 1903. 3rd Royal Bombay Sappers and Miners 1921. Royal Bombay Sappers and Miners 1923. To India 1947.
1st Bengal Native Infantry	Mutinied at Cawnpore in 1857.
2nd Bengal Native Infantry	Disarmed at Barrackpore in 1857.
3rd Bengal Native Infantry	Mutinied at Phillour in 1857, but loyal portion formed part of the Loyal Purbeah Regiment.
4th Bengal Native Infantry	Disarmed in 1857 and disbanded in 1861.
7th Bengal Native Infantry	Mutinied at Dinapore in 1857.
8th Bengal Native Infantry	Mutinied at Dinapore in 1857.
12th Bengal Native Infantry	Mutinied at Jhansi and Nowgong in 1857.
13th Bengal Native Infantry	Mutinied at Lucknow in 1857 but loyal portion helped form the Regiment of Lucknow.
14th Bengal Native Infantry	Mutinied at Jhansi in 1857.
15th Bengal Native Infantry	Mutinied at Nasirabad in 1857.
16th Bengal Native Infantry	Disarmed at Meean Meer in 1857.
18th Bengal Native Infantry	Mutinied at Bareilly in 1857.
20th Bengal Native Infantry	Mutinied at Meerut in 1857.
22nd Bengal Native Infantry	Mutinied at Fyzabad in 1857.
24th Bengal Native Infantry	Disarmed at Peshawar in 1857.
25th Bengal Native Infantry	Disbanded in 1857.
26th Bengal Native Infantry	Mutinied at Meean Meer in 1857.
29th Bengal Native Infantry	Mutinied at Moradabad in 1857.
30th Bengal Native Infantry	Mutinied at Nasirabad in 1857.
31st Bengal Native Infantry	31st Bengal Light Infantry 1856. Greater part remained loyal in 1857. 2nd Bengal Light Infantry 1861. 2nd (Queen's Own) Bengal Native Light Infantry 1876.* 2nd (Queen's Own) Regiment Rajput Bengal Light Infantry 1897. 2nd (Queen's Own) Rajput Light Infantry 1901. 2nd Queen Victoria's Own Rajput Light Infantry 1911. 1st (Queen Victoria's Own Light Infantry) Battalion. 7th Rajput Regiment 1922. To India 1947. *4th Battalion The Brigade of Guards 2009.*
33rd Bengal Native Infantry	Disarmed in 1857. 4th Bengal Native Infantry 1861. 4th (Prince Albert Victor's) Bengal Infantry 1890. 4th (Prince Albert Victor's) Rajput Infantry 1901. 4th Prince Albert Victor's Rajputs 1903. 2nd Battalion (Prince Albert Victor's) 7th Rajput Regiment 1922. To India 1947. *2nd Battalion The Rajput Regiment 2009.*

36th Bengal Native Infantry	Mutinied at Jullundur in 1857. Loyal portion went to form the Loyal Purbeah Regiment.
37th Bengal Native Infantry	Mutinied at Benares in 1857.
41st Bengal Native Infantry	Mutinied at Sitapur in 1857.
42nd Bengal Native Light Infantry	Partly mutinied at Saugor in 1857. 5th Bengal Native Light infantry 1861. 5th Light Infantry 1903. Disbanded in 1922.
43rd Bengal Native Light Infantry	Disarmed at Barrackpore in 1857. 6th Bengal Native Light Infantry 1861. 6th Jat Regiment, Bengal Light Infantry 1897. 6th Jat Light Infantry 1903. 6th Royal Jat Light Infantry 1922. 1st Royal Battalion (Light Infantry) 9th Jat Regiment 1922. To India 1947. *2nd Battalion The Mechanized Regiment (1 Jat) 2009.*
45th Bengal Native Infantry	Mutinied at Ferozepore in 1857.
46th Bengal Native Infantry	Mutinied at Sialkot in 1857.
47th Bengal Native Infantry	Partially disarmed at Mirzapur but remained loyal 1857. 7th Bengal Native Infantry 1861. 7th (Duke of Connaught's Own) Bengal Native Infantry 1883. 7th Rajput (Duke of Connaught's Own) Regiment of Bengal Infantry 1897. 7th Duke of Connaught's Own Rajputs 1903. 3rd Battalion (Duke of Connaught's Own) 7th Rajput Regiment 1922. To India 1947. *3rd Battalion The Rajput Regiment 2009.*
48th Bengal Native Infantry	Mutinied at Lucknow in 1857 but loyal portion became part of The Regiment of Lucknow.
49th Bengal Native Infantry	Disarmed at Meean Mir in 1857 and later disbanded.
50th Bengal Native Infantry	Mutinied at Nagode in 1857.
51st Bengal Native Infantry	Disarmed at Peshawar in 1857.
52nd Bengal Native Infantry	Mutinied at Jubbulpore in 1857.
53rd Bengal Native Infantry	Mutinied at Cawnpore in 1857.
54th Bengal Native Infantry	Mutinied at Delhi in 1857.
56th Bengal Native Infantry	Mutinied at Cawnpore in 1857.
59th Bengal Native Infantry	Disarmed at Amritsar in 1857. 8th Bengal Native Infantry 1861. 8th Rajput Regiment Bengal Infantry 1897. 8th Rajput Infantry 1901. 8th Rajputs 1903. 4th Battalion 7th Rajput Regiment 1922. To India 1947. *4th Battalion The Rajput Regiment 2009.*
63rd Bengal Native Infantry	Disarmed at Behrampore in 1857. 9th Bengal Native Infantry 1861. 9th (Gurkha Rifles) Regiment Bengal Infantry 1894. 9th Gurkha Rifles 1901. To India 1947. *1st Battalion The 9th Gurkha Rifles 2009.*
68th Bengal Native Infantry	Mutinied at Bareilly in 1857.
69th Bengal Native Infantry	Disarmed at Multan in 1857.
70th Bengal Native Infantry	Disarmed at Barrackpore in 1857. 12th then 11th Bengal Native Infantry 1861. 11th (Rajput) Regiment Bengal Infantry 1897. 11th Rajput

	Infantry 1901. 11th Rajputs 1903. 5th Battalion 7th Rajput Regiment 1922. To India 1947. *5th Battalion The Rajput Regiment 2009.*
71st Bengal Native Infantry	Mutinied at Lucknow in 1857 but loyal portion became part of the Regiment of Lucknow.
72nd Bengal Native Infantry	Mutinied at Neemuch in 1857.
73rd Bengal Native Infantry	Two companies mutinied at Dacca in 1857, but rest remained loyal. Ultimately disbanded.
Infantry of Shekhawati Brigade	Shekhawati Battalion 1847. 14th then 13th Bengal Native Infantry 1861. 13th (Shekhawati Regiment) Bengal Native Infantry 1884.* 13th Rajputs (The Shekhawati Regiment) 1903. 10th (Shekhawati) Battalion, 6th Rajputana Rifles 1922. To India 1947. *6th Battalion The Rajputana Rifles (Shekhawati) 2009.*
The Nasiri Battalion	66th or Gurkha Regiment of Bengal Native Infantry 1850. 66th or Gurkha Light Infantry 1858. 11th Bengal Native Infantry and then 1st Gurkha Regiment of Light Infantry 1861. 1st Gurkha (Rifle) Regiment 1890. 1st Gurkha Rifles 1901. 1st Gurkha Rifles (The Malaun Regiment) 1906. 1st King George's Own Gurkha Rifles (The Malaun Regiment) 1910. 1st King George Vs Own Gurkha Rifles (The Malaun Regiment) 1937. To India 1847. *1st Battalion The 1st Gurkha Rifles (Malaun) 2009.*
The Sirmoor Battalion	The Sirmoor Rifle Regiment 1858. 17th Bengal Native Infantry and then 2nd Gurkha Regiment 1861. 2nd Gurkha (Sirmoor Rifles) Regiment 1864. 2nd (Prince of Wales's Own) Gurkha Regiment (The Sirmoor Rifles) 1876. 2nd King Edward's Own Gurkha Rifles (The Sirmoor Regiment) 1906. 2nd King Edward's VII Own Gurkha Rifles (The Sirmoor Rifles) 1927. To the United Kingdom. *2nd King Edward VII's Own Gurkha Rifles (The Sirmoor Rifles) 2009.*
Corps of Guides (Infantry)	Corps of Guides, Punjab Irregular Force 1851. Corps of Guides, Punjab Frontier Force 1865. The Queen's Own Corps of Guides, Punjab Frontier Force, 1876. Queen's Own Corps of Guides (Lumsden's) 1904. Queen Victoria's Own Corps of Guides (Frontier Force) (Lumsden's) Infantry 1911. 5th Battalion (Queen Victoria's Own Corps of Guides) 12th Frontier Force Regiment 1922. 5th Battalion 12th Frontier Force Regiment (Queen Victoria's Own Corps of Guides) (Lumsden's) 1927. To Pakistan 1947. *2nd Battalion The Frontier Force Regiment (Lumsden's Guides) 2009.*
1st Sikh Local Infantry	1st Sikh Infantry, Punjab Irregular Force 1857. 1st Sikh Infantry, Punjab Frontier Force 1865. 1st Sikh

	Infantry 1901. 51st Sikhs (Frontier Force) 1903. 51st (Prince of Wales's Own) Sikhs (Frontier Force) 1921. 1st Battalion (Prince of Wales's Own) (Sikhs). 12th Frontier Force Regiment 1922. To Pakistan 1947. *3rd Battalion The Frontier Force Regiment 2009.*
2nd or Hill Regiment Sikh Local Infantry	2nd, or Hill, Sikh Infantry, Punjab Irregular Force 1857. 2nd, or Hill, Sikh Infantry Punjab Irregular Force 1865. 2nd, or Hill, Sikh Infantry 1901. 52nd Sikh (Frontier Force) 1903. 2nd Battalion (Sikhs) 12th Frontier Force Regiment 1922. To Pakistan 1947. *4th Battalion The Frontier Force Regiment 2009.*
3rd Bombay Native Infantry	3rd Bombay Native Light Infantry 1871. 103rd Mahratta Light Infantry 1903. 1st Battalion The 5th Mahratta Light Infantry 1922. To India 1947. *1st Battalion The Mahratta Light Infantry (Jangi Paltan) 2009.*
4th Bombay Native Infantry	4th Regiment, 1st Battalion Rifle Regiment, of Bombay Infantry 1889. 4th Bombay Rifles 1901. 104th Wellesley's Rifles 1903. 1st Battalion (Wellesley's) 6th Rajputana Rifles 1922. To India 1947. *3rd Battalion The Brigade of Guards 2009.*
9th Bombay Native Infantry	109th Infantry 1903. 4th Battalion 4th Bombay Grenadiers 1922. Disbanded in 1930.
19th Bombay Native Infantry	119th Infantry (The Mooltan Regiment) 1903. 2nd Battalion (Mooltan Regiment), 9th Jat Regiment 1922. To India 1947. *2nd Battalion The Jat Regiment 2009.*
Marine Battalion Bombay Native Infantry	21st Bombay Native Infantry (The Marine Battalion) 1861. 21st Bombay Pioneers and then 121st Pioneers 1903. 10th Battalion 2nd Bombay Pioneers (Marine Battalion) 1922. 1st (Marine) Battalion, Corps of Bombay Pioneers 1929. Disbanded in 1933.

* The word 'native' was omitted from regimental titles from 1885.

Note 1: The Bengal and Bombay Artillery ceased to exist after the Indian Mutiny.

Note 2: The Regiment of Lucknow became the 20th and then 16th Bengal Native Infantry in 1861. 16th (The Lucknow Regiment) Bengal Native Infantry 1864. 16th (The Lucknow) Rajput Regiment, Bengal Infantry 1897. 16th (Lucknow) Rajput Infantry 1901. 16th Rajputs (The Lucknow Regiment) 1903. 10th Battalion (The Lucknow Regiment) 7th Rajput Regiment 1922. To India 1947.

Note 3: The Loyal Purbeah Regiment became the 21st and then 17th Bengal Native Infantry in 1861. 17th (Loyal Purbeah) Regiment Bengal Native Infantry 1864. 17th (The Loyal) Regiment Bengal Infantry 1898. 17th Mussulman Rajput Infantry (The Loyal Regiment) 1902. 17th The Loyal Regiment 1903. Disbanded 1922.

ANNEXURE XV

MEMORANDUM: BY MR CHARLES WOOD AND THE COUNCIL OF INDIA, 21 MARCH 1860

AT the close of the second Sikh war it was determined to annex the Punjaub to British territory, and to put an end to the separate Khalsa Government of the Sikhs. The form in which the arrangement for this purpose was recorded, was a paper of terms granted and accepted at Lahore in 1849, and notified by the Governor General.

The provisions in favour of the Maharajah are contained in the fourth and fifth Articles of those terms (the first three being all declaratory of the surrender) as follows:-

'4. His Highness Duleep Singh shall receive from the Honorable East India Company, for the support of himself, his relatives, and the servants of the State, a pension not less than four and not exceeding five lakhs of the Company's rupees per annum.

'5. His Highness shall be treated with respect and honour. He shall retain the title of Maharajah Duleep Singh Bahadoor, and he shall continue to receive during his life such portion of the above-named pension as may be allowed to himself personally, provided he shall remain obedient to the British Government, and reside at such place as the Governor General of India may select.'

The terms were signed by the young Maharajah, and by six of the principal Sirdars and people of his Court.

The first question is, What are the Maharajah's rights under the two Articles, and what are the obligations which the Government of India came under towards him personally.

It is clear that being a minor, required to live where the Governor General might determine, he was not intended to be the recipient of the 'pension not less than four and not exceeding five lakhs of Company's rupees per annum,' which was to form the provision for 'himself, his relatives, and the servants of the State.'

This Article, though using his name as the head of the State at the time that the arrangement was made, must be construed with the following Article, which provides that 'he shall continue to receive during his life such portion of the above-named pension as may be allotted to himself personally,' under the condition of good behaviour.

The personal claim of the Maharajah is here limited to the receipt for his life of his personal stipend, and the amount to be allotted to him was left entirely to the Government of India.

During the first year of the Maharajah's minority, the annual sum allotted for his personal allowance was 120,000 rupees per annum. It was afterwards increased to 250,000 rupees per annum, the increase taking effect from the date of his attaining the age of eighteen.

The Indian government recommended that, on his attaining the age of twenty-one, £25,000 should be allotted to the other recipients of allowances under the fourth Article, will exceed the amount of four lakhs.

Some of these allowances will necessarily fall in sooner or later, and the amount of allowances will again be reduced below four lakhs.

A question may arise as to the obligations under the terms of 1849, as to the disposal of any such annual sums so falling in.

The Maharajah seems to expect that he may be considered entitled to benefit from such lapses. But this claim has been distinctly negatived by Lord Dalhousie,* who cannot be mistaken as to the meaning of the terms which he granted, and the provision that the Maharajah shall only receive what may be specifically allotted to him is so clear in the fifth Article that he can evidently have no right to any increase of his stipend consequently.

It is evident that the portion of the pension allotted to others can only be for their respective lives.

The provision in the Maharajah's favour is only for life. This is expressly provided for.

It cannot be supposed that the allowance to be assigned to the other persons were for any other term than that assigned for the Maharajah's, namely, for their respective lives.

The only other possible construction of the terms would be that the allowances of the other parties were to be for the period of the Maharajah's life.

But it would be an absurdity to suppose because Article 4 uses the Maharajah's name as the recipient of the entire provision, that the pensions assigned to other members of the family and State servants would at once have ceased if the Maharajah had happened to die during his minority. All of them, like the personal stipend of the Maharajah, must be regarded as assured life stipends, but not extending beyond life.

The amount, therefore, of any stipends so falling in hereafter must, according to the terms of 1849, fall the British government.

There is no doubt, however, but that up to the present time the difference between the sums allotted to the Maharajah, his relatives and the servants of the State, and the amount of four lakhs, which was the. smallest sum which it was provided that the British government should apply to the purposes mentioned, has not been so expended.

What the amount of the accumulation is we have no means of ascertaining in England; but it is understood that there may be a balance of between £150,000 and £200,000.

The Maharajah supposes that he is entitled to claim this as payable to himself personally; first because the fourth Article of the terms of 1849 uses his name as recipient of the whole four lakhs, and therefore that, whatever has not been paid to other recipients, ought to be paid to him;

and secondly, because he alleges that the balance is composed mainly, if not entirely, of short payments to himself of what he considers to have been due to him during his minority.

The simple answer to this claim is afforded by the fifth Article, which specifically provides that he is only to receive the 'portion of the above-named pension' that might be allotted 'to himself personally,' and the Government of India might allot to him whatever sum it thought proper, as it might in like manner to the other persons referred to in the fourth Article.

Any part of the £40,000 per annum, which has not been allotted and has accumulated in the treasury of the British government, is at their disposal, but they are bound to apply it for the purposes stated in the terms of 1849.

It is a fair question, however, what is the best method of disposing of any balance that the British government has now in its hands, and which it is under obligation to spend for the benefit of these parties; and it would certainly seem that the most appropriate disposition will be to make a provision for the families of the life stipeudiaries.

It is to be observed that it is the practice in India in dealing with political stipendiaries, to leave the provision for the family to be settled after the stipendiary's decease, and not to place it in the hands of the annuitant.

The Maharajah has felt the precarious position in which any family which he might leave would be placed in this respect, and has asked us to give him security on this point.

The Committee of the Council proposed a scheme on this especial point, namely, that a sum should be capitalized, sufficient to produce an annual sum of £10,000 per annum as a trust fund, for the benefit of his family. The case will be referred to the Governor General of India desiring him to ascertain what the real balance of unappropriated 'pension' payable under the fourth Article of the terms of 1849 now is, and also to determine the proportion of that balance which may fairly be assigned to the Maharaja. This is strictly conformable with those terms.

The Council of India are of opinion that the proposal to capitalize the proportion of the stipend of £25,000 per annum – i.e., £10,000 per annum as a trust provision for his family – is the most beneficial arrangement for the Maharajah. They will, however, willingly accede to whichever of these arrangements he may prefer.

MINUTE OF LORD DALHOUSIE ON QUITTING OFFICE IN 1856.
(Referred to in the above-written Memorandum.)*

When the Maharajah quitted India, the object which the Superintendent had in view was to obtain for His Highness a grant of land in the Eastern Dhoon, near Deyrali, with the expectation, I presume, that, the Maharajah would live at Mussoorie during the hot season, as he had been in the habit of doing, and would occupy himself, and interest himself, in the cultivation and improvement of the estate which was to be granted to him. The Superintendent appeared to be under the impression that the Maharajah himself very strongly desired the settlement of his future position. It seemed to me to be very unlikely that a boy of his years would have a strong feeling of any kind on such a subject, and quite certain that he could not as yet know his own mind.

In correspondence with Dr Login since the Maharajah has resided in England, I have learned that upon being questioned further upon the subject, His Highness did not seem to desire an estate at all, but preferred a money stipend, and spoke as if he were under the impression that the four lac which were mentioned in the paper of terms which were granted on the annexation of the Punjab would all ultimately lapse to him. The view which was taken by His Highness of this subject was entirely erroneous. The terms granted did not secure to the Maharajah four lacs, out of which His Highness was to grant pensions to relatives and followers, which on the death of the recipients were to revert to the Maharajah. The terms simply set apart four lacs of rupees at the time of the annexation, as provision for the Maharajah, for the members of his family, and for the servants of the State.

SHUKARCHAKIAS

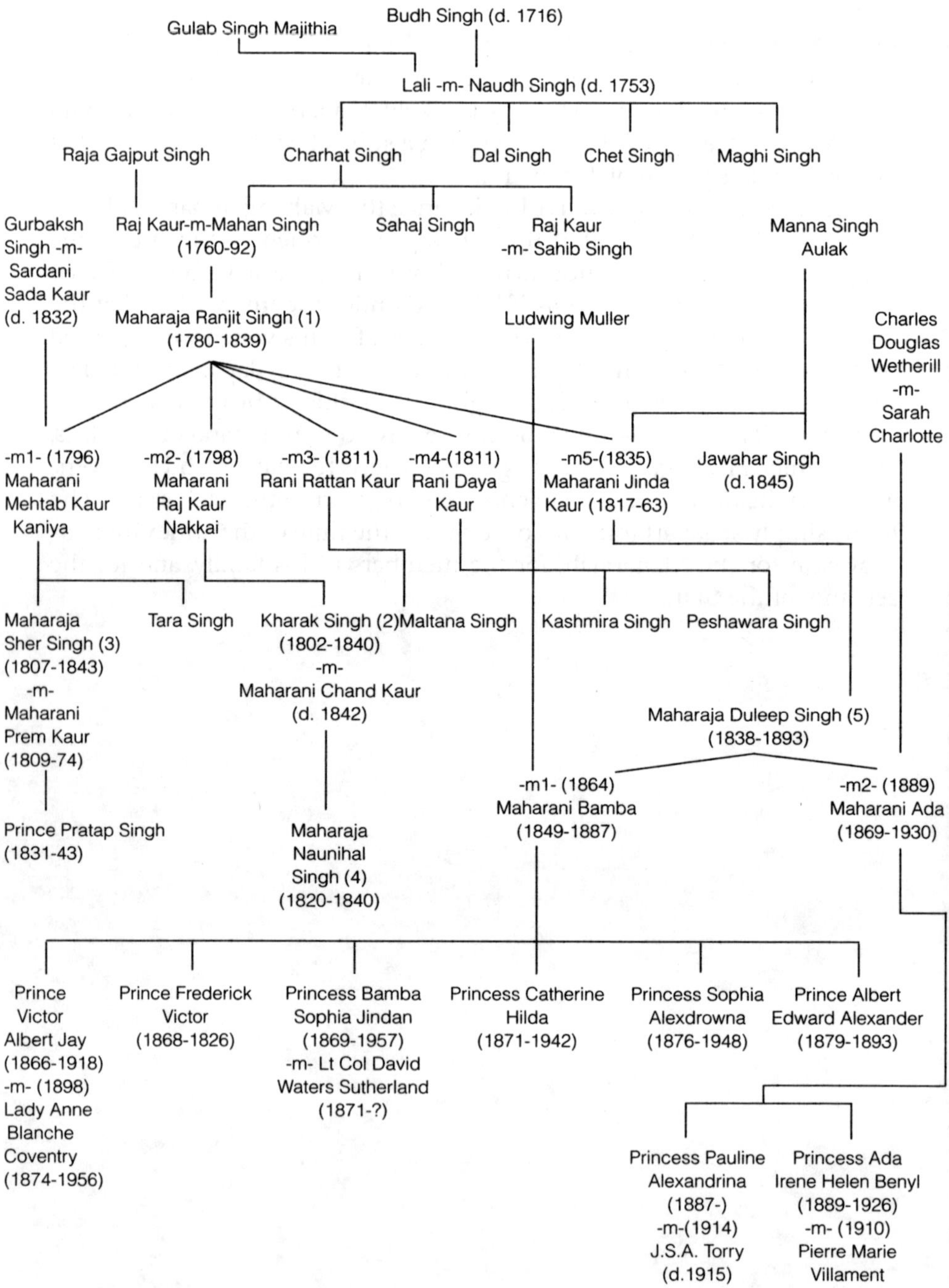

NALWA

- Hardas Singh (d. 1762)
  - Gurdayal Singh (d. 1798)
    - **General Hari Singh** (d. 1837)
      - Sardar Gurdit Singh (d. 1882)
      - Sardar Jawahir Singh (d. 1877)
      - Sardar Punjab Singh (d. 1854)
      - Sardar Arjun Singh (d. 1848)
        - Sardar Icchhra Singh (d. 1908)
          - Sardar Bahadur Nabayab Singh Honorary Magistrate (b. 1857)
            - Kartar Singh (d. 1896)
            - Mul Singh (d. 1897)
            - Balwant Singh PCS (b. 1894)
              - Kuldip Singh (b. 1922)
              - Amarjit Singh (b. 1926)
            - Iqbal Singh Capt., IMS
            - Sant Singh
            - Bakshish Singh
            - Kalwant Singh (b. 1910)
            - Inder Singh (b. 1913)
        - Sampuran Singh (d. 1874)
          - Sardar Kartar Singh (d. 1868)

JIND

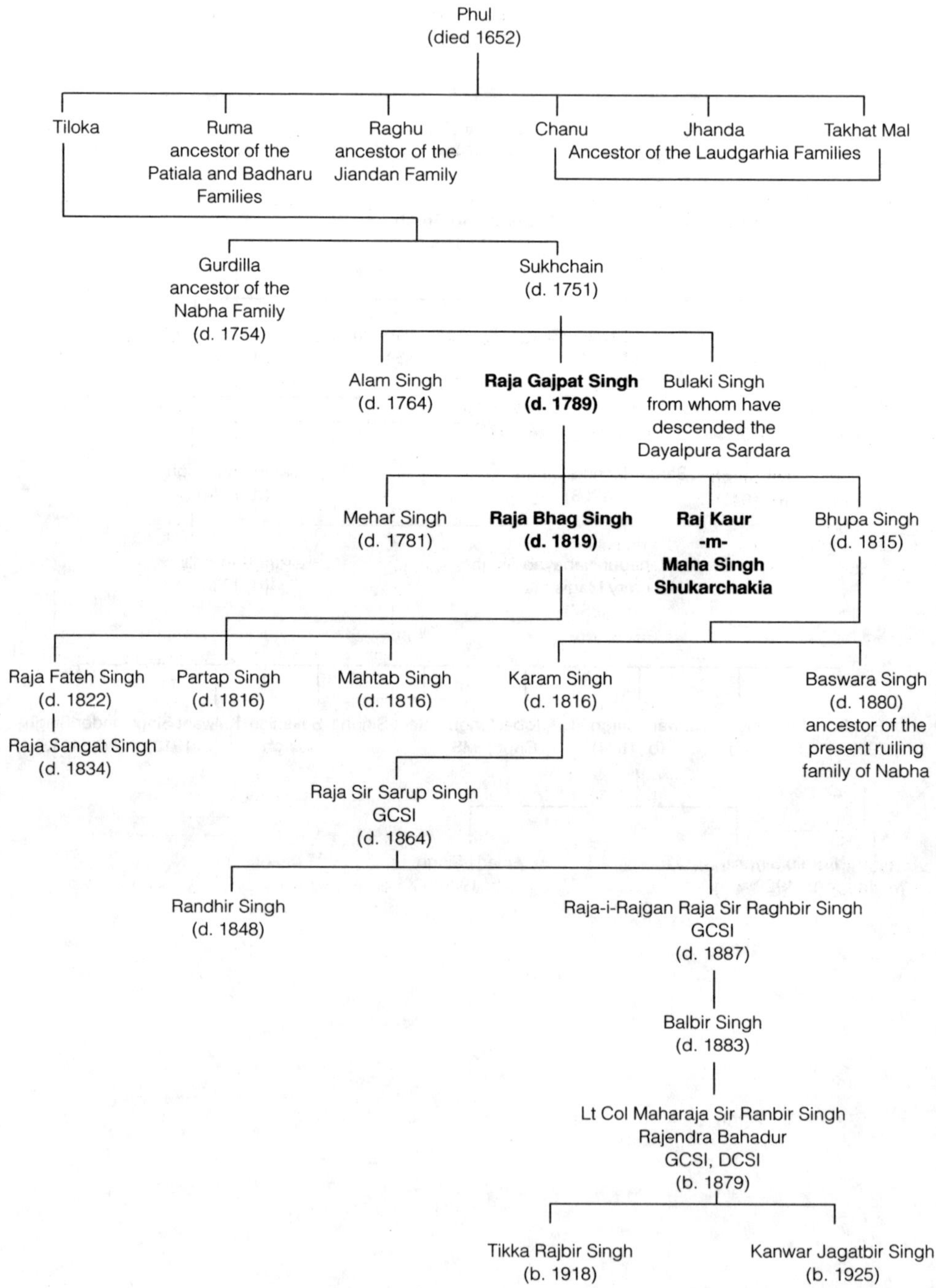
Phul
(died 1652)
Tiloka
Ruma
ancestor of the
Patiala and Badharu
Families
Raghu
ancestor of the
Jiandan Family
Chanu
Jhanda
Takhat Mal
Ancestor of the Laudgarhia Families
Gurdilla
ancestor of the
Nabha Family
(d. 1754)
Sukhchain
(d. 1751)
Alam Singh
(d. 1764)
Raja Gajpat Singh
(d. 1789)
Bulaki Singh
from whom have
descended the
Dayalpura Sardara
Mehar Singh
(d. 1781)
Raja Bhag Singh
(d. 1819)
Raj Kaur
-m-
Maha Singh
Shukarchakia
Bhupa Singh
(d. 1815)
Raja Fateh Singh
(d. 1822)
Raja Sangat Singh
(d. 1834)
Partap Singh
(d. 1816)
Mahtab Singh
(d. 1816)
Karam Singh
(d. 1816)
Baswara Singh
(d. 1880)
ancestor of the
present ruiling
family of Nabha
Raja Sir Sarup Singh
GCSI
(d. 1864)
Randhir Singh
(d. 1848)
Raja-i-Rajgan Raja Sir Raghbir Singh
GCSI
(d. 1887)
Balbir Singh
(d. 1883)
Lt Col Maharaja Sir Ranbir Singh
Rajendra Bahadur
GCSI, DCSI
(b. 1879)
Tikka Rajbir Singh
(b. 1918)
Kanwar Jagatbir Singh
(b. 1925)

SANDHANWALIA

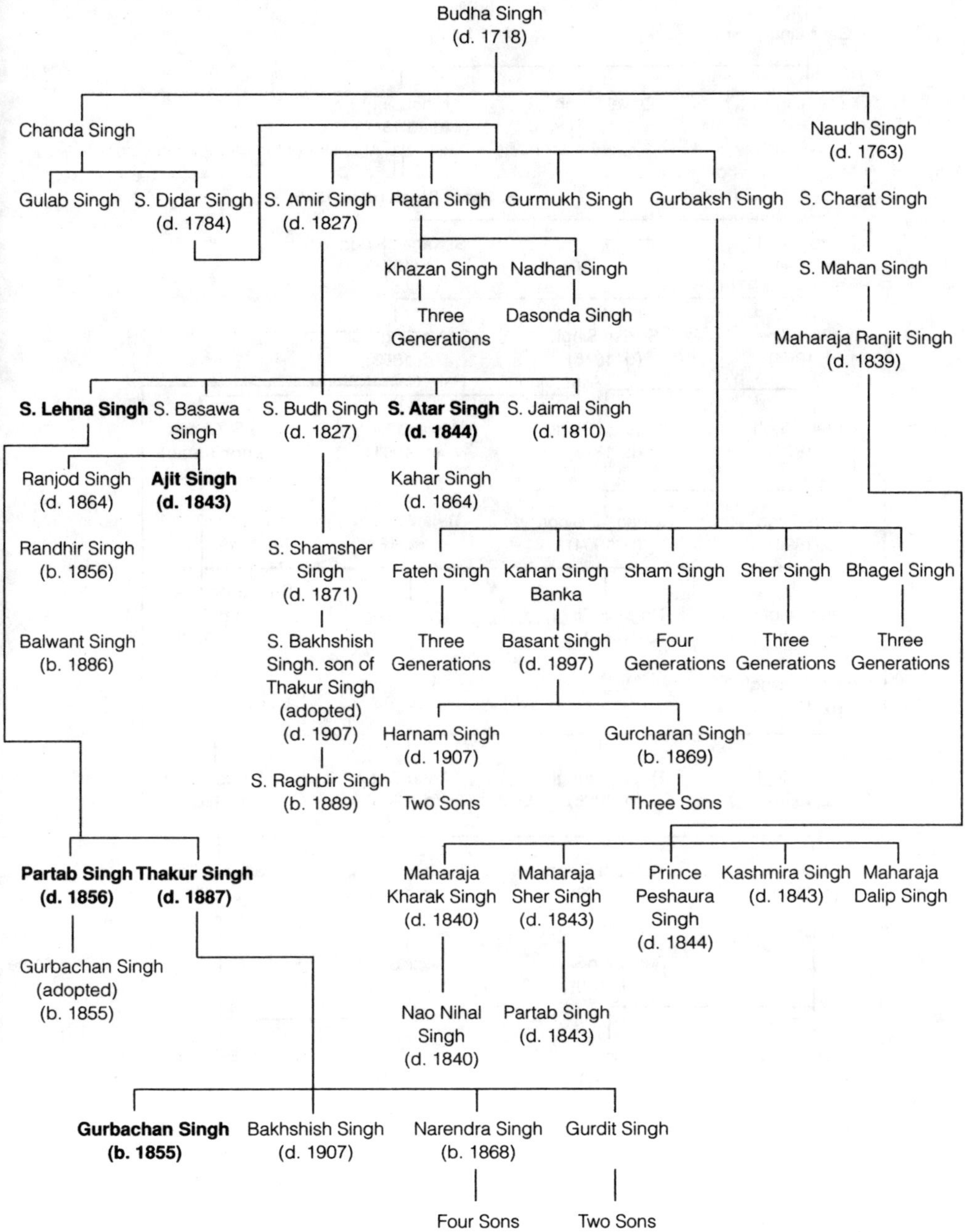

ATTARI

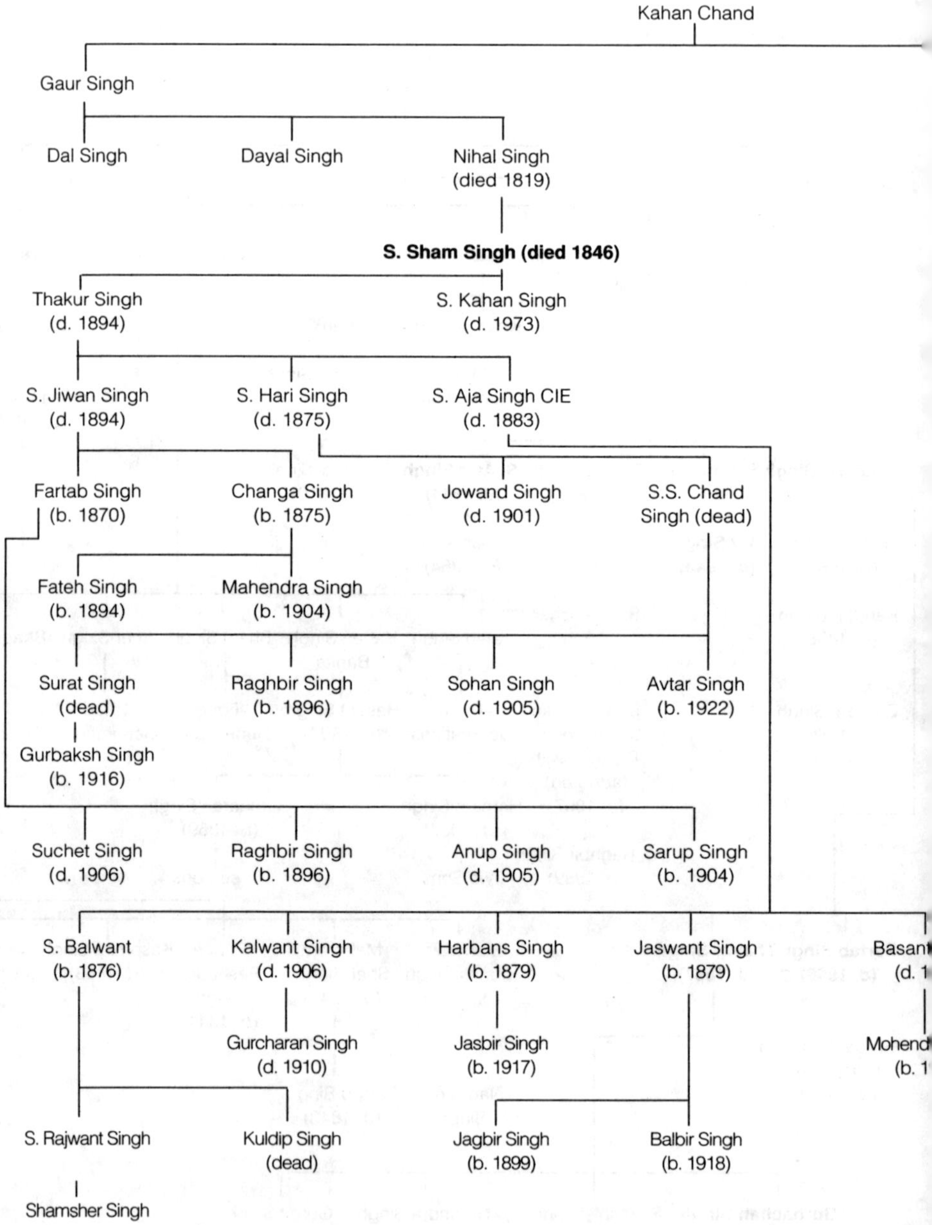
Kahan Chand
Gaur Singh
Dal Singh
Dayal Singh
Nihal Singh (died 1819)
S. Sham Singh (died 1846)
Thakur Singh (d. 1894)
S. Kahan Singh (d. 1973)
S. Jiwan Singh (d. 1894)
S. Hari Singh (d. 1875)
S. Aja Singh CIE (d. 1883)
Fartab Singh (b. 1870)
Changa Singh (b. 1875)
Jowand Singh (d. 1901)
S.S. Chand Singh (dead)
Fateh Singh (b. 1894)
Mahendra Singh (b. 1904)
Surat Singh (dead)
Raghbir Singh (b. 1896)
Sohan Singh (d. 1905)
Avtar Singh (b. 1922)
Gurbaksh Singh (b. 1916)
Suchet Singh (d. 1906)
Raghbir Singh (b. 1896)
Anup Singh (d. 1905)
Sarup Singh (b. 1904)
S. Balwant (b. 1876)
Kalwant Singh (d. 1906)
Harbans Singh (b. 1879)
Jaswant Singh (b. 1879)
Gurcharan Singh (d. 1910)
Jasbir Singh (b. 1917)
S. Rajwant Singh
Kuldip Singh (dead)
Jagbir Singh (b. 1899)
Balbir Singh (b. 1918)
Shamsher Singh

ATTARI

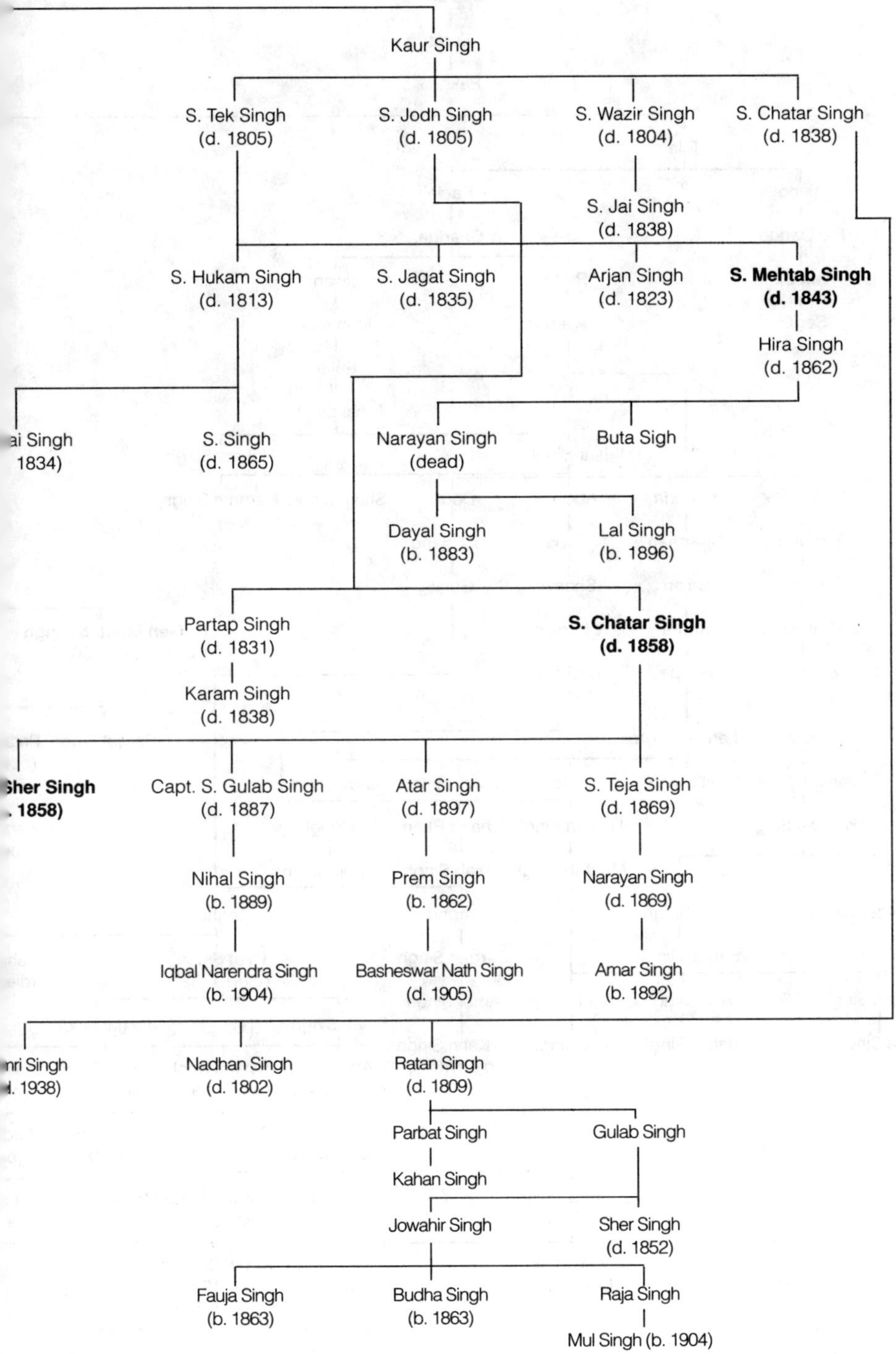

Kaur Singh
S. Tek Singh (d. 1805)
S. Jodh Singh (d. 1805)
S. Wazir Singh (d. 1804)
S. Chatar Singh (d. 1838)
S. Jai Singh (d. 1838)
S. Hukam Singh (d. 1813)
S. Jagat Singh (d. 1835)
Arjan Singh (d. 1823)
S. Mehtab Singh (d. 1843)
Hira Singh (d. 1862)
ai Singh
1834)
S. Singh (d. 1865)
Narayan Singh (dead)
Buta Sigh
Dayal Singh (b. 1883)
Lal Singh (b. 1896)
Partap Singh (d. 1831)
S. Chatar Singh (d. 1858)
Karam Singh (d. 1838)
Sher Singh
1858)
Capt. S. Gulab Singh (d. 1887)
Atar Singh (d. 1897)
S. Teja Singh (d. 1869)
Nihal Singh (b. 1889)
Prem Singh (b. 1862)
Narayan Singh (d. 1869)
Iqbal Narendra Singh (b. 1904)
Basheswar Nath Singh (d. 1905)
Amar Singh (b. 1892)
nri Singh
1938)
Nadhan Singh (d. 1802)
Ratan Singh (d. 1809)
Parbat Singh
Gulab Singh
Kahan Singh
Jowahir Singh
Sher Singh (d. 1852)
Fauja Singh (b. 1863)
Budha Singh (b. 1863)
Raja Singh
Mul Singh (b. 1904)

MAJITHIA

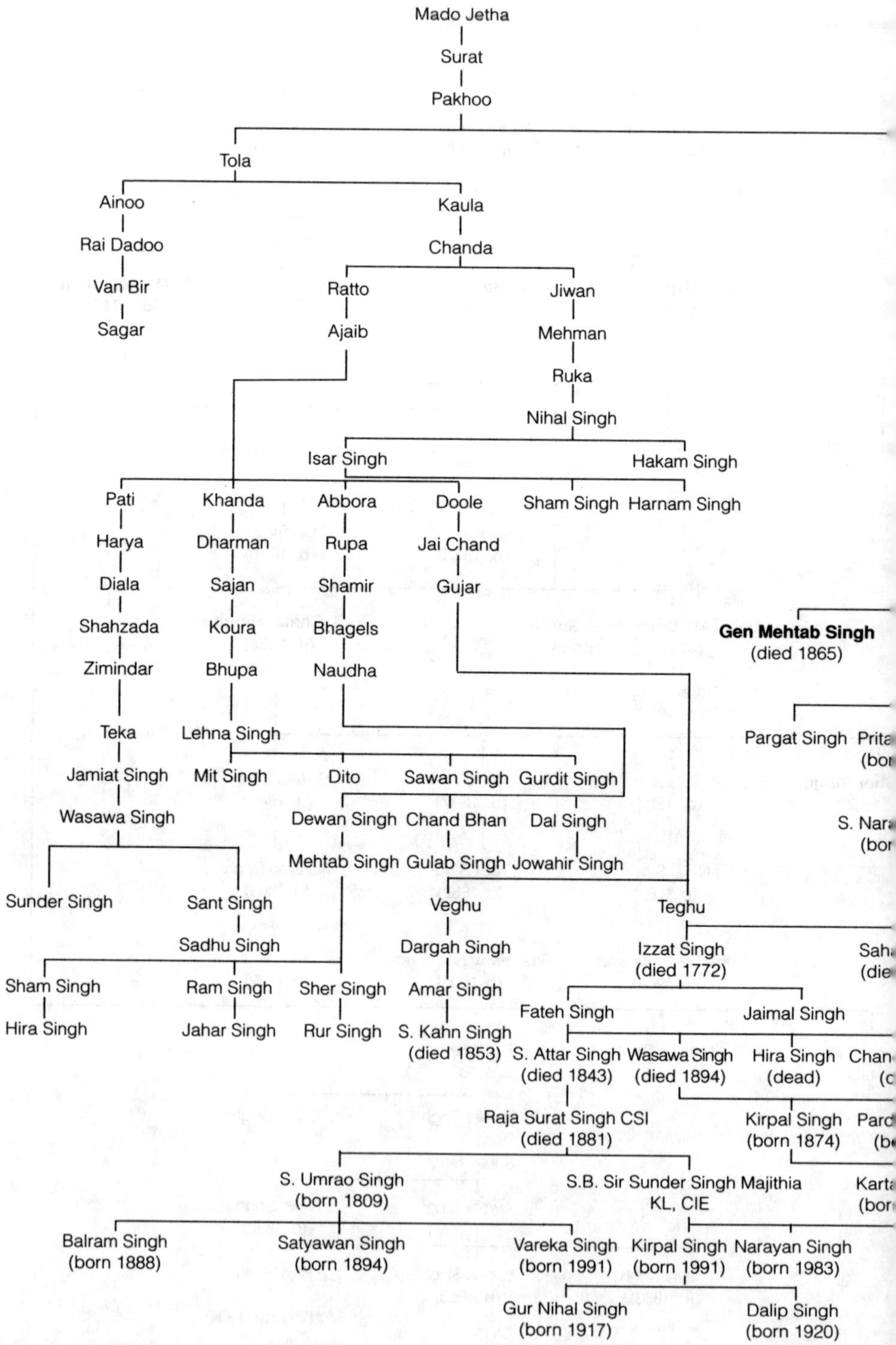
Mado Jetha
Surat
Pakhoo
Tola
Ainoo
Kaula
Rai Dadoo
Chanda
Van Bir
Ratto
Jiwan
Sagar
Ajaib
Mehman
Ruka
Nihal Singh
Isar Singh
Hakam Singh
Pati
Khanda
Abbora
Doole
Sham Singh
Harnam Singh
Harya
Dharman
Rupa
Jai Chand
Diala
Sajan
Shamir
Gujar
Shahzada
Koura
Bhagels
Gen Mehtab Singh
(died 1865)
Zimindar
Bhupa
Naudha
Teka
Lehna Singh
Pargat Singh
Prita
(bor
Jamiat Singh
Mit Singh
Dito
Sawan Singh
Gurdit Singh
Wasawa Singh
Dewan Singh
Chand Bhan
Dal Singh
S. Nara
(bor
Mehtab Singh
Gulab Singh
Jowahir Singh
Sunder Singh
Sant Singh
Veghu
Teghu
Sadhu Singh
Dargah Singh
Izzat Singh
(died 1772)
Saha
(die
Sham Singh
Ram Singh
Sher Singh
Amar Singh
Fateh Singh
Jaimal Singh
Hira Singh
Jahar Singh
Rur Singh
S. Kahn Singh
(died 1853)
S. Attar Singh
(died 1843)
Wasawa Singh
(died 1894)
Hira Singh
(dead)
Chan
(c
Raja Surat Singh CSI
(died 1881)
Kirpal Singh
(born 1874)
Pard
(b
S. Umrao Singh
(born 1809)
S.B. Sir Sunder Singh Majithia
KL, CIE
Karta
(bor
Balram Singh
(born 1888)
Satyawan Singh
(born 1894)
Vareka Singh
(born 1991)
Kirpal Singh
(born 1991)
Narayan Singh
(born 1983)
Gur Nihal Singh
(born 1917)
Dalip Singh
(born 1920)

MAJITHIA

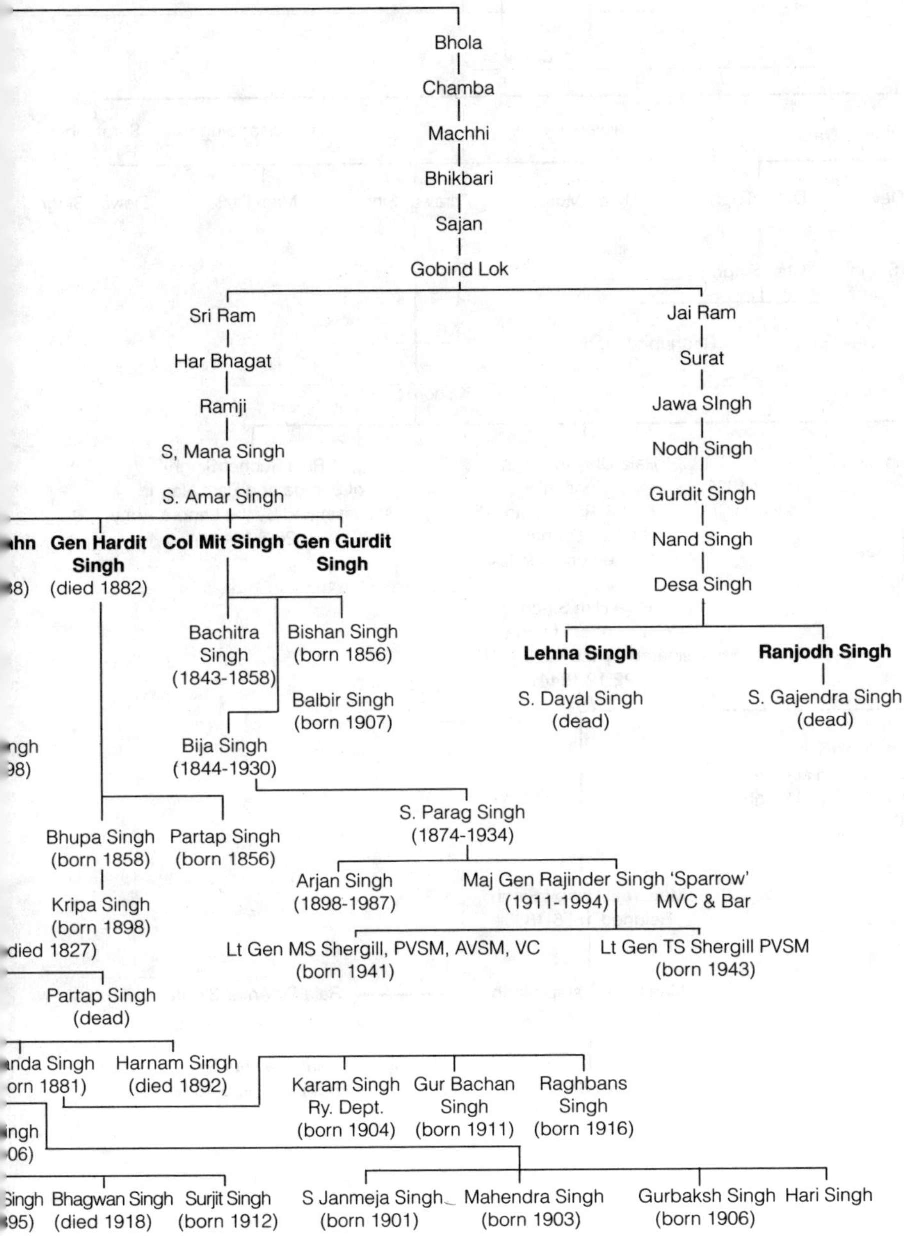

From *Chiefs & Families of note in Punjab* by Griffin & Massey 1930 edition

THE JAMMU FAMILY

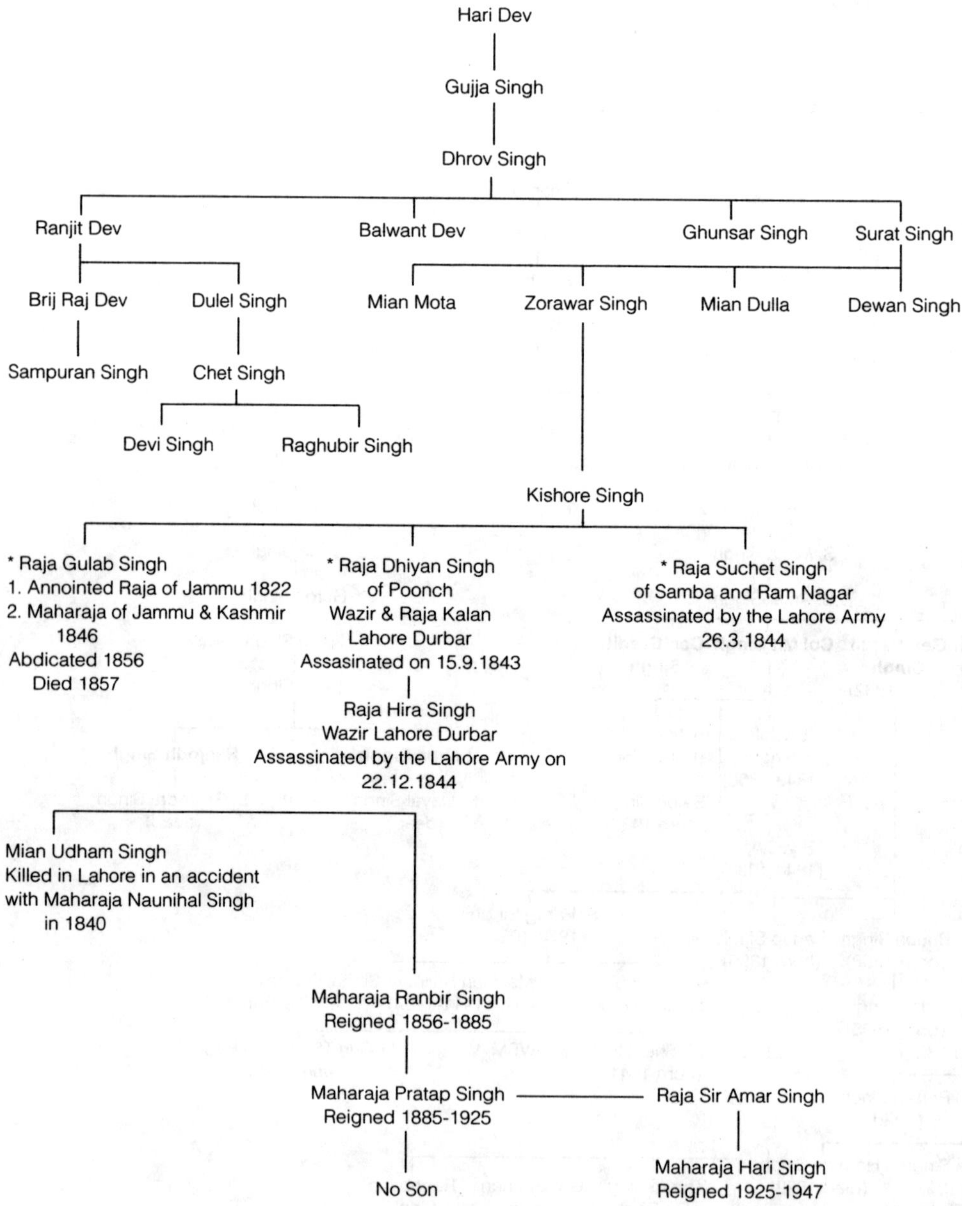

* All three were appointed Rajas by Maharaja Ranjit Singh and given their respective territories to rule over.

Notes

1. The Sikhs had twelve confederacies known as *Misls* (much like the Scottish clans). The Shukarchakia Misl, to which Ranjit Singh belonged, was one of them.
2. *Sati* was a ritual where on the death of her husband, a wife could immolate herself along with him on his funeral pyre.
3. Jwalamukhi is one of north India's holiest Hindu shrines. It is situated in the foothills of the Himalayas, in the Indian state of Himachal Pradesh.
4. A *maund* is a measure of weight. 1 *maund* is equivalent to 40 kilograms.
5. During the ritual of *sati*, the dead husband's head lies in the wife's lap.
6. Punjab is broken up into regions by its five rivers. South of the River Sutlej lies the 'Malwa' region. The 'Do-ab' region lies between the River Sutlej and the River Beas. The 'Majha' falls between the River Beas and the River Ravi.
7. The Fyzulpuria Misl is one of the twelve *misl*s of the Sikhs. The Shukarchakia Misl was formed as a breakaway *misl* from this one.
8: Syad Muhmmad Latif, *History of the Punjab from the Remotest Antiquities to the Present Time.* Calcutta: Calcutta Central Press Co., 1891.
9. The twelve misls are: Ahluwalia, Bhangi, Dallewalia, Fyzulpuria or Singhpuria, Kanhiya, Karorsinghia, Nakkai, Nishanwalia, Ramgarhia, Shahid, Shukarchakia, and Phulkian. Other than the Phulkians who were south of the River Sutlej, the rest were west of it.
10. The Khalsa was created by Sri Guru Gobind Singh in 1699 at Keshgarh Sahib, Sri Anandpur. The Sikhs were baptized and were given an identity by the Tenth Guru. They had to observe the five 'Ks' to ensure their identity. *Kesh* – long hair, *Kara* – a steel bangle, *Kuch* – drawers, *Kirpan* – a dagger or sword, and *Kanga* – a comb to keep one's hair and beard in order.
11. The clan originated in Japanese Manchuria. It then shifted to China and was better known there as the clan that grew long hair, plaited into pigtails. They moved south to Asia during the period of the Tsing dynasty.
12. The Zamzama or 'Bhangian di Top' was cast in Lahore by Shah Nazir, under the orders of Shah Wali Khan, prime minister of Ahmed Shah Durrani at Lahore. After the third battle of Panipat, where it was first deployed in 1761, Ahmed Shah left it at Lahore with his governor, Khwaja Ubed. It was left behind as it was too large to be transported to Kabul. It was 14 ft long with a muzzle diameter of 9.5 inches and it fired an 84 pound projectile.

    In 1762, Hari Singh Bhangi captured this gun from Khwaja Ubed. Two years later it was given to Charat Singh Shukarchakia, Ranjit Singh's grandfather, by the Bhangis as his share of plunder in one of their joint campaigns. In a later battle against the Chathas, the Chathas captured the gun from Charat Singh. The two Chatha brothers,

Ahmed Khan and Pir Mohammad then transported the gun to Ahmadnagar, where they then fought over the possession of the gun. The former lost two sons in this battle and the latter one. In this battle, Gujjar Singh Bhangi sided with Pir Mohammad who then gave him this gun in gratitude for his assistance.
Two years later Charat Singh captured it from Gujjar Singh Bhangi. Yet, once again in battle, the Chathas took the gun from Charat Singh. And yet again the Bhangis once more captured the gun from the Chathas. In 1778, Maha Singh captured the gun from the Bhangis, which he then left in the care of the Chathas, as it was too heavy for him to transport. Jhanda Singh Bhangi then forced the Chathas to part with the gun and this time transported it to his estate in Amritsar. In 1802, Maharaja Ranjit Singh captured it after occupying Amritsar and dislodging the Bhangis under Mai Sukhan. It was deployed by him in the battles of Daska, Kasur, Sujanpur, Wazirabad, and Multan. After facilitating the capture of Multan, the gun damaged during the battle was decommissioned in 1818. It is currently on display at the Lahore Museum.

13. Syad Muhmmad Latif, *History of the Punjab*.
14. The 'Majha' region lies between the rivers Beas and Ravi.
15. Syad Muhmmad Latif, *History of the Punjab*. And Major George Carmichael Smyth (ed.), *A History of the Reigning Family of Lahore, with Some Account of the Jummoo Rajahs, the Seik Soldiers and their Sirdars.* Calcutta: W. Thacker and Co., 1847.
16. Smyth, *A History of the Reigning Family of Lahore*.
17. Hari Ram Gupta, *History of the Sikhs from Nadir Shah's Invasion to the Rise of Ranjit Singh, 1739-1799.* Simla: Minerva Book Shop, 1952.
18. Najibs were Muslim garrison troops, from the Saharanpur region.
19. Gupta, *History of the Sikhs*, vol. 5.
20. Baron Von Hugel and Charles Freiherrn. *Travels in Cashmere and the Punjab*, translated from German by Major T.B. Jervis. First published in 1845. Reprint, Patiala: The Punjab Languages Department, 1970.
21. Gupta, *History of the Sikhs*, vol. 5.
22. Victor Jacquemont, *Letters from India: Describing a Journey in the British Dominions of India, Tibet, Lahore and Cashmere during the years 1828–1831. Undertaken by orders of the French Government* – 2 volumes (translated from French by Edward Churton, London 1834). Quoted in 'Introduction' by Khushwant Singh in W.G. Osborne's *Court and Camp of Ranjeet Singh with an Introductory Sketch of the Origin and Rise of the Sikh State.* First published 1840. Reprint, Patiala: The Punjab Languages Department, 1970.
23. W.G. Osborne, *The Court and Camp of Ranjeet Singh*.
24. Emily Eden, *Up The Country: Letters Written to the Sister from the Upper Provinces of India,* quoted in 'Introduction' by Khushwant Singh in W.G. Osborne's *Court and Camp of Ranjeet Singh.*
25. A *nazarana* is an offering made by an individual to a ruler signifying submission and loyalty.
26. A *khilat* is a return gift made to a person offering a *nazarana*, to signify that the ruler accepts his submission and offer of loyalty.
27. Sir Lepel Griffin, *Ranjit Singh* (Rulers of India Series). Delhi: National Book Shop, 2002.
28. Sir Edward Benjamin Edwardes, *The Life of Sir Henry Lawrence, by the Late Major-General Sir Herbert B. Edwardes and Herman Merivale.* 2 vols. London: Smith, Elder & Co., 1872.
29. Syad Muhmmad Latif, *History of the Punjab*.
30. Cis-Sutlej Resolution
31. Gupta, *History of the Sikhs*.
32. Ibid.
33. W.G. Osborne, *The Court and Camp of Ranjeet Singh*.
34. Emily Eden, *Up the Country*.
35. On the demise of an individual, a person closely related to him, or otherwise close to him, such as a male relative or a friend, could put a *chaddar* (veil) over his widow, with her consent, from when onwards she would be considered his lawfully wedded wife.

36. Hari Ram Gupta, *History of the Sikhs*.
37. The Jathedar of the Akal Takht, the highest temporal seat of the Sikhs was established by the sixth guru, Sri Guru Hargobind Sahib. He put up two flags, *nishans*, close to it to indicate that religion must guide the State and in turn the State must protect the religion. This Seat then became the arbitrator of all disputes amongst the Sikh *misls* and sects of that period, and continues to be so even today. The Akal Takht issues 'Hukamnamas' or edicts on Sikh matters of day-to-day functioning, etc.
38. Hari Ram Gupta, *History of the Sikhs*.
39. Fakir Waheeduddin, *The Real Ranjit Singh*. Patiala: The Publication Bureau, Punjabi University, 2001.
40. W.G. Osborne, *The Court and Camp of Ranjeet Singh*.
41. Captain Osborne, in *The Court and Camp of Runjit Singh*, writes about Sher Singh, 'He is a twin son of one of Runjeet's wives, named Mehtab Keonwar, who, in 1807, (on his return to Lahore, after an absence of some duration,) presented him with two boys, Sher Singh and Tara Singh. The lady's conjugal fidelity had been already suspect, and her husband would not own them. He appears, however, in some degree to have acknowledged Sher Singh, by the distinction with which he treated him; but Tara Singh experienced uniform neglect.' The possible reason for accepting Sher Singh was that he had by the time of acceptance, distinguished himself as a soldier and a general.
42. Alexander Burnes, *Travels into Bokhara*. Volume 1 of 3 vols. London: Oxford University Press, 1973.
43. Fauja Singh Bajwa, *Military System of the Sikhs: During the Period 1799-1849*. Delhi/ Varanasi/Patna: Motilal Banarsidass, 1964.
44. Hari Ram Gupta, *History of the Sikhs*.
45. Major Hugh Pearse (ed.), *Soldier and Traveller: Memoirs of Alexander Gardner*. Edinburgh/ London: William Blackwood and Sons, 1898.
    A booklet titled *Sher-e-Punjab Maharaja Ranjit Singh* produced by Faqir Syed Saifuddin of the Fakir Khana Museum, Lahore, on the occasion of Ranjit Singh's 225th birthday, puts the European officer strength at 54 and has included 4 Russians. In this book, however, I am going by the *Memoirs* of Colonel Gardner. Col Gardner was one of the European officers in Ranjit Singh's army, as a colonel of Artillery.
46. Major Hugh Pearse, *Soldier and Traveller: Memoirs of Alexander Gardner*.
47. Andrew Preziosi, *The First Sikh War 1845-1846: Order of Battle Book*. Miami: Khyber Pass Games and Books, 2004.
48. Ibid.
49. Ibid.
50. Ian Heath and Micheal Perry, *The Sikh Army 1799-1849 (*Men at Arms Series). Oxford: Osprey Publishing, 2005.
51. Major Hugh Pearse, *Soldier and Traveller: Memoirs of Alexander Gardner*.
52. Sir Claude Wade was the British political agent at Lahore. He was on very friendly terms with Ranjit Singh.
53. Griffen et al., *Chiefs and Families of Note in Punjab*, vol. 2. Lahore: Government Printing, 1940.
54. Hari Ram Gupta, *History of the Sikhs,* Vol 5.
55. Major Hugh Pearse, *Soldier and Traveller: Memoirs of Alexander Gardner*.
56. Fauja Singh Bajwa, *Military System of the Sikhs*.
57. Ibid.
58. Ibid.
59. Andrew Preziosi, *The First Sikh War 1845-1846: Order of Battle Book*.
60. Mohanlal, *Travels in the Punjab, Afghanistan and Turistan, Khorasan and part of Persia in the company of Lt Burns and Dr Gerrard*. Calcutta, 1843.
61. Hari Ram Gupta, *History of the Sikhs*, vol 5.
62. Syad Muhmmad Latif, *History of the Punjab*.
63. Major G. Carmichael Smyth, *Reigning Family of Lahore*.
64. Major Hugh Pearse, *Soldier and Traveller: Memoirs of Alexander Gardner*.

65. A summerhouse built in marble.
66. The army by this time had become rebellious and had elected representatives, called *panches*, who decided on matters, earlier looked after by the senior military hierarchy. Each company elected five *panches*. In Punjabi, a *panch* means an elected member of a committee of five.
67. Syad Latif in his *History of the Punjab*, puts this figure at 4,786 soldiers, 610 horses and 320 bullocks killed. While the besiegers took 130 casualties. I have, however, taken Colonel Gardner's figures in my narrative.
68. Syad Muhmmad Latif, *History of the Punjab*.
69. Major Hugh Pearse, *Soldier and Traveller: Memoirs of Alexander Gardner.*
70. Major G. Carmichael Smyth, *A History of the Reigning Family of Lahore*. Appendix xiv.
71. Major Hugh Pearse, *Soldier and Traveller: Memoirs of Alexander Gardner.* Appendix xxxix.
72. Ian Heath and Micheal Perry. *The Sikh Army 1799-1849.*
73. H.C.B. Cook, *The Sikh Wars: British Army in the Punjab, 1845-49.* London: Leo Cooper, 1975.
74. Major G. Carmichael Smyth, *A History of the Reigning Family of Lahore.*
75. Henry Hardinge, Hugh Gough, and Sir Harry George Wakwlyn Smith, *The War in India: Despatches of Viscount Hardinge, Lord Gough, Sir Harry Smith ... and other documents; comprising the engagements of Moodkee, Ferozshah, Aliwal, and Sobraon.* Smith. London: J Oliver, 1846.
76. Donald Featherstone, *At Them with the Bayonet: The First Sikh War.* London: Jarrolds, 1968.
77. Ibid.
78. George Bruce, *Six Battles for India: The Anglo-Sikh Wars, 1845-46, 1848-49*. London: Arthur Barker Ltd, 1969.
79. Andrew Preziosi, *The First Sikh War 1845-1846:- Order of Battle Book.* Quoting Cunningham, Bajwa, Sita Ram Kholi, and Lt Col Majumdar.
80. Sir Charles Gough and Arthur D. Innes, *The Sikhs and the Sikh Wars: The Rise, Conquest, and Annexation of the Punjab State.* London: A.D. Innes & Co. 1897. The Sikhs never operated in Divisions. Though Major Broadfoot did send a report of the Sikhs having 7 Divisions, it was incorrect. Three Divisions were approved by the Durbar but were never formed. The war was fought in Brigade Groups and Brigades.
81. Joseph Davey Cunningham, *A History of the Sikhs: From the Origin of the Nation to the Battle of the Sutlej.* Delhi: Chand & Co., 1966.
82. All political correspondence, decision making, etc., was done by the Governor General with the 'Secret Committee' of the East India Company.
83. Hardinge, *The War in India, Despatches of Viscount Hardinge.*
84. The region of the First Sikh War had approximately 28 types of shrubs and trees in it as listed below (based on Forest Department records)

1.	Reru (*Acacia Leucophloea*)	2.	Phulia (*Acacia modesta*)
3.	Kikar (*Acacia nilotica*)	4.	Sirris Kala (*Albizzia lebbeck*)
5.	Neem (*Azadirachta indica*)	6.	Simal (*Bombax Malabaricum*)
7.	Dhak (Butea *monosperma*)	8.	Karir (*Capparis aphylla*)
9.	Karonda (Carissa carundus)	10.	Amaltas (*Cassia fistula*)
11.	Lasoora (*Cordia dichotoma*)	12.	Tahli (*Dalbergia sissoo*)
13.	Bohar (*Ficus bengalensis*)	14.	Gular (*Ficus glomerata*)
15.	Pilkan (Ficus infectoria)	16.	Pipal (*Ficus religiosa*)
17.	Bakain (*Melia azedarach*)	18.	Suhanjana (*Moringa oleifera*)
19.	Kahjoor (*Phoenix sylvestris*)	20.	Jangal Jalebi (Pithecelobium dulce)
21.	Jand (*Prosopis cineraria*)	22.	Mosquite (*Prosopis julifera*)
23.	Imli (*Tamarindus indica*)	24.	Frash (*Tamarix aphylla*)
25.	Rohera (*Tecomella undulata*)	26.	Mallah (*Zyziphus nummularia*)
27.	Beri (*Zyziphus zuzuba*)	28.	Ban (*Salvadora oleoides*)

85. Major G. Carmichael Smyth, *A History of the Reigning Family of Lahore.*
86. See Appendices.

87. George Bruce, *Six Battles for India.*
88. In Gough's despatch to the GG,
89. George Bruce, *Six Battles for India.*
90. Ibid.
91. Andrew Preziosi, *The First Sikh War 1845-1846: Order of Battle Book.* Quoting Cunningham, Bajwa, Sita Ram Kholi, and Lt Col Majumdar.
92. George Bruce, *Six Battles for India.*
93. J.D. Cunningham, *A History of the Sikhs.*
94. Major G. Carmichael Smyth, *A History of the Reigning Family of Lahore.*
95. H.C.B. Cook, *The Sikh Wars.*
96. George Bruce, *Six Battles for India.*
97. Donald Featherstone, *At Them with the Bayonet.*
98. George Bruce, *Six Battles for India.*
99. G.B. Malleson, *The Decisive Battles of India. From 1746 to 1819 Inclusive. With A Portrait of the Author, A Map, and Three Plans.* London: W.H. Allen & co., 1883.
100. H.C.B. Cook, *The Sikh Wars.*
101. Donald Featherstone, *At Them with the Bayonet.*
102. Richard Cannon, *Historical record of the Third, or the King's Own Regiment of Light Dragoons: Containing an account of the formation of the regiment in 1685, and of its subsequent services to 1846.* London: Parker, Furnivall, & Parker, 1847.
103. Donald Featherstone, *At Them with the Bayonet.*
104. H.C.B. Cook, *The Sikh Wars.*
105. Ibid.
106. George Bruce, *Six Battles for India.*
107. Ibid.
108. Ibid.
109. Ibid.
110. Ibid.
111. Ibid.
112. Charles Gough and Arthur D. Innes, *The Sikhs and the Sikh Wars.*
113. H.C.B. Cook, *The Sikh Wars.*
114. Charles Gough and Arthur D. Innes, *The Sikhs and the Sikh Wars.*
115. Ibid.
116. Ibid.
117. George Bruce, *Six Battles for India.*
118. Andrew Preziosi, *The First Sikh War 1845-1846:- Order of Battle Book.*
119. George Bruce, *Six Battles for India.*
120. *War in India, Dispatches of the Governor General, the C-in-C and Maj. Gen.. Sir Harry Smith.*
121. J.D. Cunningham, *A History of the Sikhs.*
122. George Bruce, *Six Battles for India.*
123. Ibid.
124. H.C.B. Cook, *The Sikh Wars.*
125. George Bruce, *Six Battles for India.*
126. Harry George Wakelyn Smith and G.C. Moore, *The Autobiography of Lieutenant-General Sir Harry Smith, Baronet of Aliwal on the Sutlej, G.C.B.* London: J. Murray, 1902.
127. George Bruce. *Six Battles for India.*
128. Ibid.
129. Andrew Preziosi,. *The First Sikh War 1845-1846: Order of Battle Book.*
130. Ibid.
131. George Bruce, *Six Battles for India.*
132. H.C.B. Cook, *The Sikh Wars.*
133. Andrew Preziosi, *The First Sikh War 1845-1846: Order of Battle Book.*
134. Ibid.
135. 'The Memoirs of Field Marshal Herbert Edwards'.
136. George Bruce, *Six Battles for India.*

137. Ibid.
138. Ibid.
139. Charles Gough and Arthur D. Innes, *The Sikhs and the Sikh Wars.*
140. Donald Featherstone, *At them with the Bayonet.*
141. George Bruce, *Six Battles for India.*
142. Ibid.
143. *Historical Records of the 3rd dragoon.*
144. Charles Gough and Arthur D. Innes, *The Sikhs and the Sikh Wars.*
145. G.B. Malleson, *The Decisive Battles of India.*
146. George Bruce, *Six Battles for India.*
147. H.C.B. Cook, *The Sikh Wars.*
148. George Bruce, *Six Battles for India.*
149. Hugh Gough, *Despatches.*
150. H.C.B. Cook, *The Sikh Wars.*
151. Ibid.
152. Ibid.
153. George Bruce, *Six Battles for India.*
154. H.C.B. Cook, *The Sikh Wars.*
155. Ibid.
156. Ibid.
157. Ibid.
158. Ibid.
159. Ibid.
160. Ibid.
161. J.D. Cunningham, *A History of the Sikhs.*
162. George Bruce, *Six Battles for India.*
163. Major Evans Bell, *The Annexation of the Punjaub and the Maharajah Duleep Singh*. London: Trubner, 1882.
164. Charles Gough and Arthur D. Innes, *The Sikhs and the Sikh Wars.*
165. George Bruce, *Six Battles for India.*
166. Ibid.
167. Ibid.
168. Ibid.
169. H.C.B. Cook, *The Sikh Wars.*
170. Ibid.
171. George Bruce, *Six Battles for India.*
172. Reginald Burton, *The First and Second Sikh Wars, An Official British Army History.* Pennsylvania: Westholme Publishing, 2008.
173. Hugh Gough, *Despatches.*
174. Charles Gough and Arthur D. Innes, *The Sikhs and the Sikh Wars.*
175. Winston Churchill, *A History of the English Speaking Peoples: The Great Democracies*, vol iv. London: Cassell, 1991.
176. H.C.B. Cook, *The Sikh Wars.*
177. George Bruce, *Six Battles for India.*
178. Ibid.
179. Ibid.
180. H.C.B. Cook, *The Sikh Wars.*
181. George Bruce, *Six Battles for India.*
182. Ibid.
183. Unit Returns of the Second Sikh War. General Lumsden, Adjutant General of India
184. Reginald Burton, *The First and Second Sikh Wars.*
185. Ibid.
186. George Bruce, *Six Battles for India.*
187. Edward Joseph Thackwell, *Narrative of the Second Sikh War in 1948-49: With A Detailed Account of the Battles of Ramnugger, The Passage of the Chenab, Chillianwallah, Goojerat, &c.* Patiala: Languages Department, 1970.

188. H.C.B. Cook, *The Sikh Wars.*
189. Major Evans Bell, *The Annexation of the Punjaub and the Maharajah Duleep Singh.*
190. Ibid.
191. Ibid.
192. Ibid.
193. Sir Herbert Benjamin Edwardes, *Life of Sir Henry Lawrence*, vol 2.
194. 'Maharaja Duleep Singh and the Government – A Narrative'. The Second Treaty of Lahore 1849 – Appendix XV.
195. Michael Alexander and Sushila Anand, *Queen Victoria's Maharajah: Duleep Singh 1838-93.* London: Weidenfeld and Nicolson, 1980.
196. Lady Lena Campbell Login, *Lady Login's Recollections: Court Life and Camp Life, 1820-1904.* London: Smith, Elder, 1916. In her *Recollections*, Lady Login says that Rani Dukhnoo 'was of ancient Rajpoot lineage from the Kangra hills, and had been specially selected for her beauty for the harem of Sher Singh (later Maharaja Sher Singh) – Ranjit Singh's adopted son – on his coming to the throne. Thus the little Sheo Deo Singh was only a few months old when his father was murdered, and Duleep Singh was elected by the Khalsa (Sikh Commonwealth).'
197. Ibid.
198. Michael Alexander and Sushila Anand, *Queen Victoria's Maharajah.*
199. Ibid.
200. Ibid.
201. Peter Bance, *The Duleep Singhs: The Photograph Album of Queen Victoria's Maharajah.* Stroud: Sutton, 2004.
202. Michael Alexander and Sushila Anand, *Queen Victoria's Maharajah.*
203. Ibid.
204. Lady Lena Campbell Login, *Lady Login's Recollections.*
205. Ibid.
206. Michael Alexander and Sushila Anand, *Queen Victoria's Maharajah.*
207. Ibid.
208. Ibid.
209. Ibid.
210. Ibid.
211. Ibid.
212. Ibid.
213. Ibid.
214. Ibid.
215. Ibid.
216. Ibid.
217. Ibid.
218. Ibid.
219. Ibid.
220. Ibid.
221. Ibid.
222. Ibid.
223. Ibid.
224. Ibid.
225. Ibid.
226. Ibid.
227. Ibid.
228. Ibid.
229. Ibid.
230. Ibid.
231. Ibid.
232. Ibid.
233. Ibid.
234. Ibid.

235. Ibid.
236. Ibid.
237. Ibid.
238. Ibid.
239. Ibid.
240. Ibid.
241. Ibid.
242. Ibid.
243. Christy Campbell, *The Maharaja's Box: An Imperial Story of Conspiracy, Love, and a Guru's Prophecy*. London: Overlook Press, 2002.
244. Michael Alexander and Sushila Anand, *Queen Victoria's Maharajah*.
245. Ibid.
246. Ibid.
247. Ibid.
248. Ibid.
249. Christy Campbell, *The Maharaja's Box*.

Select Bibliography

Ahluwalia, M.L. and Prithipala Singha Kapura. *Maharani Jinda Kaur (1816-1863)*. Maharaja Duleep Singh-Raj Mata Jind Kaur Foundation (Patiala, India). Amritsar: Singh Bros., 2001.

Alexander, Michael and Sushila Anand. *Queen Victoria's Maharajah: Duleep Singh 1838-93*. London: Weidenfeld and Nicolson, 1980.

Ali, Shahamat. *Historical Account of Sikhs And Afghans*. London: Murray. N.d.

Bajwa, Fauja Singh. *Military System of the Sikhs: During the Period 1799-1849*. Delhi: Motilal Banarsidass, 1964.

Bance, Peter. *The Duleep Singhs: The Photograph Album of Queen Victoria's Maharajah*. Stroud: Sutton, 2004.

Bell, Major Evans. *The Annexation of the Punjaub and the Maharajah Duleep Singh*. London: Trubner, 1882.

Bruce, George. *Six Battles for India: The Anglo-Sikh Wars, 1845-46 and 1848-49*. London: Arthur Barker Ltd., 1969.

Burnes, Sir Alexander. *Travels into Bokhara*. (performed by order of the supreme govt. of India in the years 1831, 32, and 33). London: J. Murray, 1835.

Burton, Reginald George. *The First and Second Sikh Wars: An Official British Army History*. Pennsylvania: Westholme Publishing, 2008.

Caine, Caesar and H.M. Havelock-allan. *Barracks and Battlefields in India*. New Delhi: Nirmal Publishers & Distributors, 1986.

Campbell, Christy. *The Maharaja's Box: An Imperial Story of Conspiracy, Love, and a Guru's Prophecy*. London: Overlook Press, 2002.

Cannon, Richard. *Historical record of the Third, or the King's Own Regiment of Light Dragoons*. London: Parker, Furnivall, & Parker, 1847.

Chaudhry, Nazir Ahmad. *The Maharajah Duleep Singh and the Government – A Narrative*. Lahore: Sang-e-Meel Publications, 1999.

Churchill, Winston. *A History of the English Speaking Peoples: The Great Democracies*. London: Cassell, 1991.

Cole, John Jones. *A Sketch of The Siege of Mooltan*. Lahore: Sang-e-Meel Publications, 1999.

Cook, H.C.B. *The Sikh Wars: British Army in the Punjab, 1845-49*. London: Leo Cooper, 1975.

Cunningham, Joseph Davey. *A History of the Sikhs: From the Origin of the Nation to the Battle of the Sutlej*. Delhi: Chand & Co, 1966.

Dunlop, John and A. Maclure. *Mooltan, During and After the Siege*. London: Wm. S. Orr, 1849.

Edwardes, Sir Herbert Benjamin. *Life of Sir Henry Lawrence*. London: Smith, Elder & Co., 1872.

Featherstone, Donald F. *All For a Shilling a Day: An Account of Recruits to the 16th Lancers in the mid-1840s*. London: Jarrolds, 1966.

Featherstone, Donald. *At Them with the Bayonet: The First Sikh War*. London: Jarrolds, 1968.

Gordon, Sir John. H. *The Sikhs*. Edinburgh: W. Blackwood and Sons, 1904.

Gough, Sir Charles and Arthur D Innes. *The Sikhs and the Sikh Wars: The Rise, Conquest, and Annexation of the Punjab State*. London; A.D. Innes & Co., 1897.

Griffin, Sir Henry Lepel, Gulshan Lall Chopra, Charles Francis Massey and W.L. Conran. *Chiefs and Families of Note in Punjab*. Lahore: Government Printing, 1940.

Griffin, Sir Henry Lepel. *Ranjit Singh (Rulers of India Series)*. Delhi: National Book Shop, 2002.

Gupta, Hari Ram. *History of the Sikhs from Nadir Shah's Invasion to the Rise of Ranjit Singh, 1739-99*. Simla: Minerva Book Shop, 1952.

Hardinge, Viscount Henry; Viscount Hugh Gough and Sir Harry George Wakelyn Smith. *The War in India. Despatches of Viscount Hardinge, Lord Gough, Sir Harry Smith ... and other documents; comprising the engagements of Moodkee, Ferozshah, Aliwal, and Sobraon*. London: J. Oliver, 1846.

Heath, Ian and Perry Michael. *The Sikh Army 1799-1849 (Men at Arms Series)*. Oxford: Osprey Publishing, 2005.

Heathcote, T.A. *The Afghan Wars, 1839-1919*. London: Osprey, 1980.

Honigberger, John Martin. *Thirty-five Years in the East*. London: H. Baillie're, 1852.

Humbley, W.W.W. *Journal of a Cavalry Officer; including the memorable Sikh campaign of 1845-1946*. London: Longman, Brown, Green, and Longmans, 1854.

Kohli, Sita Ram. *Catalogue of Khalsa Darbar Records, Vols I & II*. Lahore: Superintendent, Government Press, 1927.

Kohli, Sita Ram. *The Army of Maharaja Ranjit Singh*. Bombay: Oxford University Press, 1922.

Latif, Syad Muhammad. *History of the Punjab from the Remotest Antiquities to the Present Time*. Calcutta: Calcutta Central Press Co., 1891.

Lawrence-Archer, J.H. *Commentaries on the Punjab Campaign: 1848-49*. Lahore: Universal Books, 1976.

Login, Lady Lena Campbell. *Lady Login's Recollections: Court Life and Camp Life, 1820-1904*. E. Dalhousie Login (ed.). London: Smith, Elder, 1916.

M'Gregor, William Lewis. *The History of the Sikhs*. Patiala: Languages Department, 1979.

Macmunn, Sir George Fletcher. *Vignettes from Indian Wars*. London: S. Low, Marston, 1932.

Malleson, G.B. *The Decisive Battles of India: From 1746 to 1819*. London: W.H. Allen & Co., 1883.

McLeod Innes, James J. *Sir Henry Lawrence: The Pacificator*. Oxford: Clarendon Press, 1898.

Mohan Lal. *Travels in the Punjab, Afghanistan and Turistan, Khorasan and part of Persia in the company of Lt Burns and Dr Gerrard*. Calcutta, 1843

Moorcraft, William, George Trebeck and H.H. Wilson. *Travels in the Himalayan provinces of Hindustan and the Panjab; in Ladakh and Kashmir; in Peshawar, Kabul, Kunduz, and Bokhara*. Patiala: Languages Department, 1970.

Muhammada, Shaha and P.K. Nijhawan. *The First Punjab War: Shah Mohammed's Jangnamah*. Maharaja Duleep Singh-Rajmata Jind Kaur Foundation (Patiala, India). Amritsar/Patiala: Singh Bros. in association with Maharaja Duleep Singh-Raj Mata Jind Kaur Foundation, 2001.

Osborne, W.G. *Court and Camp of Ranjeet Singh with an Introductory Sketch of the Origin and Rise of the Sikh State*. Patiala: The Punjab Languages department, 1970.

Parshad, Dewan Ajudhia. *Waqai-Jang-i-Sikhan*: *Events of the First Anglo-Sikh War* 1845-46. V.S. Suri (tr) Chandigarh: Punjab Itihas Prakashan, 1975.

Pearman, John. *Sergeant Pearman's Memoirs: Being, Chiefly, His Account of Service with the Third (King's Own) Light Dragoons in India, from 1845 to 1853, Including the First and Second Sikh Wars*, The Marquess of Anglesey (ed.). London: Jonathan Cape, 1968.

Pearse, Major Hugh (ed.). *Soldier and Traveller: Memoirs of Alexander Gardner*. Edinburgh/London: William Blackwood and Sons, 1898.

Preziosi, Andrew. *The First Sikh War 1845-1846 – Order of Battle Book*. Khyber Pass Games and Books, 2005.

Ram, Sita. Ed. James Lunt. *From Sepoy to Subedar: Being the life and adventures of Subedar Sita Ram, a Native Officer of the Bengal Army*. London: Routledge & Kegan Paul, 1973.

Sandford, Daniel A. *Leaves from the Journal of a Subaltern, during the campaign in the Punjaub, September 1848 to March 1849*. Edinburgh: William Blackwood & sons. 1849.

Sandhawalia, Preminder Singh. *Noblemen and Kinsmen: History of a Sikh Family*. New Delhi: South Asia Books, 1999.

Sharma, Radha. *The Lahore Darbar*. Amritsar: Guru Nanak Dev University, 2001.

Singh, Bawa Satinder. *The Jammu Fox: A Biography of Maharaja Gulab Singh of Kashmir, 1792-1857*. Carbondale: Southern Illinois University Press, 1974.

Singh, Ganda, Sir Frederick Currie *Private Correspondence Relating to the Anglo-Sikh Wars, Being Private Letters of Lords Ellenborough, Hardinge, Dalhousie and Gough, and of Political Assistants, addressed to Sir Frederick Currie as British Resident at Lahore*. Amritsar: Sikh History Society, 1955.

Singh, Karnail. *Winston Churchill's Account of Anglo-Sikh Wars and Its In-side Tale*. Amritsar: Shiromani Gurdwara Parbandhak Committee, 1984.

Smith, Lieutenant-General Harry and G.C. Moore. *The Autobiography of Lieutenant-General Sir Harry Smith*. London: John Murray, 1903.

Smyth, Major George Carmichael (ed.). *A History of the Reigning Family of Lahore, with Some Account of the Jummoo Rajahs, the Seik Soldiers and their Sirdars*. Calcutta: W. Thacker and Co., 1847.

Suri, Sohan Lal and Vidya Sagar. *Umdat-Ut-Tawarikh*. Delhi: S. Chand, 1961.

Thackwell, Edward Joseph. *Narrative of the Second Sikh War in 1948-49: With A Detailed Account of the Battles of Ramnugger, The Passage of the Chenab, Chillianwallah, Goojerat, & c*. Patiala: Languages Department, 1970.

Thorburn, S.S. *The Punjab in Peace and*

War. Edinburgh/London: William Blackwood and Sons, 1904.
Von Hugel, Baron and Charles Freiherrn. *Travels in Cashmere and the Punjab*, translated from German by Major T.B. Jervis. First published in 1845. Reprint, Patiala: The Punjab Languages Department, 1970
Waheeduddin, Fakir Syed. *The Real Ranjit Singh*. Patiala: Publication Bureau, Punjabi University, 1981.

Index